Dragon Art

Inspiration, Impact & Technique in Fantasy Art

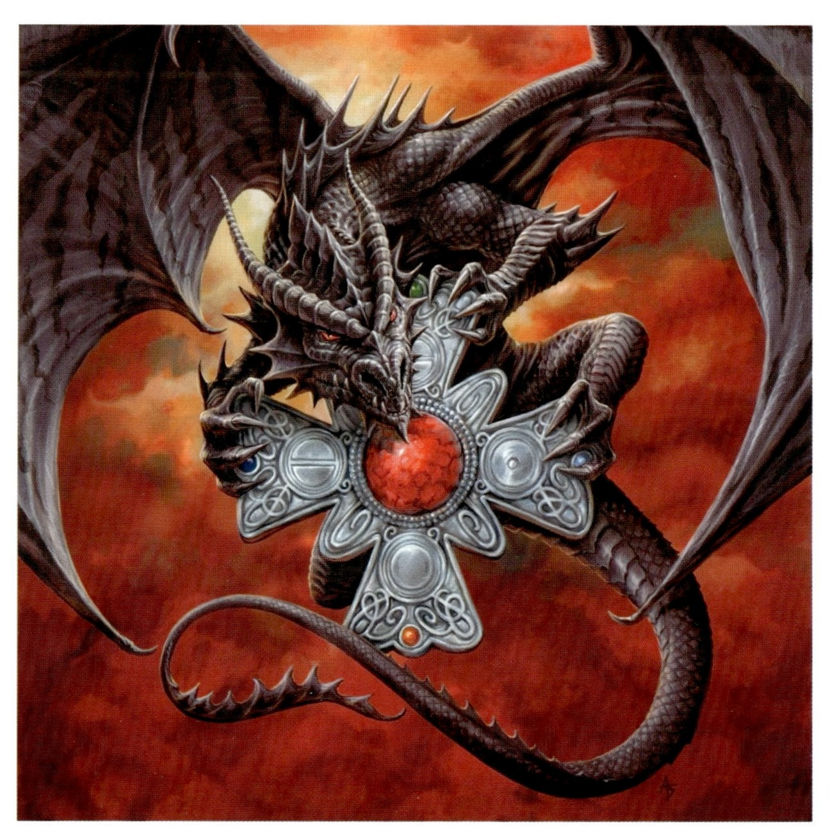

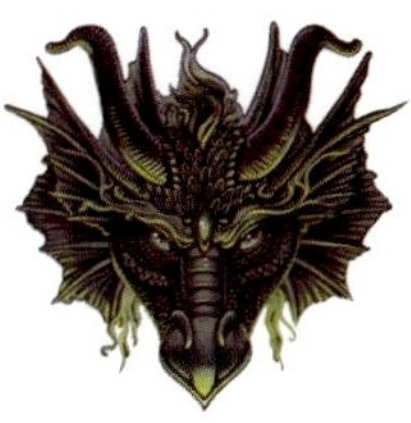

Publisher and Creative Director: Nick Wells
Project Editor and Picture Research: Cat Emslie
Art Director and Layout Design: Mike Spender
Digital Design and Production: Chris Herbert
Proofreader: Dawn Laker
Indexer: Helen Snaith

Special thanks to: John Howe, Victoria Lyle, Chelsea Edwards, Rob Carney and, most importantly, all the artists who helped make this book what it is.

13 12
5 7 9 10 8 6 4

This edition first published 2009 by
FLAME TREE PUBLISHING
Crabtree Hall, Crabtree Lane
Fulham, London SW6 6TY
United Kingdom

www.flametreepublishing.com

Flame Tree Publishing is an imprint of Flame Tree Publishing Ltd

All images without captions are courtesy of the following artists: 1, 4R, 6R, 7, 8, 45, 121, 124L, 200L, 204 © Anne Stokes (*see also* pages 124, 118); 2, 9L, 201T © Michele-lee Phelan (*see also* page 140); 3 © Andy Fairhurst (*see also* page 75); 4L, 14-15 © Todd Lockwood (*see also* page 28); 5L © Janny Wurts (*see also* page 20); 5R © (*see also* page 110); 6L © Don Maitz (*see also* page 19); 10, 12, 38, 49, 801, 951 © Kerem Beyit (*see also* pages 76, 82); 11 © Minna Sundberg (*see also* page 104); 13 © Tiago da Silva (*see also* page 188); 34-35 © Ignacio Bazán Lazcano (*see also* page 62); 144, 197, 200R © Sandra Staple (*see also* page 133); 177 © Carlos Herrera (*see also* page 179); 200B © Kirsi Salonen (*see also* page 67)

ISBN 978-1-84786-300-3

A CIP record for this book is available from the British Library upon request.

Printed in China

Dragon Art

Inspiration, Impact & Technique in Fantasy Art

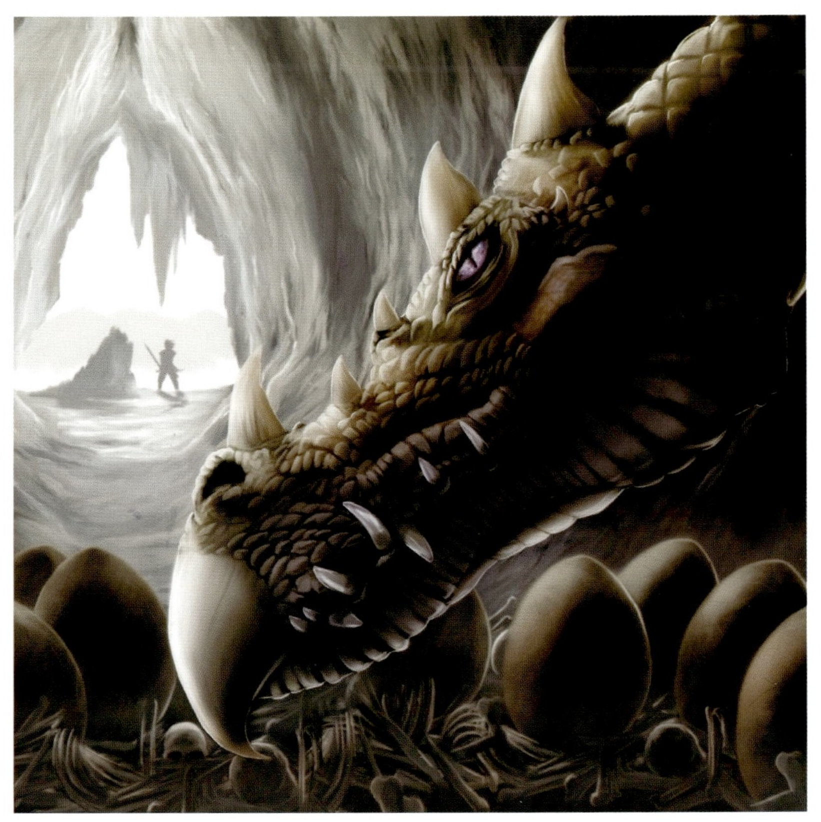

Graeme Aymer

Foreword by John Howe

FLAME TREE
PUBLISHING

Contents by Artist

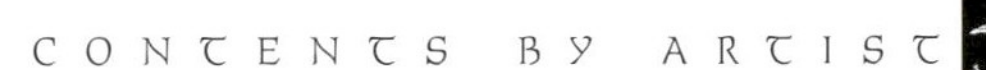

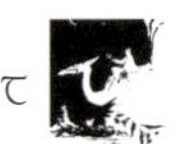

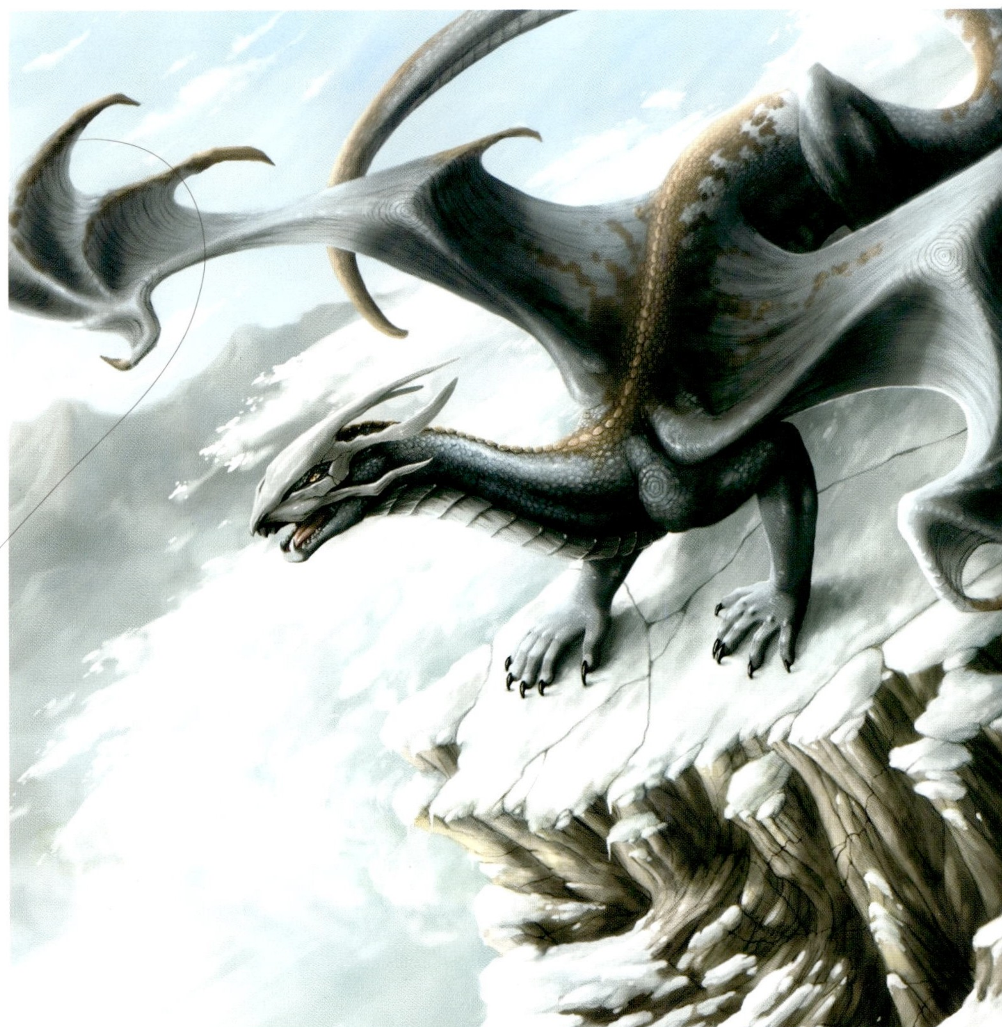

Contents by Structure

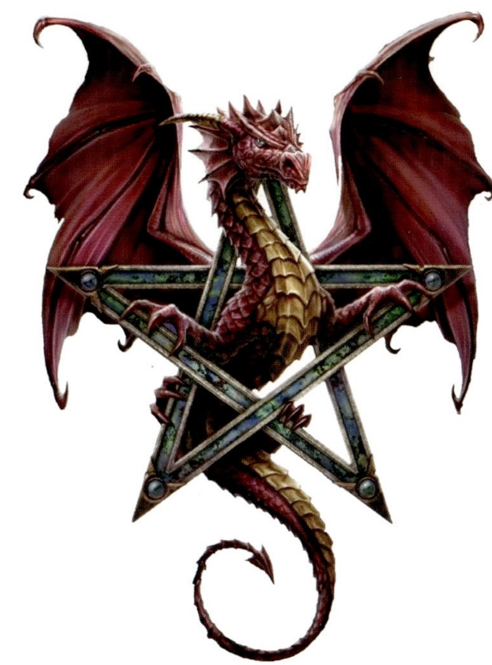

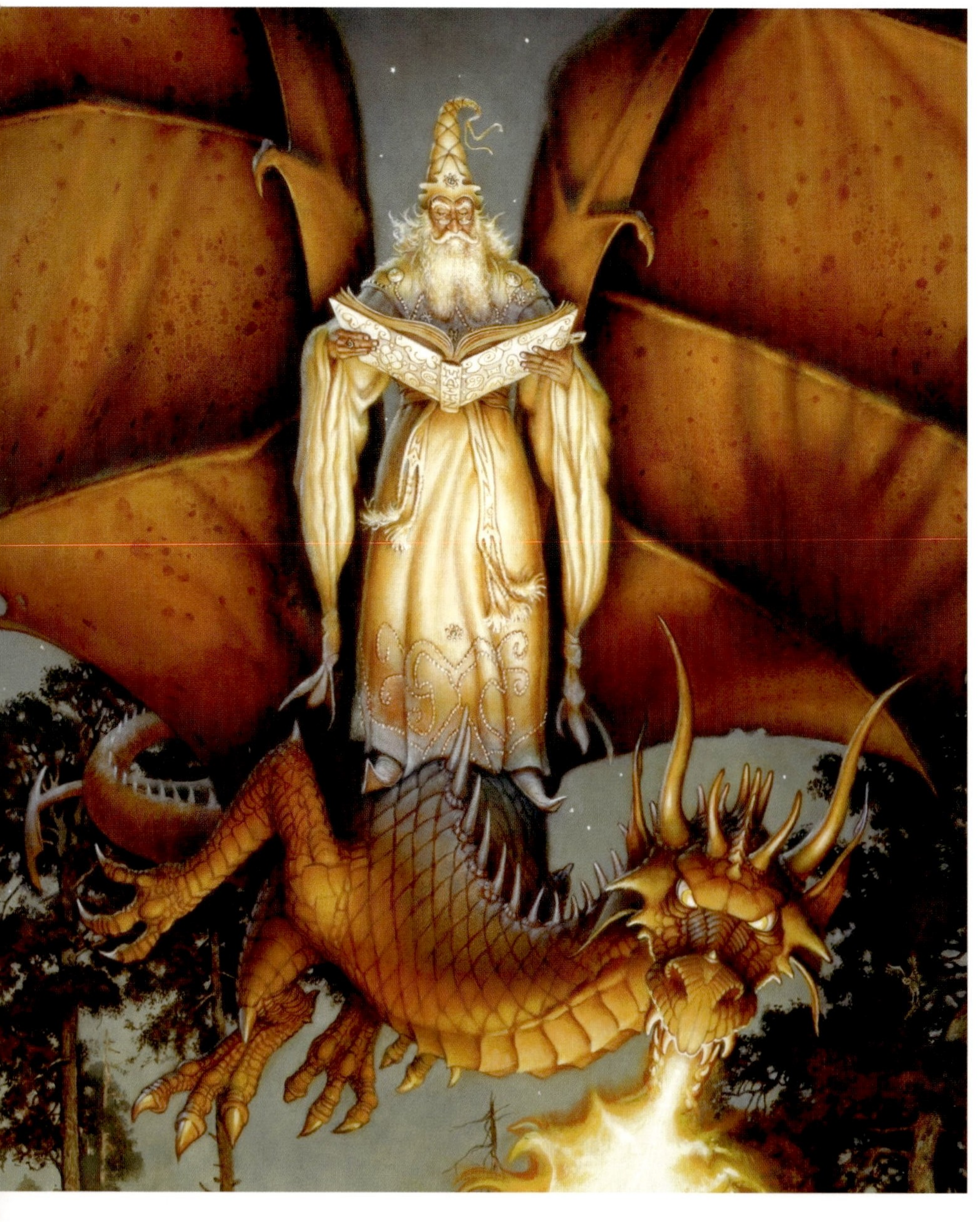

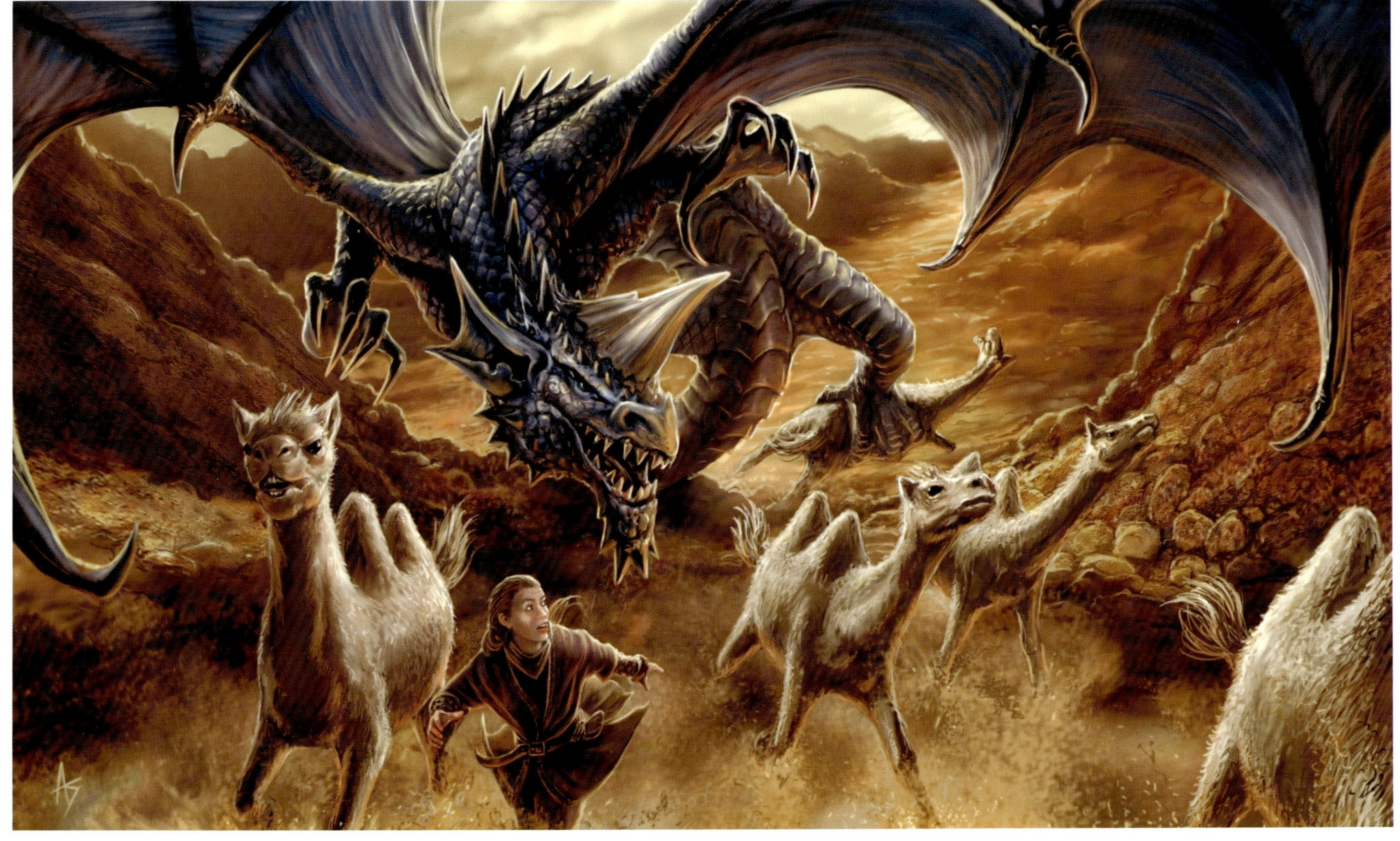

Foreword: Just What is it About Dragons?

They seem to be everywhere, their ubiquity matched only by their variety. No other creature has spread such colossal wings or dragged its scaly belly across the mythical lands of so many cultures over the aeons. They span the spectrum from devilry to divinity, from blackest evil to boundless good. They come in all configurations, they speak or they make our minds reel with the power of their thoughts, they squat athwart hoards of treasure untold. They are story. They are dragons.

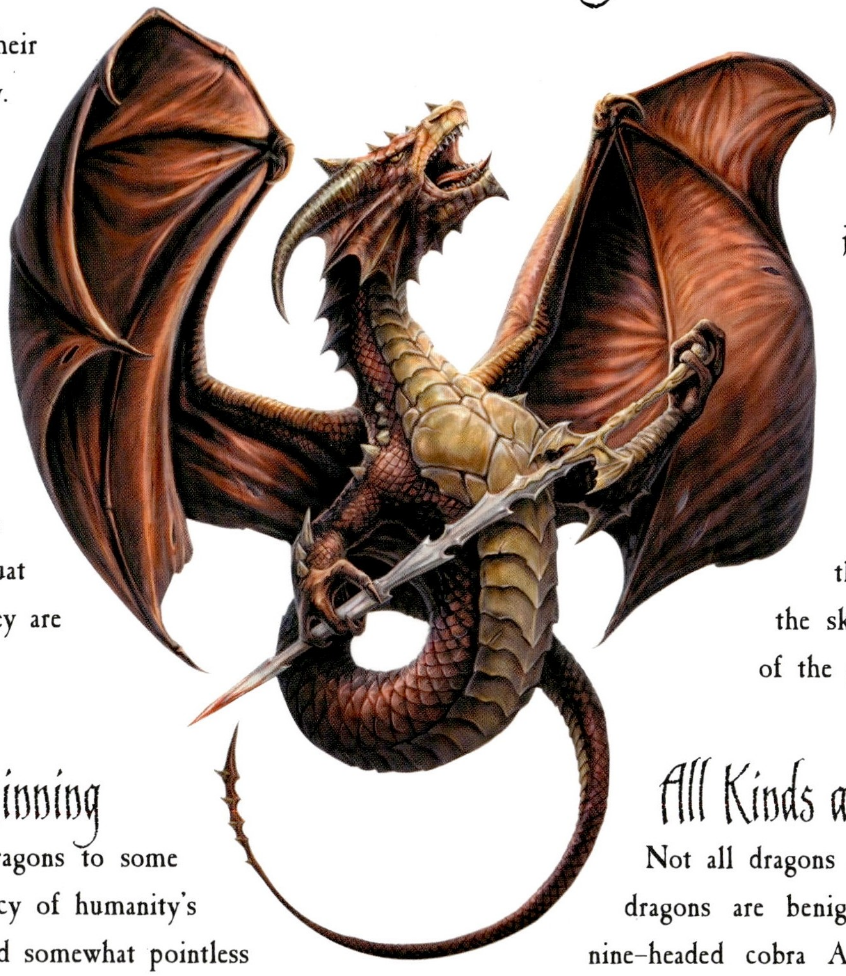

If dragons were there at the beginning, they will be there at the End. Jörmungandr will yawn wide his mighty jaws, releasing his tail, breaking the circle, breaking the world. Thor will slay him, only to die in the serpent's poison spew. Nidhoggr will gnaw so frantically at the roots of the 'world ash' Yggdrasil that it will fall, bringing down the sky-vault and heralding the end of the gods.

Mesmerizing from the Beginning

Attempts to link the existence of dragons to some proto-memory embedded in the infancy of humanity's genes seems, to me at least, a vain and somewhat pointless exercise in palaeontological euhemerism. When humans came to wonder what came *before*, they imagined dragons there.

Once upon a time, before time began, there were dragons, ur-creatures of turmoil and chaos, roiling, writhing, infinite. Against them battle the first heroes; Marduk slays Tiamat and, from her burst entrails, creates the world. But the dragon is not dead. Apep heaves his bulk after Ra as he journeys through the Underworld, renouncing only when the rays of the rising sun burn his flesh, to retire and lurk in wait for the dusk and pursue the sun once again.

All Kinds and Kindred

Not all dragons are forbidding or evil; oriental dragons are benign. The Naga, descendants of nine-headed cobra Ananta, accompanied the Indo-European tongues as they spread across Europe and Asia. Chinese dragons are multitude, a constellated hierarchy from imperial magnificence to the size of silkworms. They symbolize fertility and the dawn and have great affection for rivers.

Rivers too are loved by wyverns (that European variety of dragon) and by the dragon-like belle Melusina, who must leave her lover each Saturday to bathe alone. Despite his promises, he spies on her. It will not end well. There are many creatures that share this association with water, and share snake-like tails and fins – they are all kindred spirits of dragons. The banshee haunts the swamps and fens of Eire, luring hapless men to the water's edge and beyond. Her salt-water cousins, the mermaids, are as likely to ferry drowning sailors ashore as to take them deep, where they bare pointed teeth. Her pedigree is royal and ancient. These are beings not to be met on anything other than their own terms.

Ancient Lore and Legends

The serpent is in Eden and he knows the taste of apples. Mankind falls from grace, entwined in the coils of a dragon's wiles. Leviathan sinks, cowed but not defeated, beneath the waves of the Flood. Well, if God spurns him, the Devil will have him, and the dragon becomes his dire ally, evil coldsnake of Apocrypha's richest myths, bane of Christian knight, consort of the Old Ones that flee before the Irish missionaries. When Patrick drove the snakes from Ireland, they were likely swimming in the wakes of dragons (though the dragon Lig-na-baste would linger until tricked into submission by Saint Murrough). When Charlemagne felled Irminsul, the dragon likely heard it from where he lurked beneath the dark eaves of the Alemannen woods. The boy Merlin found the white and red wyrms whose struggles brought down the foundations of Vortigern's castle at Dinas Emrys and later dragons became the standard of king Uther 'chief-dragon' Pendragon.

The dragon sided with the Titans against the Dodekatheon; Hercules hacked manfully at Ladon until the hydra finally stopped sprouting heads and expired. A dragon slumbers beneath the apple tree from whose boughs hang the Golden Fleece.

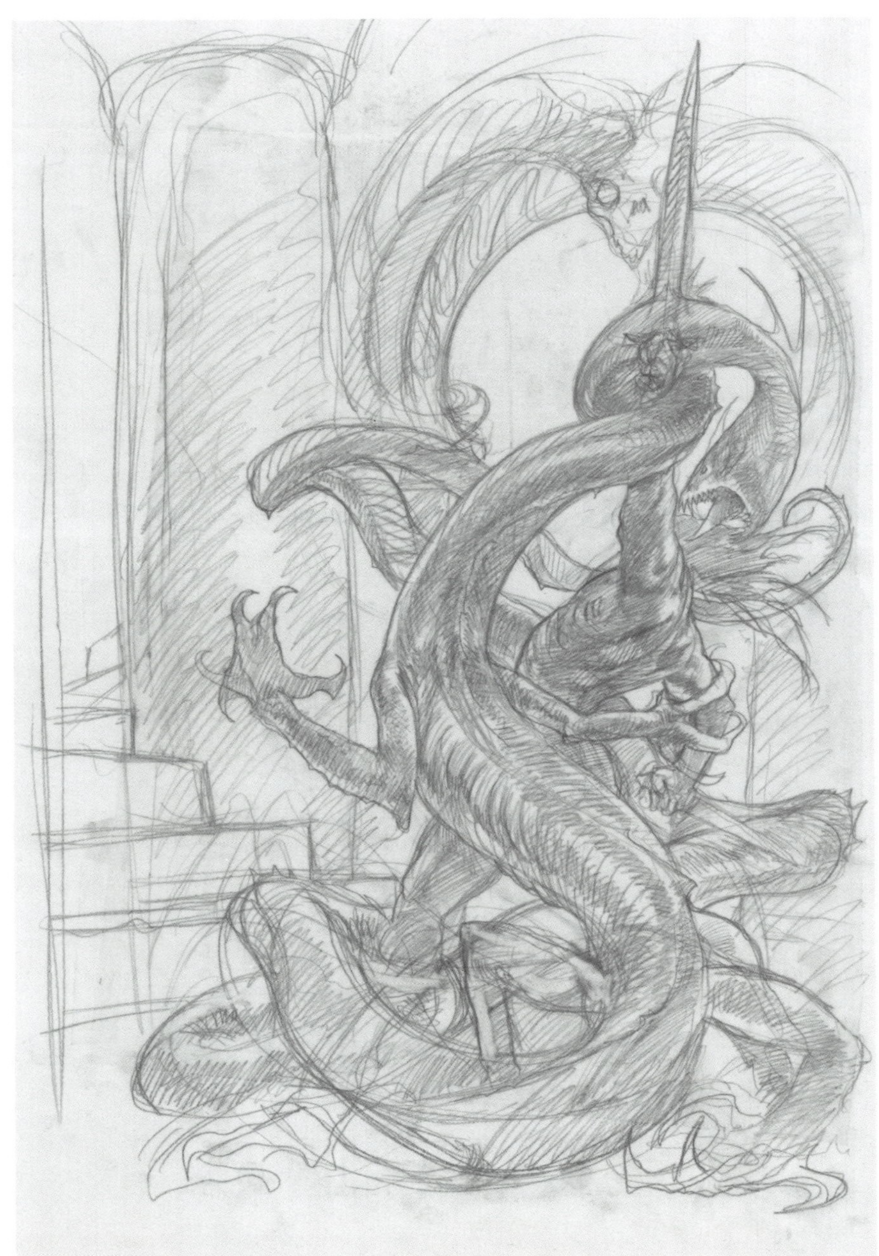

Sketch for RED NAILS by John Howe
© John Howe 2001
Traditional media: pencil on tracing paper
Sketch for the cover illustration for *The Conan Chronicles, Volume 2: The Hour of the Dragon* by Robert E. Howard, published by Gollancz – *see* page 17.

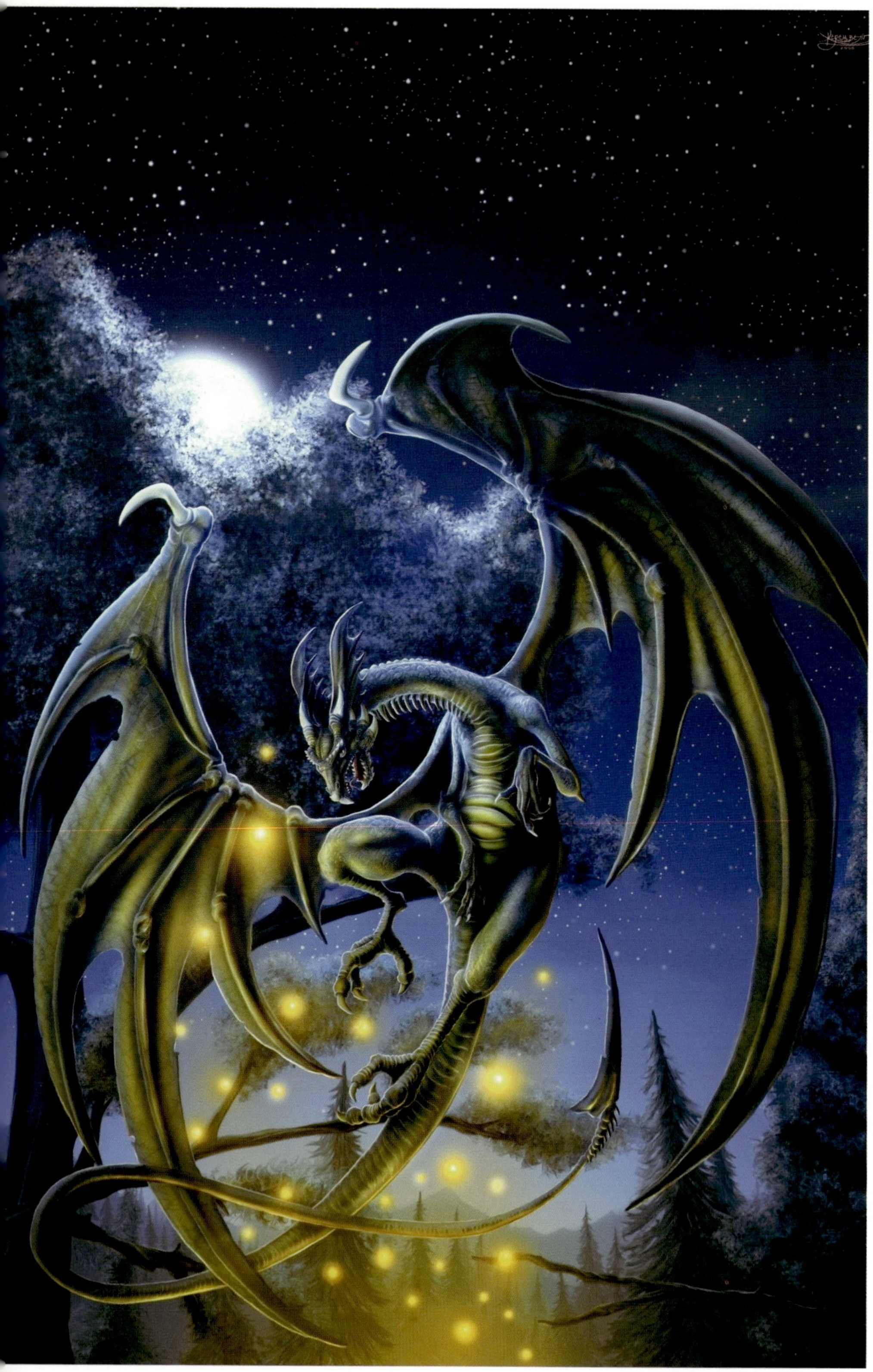

Sea monsters are the dragons of the waves: Scylla gratefully devours the ships wrecked by Charybdis, as Cetus would have swallowed Andromeda, had not Perseus captured Pegasus in time to race to her aid.

Heroes and Saints

Beowulf bravely goes to his doom against the dragon, knowing he goes to a fight he can only win in death. Fafnir the giant is so consumed by his greed for treasure that he takes on the shape of a dragon. Siegfried slays Fafnir and, in licking from his hand a drop of the creature's blood, can understand the language of birds. (There is magic in the blood of dragons, as Aesculapius might testify.) Vlad Drakul is the son of a dragon.

Saint George acquires a dragon, a charger and bright armour en route from his obscure third-century martyrdom in Cappadocia to the splendid flowering of medieval chivalry, in company of other saints who battle or overcome dragons – Michael, Margaret, Victor and Armentaire to name but a few – bequeathing us an artistic legacy of painting and sculpture unparalleled. Dragons appear in stone, wood and metal, spitting water from cathedrals and fountains, or crouch beneath darkened layers of varnish in countless canvases.

All Corners of Culture

Nor does the Renaissance dismiss dragons. Like unicorns, they haunt the marches of the not-yet-known, the high ridges, the foreign shores. Sea serpents abound in mariners' tales, and in the early 1700s Swiss polymath Johann Scheuchzer adorned his *Itinera per Helvetiae alpinas regiones* with detailed copperplates of diverse dragons sighted in the Alps.

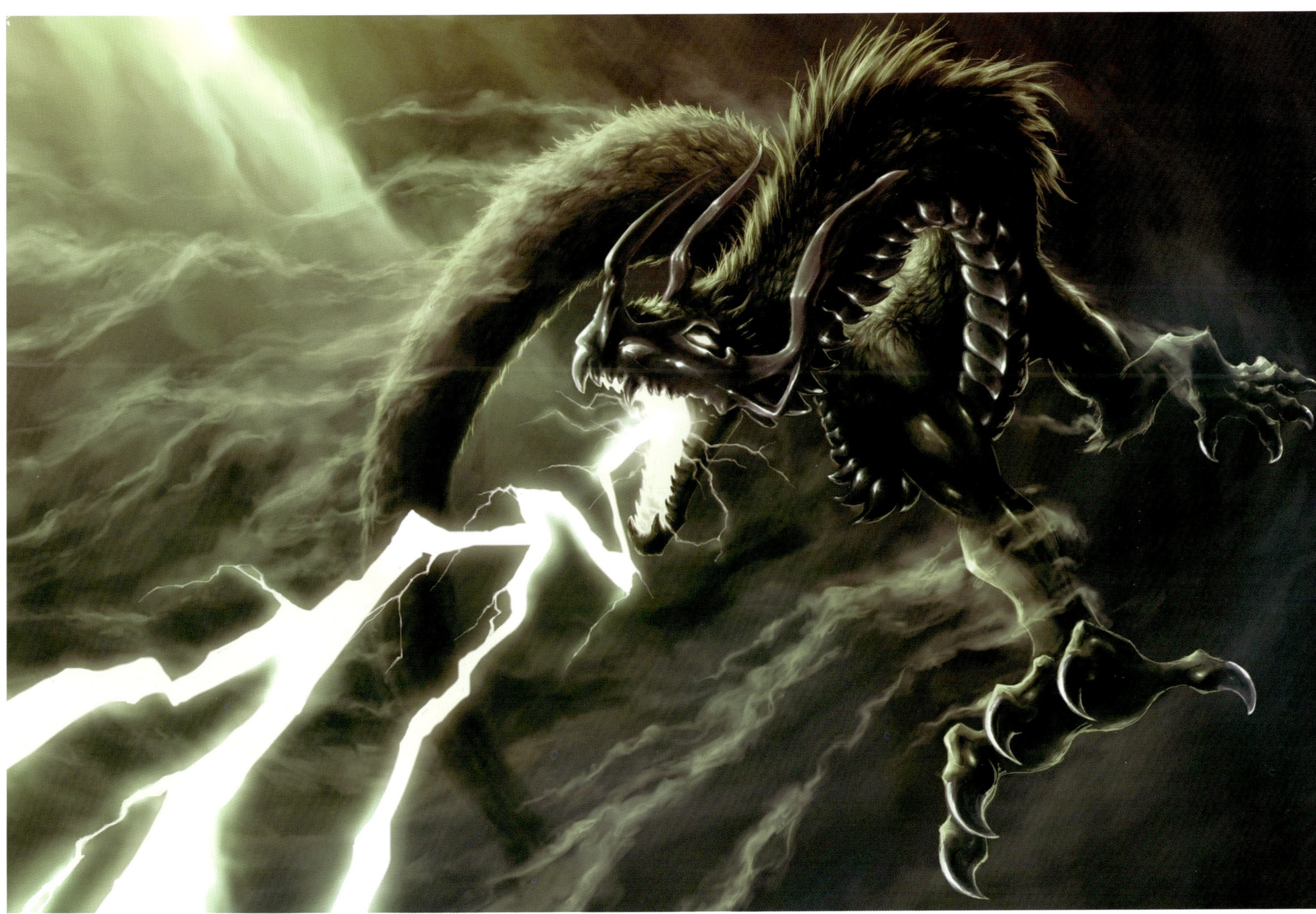

When the CERN finally makes molecules collide to give us the image of the beginning of the universe, I am confident a dragon will appear on the computer screens. After all, what is the Hadron Collider but a smaller version of the wyrm Ouroboros, the world-encompasser, the circle-snake with his tail held in his jaws?

Beyond science, dragons flex their wings in science fiction with such forceful presence they bend space-time to accommodate them whole. Few other creatures can make this quantum leap with such arrogance and poise.

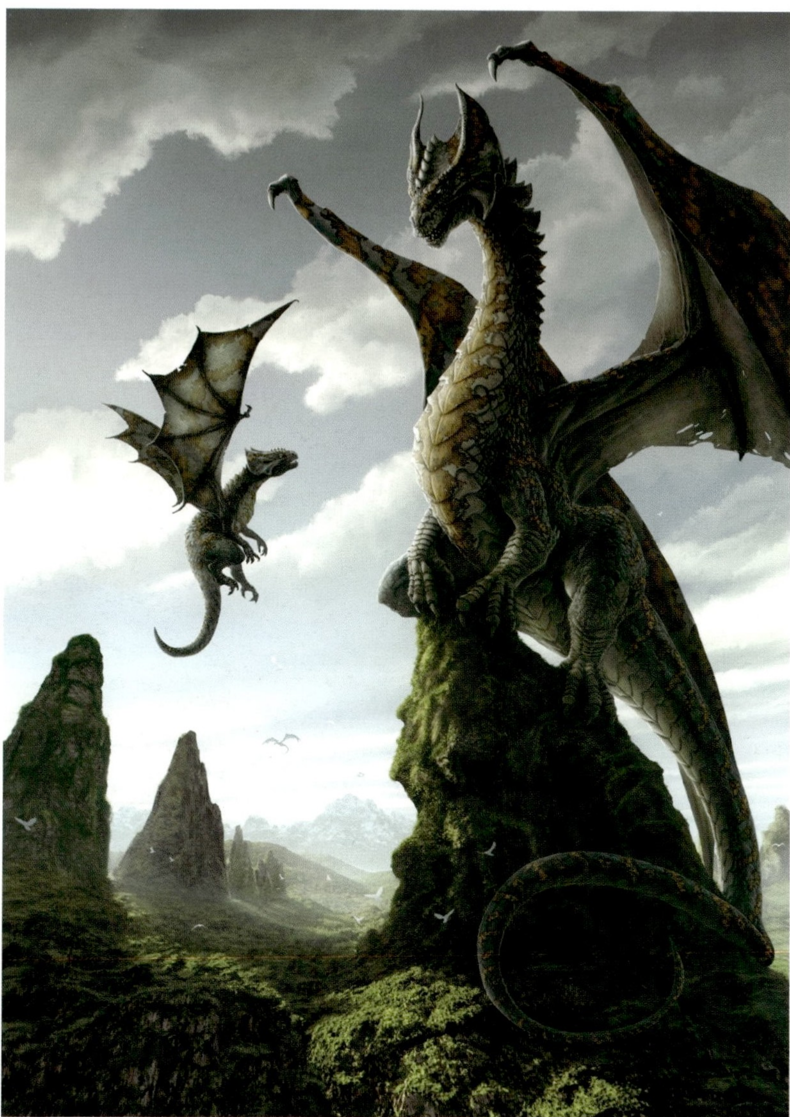

Fantasy's Dragons

But perhaps nowhere more than in modern fantasy do we encounter such a diversity of dragons. Smaug is the last descendant of Fafnir and Beowulf's bane and the father of dragons of modern fiction. His scaled and pinioned peers are legion. Icefyre, Saphira, Chrysophylax Dives, Temeraire, Errol Goodbody of Flynn and many more are witness that dragons are far from an endangered species.

Artists have been fascinated with dragons for millennia, and modern fantasy illustrators are not immune to their baleful charms. They exercise a wicked charm and a perilous glamour, offering the best of both worlds – challenges of visual representation with depth of meaning. (Dragons are not just another pretty face, they have personalities, too.) They resist easy anthropomorhizing, thus redefining the visual terms of their iconography. Dragons are irresistible.

A Personal Quest

Years of drawing and painting them have led me no nearer to truly defining dragons. Somewhere in their diversity resides an archetype that escapes me yet. Nor can I impose upon them a recognizable style of dragon, something that the enviable likes of Ciruelo, Michael Whelan or Wayne Anderson so excel at. I leaf through books of dragons painted by Rackham, Vasnetzov, Doré, Blake or Von Stuck. I have a few dozen serious non-fiction books on dragon myth, all avidly read and dog-eared, so I must be closing in. The trail is clear, but they remain elusive. Somewhere, some day, in a painting or a drawing, I know I have a rendezvous with the Dragon.

All in all, *sic hunt draconis* has never been more apt an expression. Simply, it no longer applies to those uncharted lands on maps of 'Africk' that cartographers once decorated with dragons, but to those places within our very selves we can but ill explore, the interior kingdoms of our fears and aspirations, our victories and defeats. That is where we are doomed and charmed to wander, and to face we know not what. Only one thing is certain: we will meet dragons there.

JOHN HOWE

John has published a book featuring many of his own dragon artworks: *Forging Dragons*.

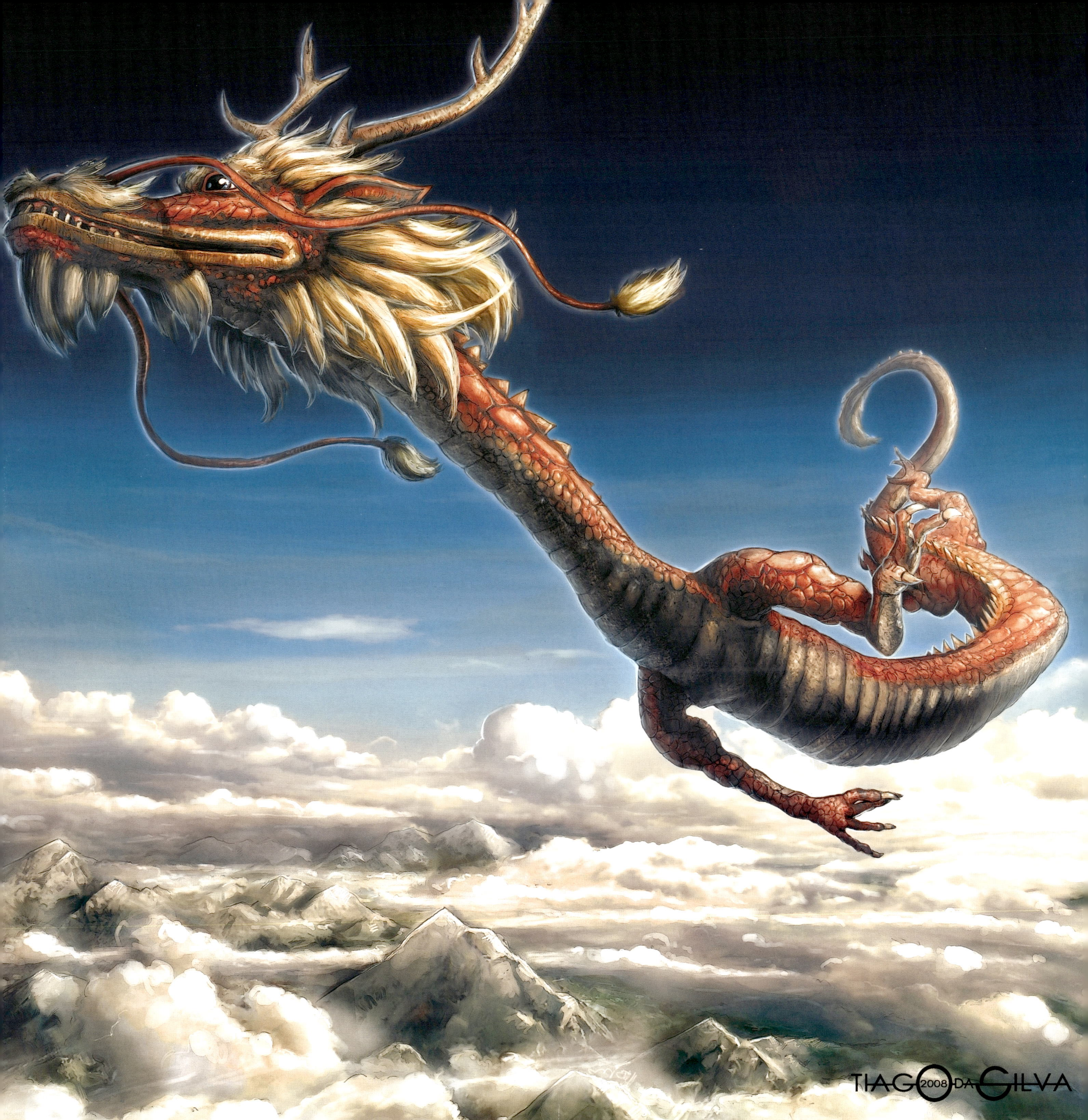
TIAGO 2008 DA SILVA

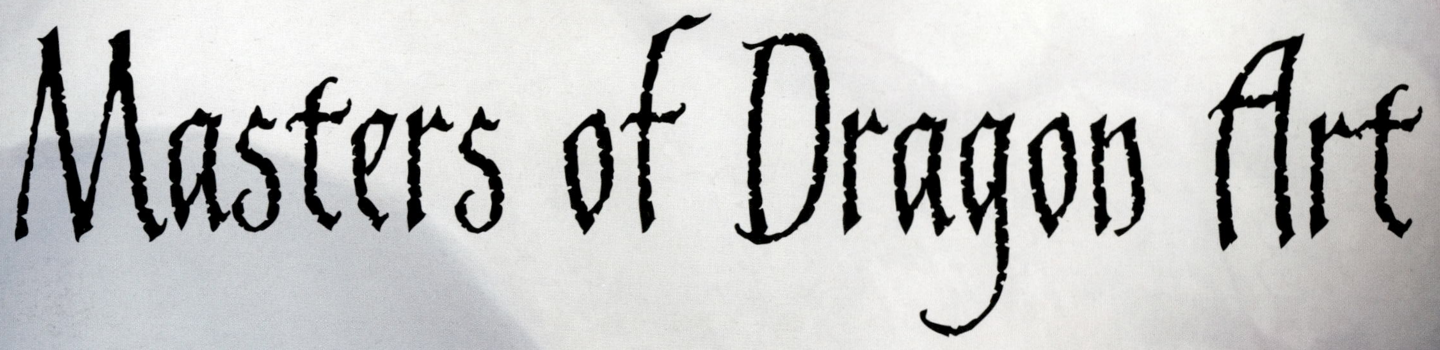

Masters of Dragon Art

To attempt to classify which artists are the 'masters' of any genre is perhaps a foolish task, as it is such a subjective and wide open debate. In a book such as this we could not hope to cover all those deserving of mention, but it is still worth highlighting a few artists who are perhaps significant, not only in their talent and success as fantasy artists, but as creators of some of the most impressive, celebrated and prolific dragons. The artists discussed over the following pages each have their own unique, distinctive style and have brought a whole range of dragon characters to life. Their work has collectively won awards aplenty and is recognizable by virtue of featuring in advertising, book covers and illustrations, album covers, games design and merchandise – the list is endless. Any fantasy fan will know the art if not the names – too infrequently do we celebrate the artists behind the work.

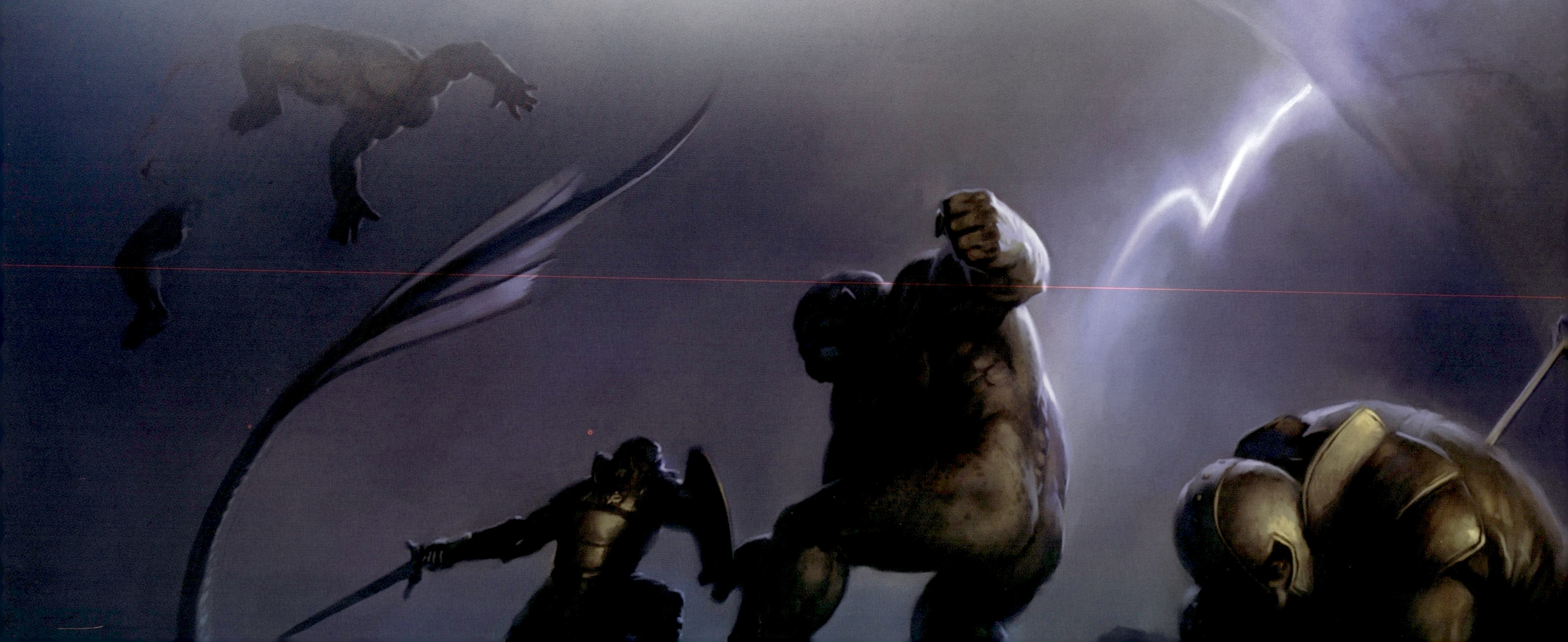

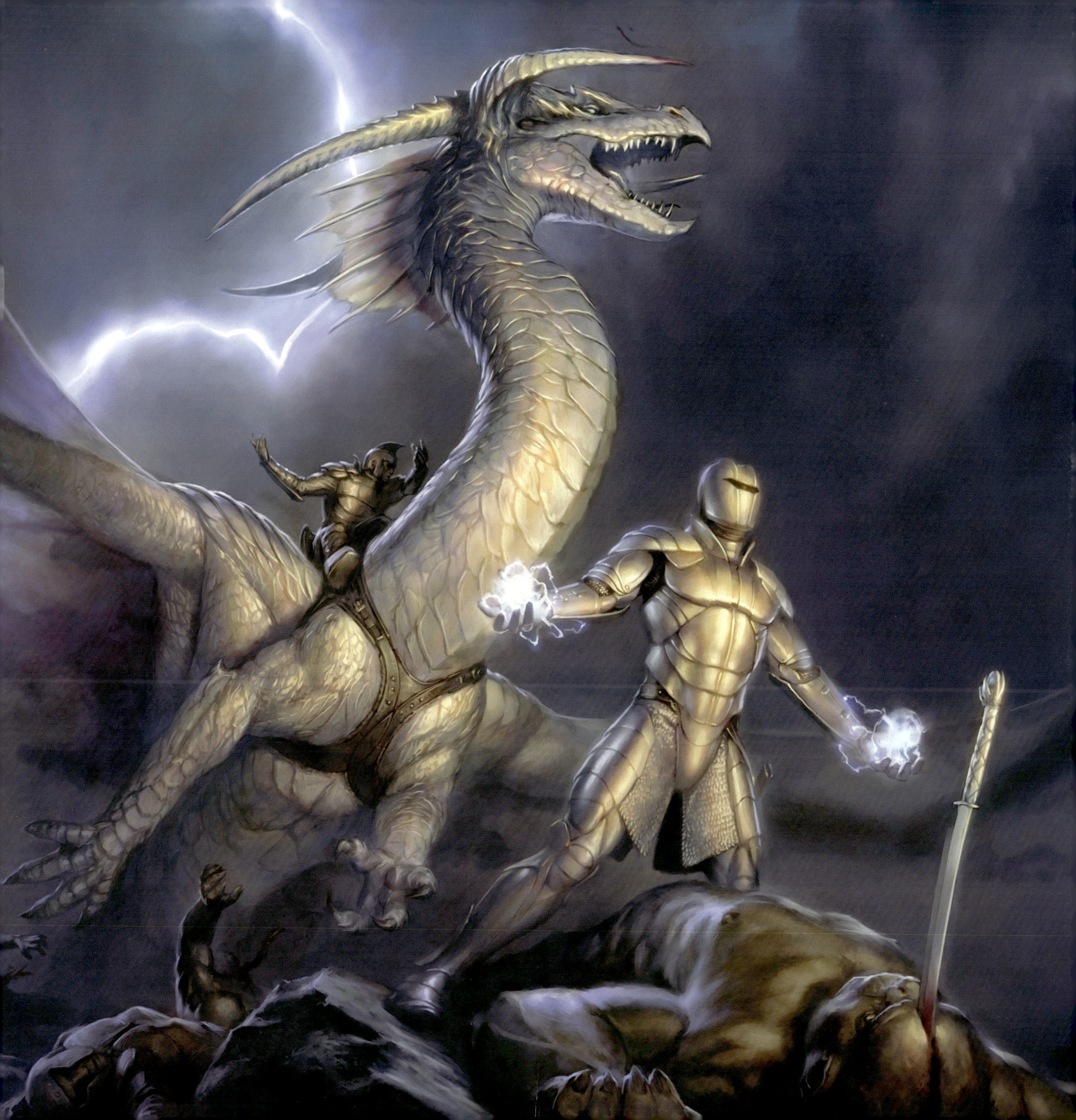

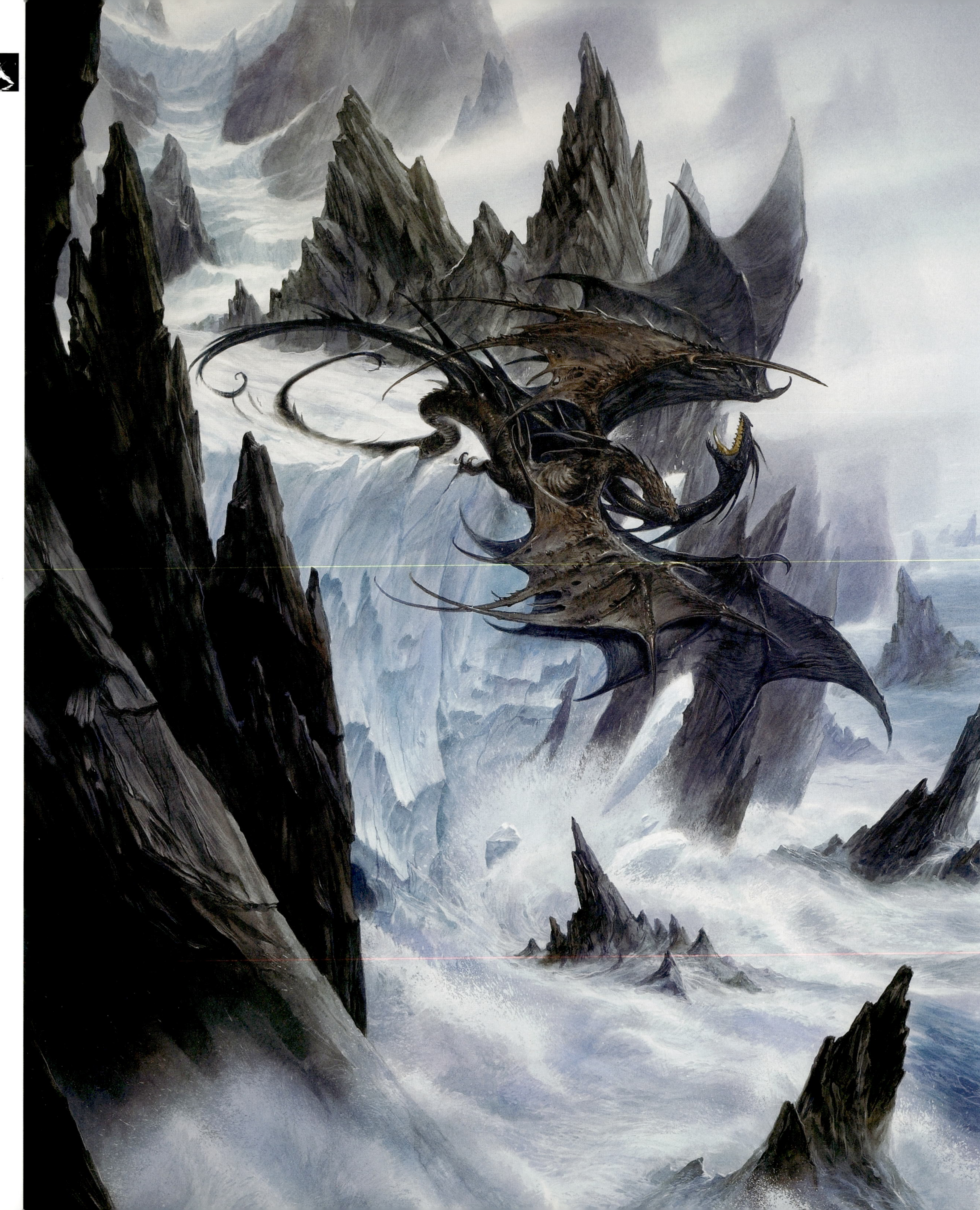

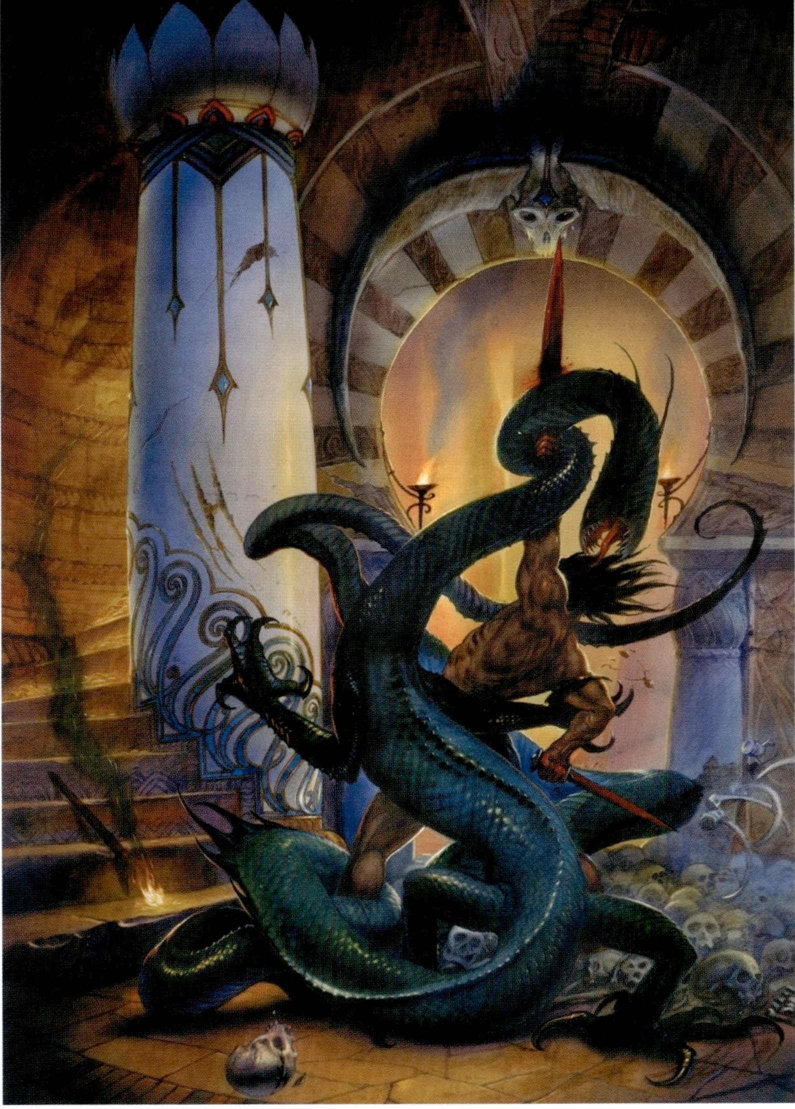

John Howe

Perhaps John Howe is an artist's artist. At the start of the decade, the Vancouver-born painter, along with Alan Lee, found himself the 'go-to' guy for film director Peter Jackson to come up with the visual tone and vision for his *Lord of the Rings* trilogy, and he has written and contributed to countless books about fantasy and mythology, again setting the standard for illustrations in such works as *The Hobbit* and *Beowulf*.

Currently residing in Switzerland, Howe recalls having a talent for drawing throughout his adolescence, inspired by, among others, Frank Frazetta comics illustrators Barry Windsor-Smith and Bernie Wrightson. He also cites a number of nineteenth- and early-twentieth-century artists and art movements for influence, such as the pre-Raphaelites and Art Nouveau. His talent took him to Strasbourg after he graduated from high school in Canada, to complete a three-year course at the École des Arts Décoratifs, which he concedes was no easy task. But it enabled him to pick up the practical skills of an artist that have come in highly useful throughout his working life.

Famously, Howe researches his work in great detail, undertaking a great deal of historical enquiry and archaeological fieldwork in pursuit of accuracy. In addition, he is not averse to donning armour himself as he strives to 'get it right'.

In terms of dragons, Howe's work for Jackson and his vision of Hobbit bête noire Smaug, as previously mentioned, are legend. But he has also worked with highly respected author Anne McCaffrey for her book *A Diversity of Dragons*. That project saw him illustrate dragons from all around the world, from the familiar European tales of St George and Sigurd all the way through to ancient Egyptian sea serpent Apophis, who would chase the sun god across the sky every day, or Tiamat, the dragon of chaos from ancient Babylonian mythology. The self-confessed watercolour fan is, without doubt, a master of fantasy illustration and a master of dragon art.

ICEFYRE & THE STONE DRAGON by John Howe
© John Howe 2003 · Traditional media: ink and watercolour
Cover illustration for *Fool's Fate*, Book Three of *The Tawny Man* by Robin Hobb, published by HarperVoyager.

RED NAILS by John Howe
© John Howe 2001 · Traditional media: ink and watercolour
Cover illustration for *The Conan Chronicles*, Volume 2: *The Hour of the Dragon* by Robert E. Howard, published by Gollancz.

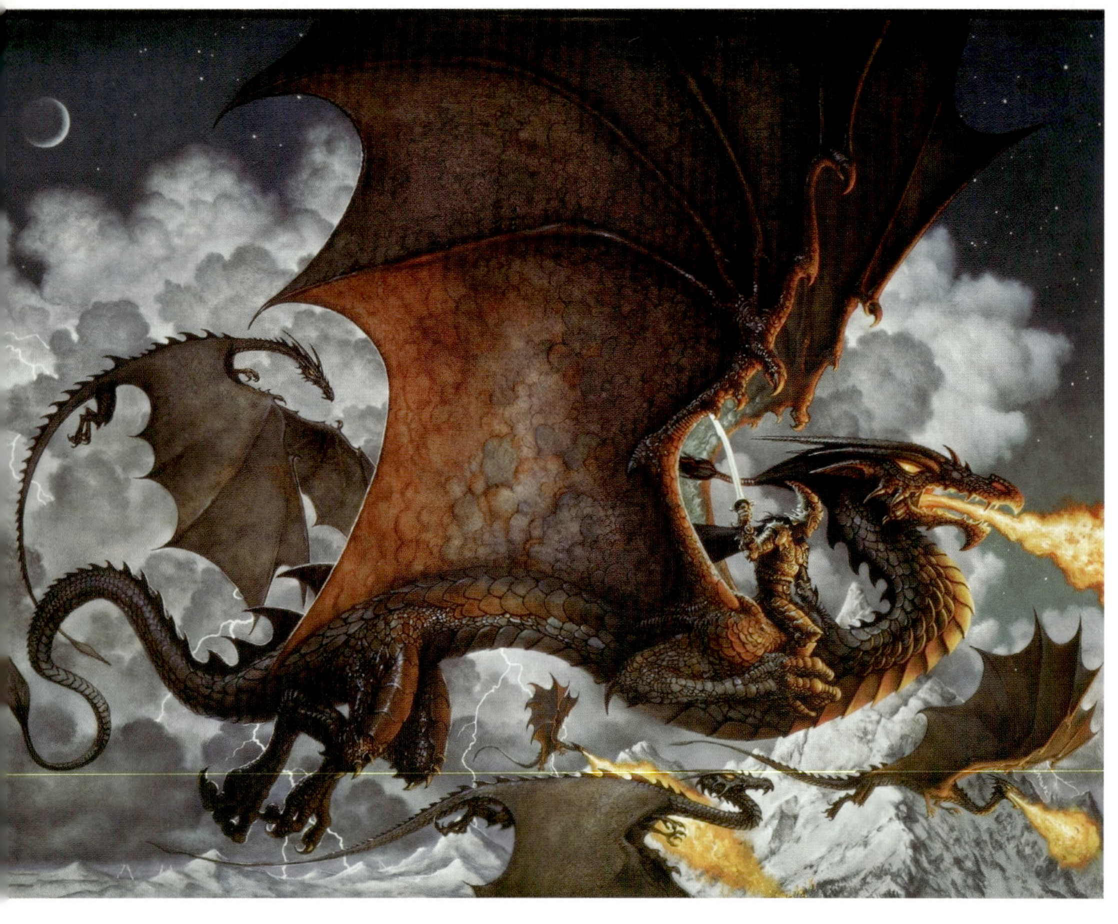

He has worked for a clientele as varied as The National Geographic Society, HarperCollins, Penguin and Warner Bros Books. He has even had his work used by NASA, at one of the space agency's twenty-fifth-year commemorative events. He has won plentiful awards, including ten Chesley awards, a silver medal from the New York Society of Illustrators and two Hugo awards. He has also produced two books of his own, *Dreamquests, The Art of Don Maitz* and *First Maitz* showcasing his art and providing insight into his working method.

Don's method is traditional, in that it is all about paint on masonite, which is prepared in such a way that he calls it, with a wink, 'Maitzonite'. Working mostly with acrylic and oil, he also uses plenty of traditional painterly technique, with glazing and scumbling particularly important to his production of rich, mysterious, character-driven work.

Don Maitz

It is not difficult to see why Don Maitz should be feted as a master of fantasy art. For one thing, there is the oft-cited fact that he created the Captain Morgan pirate character for the label of the rum of the same name, so familiar to lovers of mojitos, piña coladas and daiquiris. In fact, Maitz's portfolio is rich with pirates and similar swashbucklers.

There is more to Maitz's portfolio, though. He has painted numerous works of science fiction and fantasy, from white-bearded sorcerers and countless conjurers to helmeted heroes in outer space, adventuring in galaxies far, far away. Maitz has also collaborated with his wife, Janny Wurts, for a number of works.

Like his countless sorcerers, Maitz creates dragons of unfathomed majesty and mysticism. They have a complex relationship with their human characters, which is central to much of Maitz's paintings. These are not beasts to be slain to stave off the horror of townsfolk. They are creatures to be explored and explained to the reader or the viewer. The complexity and standard of his work easily elevates Don Maitz to the realm of the masters of fantasy art.

Dragons on the Sea of Night by Don Maitz
© Don Maitz 1996 · Traditional media: oil on masonite
www.paravia.com/DonMaitz

Booked Flight by Don Mait
© Don Maitz 1999 · Traditional media: oil on masonite
www.paravia.com/DonMaitz

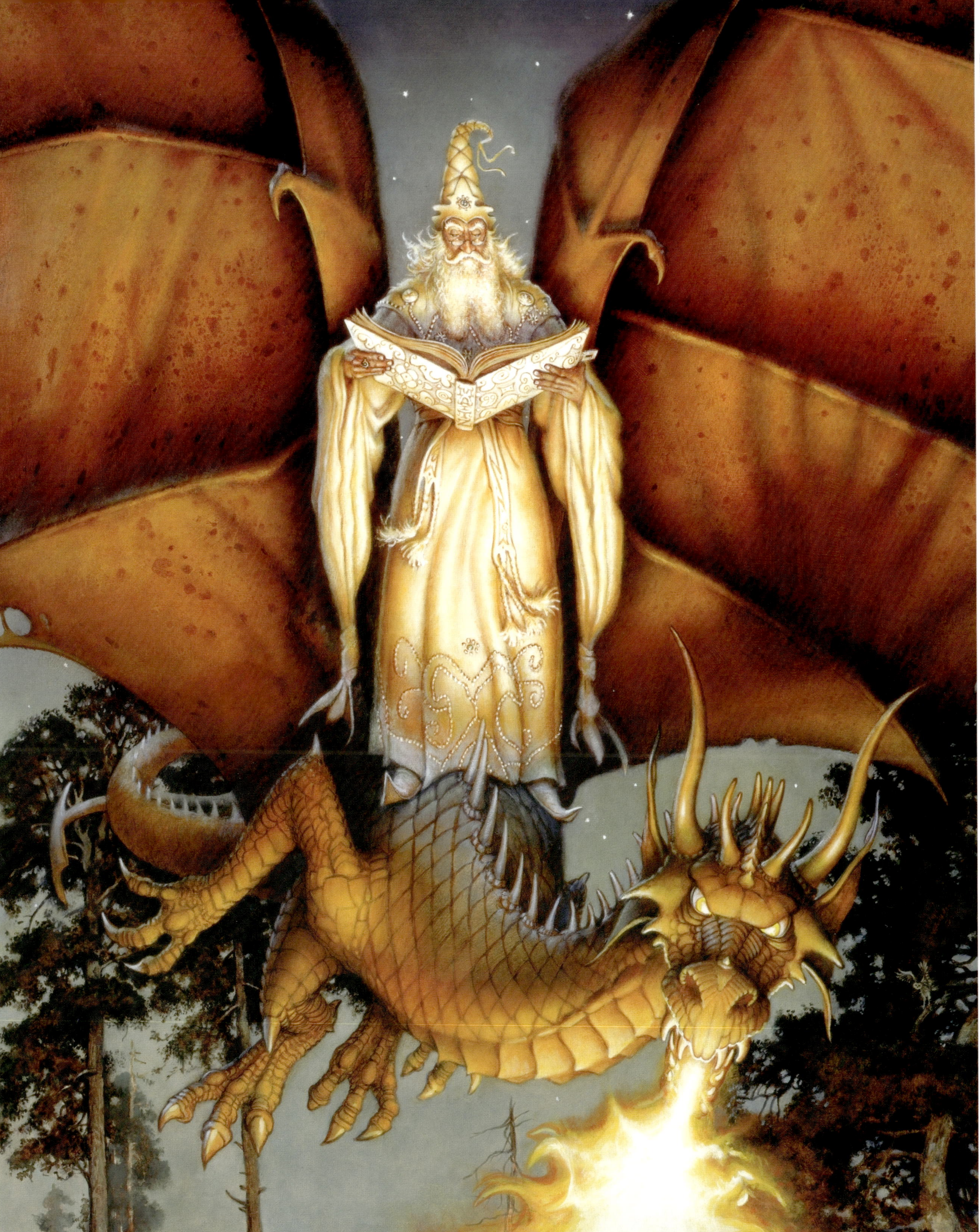

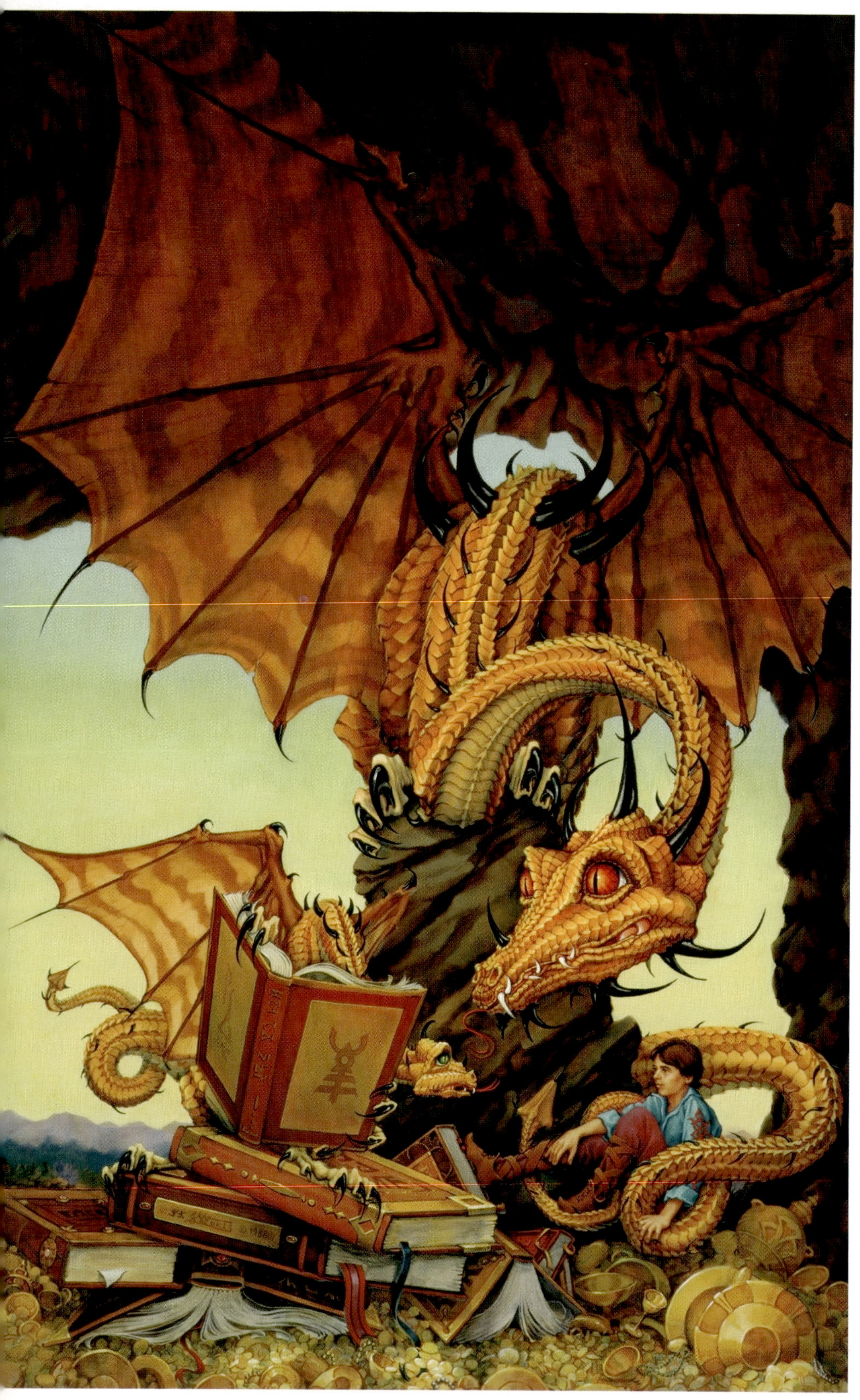

Janny Wurts

Janny Wurts is something of an unusual fantasy artist, being as she is both a writer and an artist. She has written in excess of a dozen fantasy novels in her own right, including the *Cycle of Fire* trilogy as well as the *Wars of Light and Shadow* series. Her name is found next to such titles as *Stormwarden*, *Keeper of the Keys*, *Shadowfane*, *Curse of the Mistwraith*, *Ships of Merior* and *Warhost of Vastmark*. She has in addition released several volumes of short stories and a collaboration, the *Empire Trilogy*, with author Raymond E. Feist.

As an artist, Wurts is self-taught, with Howard Pyle and Maxfield Parrish in particular as influences, alongside tales of Camelot and Greek mythology. Wurts says that her stories are less about 'the elves killing the orcs' as favoured by traditional sword-and-sorcery fanciers, and more investigations of human motivation; the moral ambiguities of right and wrong, consequences of actions undertaken for whatever rationale and so on. It is more shades of grey than black and white, good and evil, in her opinion, and fantasy enables her to delve into the issues with a depth and rigour that would be impossible to her if she were shackled by the constraints of the so-called 'real world'.

TAKEN TO TASK by Janny Wurts
© Janny Wurts 1994 · Traditional media: oil on masonite
www.paravia.com/JannyWurts

DRAGON'S RUN by Janny Wurts
© Janny Wurts 1981 · Traditional media: acrylic and oil on masonite
This piece hangs in the Delaware Art Museum.
www.paravia.com/JannyWurts

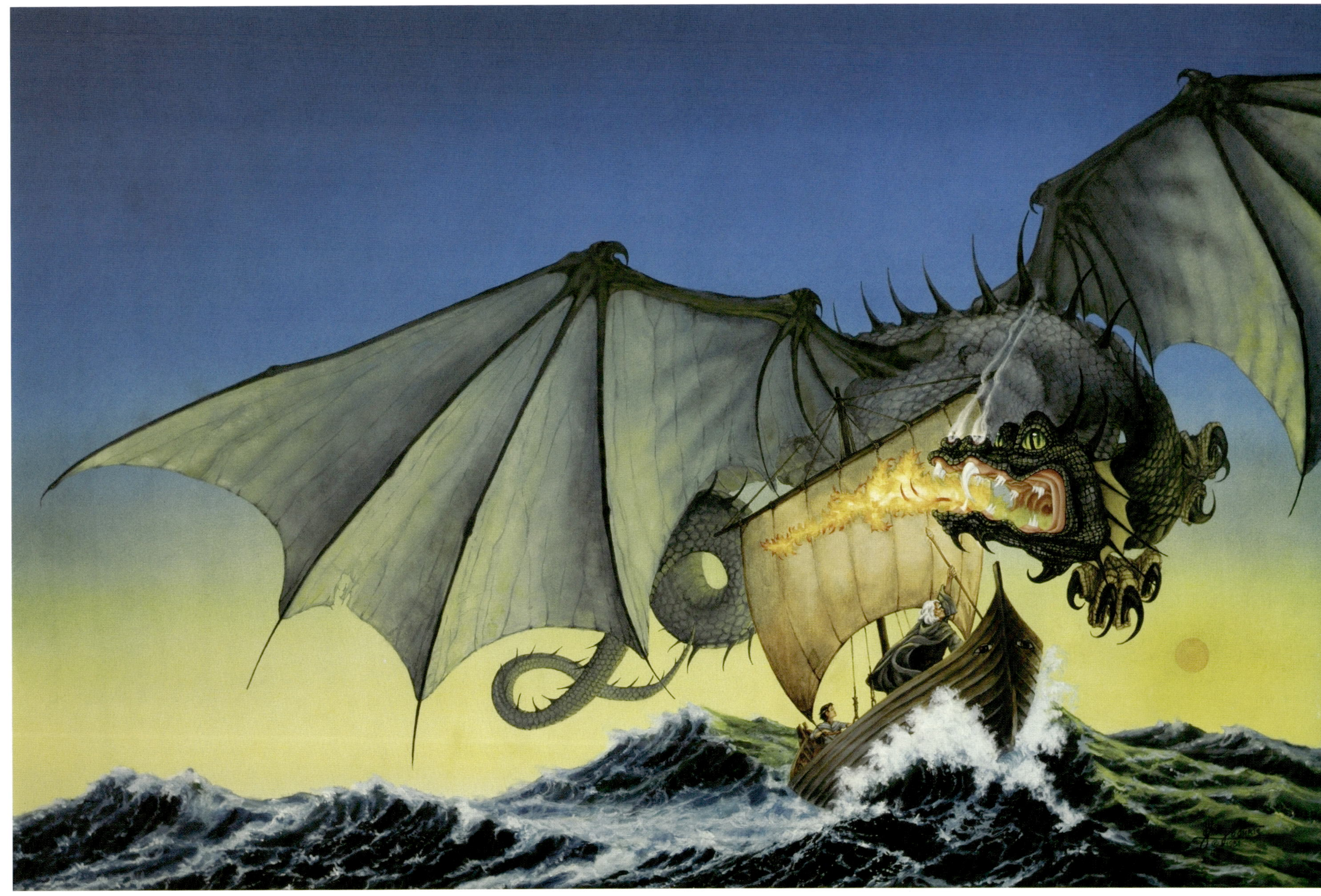

To an extent, her art reflects this. She draws almost exclusively from her imagination rather than from reference, although she does admit that to understand the properties of cloth and fabric she will sometimes get a model in to check for light and texture issues. As such, her art can feel more representational or impressionistic than the rooted-in-reality scaly-monster, muscular-hero tableaux of many a fantasy artist. That is not to assign a higher value to either style – both are equally valid. Wurts's take can, however, approach some subjects with a flexibility that more reality-based styles cannot; her dragons can at times appear large and fierce, or at others as helping wise figures, child-friendly guides, or more inspired by the Orient, for instance. Without a doubt, as author and illustrator, Janny Wurts is among the masters of fantasy art.

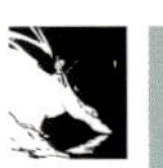

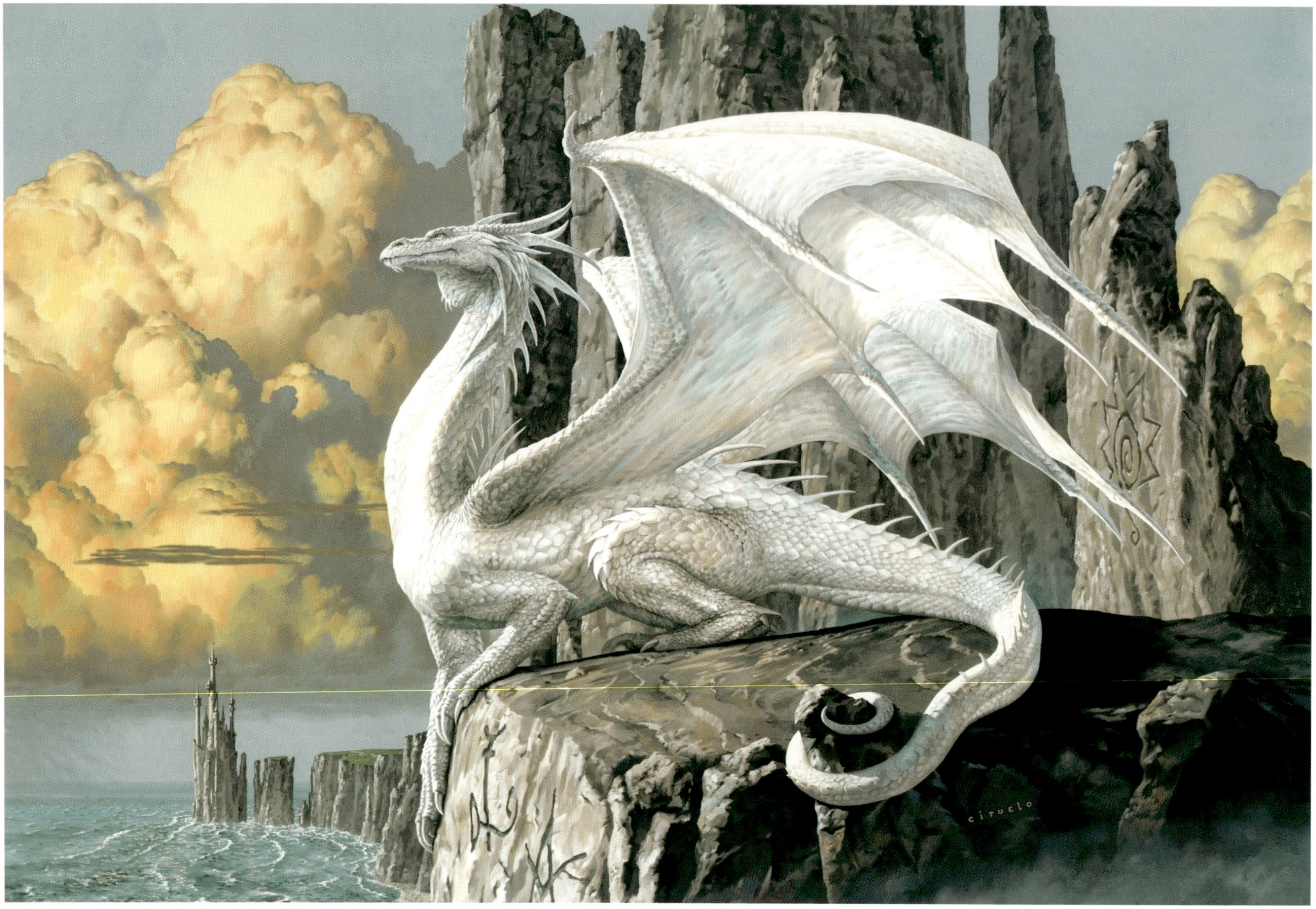

Ciruelo

Ciruelo is undoubtedly on the experimental side of fantasy art. While the debate rages between digital versus traditional art, Ciruelo has literally headed outside and found an entirely new base for his painting: stones. His 'petropictos' project has seen him literally painting on to stones he has recovered, with their shapes dictating the creatures and figures featured. It is, according to him, a cross between painting and sculpture. Appropriately, much of his painting features a marbling technique designed to give a stony texture to the subject matter.

But there is plenty more to Ciruelo. Born Ciruelo Cabral in Argentina, his working career began in advertising design in his late teens, but by the age of 21 he had embarked upon his career as a fantasy artist. For over 20 years, he has been a Barcelona resident. He has illustrated a wide selection of published material, including George Lucas's *Chronicles of the Shadow War* for Bantam and countless illustrations for Warner, *Heavy Metal* magazine, Wizards of the Coast and Tor books. He also famously designed the cover for *The 7th Song* and *The Elusive Light and Sound* for guitar virtuoso and sometime-Frank-Zappa collaborator Steve Vai. He has also produced four art books, including his very own *The Book of the Dragon.* He has recently written and illustrated a book

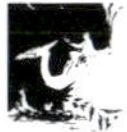

entitled *Fairies and Dragons*, inspired by his children, in which dragons play their part in the debate about nature and ecology.

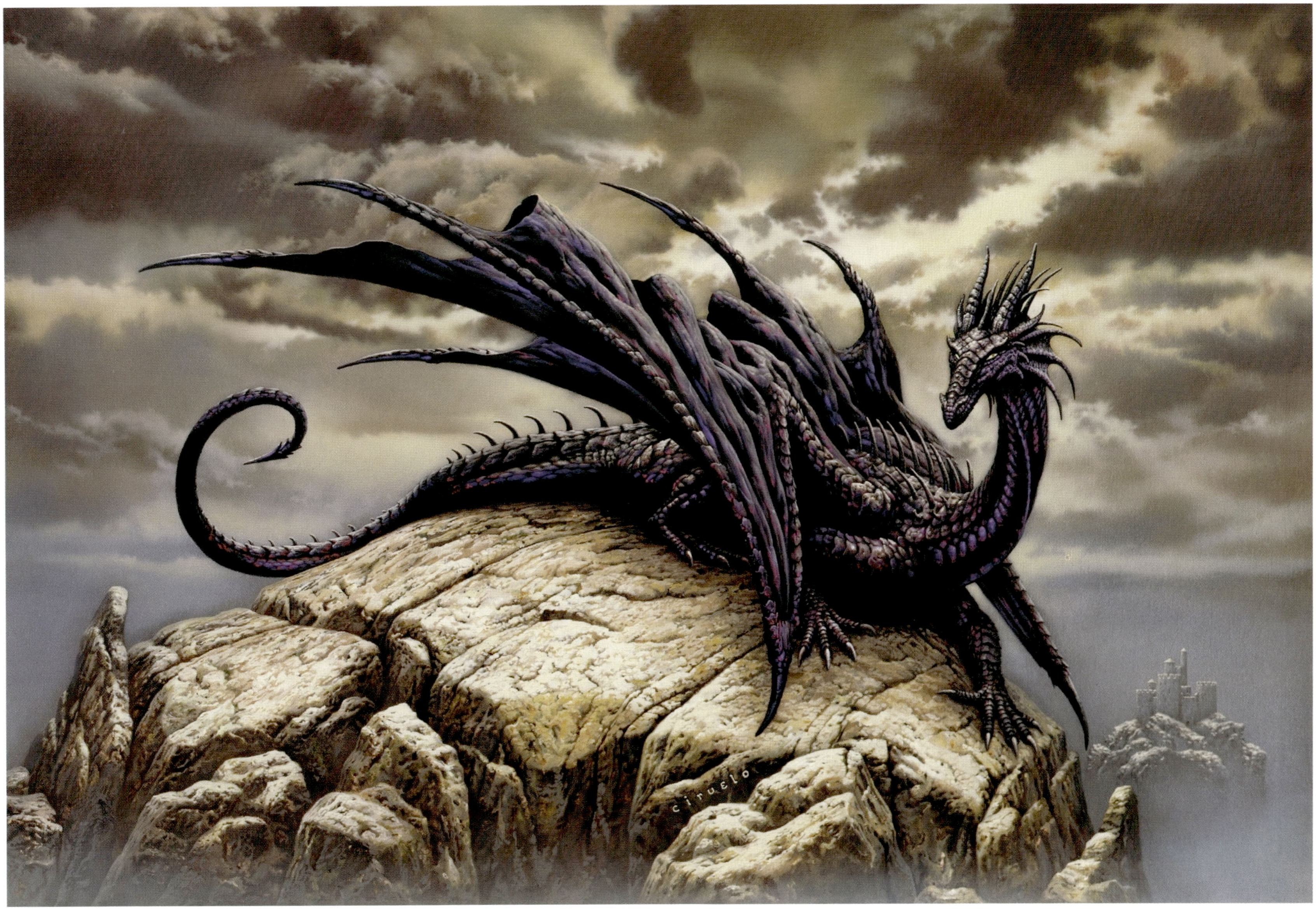

His technique is very much based on tradition, with oil his paint of choice to produce his fantasy and science fiction. His work features a fair selection of frightening dragons: large monsters to be dispatched by sword-wielding, often armour-clad heroes working in defence of castles and queens.

HOBSYLLWIN, THE WHITE DRAGON by Ciruelo
© Ciruelo 2003 · Traditional media: oil on canvas
www.dac-editions.com

DARK DSURION by Ciruelo
© Ciruelo 1997 · Traditional media: acrylic on canvas
www.dac-editions.com

But, as a South American, Ciruelo is also very much interested in New World dragons and serpents: in fact, his *Fairies and Dragons* takes place in the Americas rather than Europe. This also informs his artistic take on dragons. In particular, he cites Tren Tren and Kai Kai, benevolent and evil land and sea serpents respectively, of pre-Columbian, Patagonian Mapuche folklore, as favourites. His originality and mastery of the material ensure Ciruelo's place among the masters of fantasy art.

Bob Eggleton

From *Godzilla* to *Aliens*, Bob Eggleton is a fantasy artist who knows no boundaries. Hailing from New England, Eggleton was inspired by a range of artists old and new, including J.M.W. Turner, Eugène Delacroix, John Constable and, of course, Frank Frazetta. He is also a devotee of museums, constantly visiting them to get to grips with art of all kinds. Eggleton is also a keen reader of science fiction.

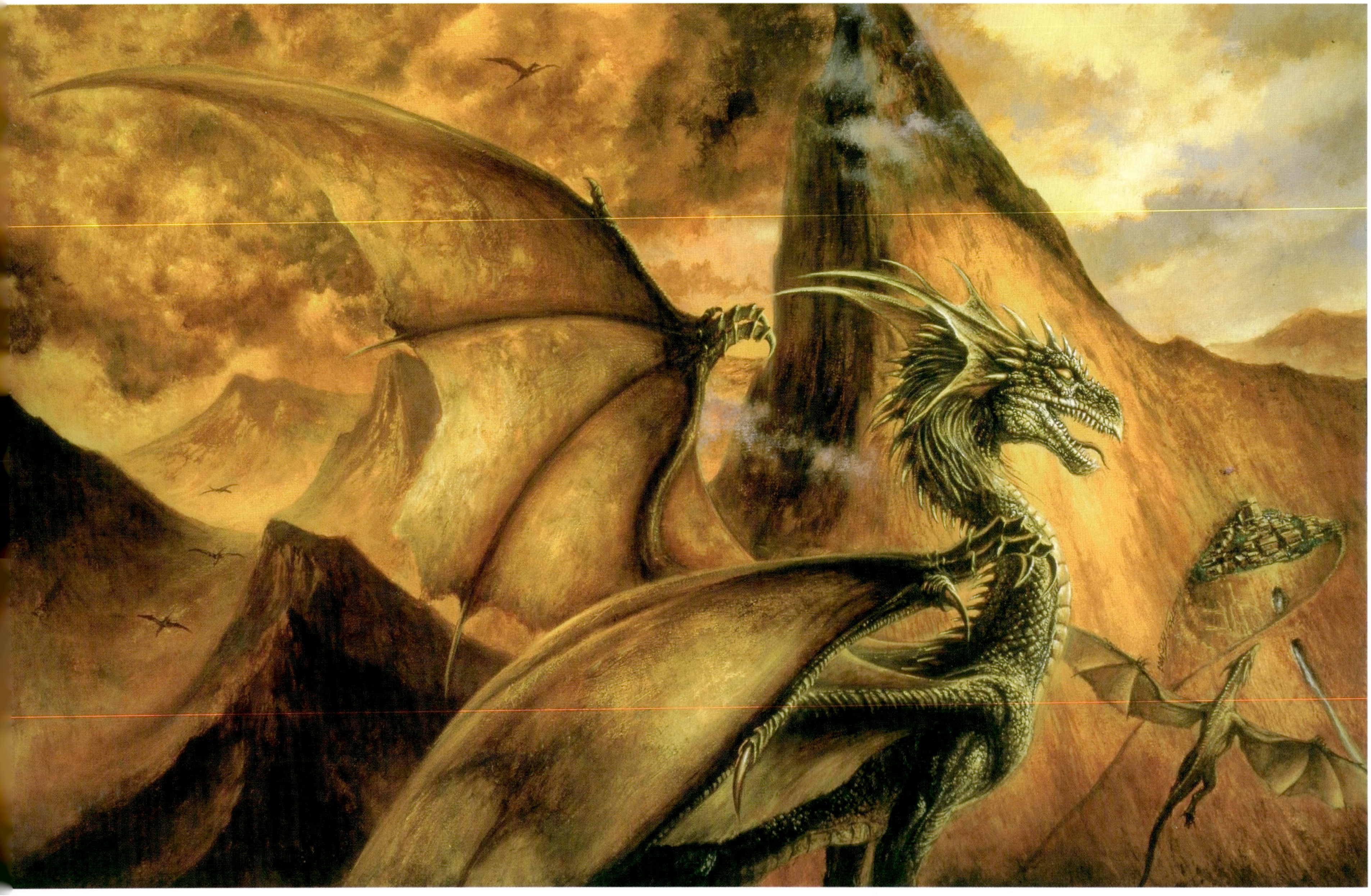

He has illustrated plenty of fiction, both sci-fi and fantasy, including classics from H.G. Wells and more modern writers like Poul Anderson and John Grant. He has also received many awards, including nine Hugos, 12 Chesley awards and two Locus awards. Increasingly, he finds himself in demand as a conceptual artist for the motion picture industry, having worked on such major releases as *Jimmy Neutron* and *The Ant Bully.*

Eggleton's art reflects a deep love of dinosaurs, which can be found throughout his fantasy portfolio. This also influences his dragons to some extent. However, his dragons are varied. Some are very much the horny-headed terrors typical in Western mythology while others are smaller and friendlier in appearance. His art does often veer into the volcanic – no bad thing – with plenty of orange denoting the fiery beasts and the almost primeval setting of much of the action.

Eggleton is also very much a 'physical painter', preferring oils on substrate to Painter and Photoshop. That said, he is a keen blogger, documenting his thoughts on art, trips to museums and working process for all to read, which also makes him a very accessible artist. He is as at home discussing Britain's controversial Turner prize as he is about his love of Godzilla, even scoring an extra role in the 2002 film *Godzilla Against Mechagodzilla.* Without doubt, Bob Eggleton is an inspiration to anyone who loves to draw or paint fantasy art and the dragons that often lurk within.

DRAGON SOCIETY by Bob Eggleton
© Bob Eggleton 2001 · Traditional media: acrylics on canvas
Cover illustration for the book of the same name by Lawrence Watt-Evans, a sequel to *Dragon Weather*, the cover of which was also illustrated by Bob, published by St Martin's Press.

DRAGON VS KRAKEN by Bob Eggleton
© Bob Eggleton 2007 · Traditional media: oil on canvas

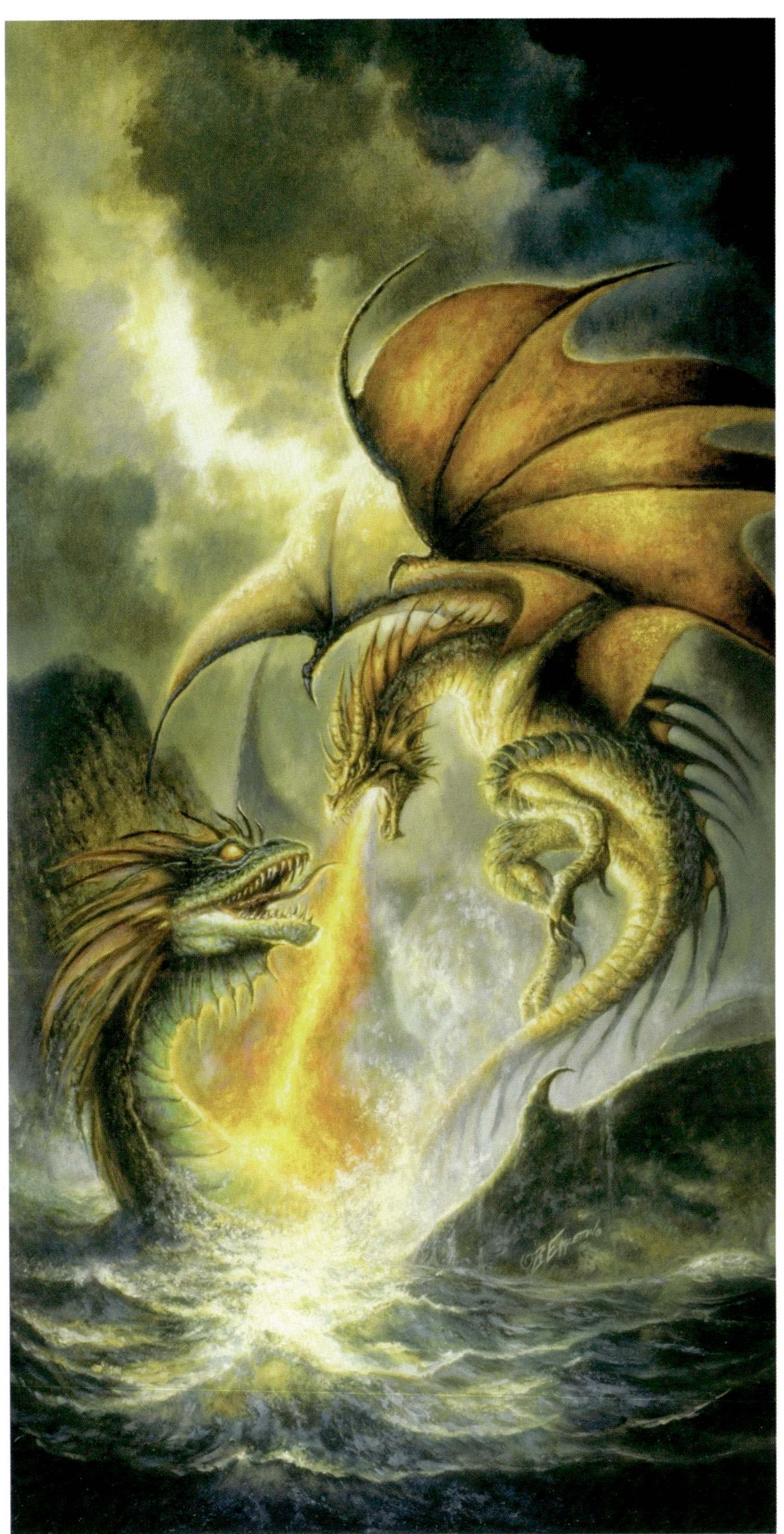

Larry Elmore

Larry Elmore's name seems to follow something of an understated fanfare, considering the influence he has had on fantasy art, dragon illustrating and the general awareness of fantasy art among the public. His work at TSR, the company behind *Dungeons and Dragons*, means that anybody who played the game back in the 1980s has probably seen and interacted with his work. Furthermore, his designs for characters and creatures set the standard for the look and feel for role players thereafter.

Larry was born in Kentucky and served briefly in the army after his graduation from Western Kentucky University in 1973 with a Bachelor's Degree in Fine Arts. In the late 1970s, his work was featured in a number of national magazines including *National Lampoon* and *Heavy Metal*. However, he began working as a staff artist in 1981 at TSR, later taken over by Wizards of the Coast, where he became the visual master of the *Dragonlance* books of Margaret Weis and Tracy Hickman in 1984. He, and later Jeff Easley and Todd Lockwood, helped to transform the *Dungeons and Dragons* game and books series into a 1980s phenomenon.

However, in 1987 he decided to move back to Kentucky, taking on more freelance work. His prodigious output has graced covers of books by the likes of Bantam, Baen Books, Warner Books and Doubleday. However, he has also worked for an eclectic collection of other companies, including Tonka Toys, Lucasfilm, DC Comics and the model-maker Mattel.

CRIMSON DAWN by Larry Elmore
© Larry Elmore 1999 · Traditional media: oil on Masonite
www.larryelmore.com

DRAGON DAWN by Larry Elmore
© TSR 1987 · Traditional media: oil on illustration board
www.larryelmore.com

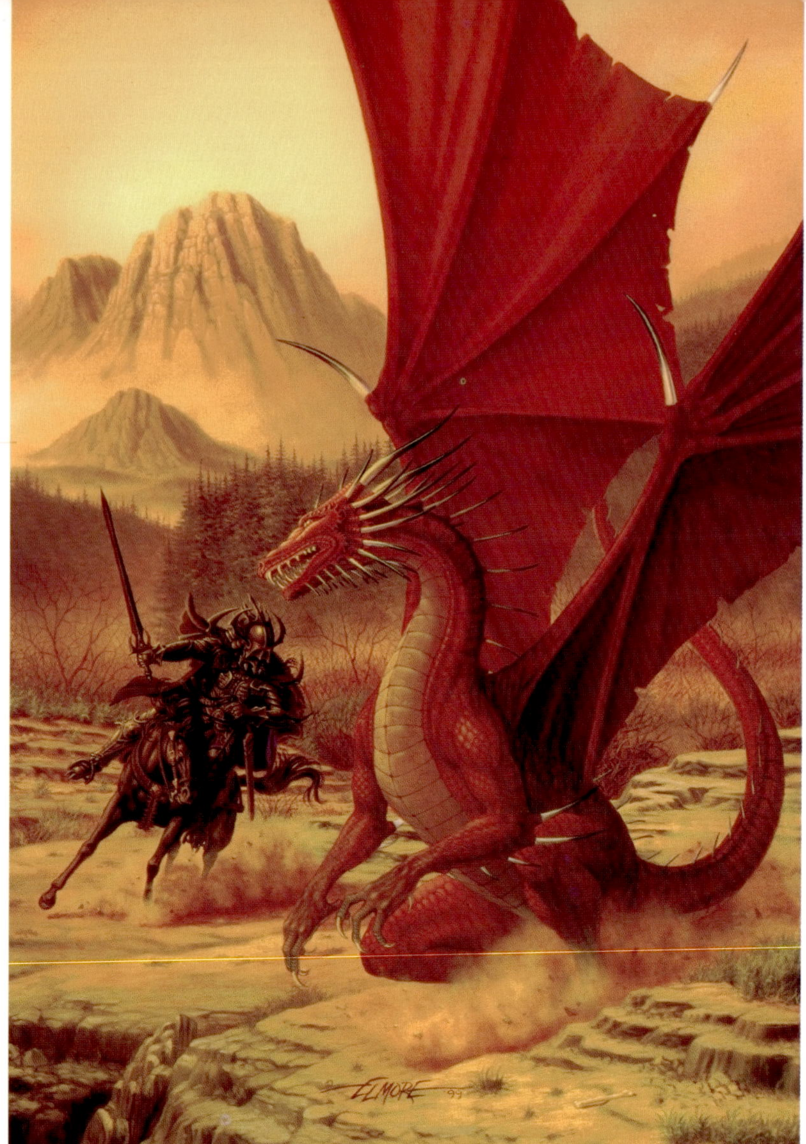

His style is certainly highly illustrative, with a nod to the medieval: plenty of armour and castles to defend from marauding, wily dragons. Much of his work seems to involve the reader or viewer on a different level from that of other illustrations; in many cases, the characters are stopped and pose, with straight-on gazes, as if for a photograph, on their way to whatever quest or adventure they are about to embark upon, inviting the viewer into the adventure as a participant rather than an observer. Elmore is unquestionably a master of fantasy art, his extensive portfolio addicting countless dragon fans for over two decades.

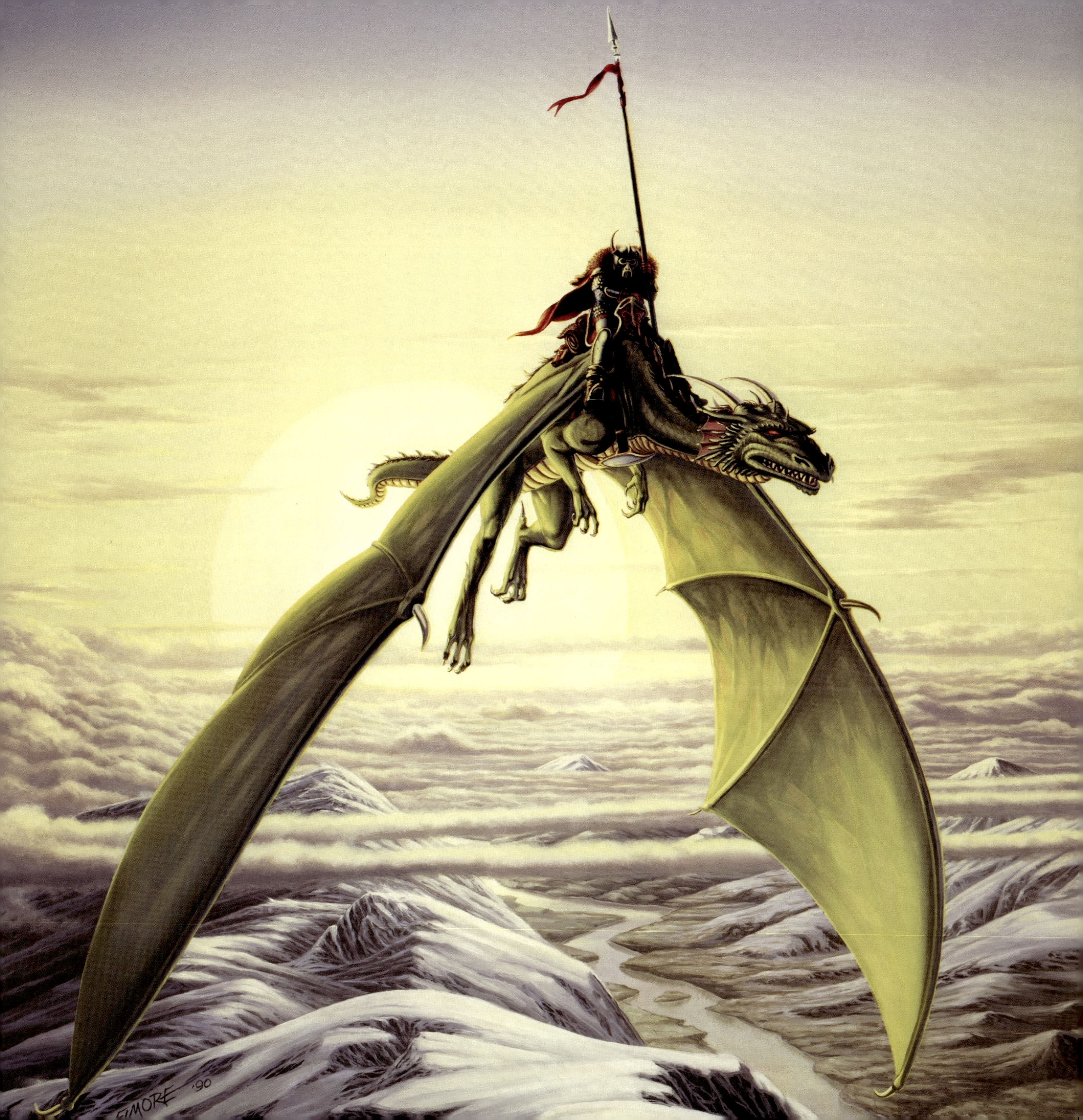
ELMORE '90

Todd Lockwood

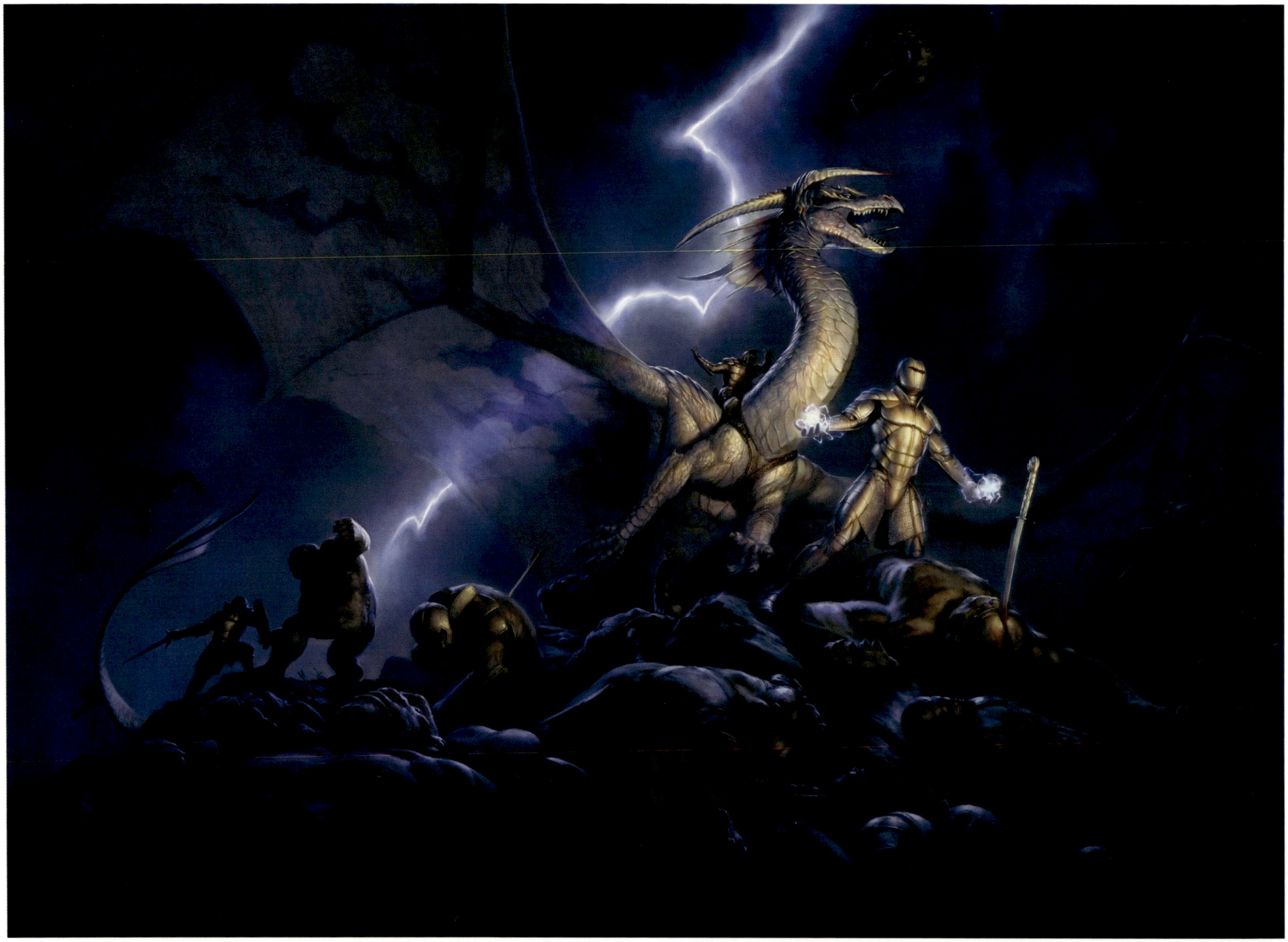

Todd Lockwood is an avid *Dungeons and Dragons* player, something that has stood him in great stead in his career as a fantasy artist. His life in art took a slightly unusual path, in that he started out as a designer for advertising after graduating from the Colorado Institute of Art in Denver. Lockwood found this career path limited and unfulfilling despite finding much success therein, leading him to eye a life as a fantasy artist. After years of hard graft, networking and pressing flesh at various fantasy art conventions, Lockwood came to the

 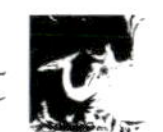

attention of TSR, who came to employ him to design for their *Dungeons and Dragons* games. He was particularly instrumental in re-imagining the games' look and feel for their dragons.

In terms of influences, he is drawn to N.C. Wyeth, Walt Disney and Jeff Easely, in particular, combined with a love of *Lord of the Rings* and mythology scholar Joseph Campbell, who has undertaken a detailed study of mythology around the world.

As an artist, Lockwood is very much a fan of referencing. In particular, he is always keen to point out that dragons' physiology should reflect their physical abilities. That is, they are very big, powerful beasts and, as such, their wings should look powerful enough to lift a large creature into the air, for instance. Because of this, there is always something very 'real' about Lockwood's art; it is almost 'reality fantasy'. While there is no doubt about his work's fantastic elements, the power and muscularity of the dragons and the physiognomy of the fighters brings a veracity to his art that makes it different from much in the genre. This sense of reality makes his fierce creatures all the more terrifying and his heroes even more physical in their activities.

Lockwood's love of global mythology means that his characters are also more culturally diverse than can be the case with much fantasy art. For him, this broadens the possibilities available to the storytelling. Whatever the case, the visceral determination that characterizes his imagery cements Todd Lockwood's place as a master of fantasy art.

STORMCALLER by Todd Lockwood
© Todd Lockwood 2008 · Digital media: Painter, Photoshop
Cover illustration for *Stormcaller: Book One of the Twilight Reign* by Tom Lloyd, published by Pyr.

TRANSITION by Todd Lockwood
© Todd Lockwood 2002 · Digital media: Painter, Photoshop
Originally done as a cover illustration for *The Dragon's Doom*, in the *Band of Four* series by Ed Greenwood. Todd removed two superfluous characters and adapted it for the cover of his first art collection, *Transitions*.

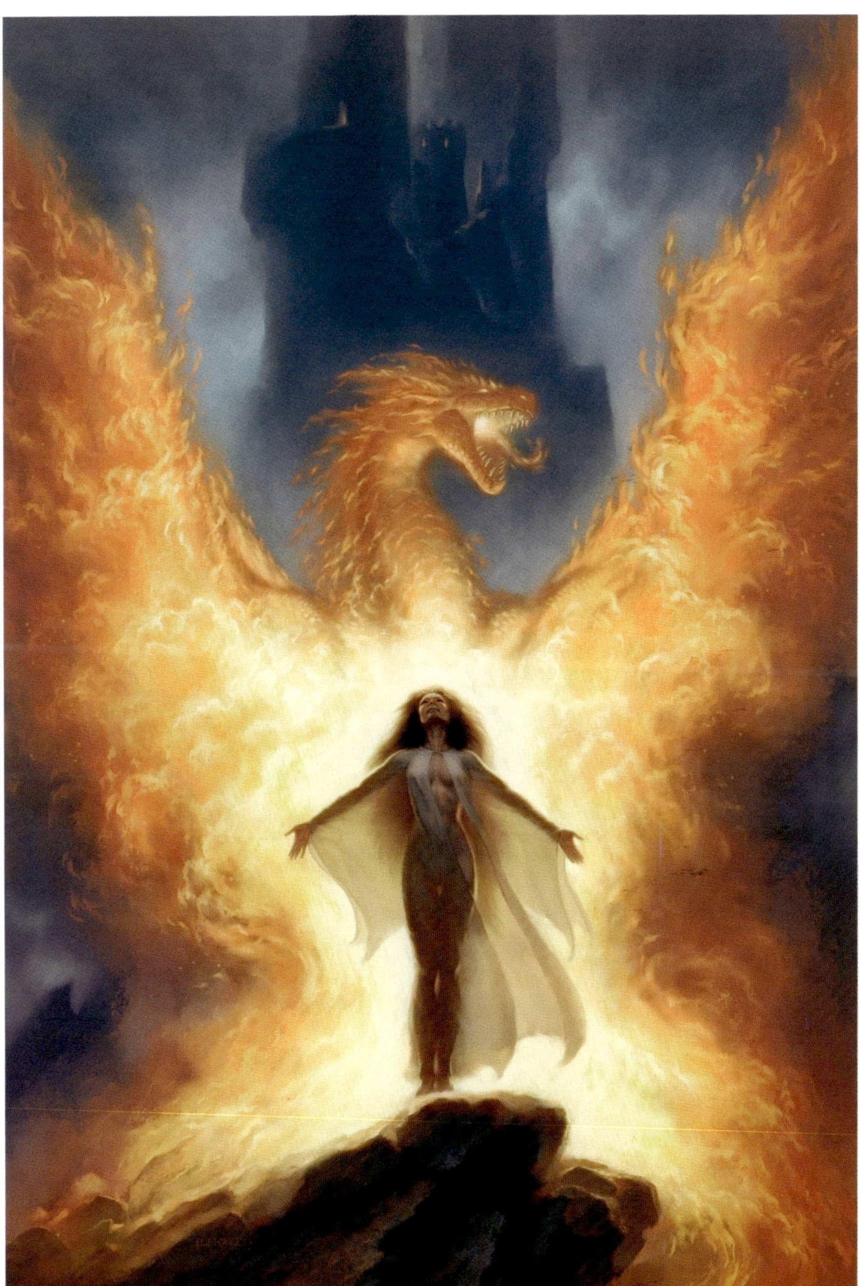

Matt Stawicki

Matt Stawicki makes no bones about his embracing of digital techniques to bring his vision to life. His tools are very much Wacom tablet, computer and software. Despite this, he is a fantasy artist firmly rooted in the tradition of painting itself. Matt may be among the countless admirers of Frank Frazetta, but does not shy away from a love of iconic American artist Norman Rockwell, whose paintings are as vivid and rich as any in fantasy, even while the subject matter is often the polar opposite. Similarly important to Stawicki are Maxfield Parrish, a fellow Pennsylvania native, and Howard Pyle protégé N.C. Wyeth, as well as the films of Walt Disney, George Lucas and Steven Spielberg.

Since graduating from the prestigious Pennsylvania School of Art and Design in 1991, Stawicki has worked on a broad range of products, from book covers for the likes of HarperCollins, Penguin, Bantam and Doubleday to various games title packaging. In addition, he has done work for the Franklin Mint, manufacturers of commemorative coins and plates. Among Stawicki's more popular assignments as far as fantasy goes, is his stint working on the *Dragonlance* novels, following in the footsteps of Larry Elmore and Jeff Easley. When publisher Wizards of the Coast re-released a number of titles, Stawicki was brought in to re-imagine a number of covers, including those of *Dragons of the Fallen Sun*, *The Dark Disciple* trilogy, *The Lost Chronicles* trilogy, *The Elven Exiles* series and *Time of the Twins*, among others.

Stawicki's art offers rich pickings for battle fans and those who like their monsters scary and creepy. There is much for armour enthusiasts, too, with plenty of posed combatants and swords wielded. The emphasis is certainly on action – action in progress or pending. As for his dragons, they are formidable beasts that strike dread into the hearts of their beholders. They are mostly good old-fashioned, scary fire-breathers in need of a good vanquishing. Stawicki is, without doubt, a pace-setter of fantasy art, untraditional in his choice of materials but absolutely timeless in his depictions of dragons, the mighty dread inspired by them in humanity from its first civilizations to this very day.

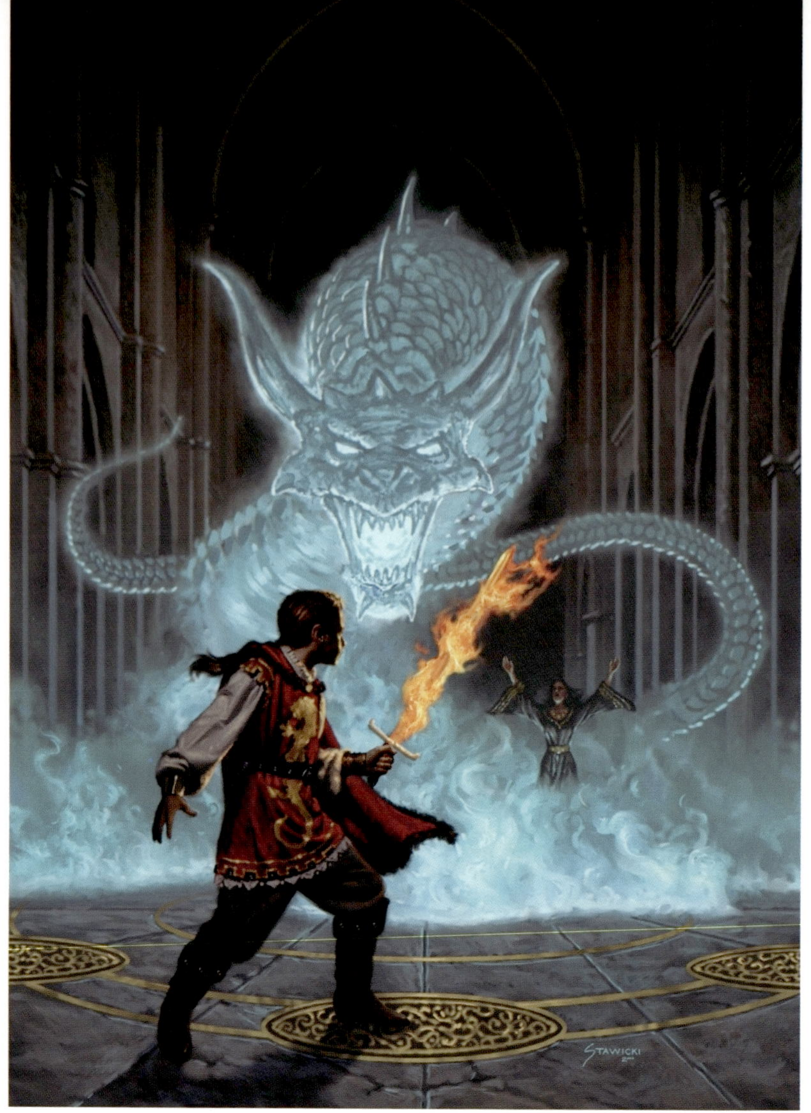

DERYNI RISING by Matt Stawicki
© Matt Stawicki 2003 · Digital media: Photoshop, Painter
www.mattstawicki.com

DRAGON'S LAIR by Matt Stawicki
© Matt Stawicki 1996 · Traditional media: oil on canvas
www.mattstawicki.com

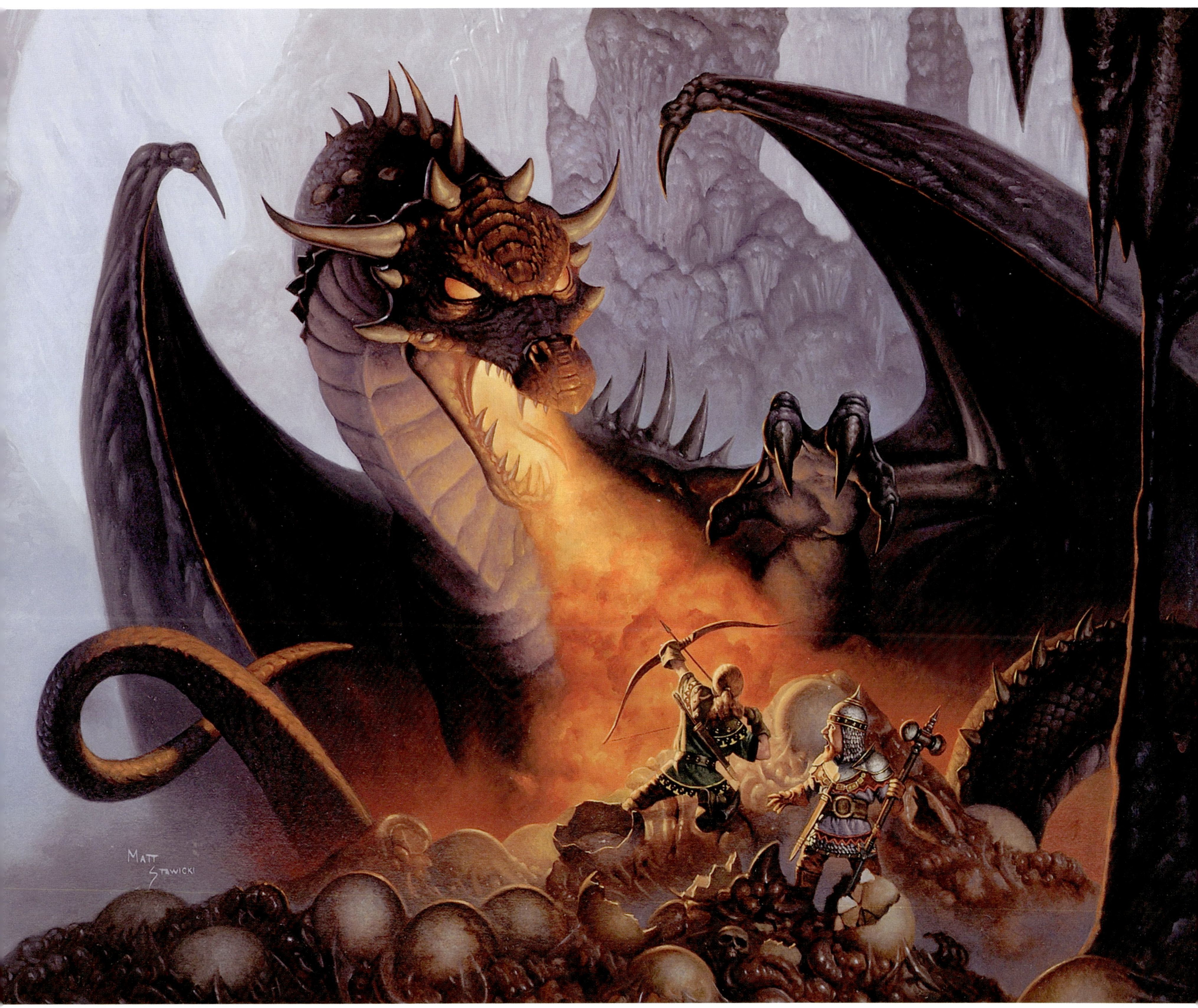
MATT
STAWICKI

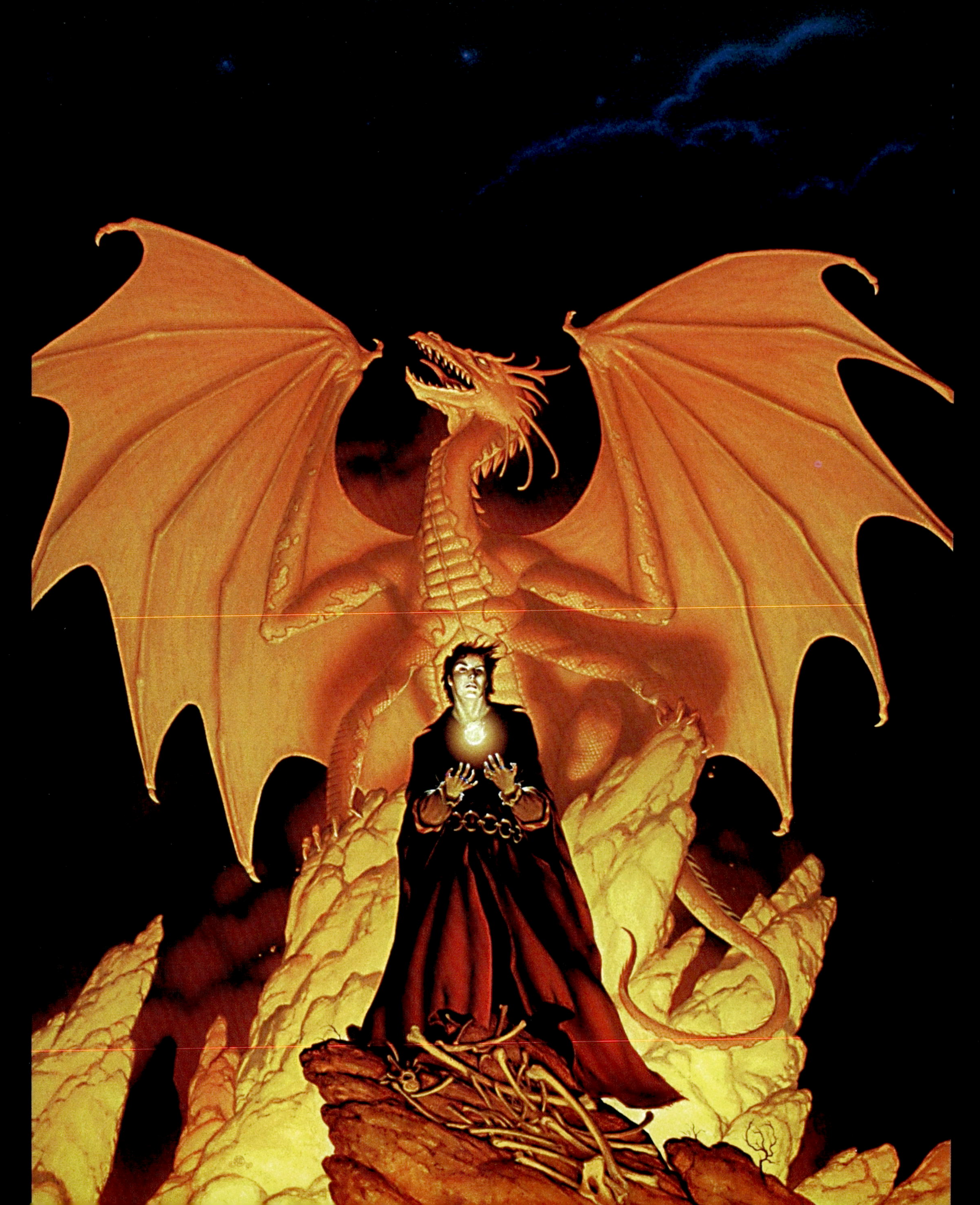

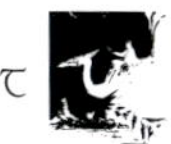

Michael Whelan

Michael Whelan is, without doubt, one of the most highly regarded fantasy artists in the world today. From sword-and-sorcery to fine art, Whelan's work is imbued with a sense of thoughtfulness, empathy and emotion that is missing from the art of many contemporary fantasy artists. His appeal goes beyond that of sword-and-sorcery masters like Frank Frazetta: he is loved equally by devotees of warrior heroes as well as by more romantic and mystical fantasy fans.

The text of this book will deal with him in far more detail, complete with assessment from those for whom he has worked, and who admire his work, including more than one of the masters in this section. But suffice it to say that Whelan is a California native whose art education ranges from summers spent at the Rocky Mountain School of Art through to San José State University and the Art Center College of Design in Los Angeles which he left in 1973 following his first professional commission.

In that time, his work has graced book covers from novelists like Stephen King, Ray Bradbury, Michael Moorcock, Poul Anderson and, most famously, Anne McCaffrey, bringing both author and artist unassailable respect among fantasy devotees. He has also won countless awards and accolades for his work, which he describes as 'communication', in a sense being an intermediary between the author's words, vision and intention and the expectation and understanding of the reader or viewer. This viewpoint means that the symbolism of his work is as important as the actions and events that make up the subject matter.

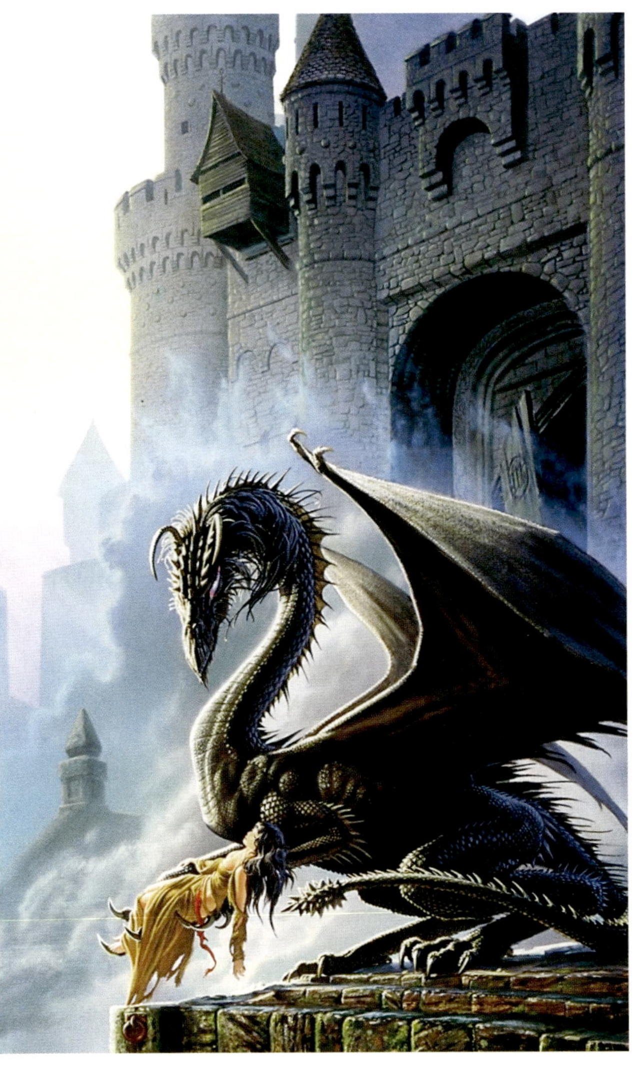

As such, his illustrated dragons are, again, wide and varied, depending on the needs and requirements of the novels for which they have been created. Regardless, they are often 'Whelan-ized', with a trademark degree of detail and emotional depth that is almost impossible to pin down, but unmistakable. These detailed, cerebral and painstaking artworks and his mould-breaking dragons mean that Michael Whelan is, without debate, among the masters of fantasy art.

DRAGONFIRE by Michael Whelan
© Michael Whelan 1989 · Traditional media: acrylics on watercolour board
Cover illustration for *Sunrunner's Fire* (*Dragon Prince*, Book 3) by Melanie Rawn. · www.michaelwhelan.com

DRAGONSBANE by Michael Whelan
© Michael Whelan 1986 · Traditional media: acrylics on watercolour board
Cover illustration for the book of the same name by Barbara Hambly.
www.michaelwhelan.com

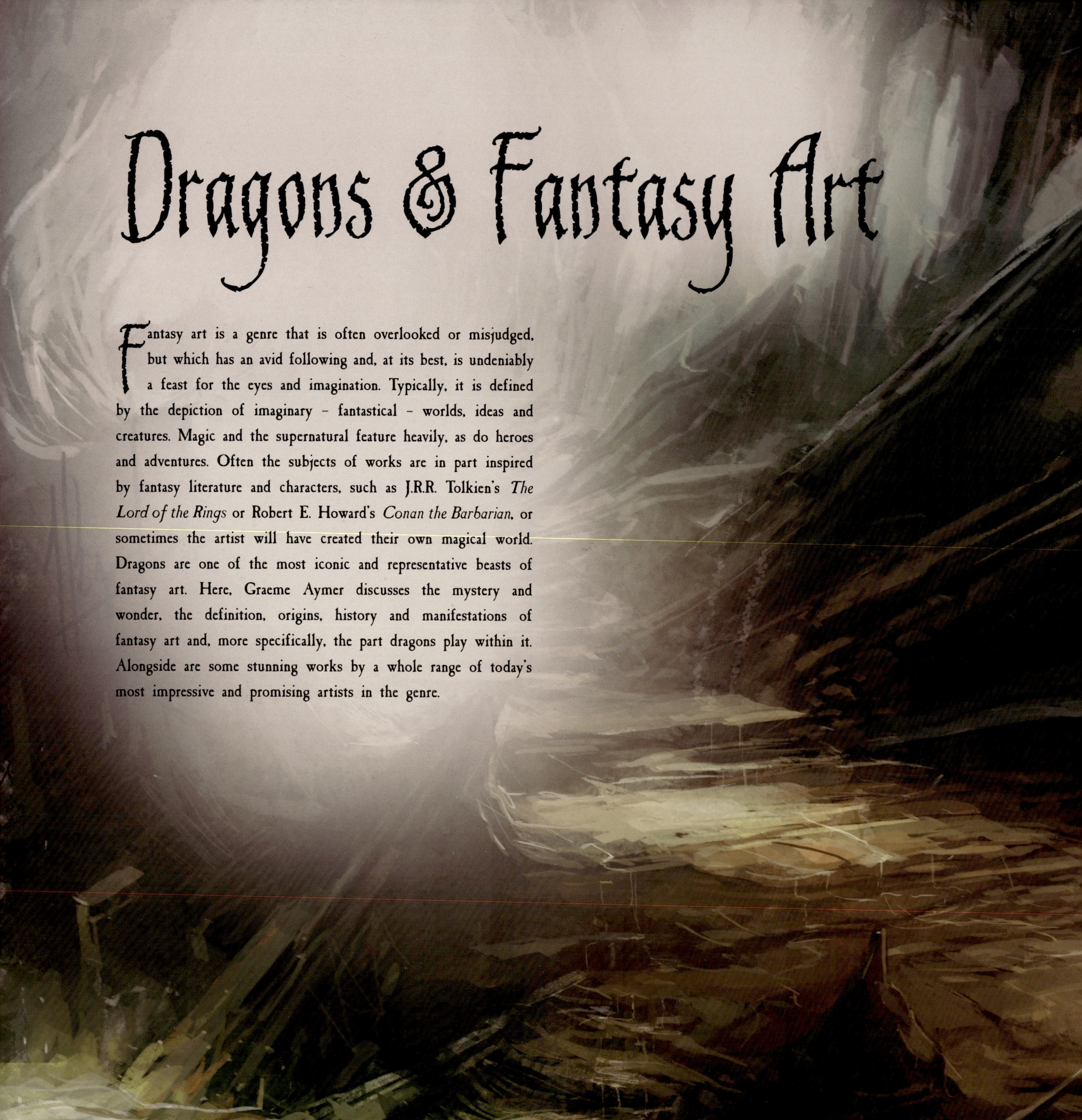

Dragons & Fantasy Art

Fantasy art is a genre that is often overlooked or misjudged, but which has an avid following and, at its best, is undeniably a feast for the eyes and imagination. Typically, it is defined by the depiction of imaginary – fantastical – worlds, ideas and creatures. Magic and the supernatural feature heavily, as do heroes and adventures. Often the subjects of works are in part inspired by fantasy literature and characters, such as J.R.R. Tolkien's *The Lord of the Rings* or Robert E. Howard's *Conan the Barbarian*, or sometimes the artist will have created their own magical world. Dragons are one of the most iconic and representative beasts of fantasy art. Here, Graeme Aymer discusses the mystery and wonder, the definition, origins, history and manifestations of fantasy art and, more specifically, the part dragons play within it. Alongside are some stunning works by a whole range of today's most impressive and promising artists in the genre.

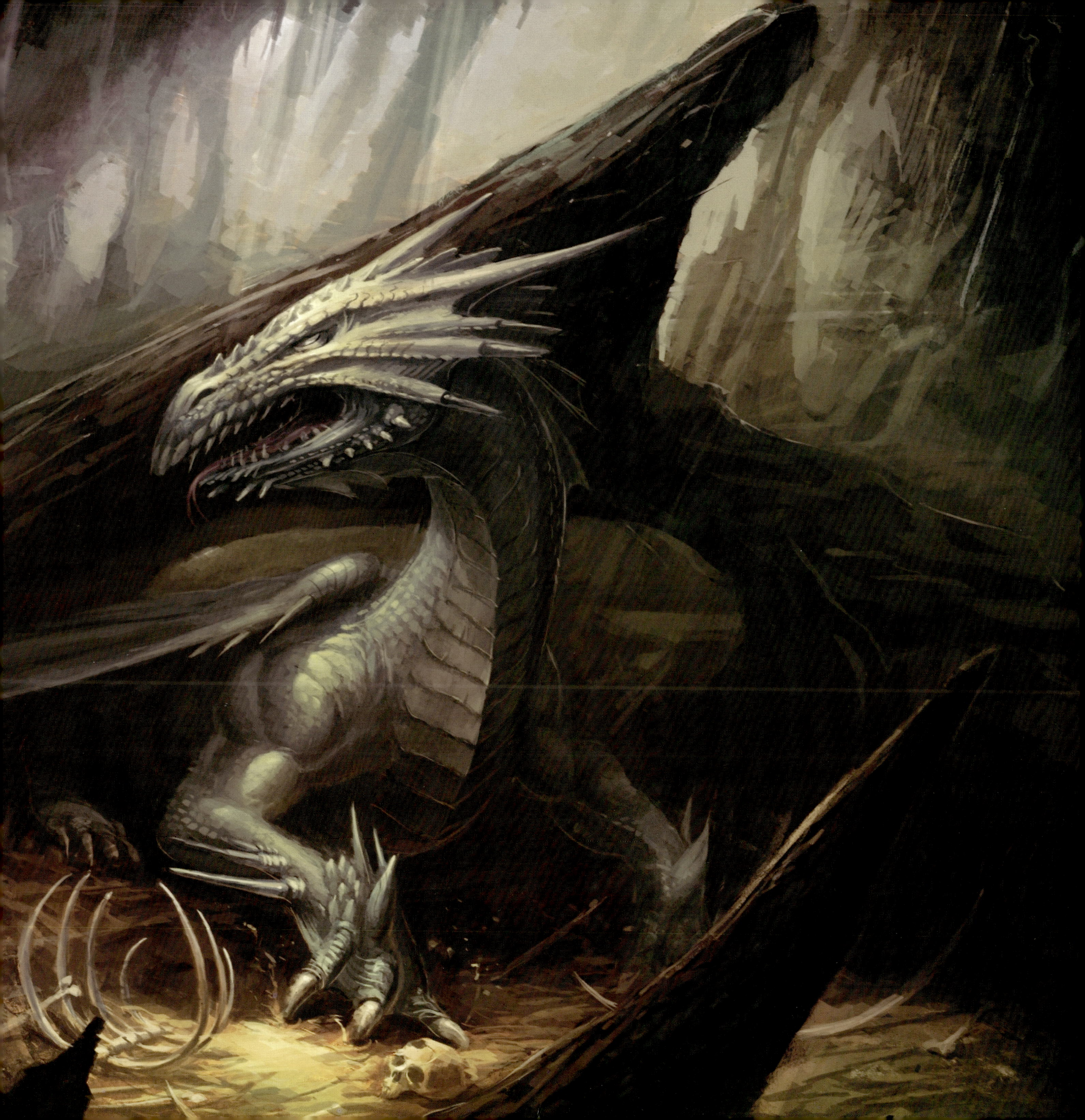

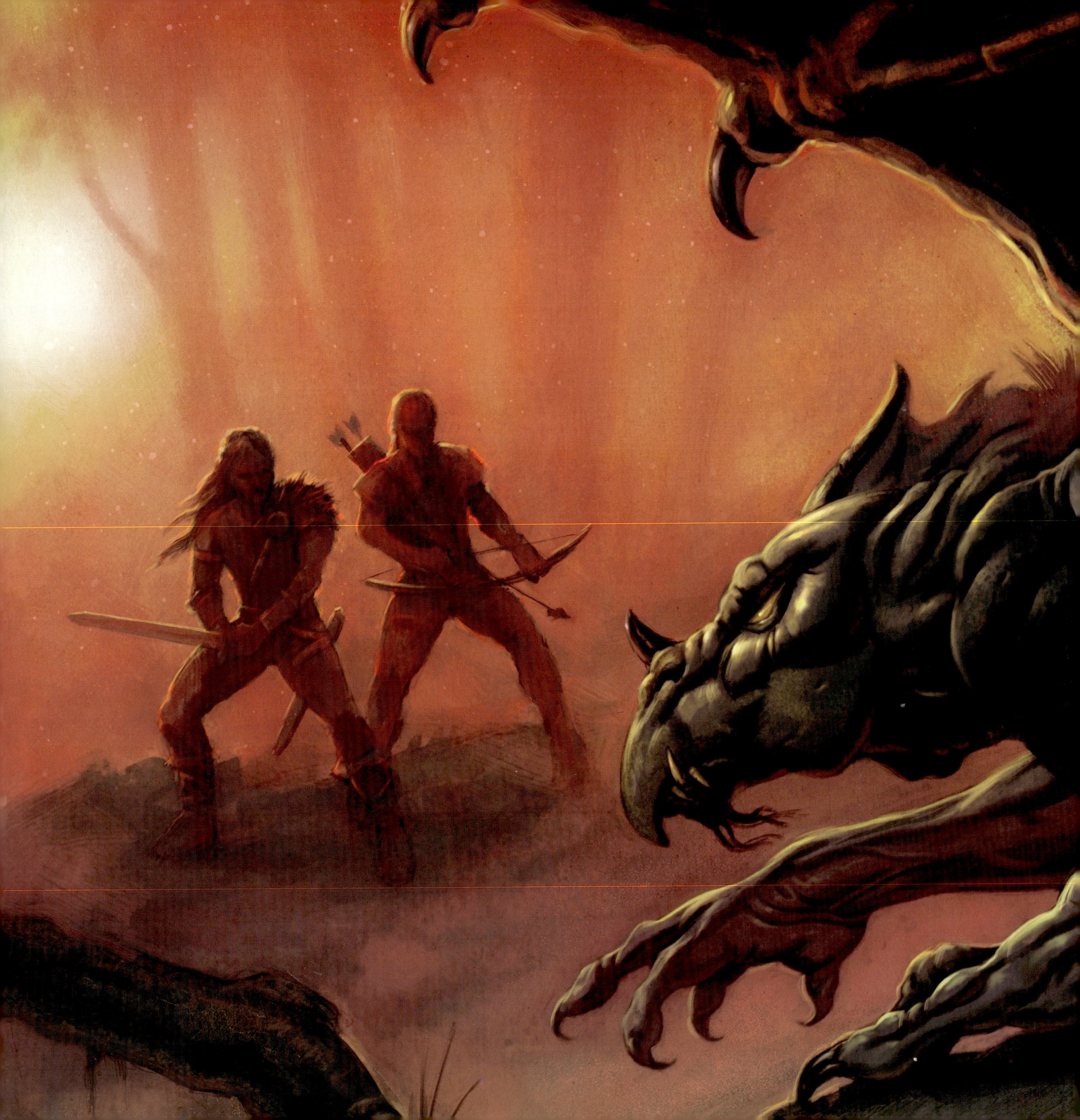

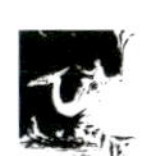

Journeys

At the time of writing, it is in vogue for people to use the word 'journey' to describe a series of circumstances surrounding their lives or a learning experience. Well, to contribute to this most modern usage, it is perhaps fitting that an extended essay all about dragons and fantasy art is something of a journey – perhaps, given the subject matter, it is more accurate to call it a 'quest', however, rather than a journey. Or perhaps, to give it a more narrative twist, it is a journey of transformation.

There are so many of these journeys here. There have been many conversations with fantasy artists about their own transformations, from imaginative children into imaginative adults, which is far more difficult than you might think! There is the quest for knowledge that has unfolded in library reading rooms and Internet chat rooms in search of the lives and times of J.R.R. Tolkien or about Robert E. Howard, to find the roots of Frodo, Gandalf, King Kull, Smaug and the Fell Beasts, to delve into the legends of Sigurd and the true nature of his dragon adversary Fafnir.

Similarly, it is fascinating to find that the cover to Sepultura's *Roots* in your CD collection is an example of the fine body of work by Michael Whelan, or to splash in the shallow water of introductions to Anne McCaffrey's *Dragonriders of Pern* series, and wishing you were in at the deep end. And then, of course, there is the chance to go leafing through the life and art of living legend Frank Frazetta.

DRAGON HUNTERS by Alan Lathwell
© Alan Lathwell 2007 · Digital media: Photoshop
http://alanlathwell.cgsociety.org/gallery

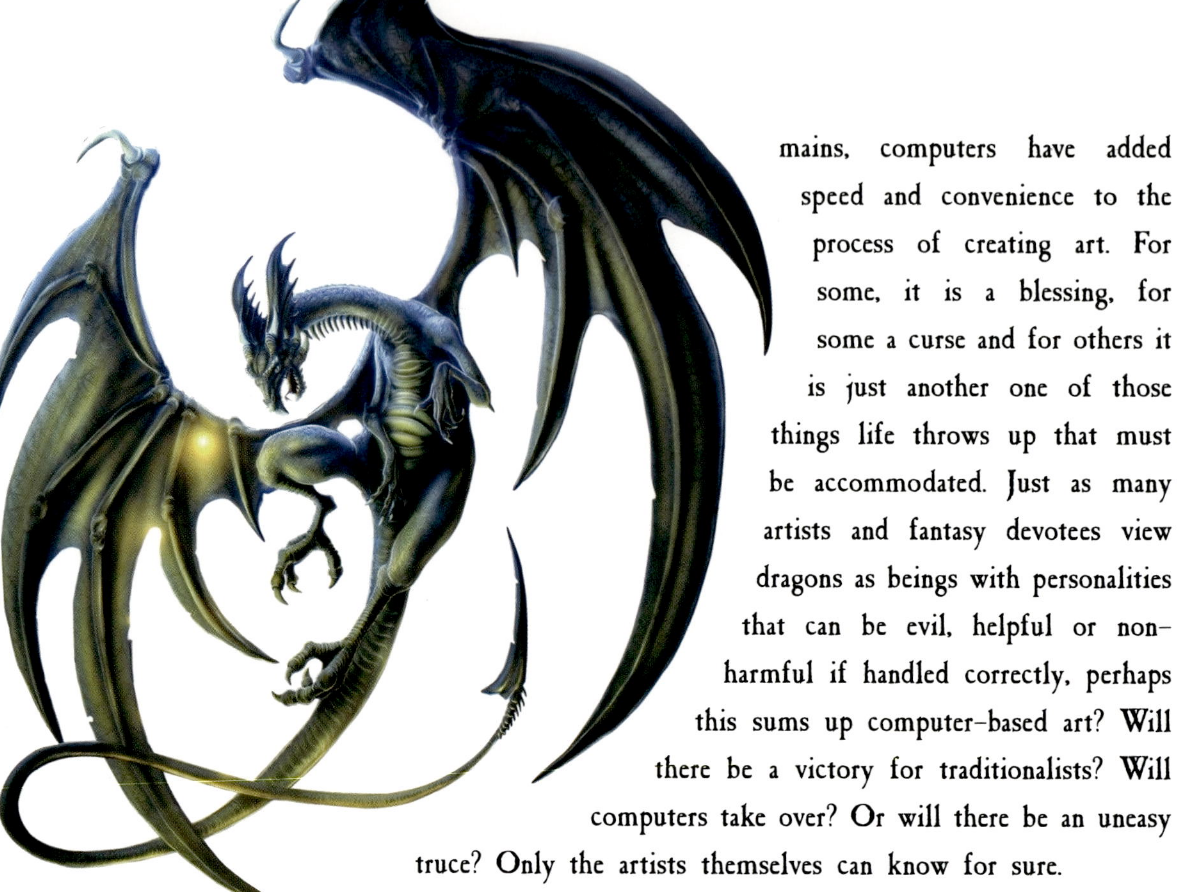

Journeys with Dragons

In terms of the discipline of fantasy and the lore of dragons, it is a similar situation. It is all about watching the documentation of beasts in a line that connects Christian Bale as Quinn in *Reign of Fire* (2002) all the way back to an ancient Mesopotamian who took 12 clay tablets and wrote down his *Epic of Gilgamesh*, and had to conjure up just how terrifying the dreaded Humbaba was, and then weaving lines from that monster to the likes of the Greeks and the Bible, to St George, Renaissance art, Smaug and back to Harry Potter. It is a long way to go!

Caves to Computers

Then again, there is another journey of transformation of note in progress that will continue to take place for quite some time. It is that of the art itself. Artists have, since the old cave paintings, mixed pigments and smeared them all over various surfaces using the best their technology could offer, from fingers to bristles to airbrushes.

That technology has, since the early 1990s, advanced with unprecedented speed. No longer is it a matter of synthesizing better pigments from our knowledge of chemistry and colour: computers can now simulate the action of painting itself. As long as there is enough battery power or a connection to the electrical mains, computers have added speed and convenience to the process of creating art. For some, it is a blessing, for some a curse and for others it is just another one of those things life throws up that must be accommodated. Just as many artists and fantasy devotees view dragons as beings with personalities that can be evil, helpful or non-harmful if handled correctly, perhaps this sums up computer-based art? Will there be a victory for traditionalists? Will computers take over? Or will there be an uneasy truce? Only the artists themselves can know for sure.

Traces of Dragons

To set the scene, it is essential to start with dragons. Dragons have accompanied humanity through its journey to civilization. Across the world, civilizations, from Africa to America, Europe to Asia, have legends of serpents, sea serpents and dragon-like

DRAGON RIDER by Alan Lathwell
© Alan Lathwell 2007 · Traditional media: oil on paper
http://alanlathwell.cgsociety.org/gallery

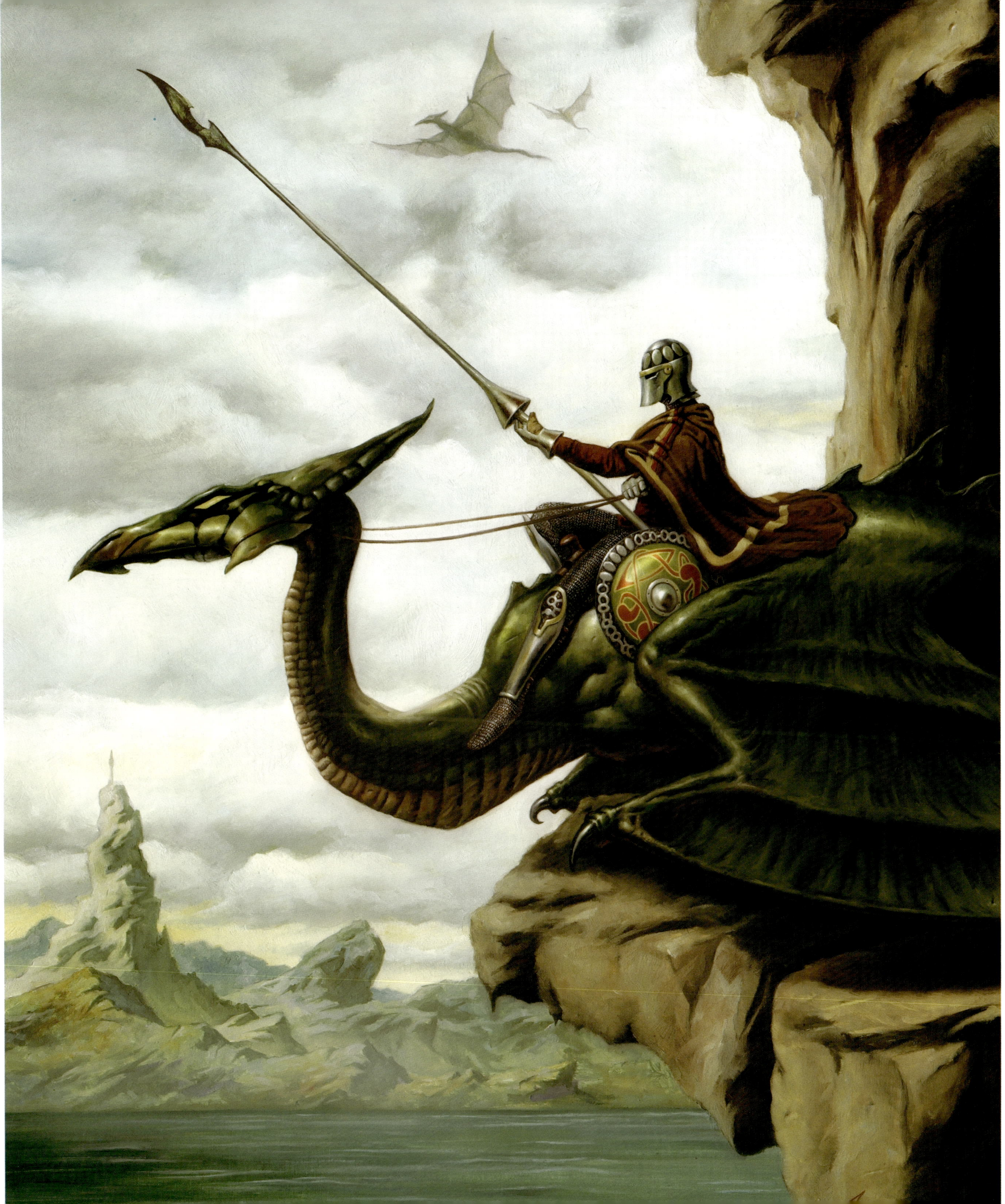

creatures, and they have had them for a very long time. There are accounts of cave paintings that depict dragon-like creatures in Altamira and Lascaux. Whether they are good or bad, these creatures are always forces to be reckoned with.

The word itself originates from the ancient Greek, *draconta* or *drakon*, meaning 'to watch'. It applied to the giant monsters that watched over various mystical, valuable items including golden apples within that culture's mythology or, in more Western European tradition, a stash of treasure.

Western Dragons

In Europe, dragons are generally identified as huge, reptilian creatures, with a body morphology that is somewhere between crocodile and snake, with the clawed feet of a lizard, a long barbed tail and a head that can be anything from beaky and bird-like to dinosaurian, complete with crests and horns. They also tend to have bat-like wings and, as if that was not terrifying enough, they breathe fire and sometimes noxious fumes.

In Western myth, they will tend to live on the outskirts of large conurbations, much to the dismay of the inhabitants. They often collect tribute, which can include anything from livestock to maidens, and are particularly difficult to kill, not just because of

WYVERN by Alan Lathwell
© Hachette Partworks Ltd 2008 · Digital media: Painter
This image was painted for *Beasts and Beings* magazine, published by Hachette Partworks Ltd.
http://alanlathwell.cgsociety.org/gallery/

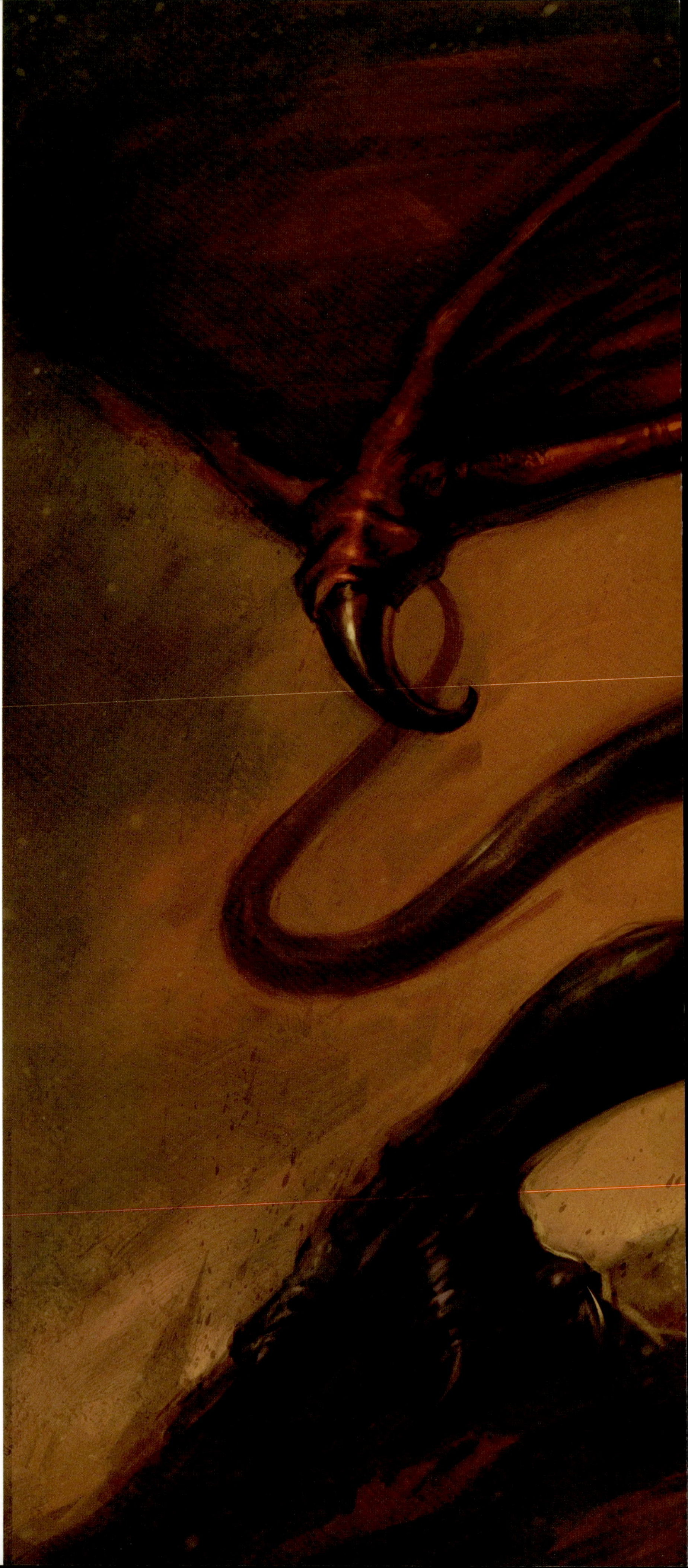

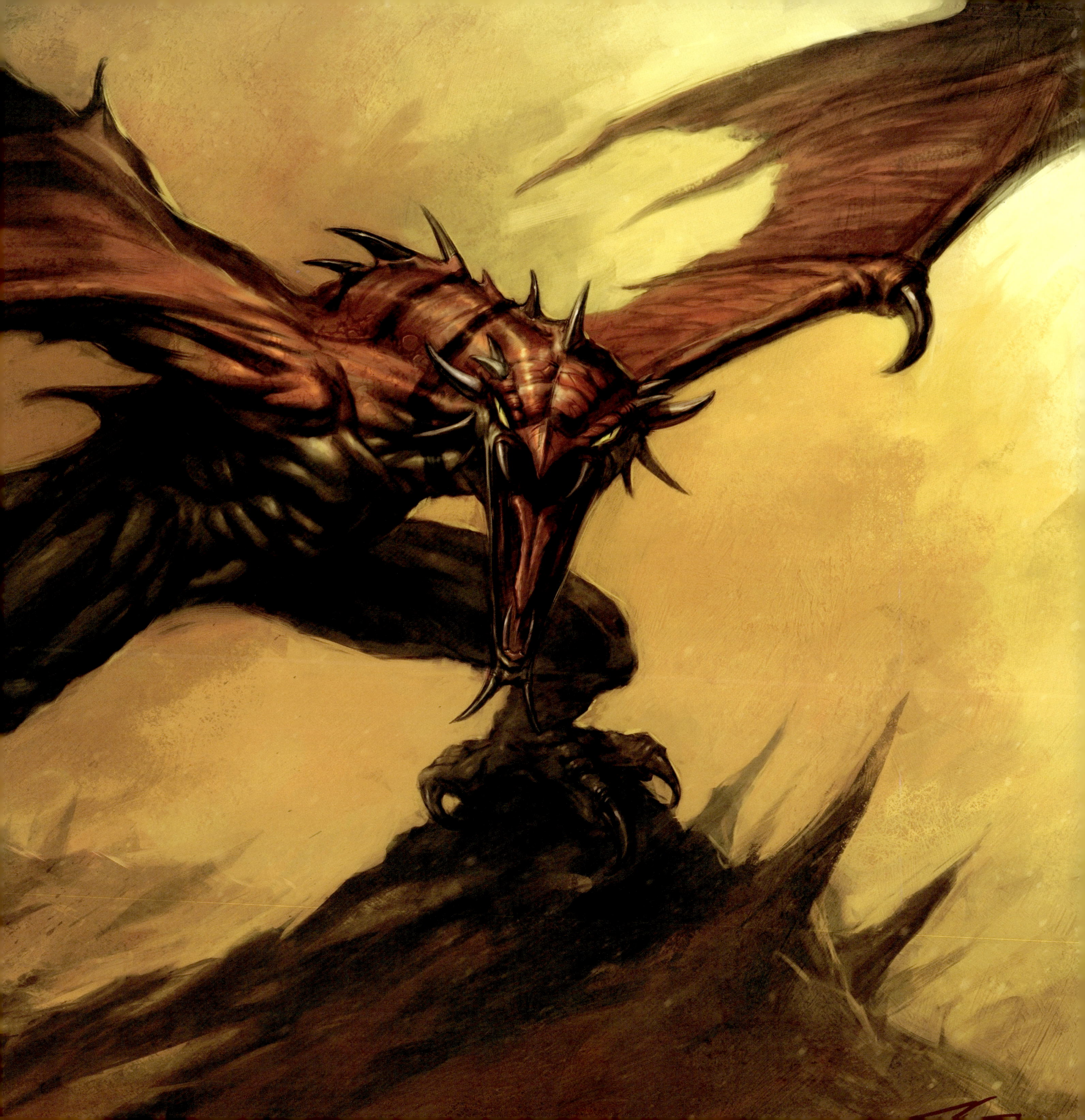

Dragon Mountains by Jason Juta

© Jason Juta 2008; Digital media: Photoshop; London-based illustrator and concept artist; www.jasonjuta.com

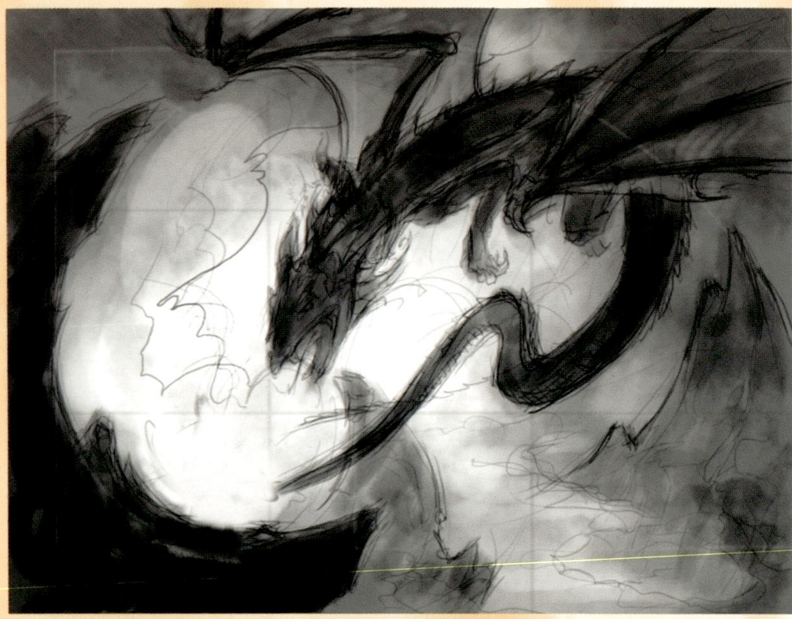

SAMPLE STEP 1. After drawing the dragon, I scan it and create a rough tonal plan. I know I'll add a human opponent at a later stage.

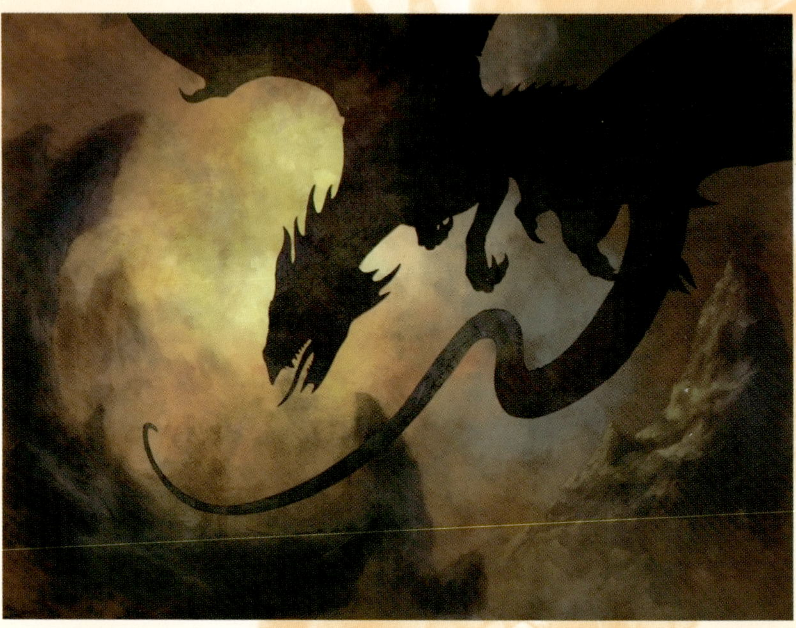

SAMPLE STEP 2. Working over the tonal plan, I lay in textured, multi-coloured brushstrokes and start painting the background.

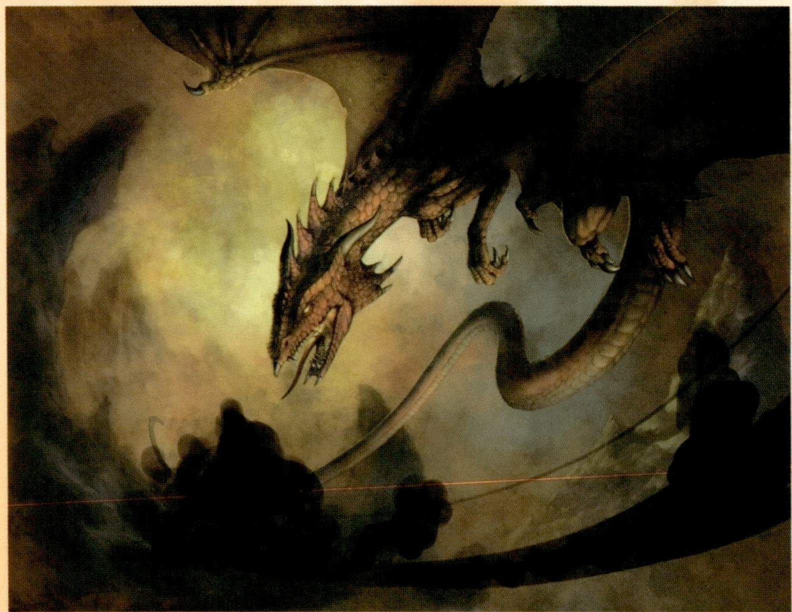

SAMPLE STEP 3. I add background detail and paint the dragon. I then play with ideas for a bridge in the foreground.

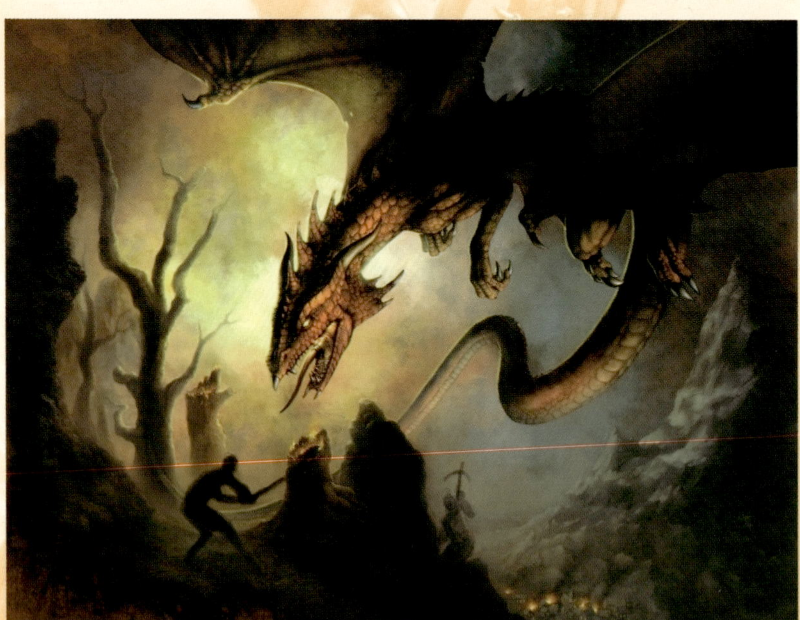

SAMPLE STEP 4. I add contrast where necessary and decide to leave the bridge out. I start thinking about the dragon's opponent.

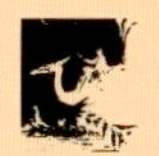

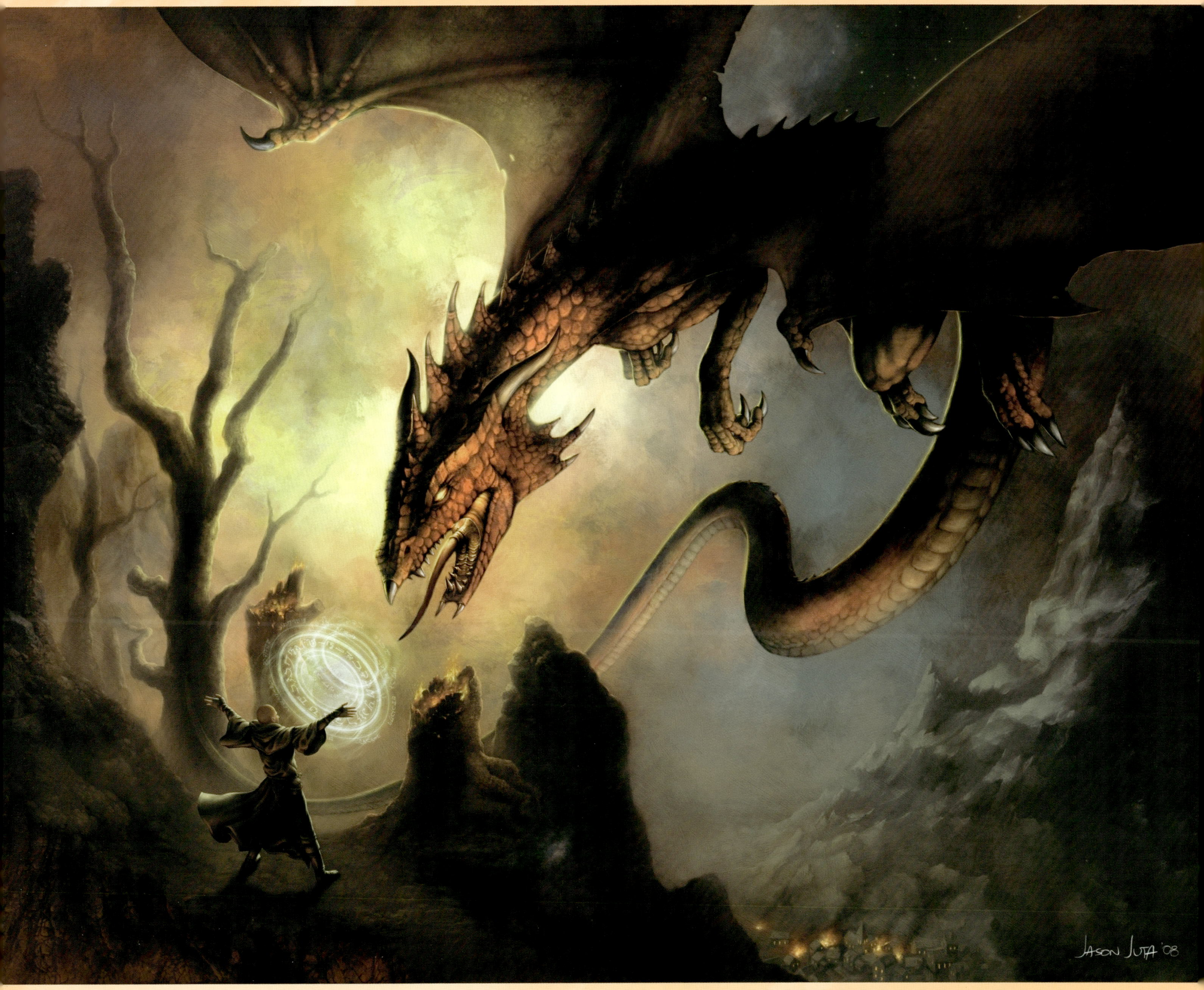

FINISHING TOUCHES. The dragon is faced by a lone, brave sorcerer – *see also* page 76.

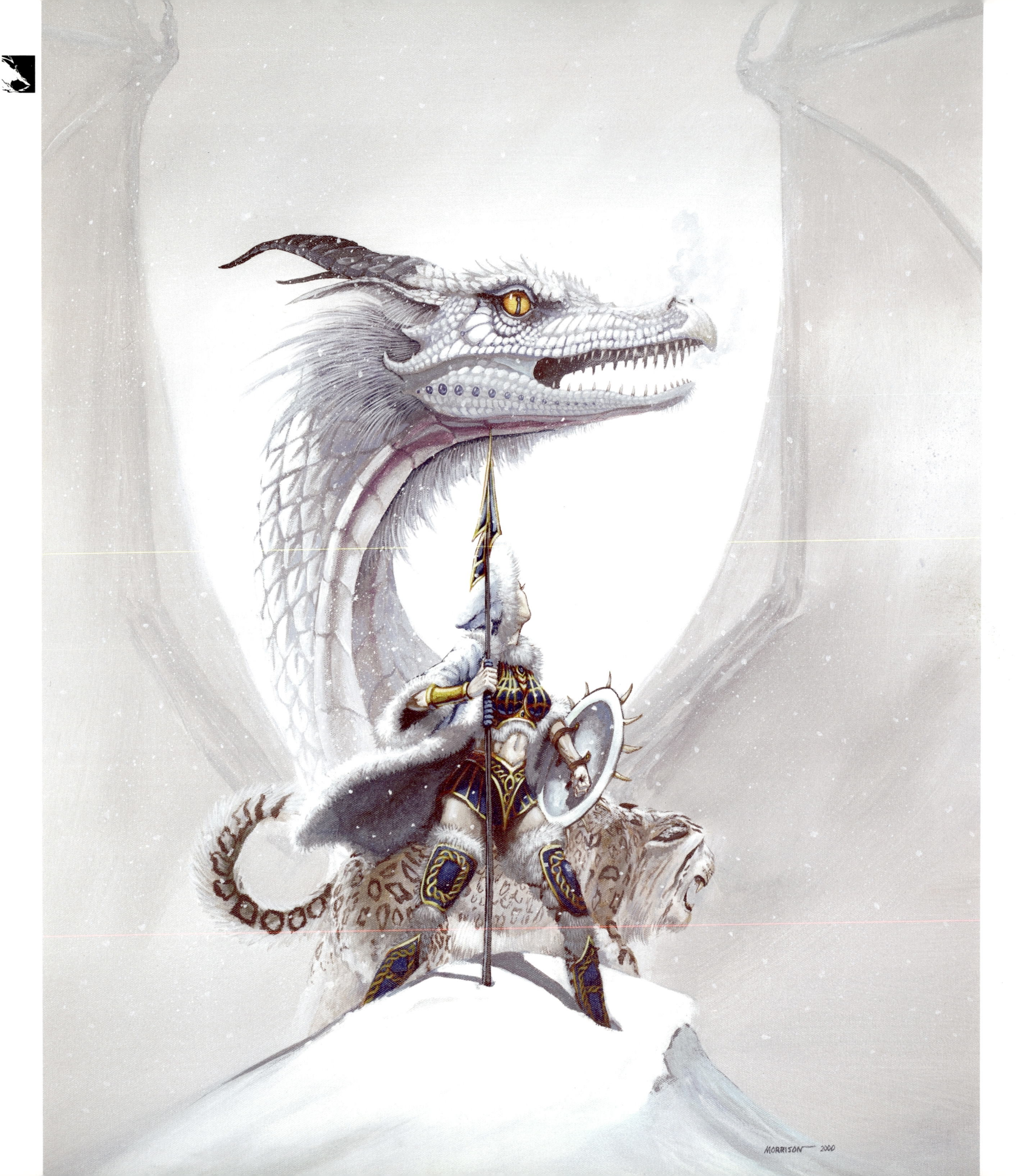
MORRISON 2000

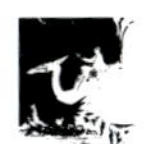

their mobility and fire-breathing, but also because their scales tend to be impervious to sharp objects. However, it should be noted that, even in the West, dragons are not always a pest. There is a long tradition of protective Celtic dragons. This will be discussed later.

Myth scholar Carol Reed discusses early evidence of the significance of dragons to human civilizatons in her book *Giants, Dragons and Monsters*. There is a dragon behind the goddess Bau, depicted on a Sumerian seal dating from 4000 BC, which she speculates is influenced by the Egyptians, who held serpents divine – such as the great serpent Aapep of the Underworld. Similarly, the Naga in the northwest area of the Indian sub-continent worshipped cobras. Antiquity is littered with tales of beasts with attributes that we associate with dragons in the modern age.

The Epic of Gilgamesh

For example, there is the *Epic of Gilgamesh*, which sees the eponymous hero, two-thirds god and one-third human, head to a cedar forest with his friend, the formerly wild man Enkidu (having been tamed by a week-long love-in with a woman sent to him by Gilgamesh). Both set off on quests to conquer monsters and gods, one particularly nasty guardian of the Cedar Forest included, by the name of Humbaba. Throughout the poem, the hero fights and bargains with other gods and monsters, helps himself to a number of brides, spurns the interests of goddesses and makes a bid for immortality.

Written sometime between 2750 and 2500 BC and thus perhaps the earliest of all fictitious tales ever written, the story describes Humbaba as 'a terror to human beings / Humbaba's roar is a Flood, his mouth is Fire, and his breath is Death / He can hear 100 leagues away any rustling in his forest! / Who would go down into his forest / Enlil assigned him as a terror to human beings, and whoever goes down into his forest paralysis will strike!'

Needless to say, hopefully this is no spoiler, Gilgamesh and Enkidu prevail over the mighty Humbaba, but not without some help from the gods that saw 'The ground split open with the heels of their feet, as they whirled around in circles Mt Hermon and Lebanon split. / The white clouds darkened, death rained down on them like fog.'

The Odyssey

Not a million miles away, there is Homer's *Odyssey*. Written some time around 800 BC, it is a tale of the return to Ithaca of protagonist Odysseus, and his trials and tribulations, again, at the hands of gods and monsters, with a fair bit of 'lady action' thrown in. Like the *Epic of Gilgamesh*, there is a quest, this time to get back home.

En route, there is a Cyclops to kill, plenty of magical goddesses both to evade and to keep company with and, of course, Scylla, 'a dreadful monster and no one – not even a god – could face her without being terror-struck. She has twelve misshapen feet, and

POLAR PRINCESS by Stanley Morrison
© Stanley Morrison 2000 · Traditional media: acrylic on canvas
Part of a four seasons dragon series. Stanley is an accomplished, award-winning fantasy artist who works in numerous media including digital, but is best known for his work with scratchboard and acrylics.
www.stanleymorrison.com

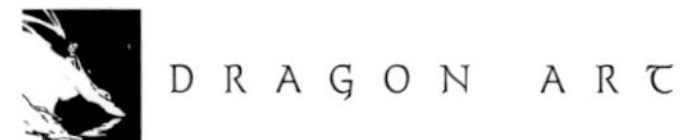

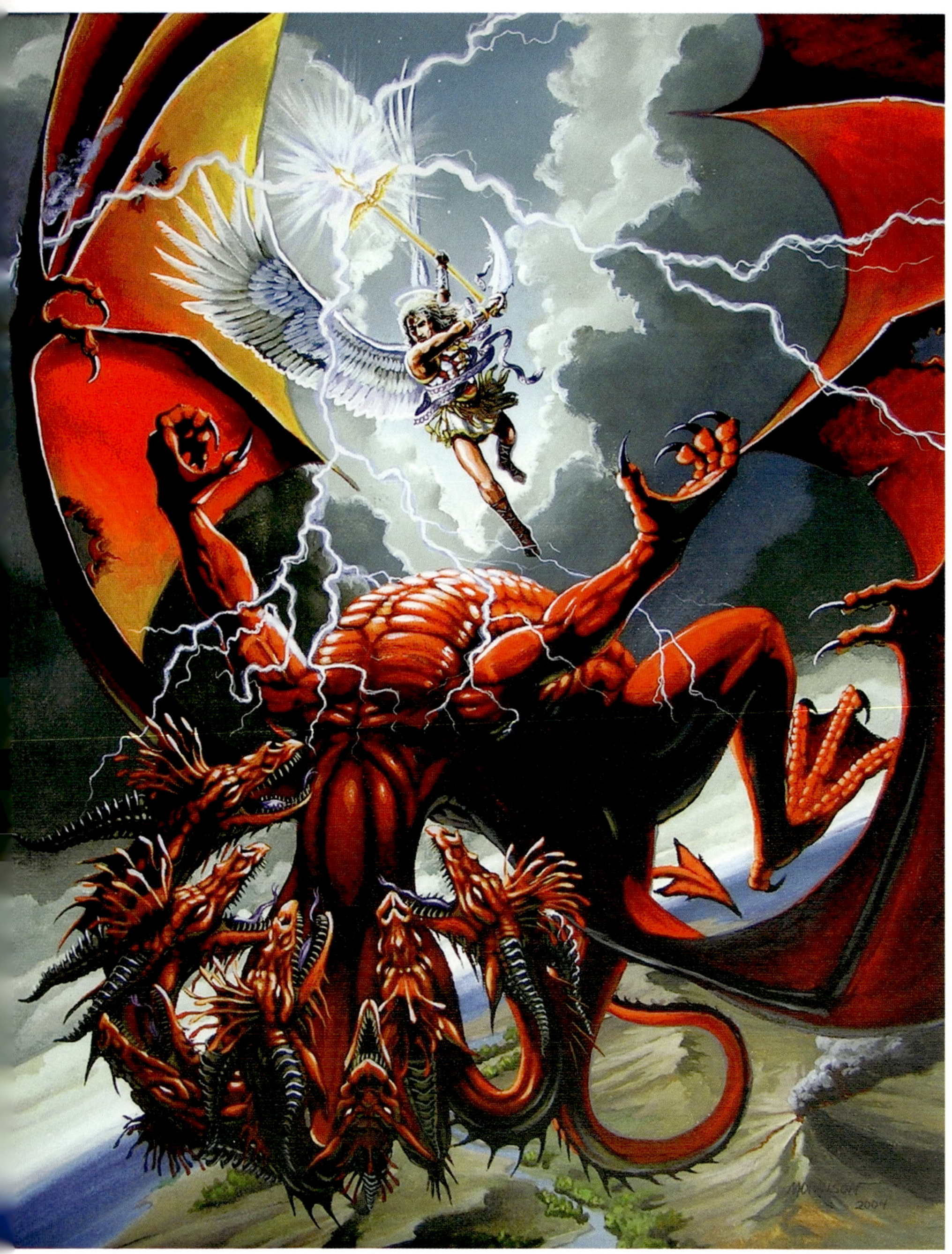

Fall of the Hydra by Stanley Morrison
© Stanley Morrison 2004 · Traditional media: acrylic on canvas board
'I wanted to paint a different looking hydra and found the story in the Bible of an angel defeating the seven-headed dragon. The heads represent the seven deadly sins.'
www.stanleymorrison.com

Copper Dragon by Stanley Morrison
© Stanley Morrison 2007 · Digital media: Photoshop
'I started a series of element dragons as a speed painting to loosen up my digital paintings. I kept each one under two hours from sketch to finish.'
www.stanleymorrison.com

six necks of the most prodigious length; and at the end of each neck she has a frightful head with three rows of teeth in each, all set very close together, so that they would crunch any one to death in a moment, and she sits deep within her shady cell thrusting out her heads and peering all round the rock, fishing for dolphins or dogfish or any larger monster that she can catch, of the thousands with which Amphitrite teems. No ship ever yet got past her without losing some men, for she shoots out all her heads at once, and carries off a man in each mouth.'

Jason and the Argonauts

In a similar vein, is the tale of Jason and the Argonauts, all of which feature similar quests, gods and monsters. In fact, Jason finds himself having to complete three tasks at the end, including the yoking of fire-breathing oxen, and even sows a field with dragons' teeth to create a race of super warriors.

The Bible

But it's not only the quests that bear these fantastical visions. The Old Testament makes a number of references to Leviathan, the giant sea monster that is described as fish and reptile, certainly serpentine in many places, sometimes with smoke coming from its nostrils and other times with seven heads. Whatever it is and

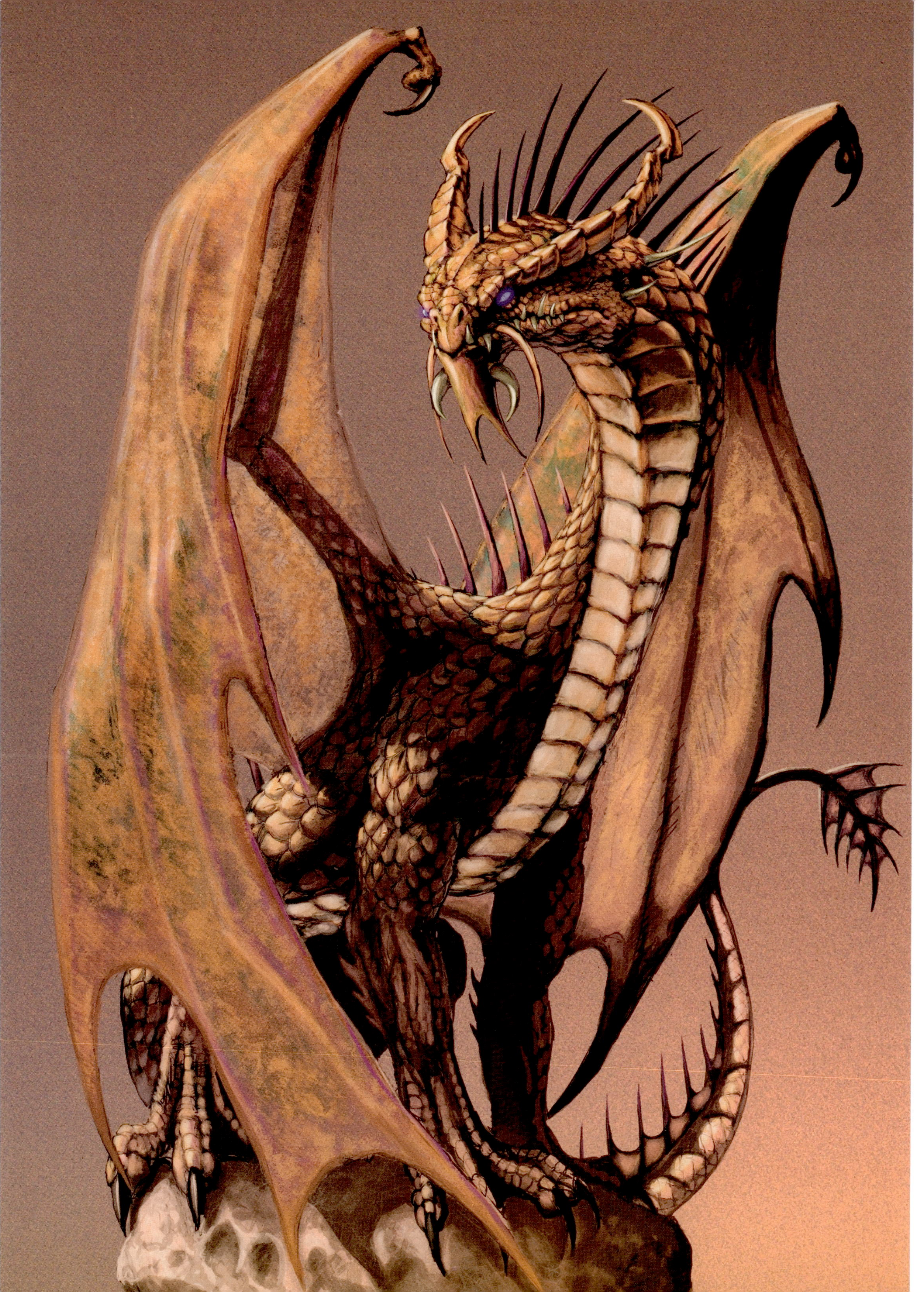

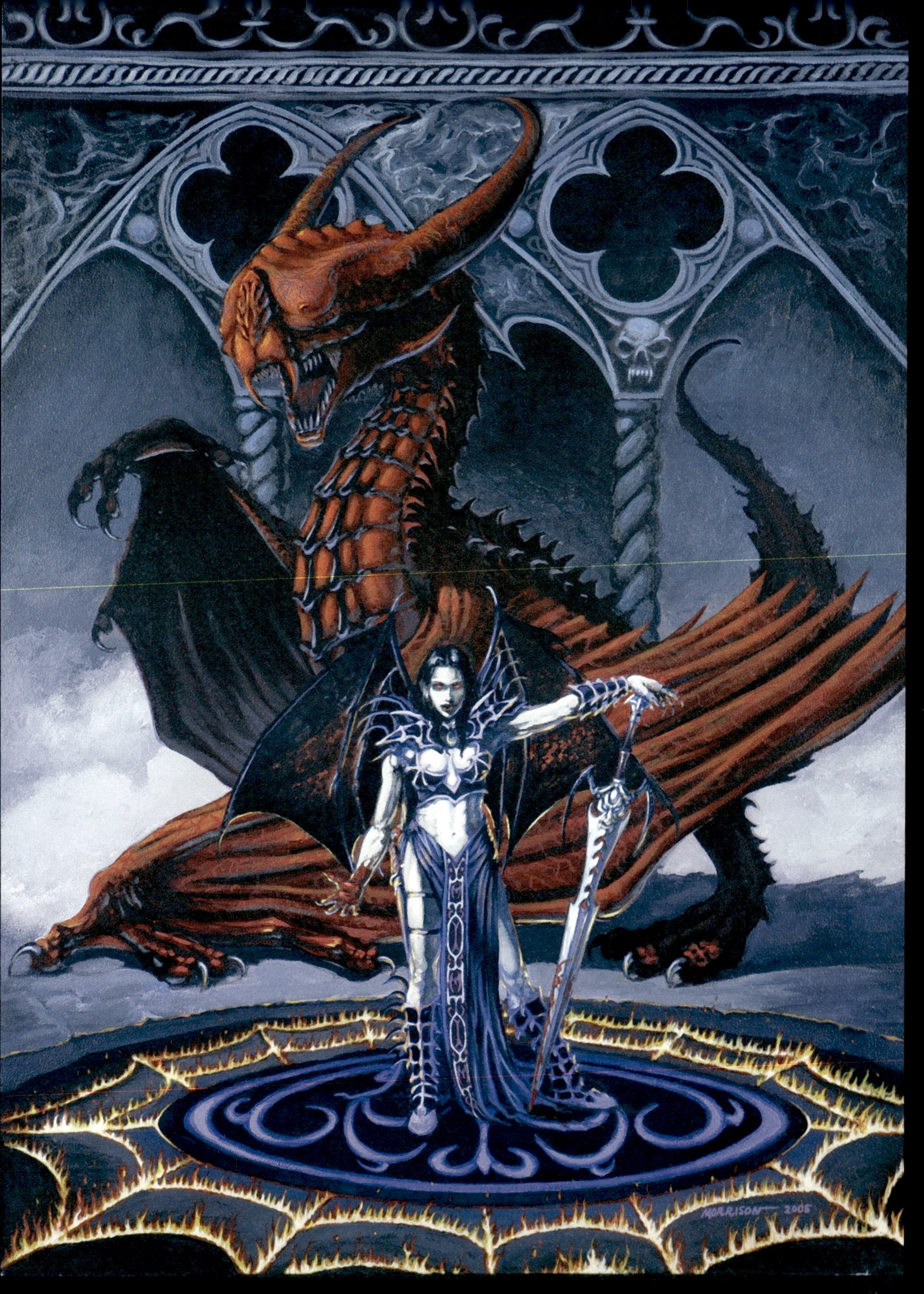
MORRISON 2005

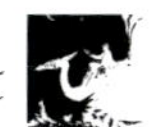

however many heads there are, one thing is for sure: Leviathan is huge. And Leviathan appears in several texts, including the Talmud and even the literature of Sumeria.

Even the serpent that tells the first woman, Eve, to eat the forbidden fruit is sometimes referred to as 'dragon'. There are several mentions of dragons in the Book of Revelations, the most famous perhaps being the Beast itself, described as a giant creature with seven heads and ten horns that has so captured the imagination for generations.

There are countless more characters from throughout the ages who have battled with dragon-like creatures, not forgetting tales such as Ovid's *Metamorphoses*, those featuring Hercules, Beowulf and countless more that have been themes for fantasy art over the years. The attraction of dragons for fantasy artists is not difficult to imagine. Turn to page 121 for further discussion of influential dragons of literature and legend.

What is Fantasy Art?

The West has a fine tradition: experience something and find a way to classify and define it so that it fits, quantified and conquered, into a cabinet, complete with index card. That is pretty difficult to do with some things, fantasy art among them.

There is fantasy art that is characterized by representations of rippling musclemen and Amazonian women in relatively flimsy outerwear gritting teeth, swords in hand, preparing for various kinds of battles, either with other similarly represented individuals or with monsters, especially dragons – elements like this are arguably some of what makes up 'sword-and-sorcery' fantasy. There is also a calmer side to this, where the emphasis is on the magic, stated or implied, of an arboreal setting. There are also images which seem almost dream-like and symbolic rather than fantasy-set to show something that may or may not have happened. There are representations that appear to be drawn from meticulous study of people and animals to make sure they are all anatomically sound and in proportion, to add almost a reality, through to fantasy that feels more inspired and spontaneous, where a literalness is not intended. Fantasy art that aspires to some sort of epic and meaningful, magical world that is on a higher plane than rough and ready sword and sorcery, is often referred to as 'high fantasy'.

Undefinable

However, it is impossible to concretely define 'fantasy' let alone to define its sub-genres; you cannot say 'it is this thing' or 'that thing'. For instance, artist Bob Eggleton describes it as an other-worldliness, beyond the rules of science fiction. This of course hints at a relationship between science fiction and fantasy art; while the two are certainly separate genres, they definitely do share something of their unbridled and unashamed reliance on the 'what ifs' of the imagination. However, science fiction is, unsurprisingly, drenched in scientific theory; whatever magic there

AKASHA AND THE BLOOD DRAGON by Stanley Morrison, 2005
© Stanley Morrison 2005 · Traditional media: acrylic on textured clayboard · 'I gave the dragon more of a vampire-bat look to go with the queen of vampires.'
www.stanleymorrison.com

may be is a matter of scientific explanation. You can create all sorts of weird and wonderful worlds, beings and events, but only as long as the reason that this is possible is explained relatively thoroughly and scientifically. Fantasy does not need any of that 'plausibility'. It merely needs to have an individual or substance capable of bestowing a certain kind of magic. There is no reason for it; it just is that way.

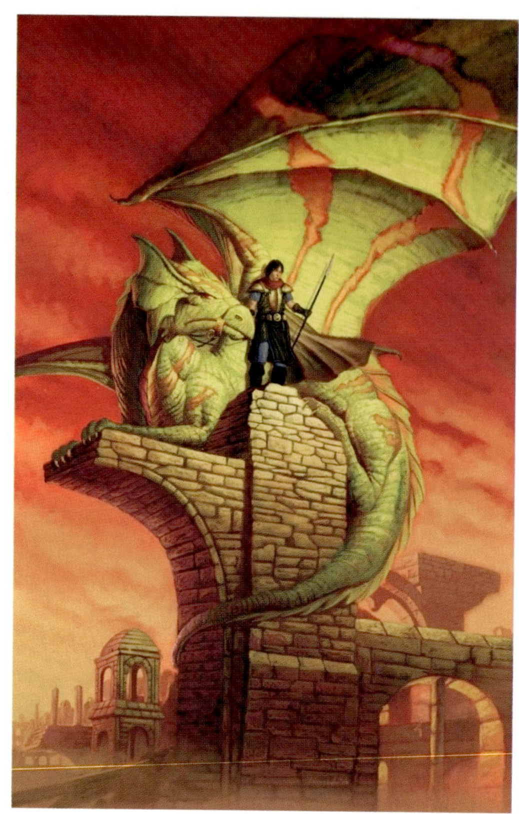

At its best, fantasy and fantasy art has a sense of the plausible. It may be way out there, but somehow it hints at the fact that it could be true. It does this by taking surroundings we are relatively familiar with and consider normal, and addinbg something particularly fantastical or miles out of the ordinary, such as monsters, warriors or elves.

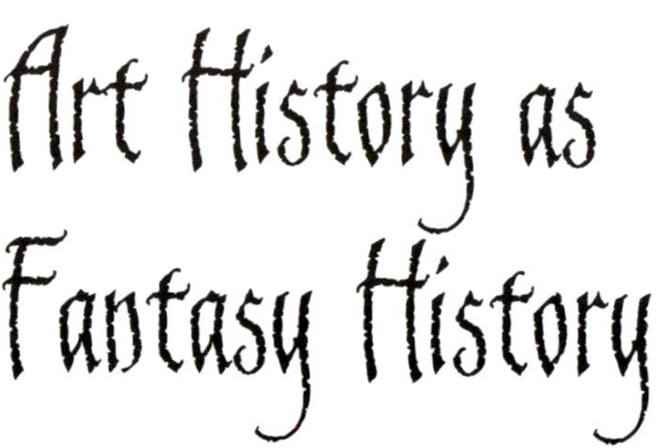

Art History as Fantasy History

One of the many things that fantasy artists will tell you is that the history of fantasy art is actually a history of art itself. For those used to viewing those otherworldly scenarios as set up by the likes of Frank Frazetta or Larry Elmore, this notion may seem strange and confusing at best, or misguided and pretentious at worst.

But hear them out. Certainly the Old Masters created a vast body of portraits of seated subjects or recreated scenes from their patrons' lives and deaths. But what is equally true is that they created work inspired by the imagination, Greek and Roman myth and, of course, the Bible.

Biblical Visions

It does not matter whether you are a Dawkins-esque atheist or a devout Christian, there is no doubt that the Bible is loaded with scenery to whet the appetite of any artist. From descriptions of God's scorched earth policy regarding Sodom and Gomorrah to St John's vision of the Beast incarnate, a dragon with seven heads and ten horns.

So it is no surprise that artists like Argentinian-born Ciruelo see the likes of Michelangelo as part of the tradition of fantasy artists. He is keen for all who will listen to consider the Sistine chapel. It is immaterial whether you are a devout believer or a dyed-in-the-wool atheist: there is no denying a sort of fantastical element to Michelangelo's famous rendering.

THE PATROL by Leonardo Borazio
© Leonardo Borazio 2007 · Mixed media: pencil, Photoshop
www.leonardoborazioart.com

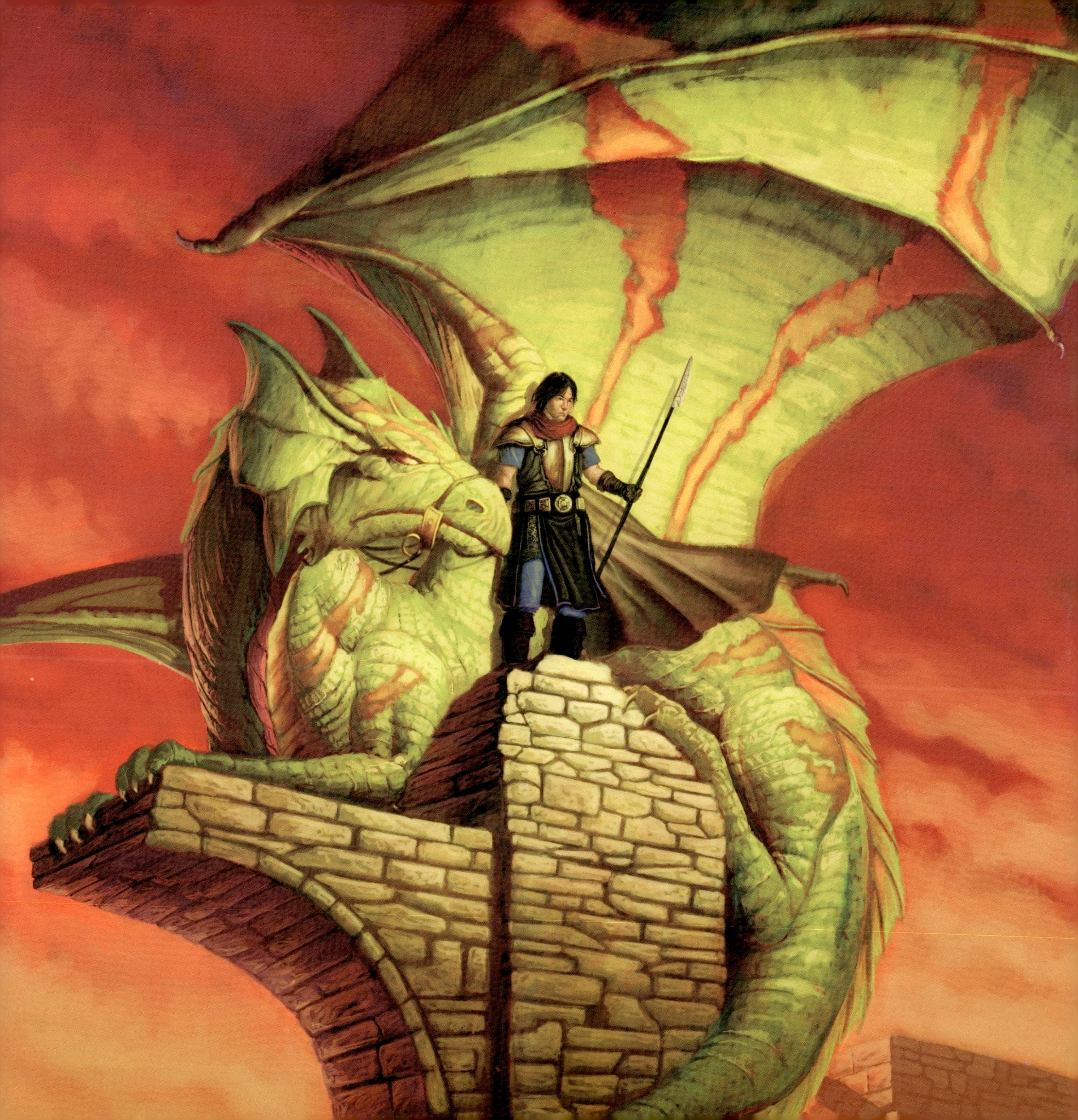

Leighton, the Fantasy Artist

In fact, there are plenty of pre-twentieth-century artists who have made their mark on today's generation of fantasy artists. Frederic Leighton is one such example. Born in Scarborough, England, in 1830, his education was bathed in a strong European tradition, spending a great deal of time in Paris, Frankfurt and Rome, among other places, learning how to paint. He made a name for himself showing his painting *Cimabue's Madonna Carried in Procession through the Streets of Florence*, in 1855 upon his return to Britain. It is a magnificent, almost photographically realistic piece, currently part of the National Gallery's collection in London. So powerful was the image that, on its first showing, Queen Victoria bought it. She said in her diary: 'There was a very big picture by a man called Leighton. It is a beautiful painting, quite reminding one of a Paul Veronese, so bright and full of light. Albert was enchanted with it – so much so that he made me buy it.'

Of particular note, however, is Leighton's 1891 work *Perseus and Andromeda*. This is arguably the work of a fantasy artist in the tradition of the twenty-first century. Currently on display at Liverpool's Walker Art Gallery, it depicts Andromeda, daughter of the Queen of Ethiopia, about to be rescued by Perseus riding Pegasus the winged horse. And what is Andromeda being rescued from? A rather black, fire-breathing dragon.

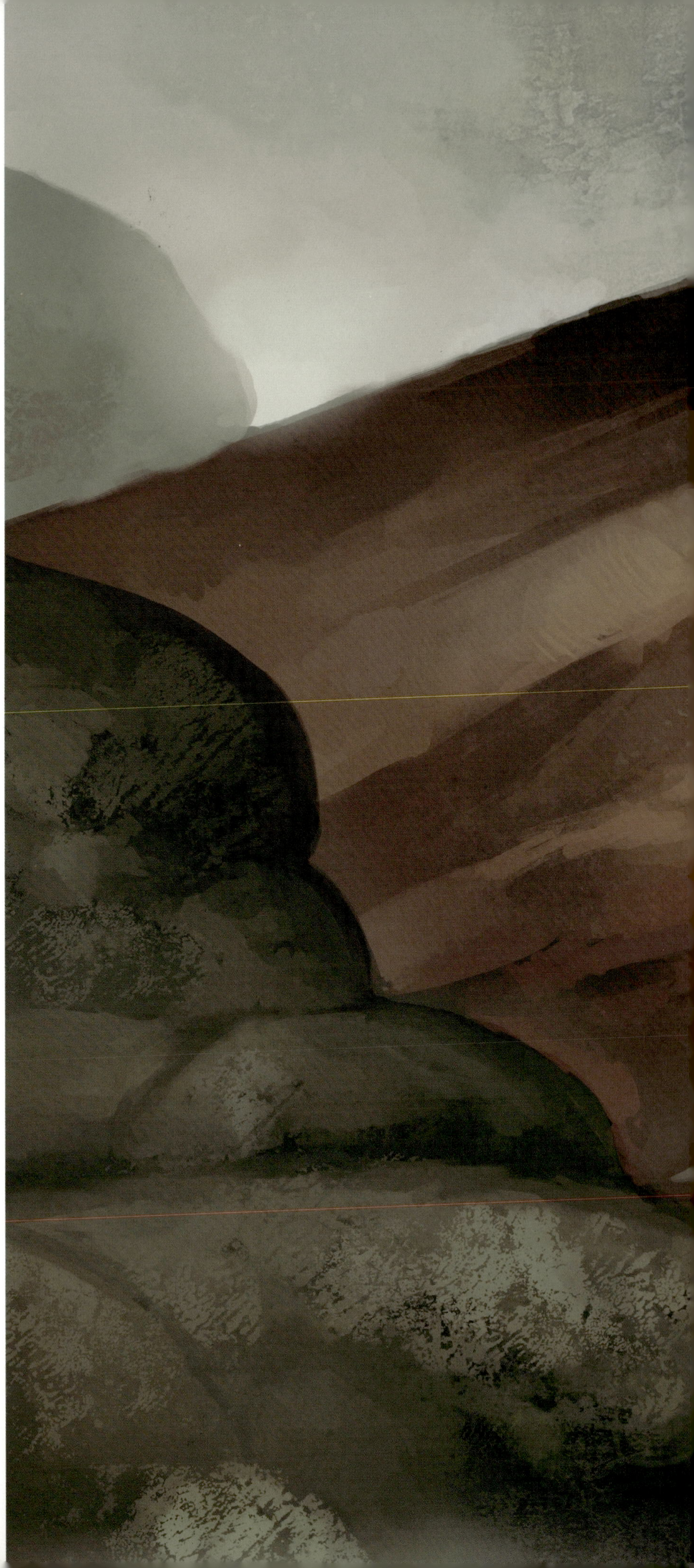

DRAGON REIGN by Jon Hodgson
© Jon Hodgson 2008 · Digital media: Artrage, Painter, Photoshop
Jon Hodgson is a full-time freelance artist working in Scotland.
www.jonhodgson.com

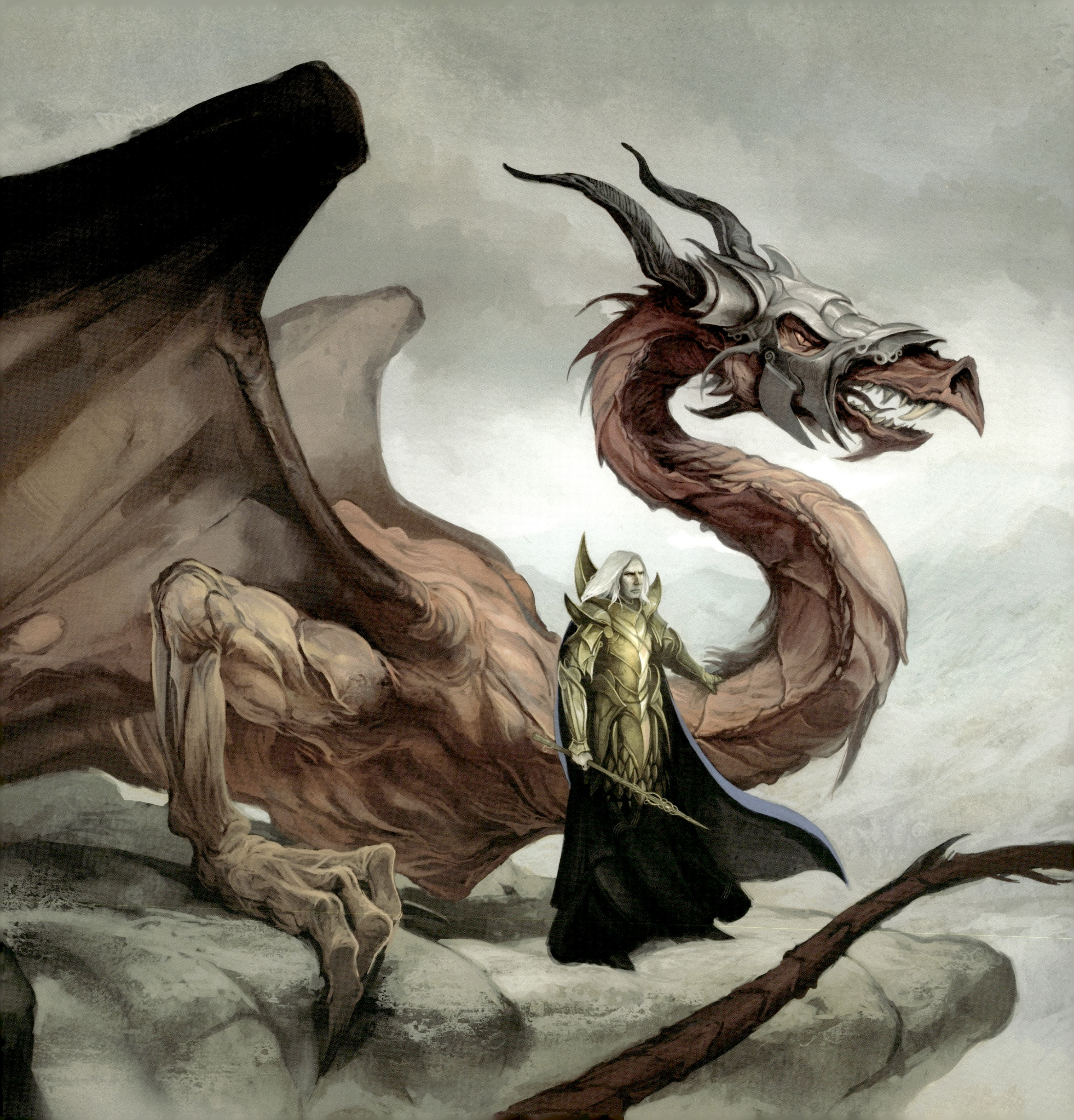

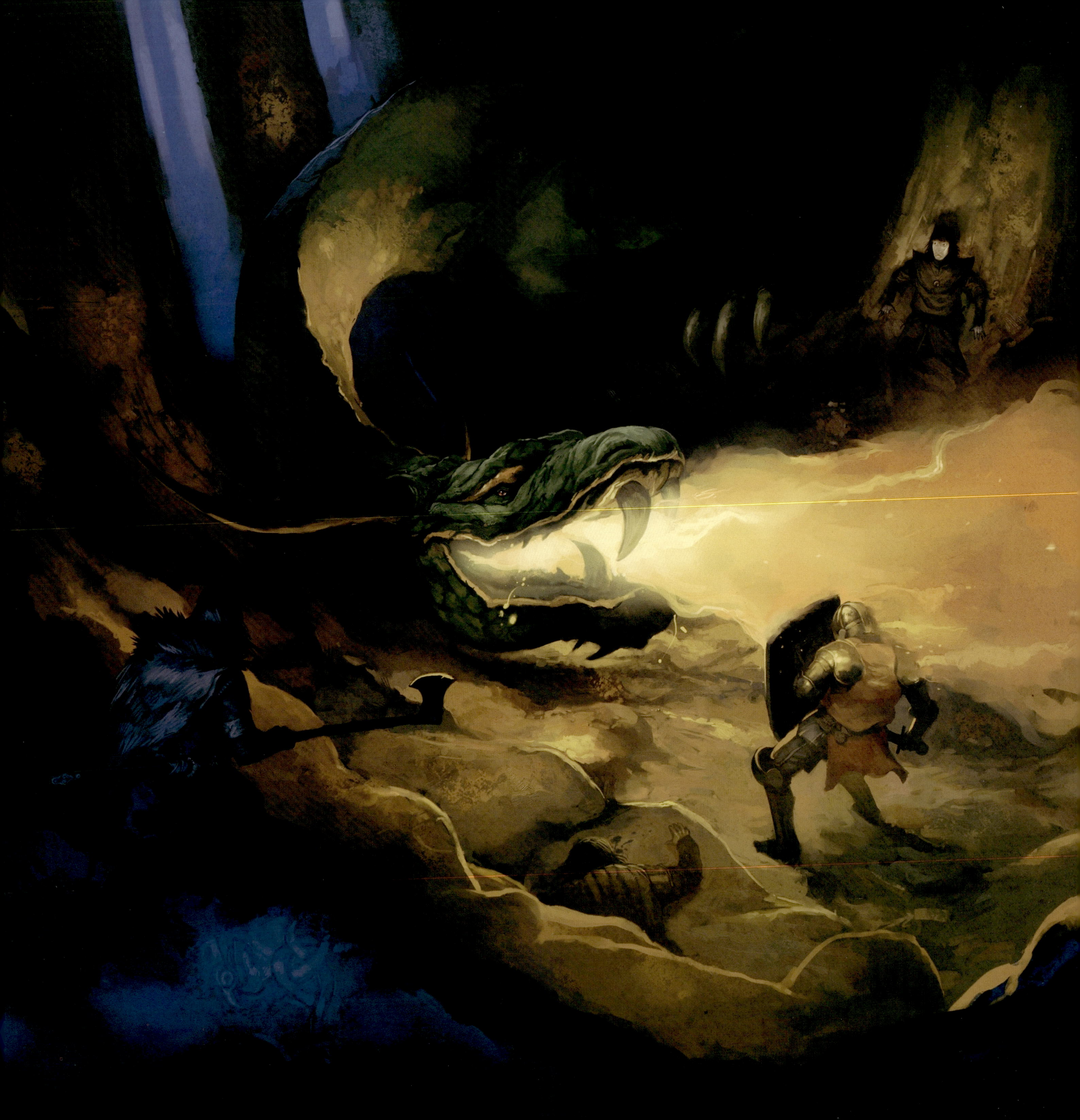

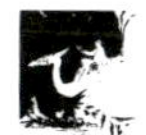

Turner's Influence

Among other highly influential artists is Joseph Mallord William Turner. Born in 1775 in Covent Garden, London, Turner began his career as an artist in a manner similar to his contemporaries, with a strong emphasis on representing space. The idea was to provide a space with which the viewer could identify, perhaps play the part of God in a hierarchy of creativity: God created us and looks down from heaven while man creates art and viewers are able to look at this creativity from a sort of heavenly perspective.

Turner's attraction for fantasy artists is not so much his subject matter as his use of light. As his career progressed, Turner became more and more concerned with light, rather than space, in his paintings, giving his work a more impressionistic feel. In fact, Turner would later go on to influence the impressionist movement of the late 19th and early 20th Centuries. Bob Eggleton says: 'I'm very influenced by that kind of work, the way of thinking, the stylistic influence.'

Delacroix's Darkness

Also cited by many fantasy artists as influential is the art of Eugène Delacroix, born near Paris in 1798. Like Turner, he's considered a Romantic artist, although he often referred to himself as a Classicist. Among his influences was Michelangelo, with whom he shared a penchant for depicting some of the darker side of human existence. He caused something of a sensation with the desolate *Le Massacre de Scio* in 1824. It depicts a multitude of starving Greeks on the verge of slaughter at the hands of the Turks in an event on the island of Scio that occurred two years before.

Delacriox was in no doubt of the potential power of painting. In fact, he once noted in a journal that, 'Materially speaking, painting is nothing but a bridge set up between the mind of the artists and that of the beholder'. What was particularly important, he believed, was the mood and feeling behind a work of art and not necessarily its content. He was also a great man of ideas, cultivating friendships with the likes of George Sand and Chopin, as well as at least strong acquaintance with Baudelaire and Stendhal.

He was also highly regarded by Manet, Cézanne and Van Gogh – in fact, the latter said that Delacroix's 'portraits of the soul' were essential for his own artistic development. Later, Picasso would also cite Delacroix as essential to his artistic development.

Emotion is Key

Delacroix immersed himself in his subject matter, attempting not just to render a depiction on the canvas but also to wring out its emotional core. For example, his lithographs for *Faust* led Goethe himself to remark that Delacroix's interpretation of his work had

DRAGON WARRIORS BESTIARY by Jon Hodgson
© Magnum Opus Press and Jon Hodgson 2008
Digital media: Artrage, Painter, Photoshop
Jon Hodgson is a full-time freelance artist working in Scotland.
www.jonhodgson.com

surpassed his own role as writer, and forced him to discover new meanings in what he had written.

Strongly influenced by Michelangelo, fantasy artists would certainly be interested in Delacroix's decoration of the ceiling of the Louvre with his rendering of *Apollo Conquering The Serpent Python* (1850). Essentially, the goodness and light, Apollo, battles the darkness and chaos, as represented by the serpent in another depiction of the dragon slayer.

Böcklin's Beasts

And then, of course, there is Swiss painter Arnold Böcklin, born in Basel in 1827, who had more than a passing interest in mythical beasts. Centaurs, fauns, mermaids and cherubs are all subjects for his work, and many are based in the very sorts of forests that are present in much fantasy work. There is humour, too: how else do you explain an engraving of a centaur visiting a blacksmith in search of new shoes? His 1880 *Isle of the Dead* is an eerie peaceful vision of a dream that is perhaps his most influential work, inspiring works of music and visual art, including output from surrealists such as Salvador Dalí and H.R. Giger.

Rather disturbing is his representation of the plague, painted in 1898, in which the disease is represented as a harrowing, corpse-like figure riding a mysterious winged beast resembling a reptile swan with batwings.

RODIN by Scott Altmann
© Scott Altmann 2008 · Digital media: Painter, Photoshop
www.scottaltmann.com

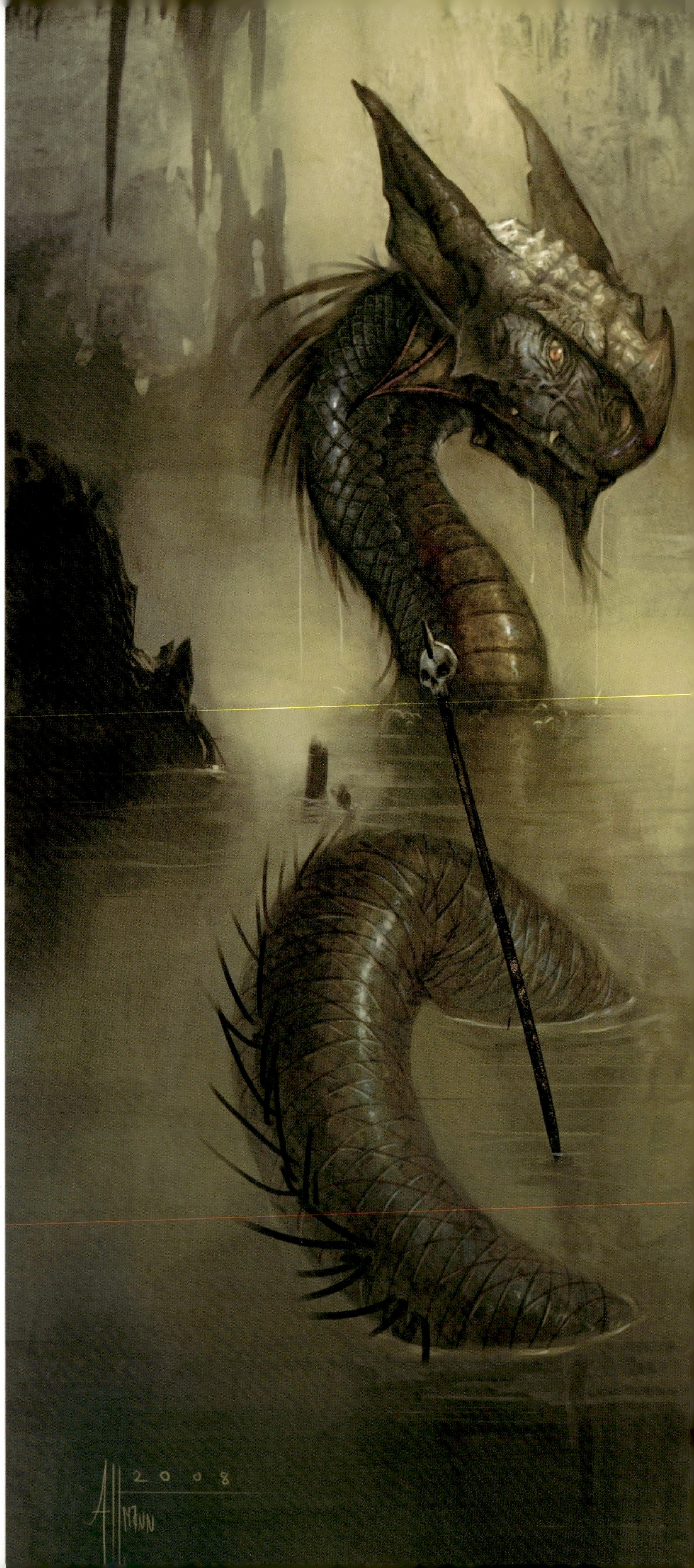

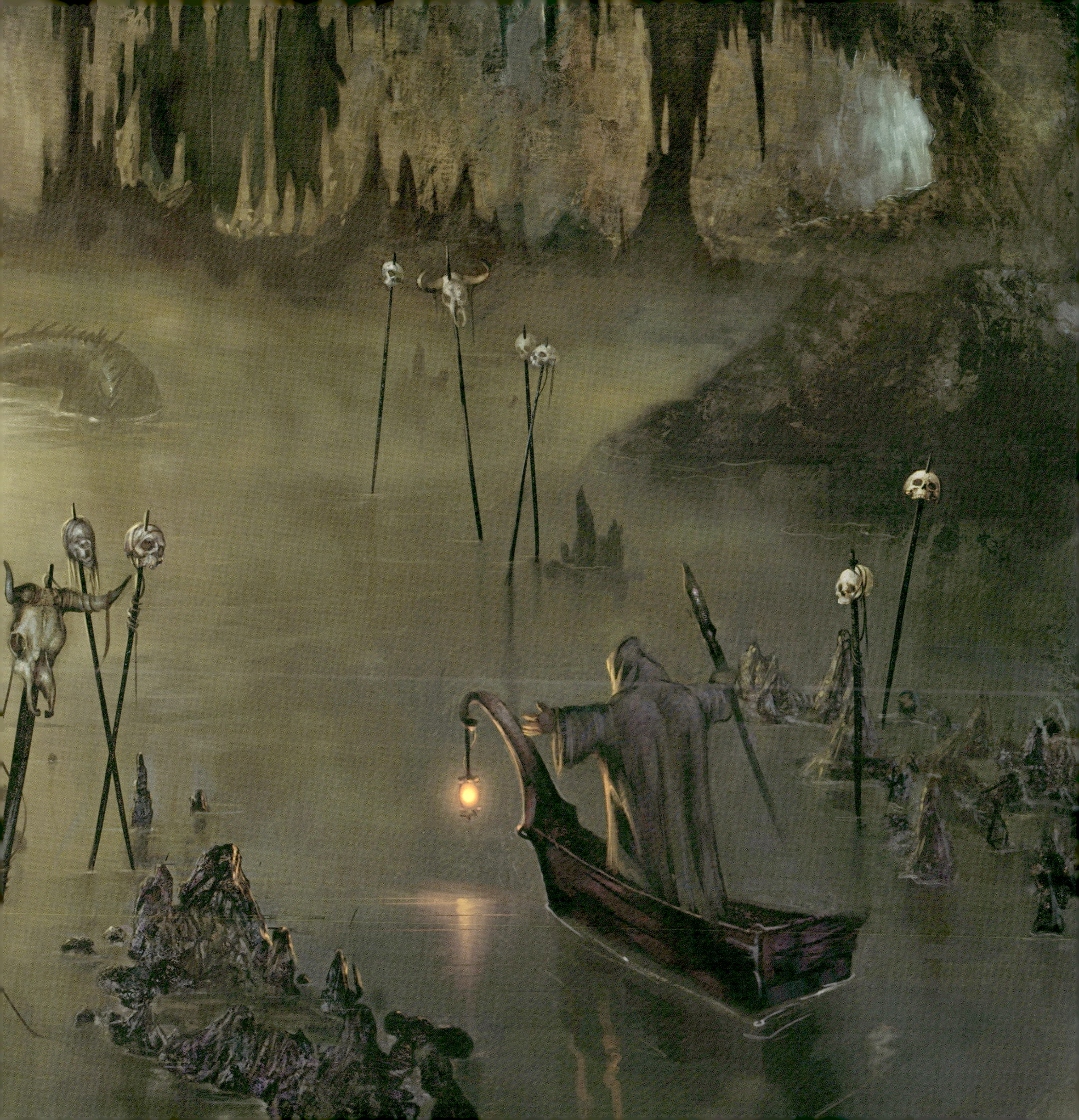

Fast Ships, Black Sails by Scott Altmann

© Scott Altmann 2008; Digital media: Painter, Photoshop; Cover illustration for *Fast Ships, Black Sails*, published by Night Shade Books; www.scottaltmann.com

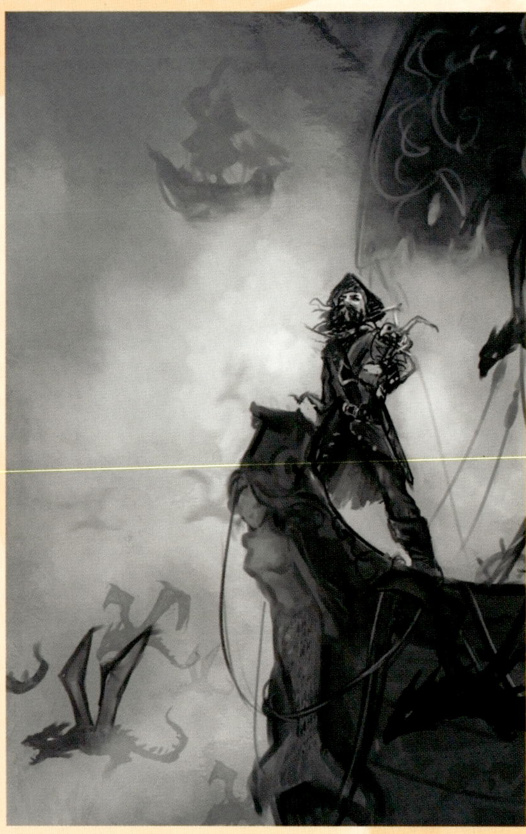

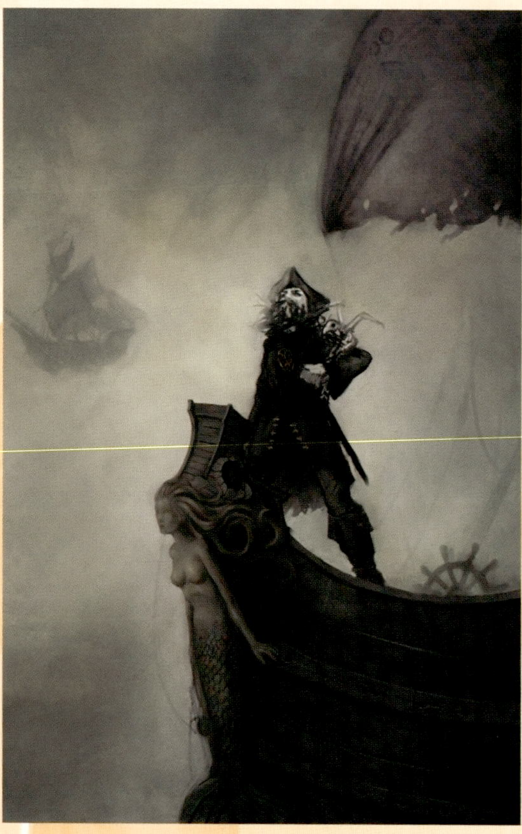

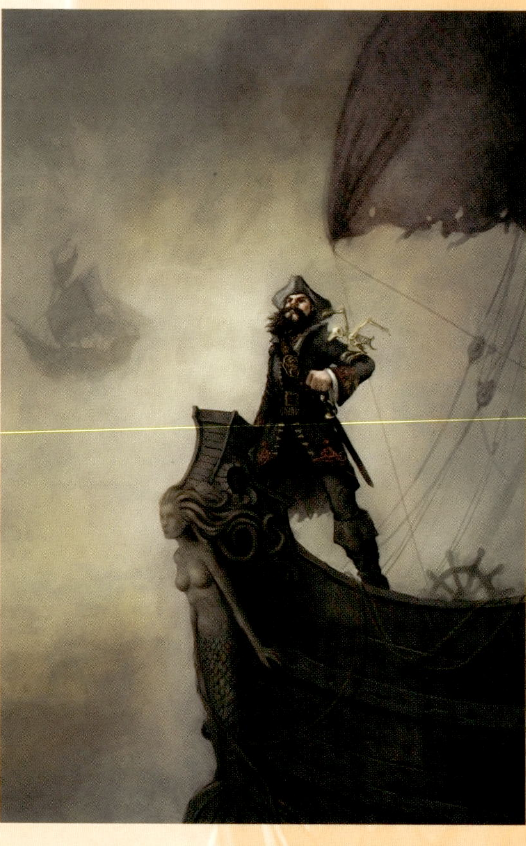

SAMPLE STEP 1. After exploring several ideas along the client's 'pirates and fantasy/sci-fi' brief, this was the sketch that was selected. It is important to only submit sketches you would be satisfied in taking to final.

SAMPLE STEP 2. I wanted the piece to have very muted, yet clean colour, with just a few, key spots of intense hue. I removed all the dragons from the initial painting as I planned to add them in later – keeping some of the elements separate can make your life easier, but you have to be careful that all the elements still look as if they belong in the same picture. After laying down some broad and large masses of colour I started in on the ship.

SAMPLE STEP 3. At this point, it was time to get working on the focal point of the image. Since his face was going to be printed somewhat small, I wanted the values to be strong in contrast. I started to flesh out some of the details, and added bright red embroidery to the pirate's jacket to add a little punch. I digitally painted the dragon skeleton on the pirate's shoulder directly from observation of a pigeon skeleton I own.

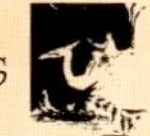

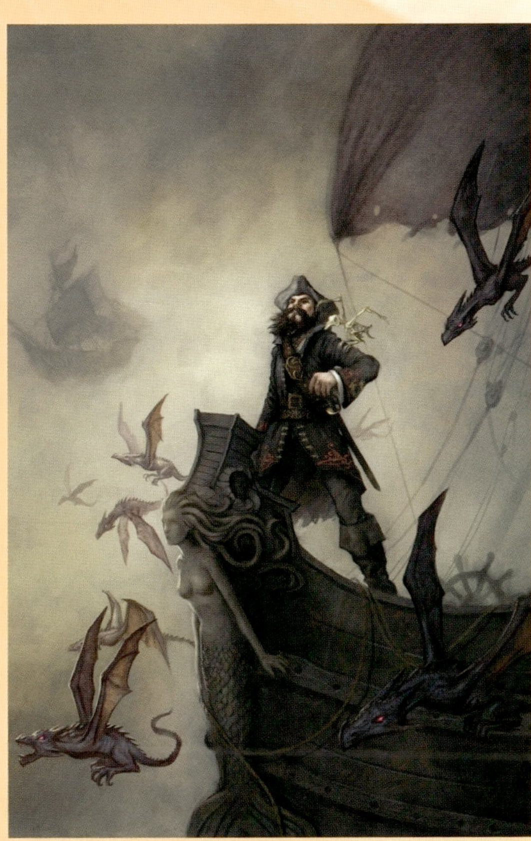

SAMPLE STEP 4. I painted the dragons fairly loose because I wanted to convey a sense of movement in them. Here, I added another spot of intense colour in their eyes, just to give another area for the viewers' eyes to jump around the image. I then felt the image needed more dragons to fill up the big gaps in negative space and enhance the sense of depth in the painting.

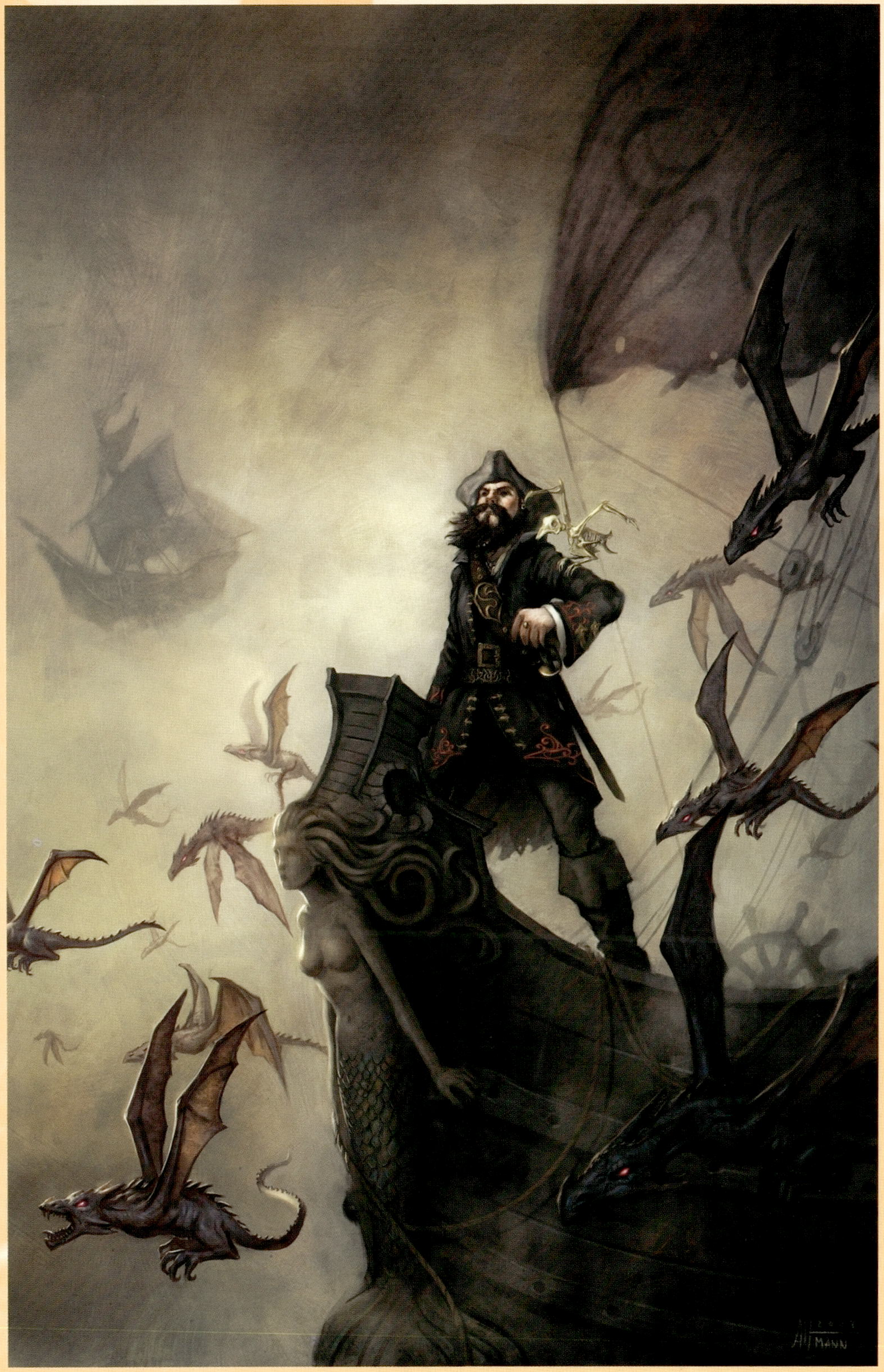

FINISHING TOUCHES. A few more details were added, and some atmospheric haze towards the bottom of the ship. Then I adjusted the levels ever so slightly and began my usual staring process, looking for anything jumping out at me. If no additional work is needed, it's off to the art director and the job is done.

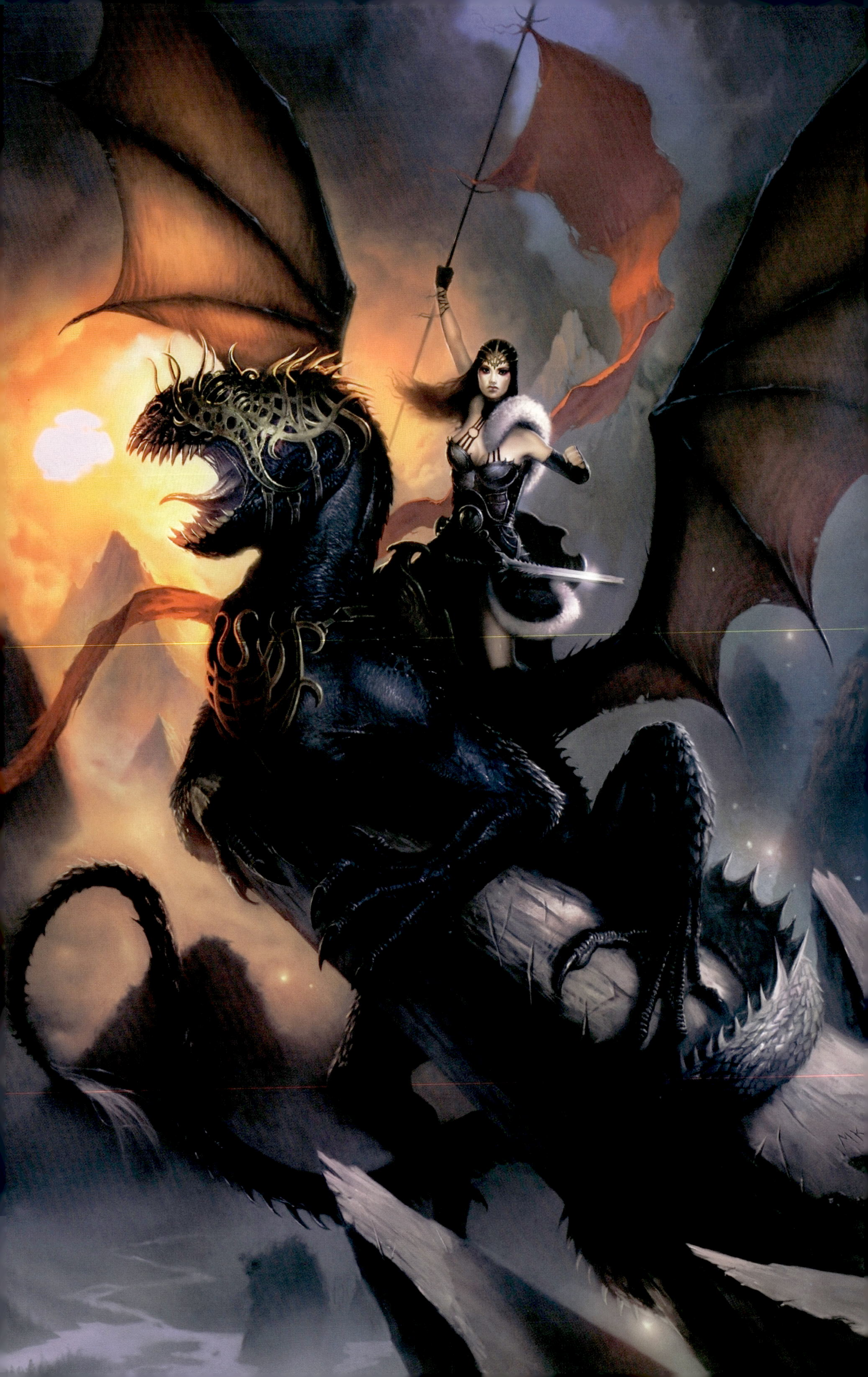

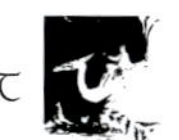

RIDER by Mathias Kollros
© Mathias Kollros 2008 · Digital media: Photoshop
Mathias is available for commissions.
www.guterrez.com

The Rise of Fantasy

Modern fantasy, as a genre of literature and art, arose largely at the start of the last century. Advances in publishing techniques at the end of the 1800s, particularly offset lithography and the rise of the linotype machine, led to something of a publishing revolution not unlike the one that would occur nearly 100 years later with the rise of desktop and Internet publishing. Suddenly it became possible for would-be magazine publishers to put together volumes of weird and wonderful tales and spooky ghost stories. They would rely on the likes of H.P. Lovecraft, Edgar Rice Burroughs, Robert E. Howard, Dashiell Hammet, Fritz Leiber and a range of others to fill their pages with words.

But if you had a magazine, you also needed a cover, and it is this requirement that has been the catalyst for the rise of much fantasy art. Typically, covers would try their best to show something strange and eerie: demon eyes, a couple in peril, strange menacing 'people from the east' hypnotizing or inveigling hapless all-American couples.

DRAGONSTYLE by Mathias Kollros
© Mathias Kollros 2008 · Digital media: Photoshop
Mathias is available for commissions.
www.guterrez.com

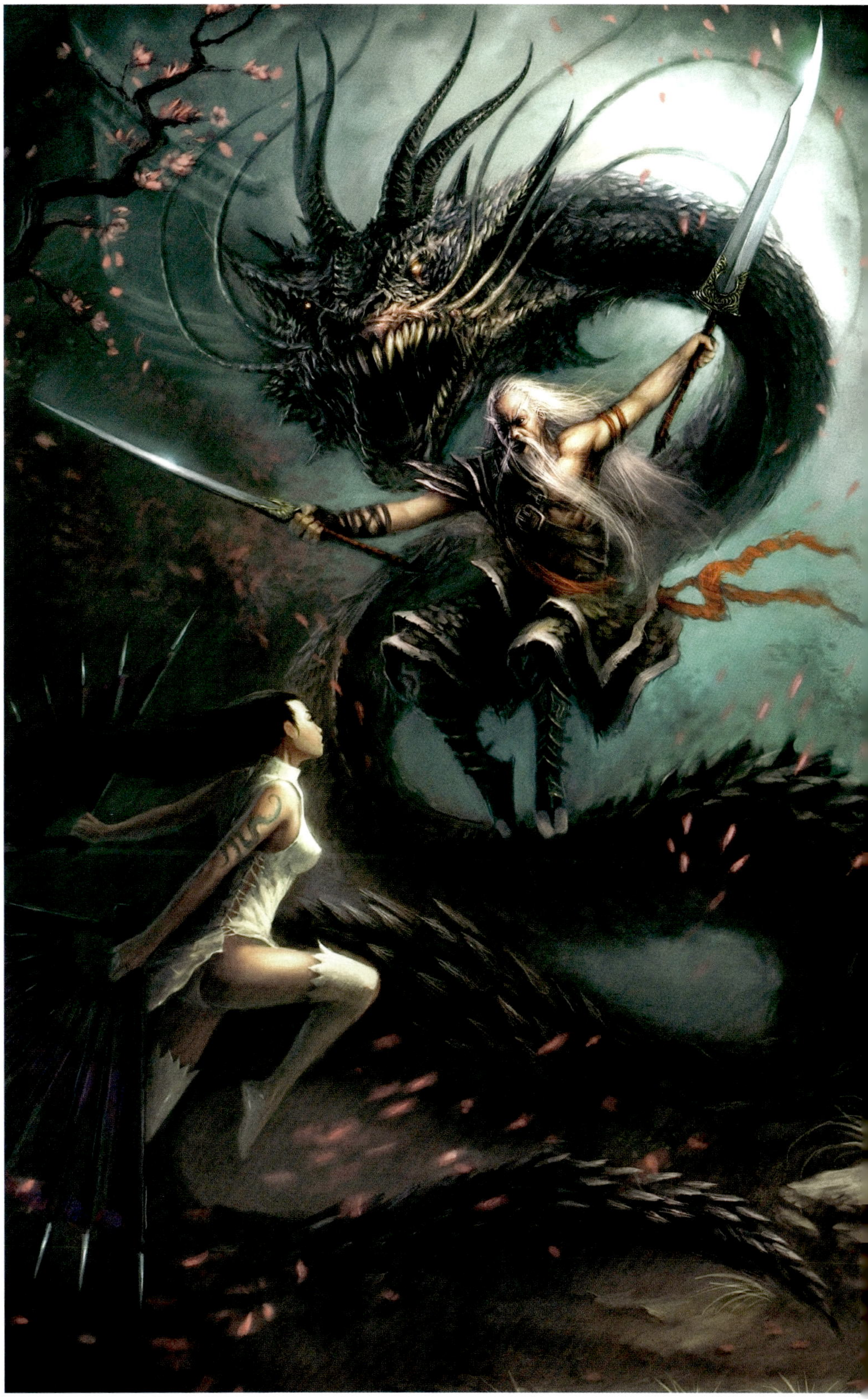

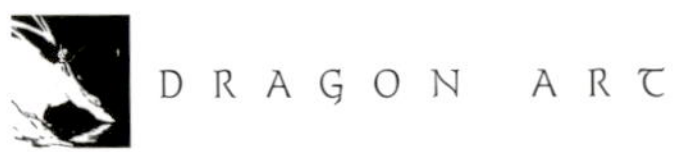

The Mother of Fantasy Art?

In the mid-1930s, *Weird Tales* broke the mould by employing one M. Brundage to illustrate their covers. Mrs Margaret Brundage was an out-of-work fashion designer looking for work and hoping to find an opportunity to illustrate in colour. A Chicago local, she happened upon the offices of *Weird Tales* and began a tenure that lasted between 1932 and 1939.

Her covers were dynamite. Rather than depicting horror and peril, her pastel-drawn covers were pure titillation: her whip-wielding, leather-clad dominatrices, scantily clad damsels awaiting rescue, buxom maidens walking, crawling, curling up or creeping all but naked would pique the curiosity of teenage boys and ensured *Weird Tales* managed to stay afloat despite the depths of the American depression at the time.

Moral Qualms

In the 1940s, however, any moral outcry over the world of comics was legitimized by the publication of *The Seduction of the Innocent* by Dr Frederic Wertham. The psychiatrist argued that comics were a leading cause of the recently defined notion of 'juvenile delinquency', and a senate sub-committee, headed by Senator Estes Kefauver, was convened to investigate. There

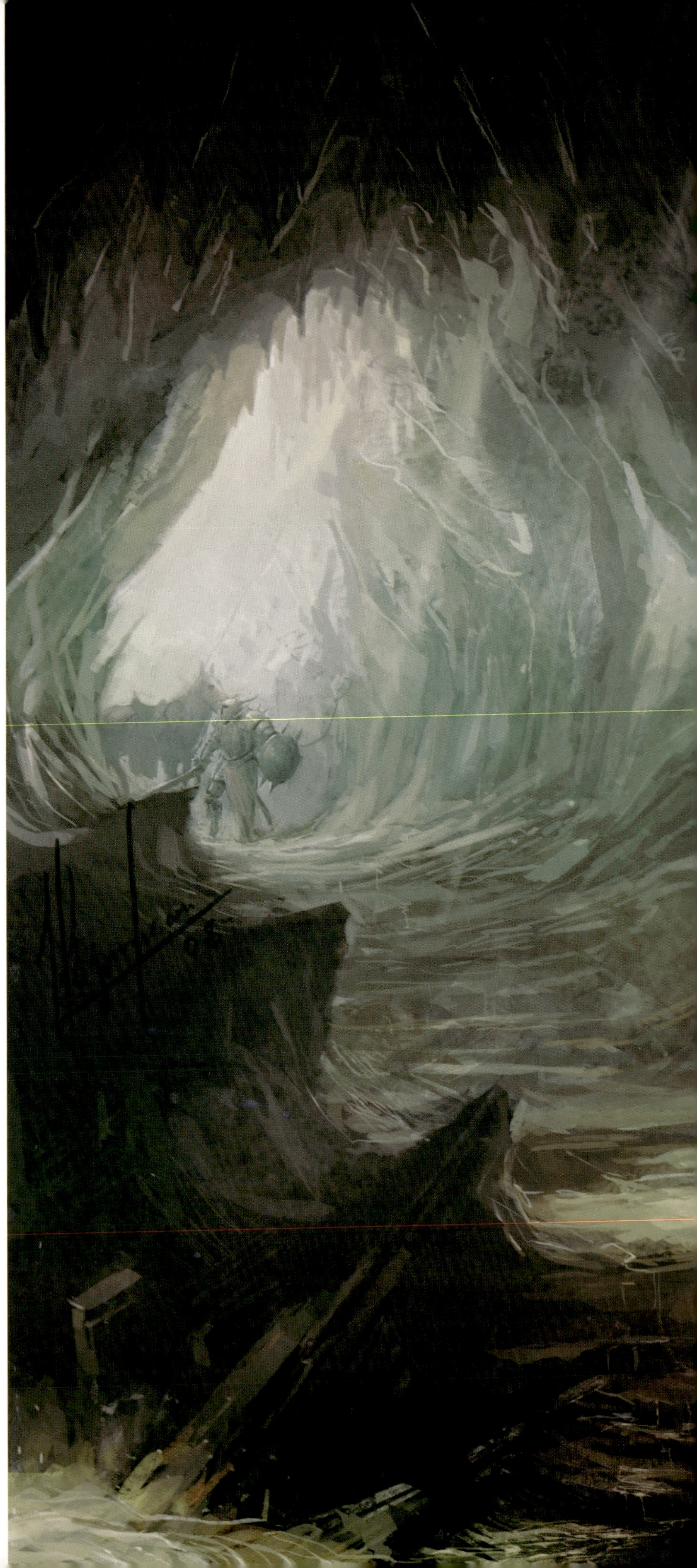

CAVERN DRAGON by Ignacio Bazán Lazcano
© Ignacio Bazán Lazcano 2008 · Mixed media: pencil, Photoshop
Ignacio works as a concept artist in the video game industry in Argentina.
www.neisbeis.deviantart.com

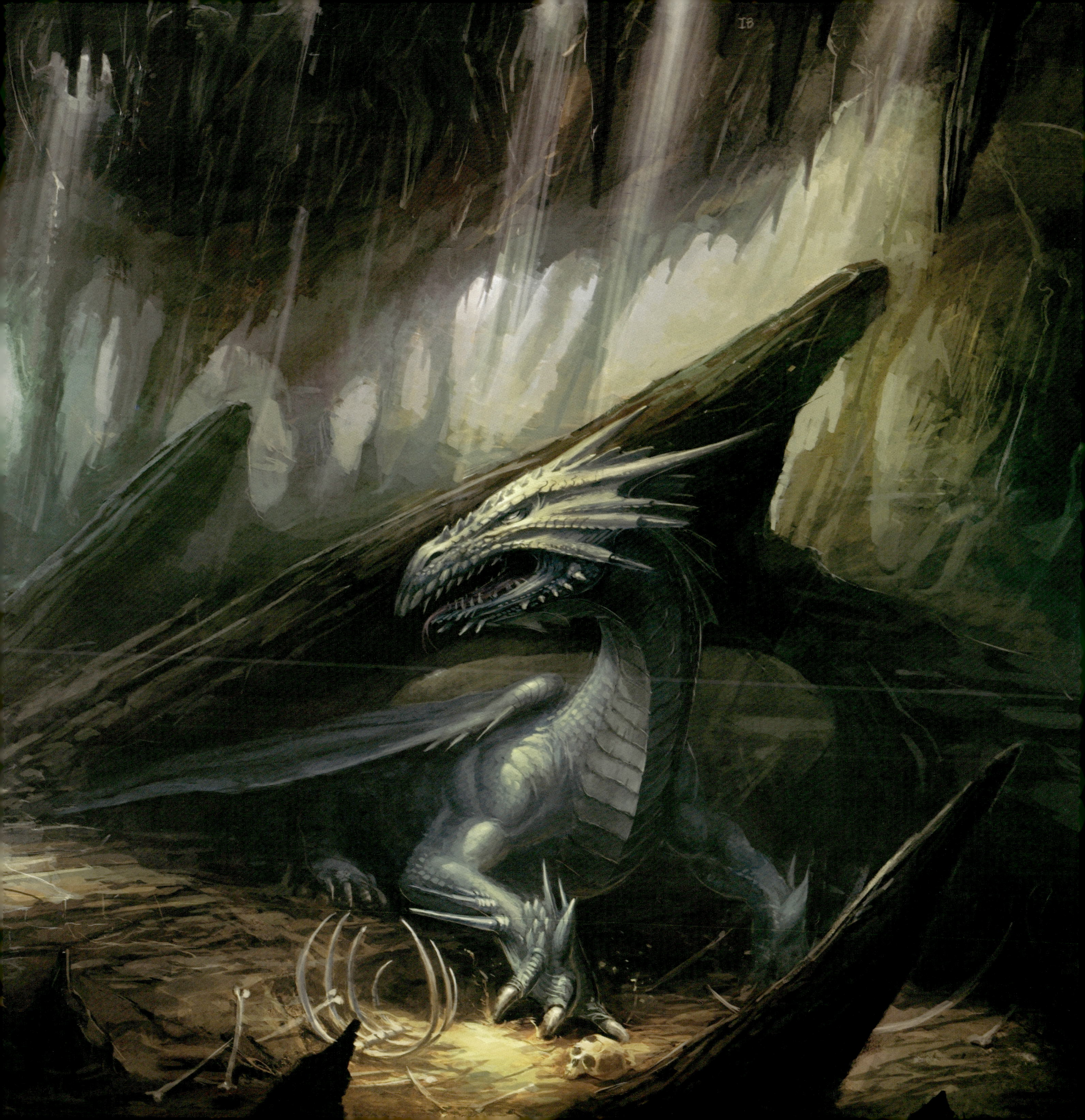

Cardinal Dragon by Chuck Wadey

© Chuck Wadey 2007; Mixed media: traditional watercolour washes and Photoshop; Chuck Wadey is the art director for Challenge Online Games' Duels.com, Planetstorm.com and Warstorm.com.

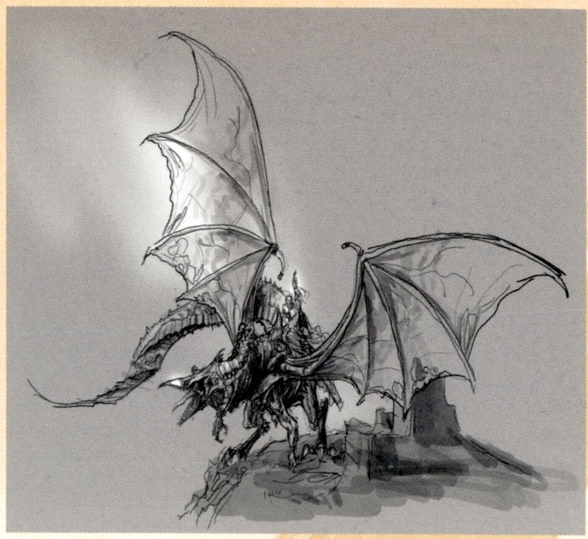

SAMPLE STEP 1. Cardinal Dragon started as a rough sketch in Photoshop. I like to add new layers to refine a drawing and then merge back down to flat when I'm happy with it.

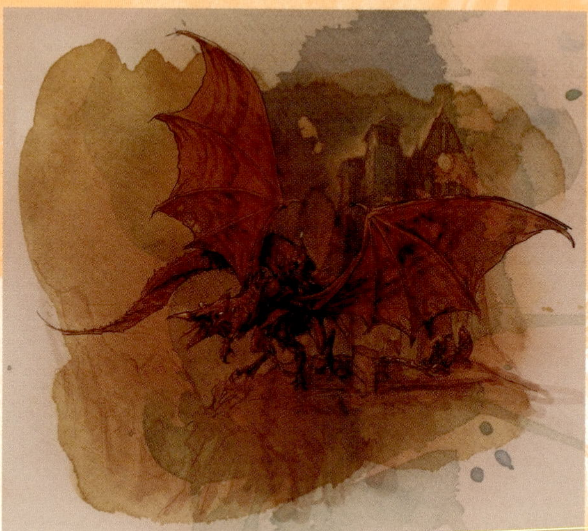

SAMPLE STEP 2. Once I had a solid drawing, I painted a handful of random watercolour washes on paper, and scanned them at a high resolution to use as my painting base in Photoshop. I think it gave the piece a stronger natural media feel than the usual Photoshop brush textures.

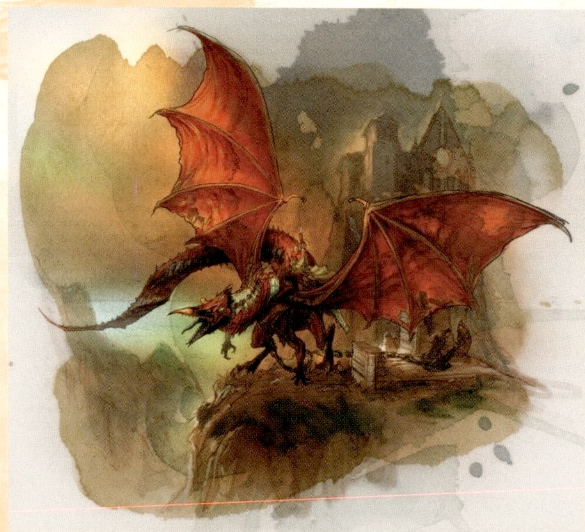

SAMPLE STEP 3. This piece continued to evolve. Cardinals on my bird feeder inspired the dragon's red colour and dark spot around the eye. From cardinal bird to Catholic Cardinal, I leapt to the idea that this could be a dragon in the service of the church. For more realism, I posed for photos to use as reference for all of the characters.

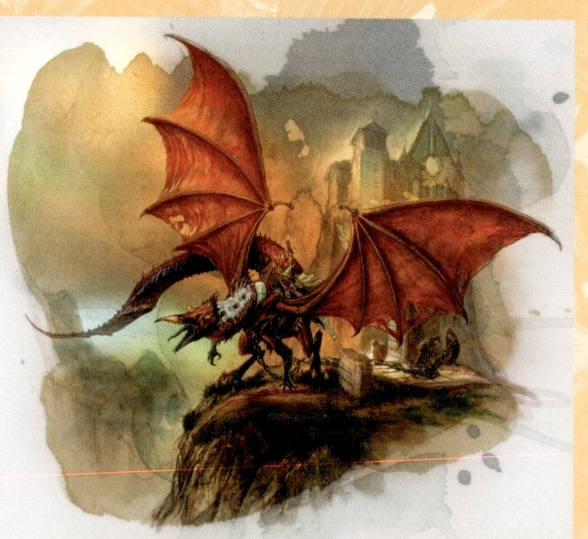

SAMPLE STEP 4. The first half of a painting is fast and fun, the second half is more time consuming with tuning small details. Paradoxically, I feel like the more finished a painting like this starts to look, the further away the finish line seems because I notice more areas that could use some tightening.

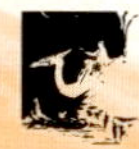

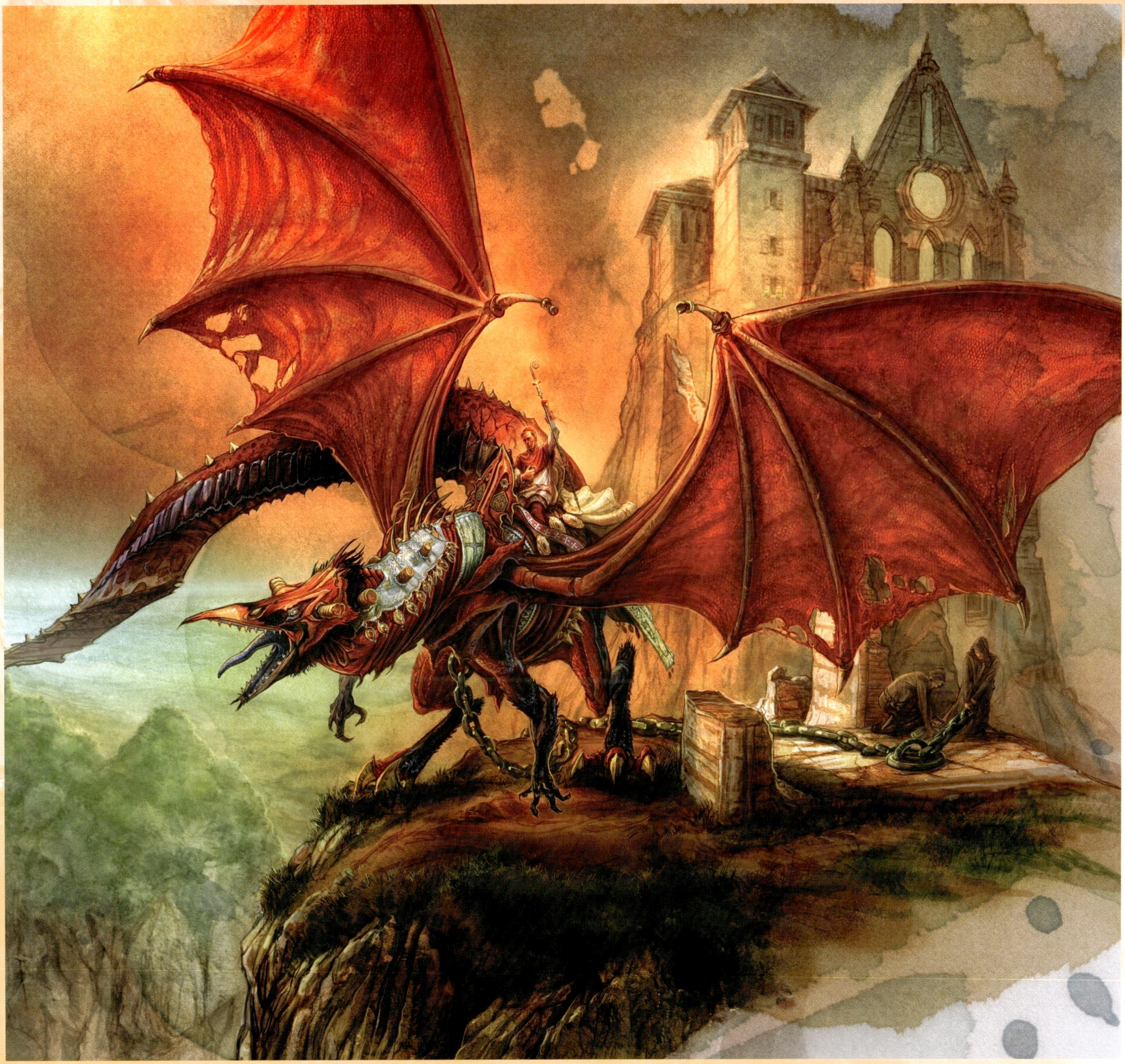

FINISHING TOUCHES. It's a hard thing to stop a painting at the right moment when it's still fresh and before it becomes overworked. Here's hoping I got this one right.

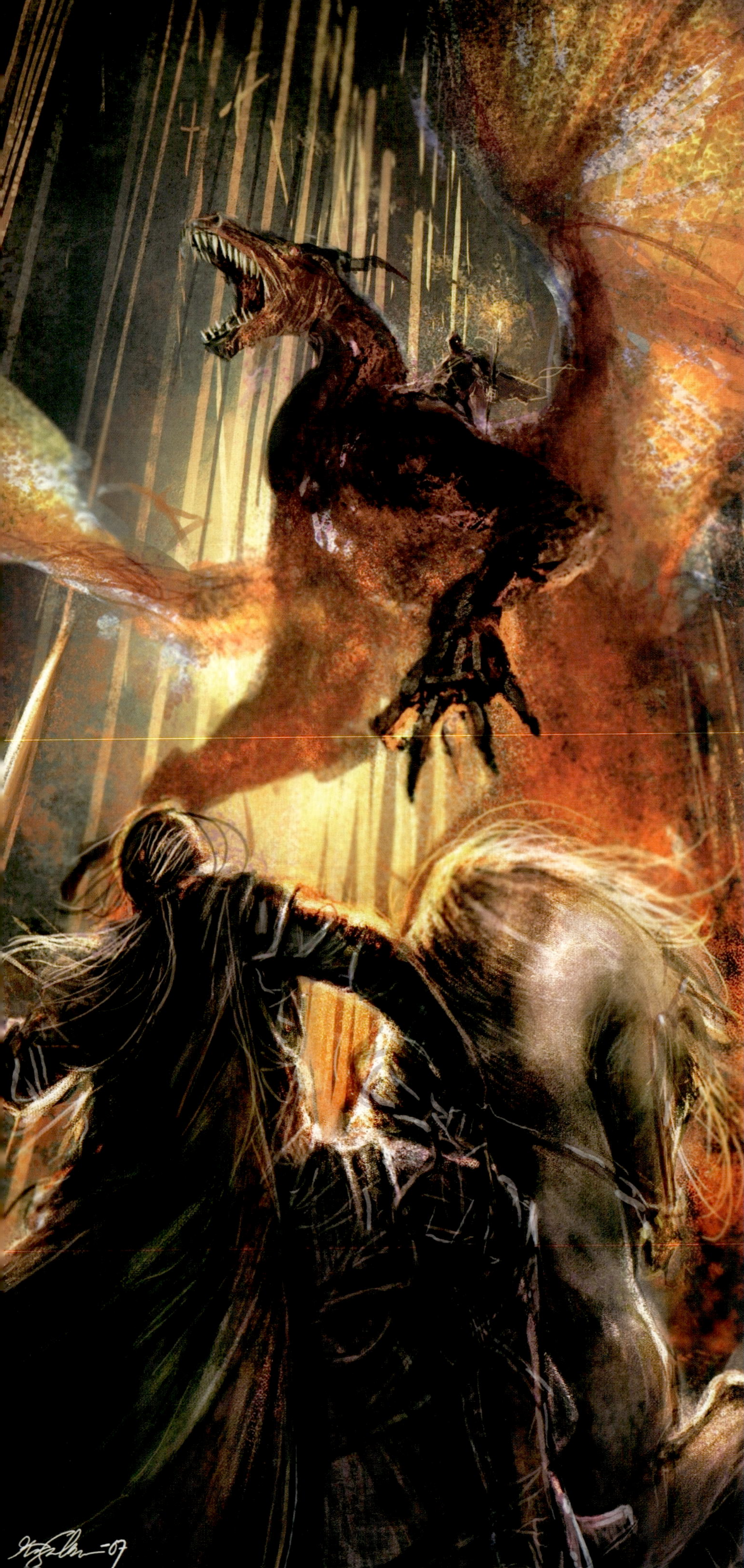

followed a voluntary code of practice that made it very difficult for magazines and comics to publish anything that might be construed as corrupting.

Frazetta Arrives

Something happened in the late 1960s, however. New York artist Frank Frazetta revisited stories by Edgar Rice Burroughs and Robert E. Howard and changed the viewer's perception of the stories completely. Frazetta's paperback book covers for Lancer did away with Mrs Brundage's burlesque and introduced masculine grit. In came rippling muscles, death and dynamism, kinetic carnage and strong, wide-hipped women that, though they clung to their men determinedly, would no doubt be capable of laying low a beast or two. If Mrs Brundage was suggestive and 'Boogie Woogie Bugleboy', Frazetta was explicit and 'Steppenwolf': pure heavy metal thunder.

Frazetta was born in Brooklyn in 1928 and took to art as a very young child. Identified as something of a child prodigy before his sixth birthday, young Frank was sent to the Brooklyn Academy of Fine Arts when he was eight years old. So impressed was his art teacher, Michele Falanga, with the young Frazetta's ability, he made plans to send the boy to study fine art in Italy, but unfortunately died before this could be achieved. While Frazetta was less than enamoured with fine art – he instead really

THE BRAVE ONE by Kirsi Salonen
© Kirsi Salonen 2007 · Digital media: Photoshop
A speedpainting.
www.kirsisalonen.com

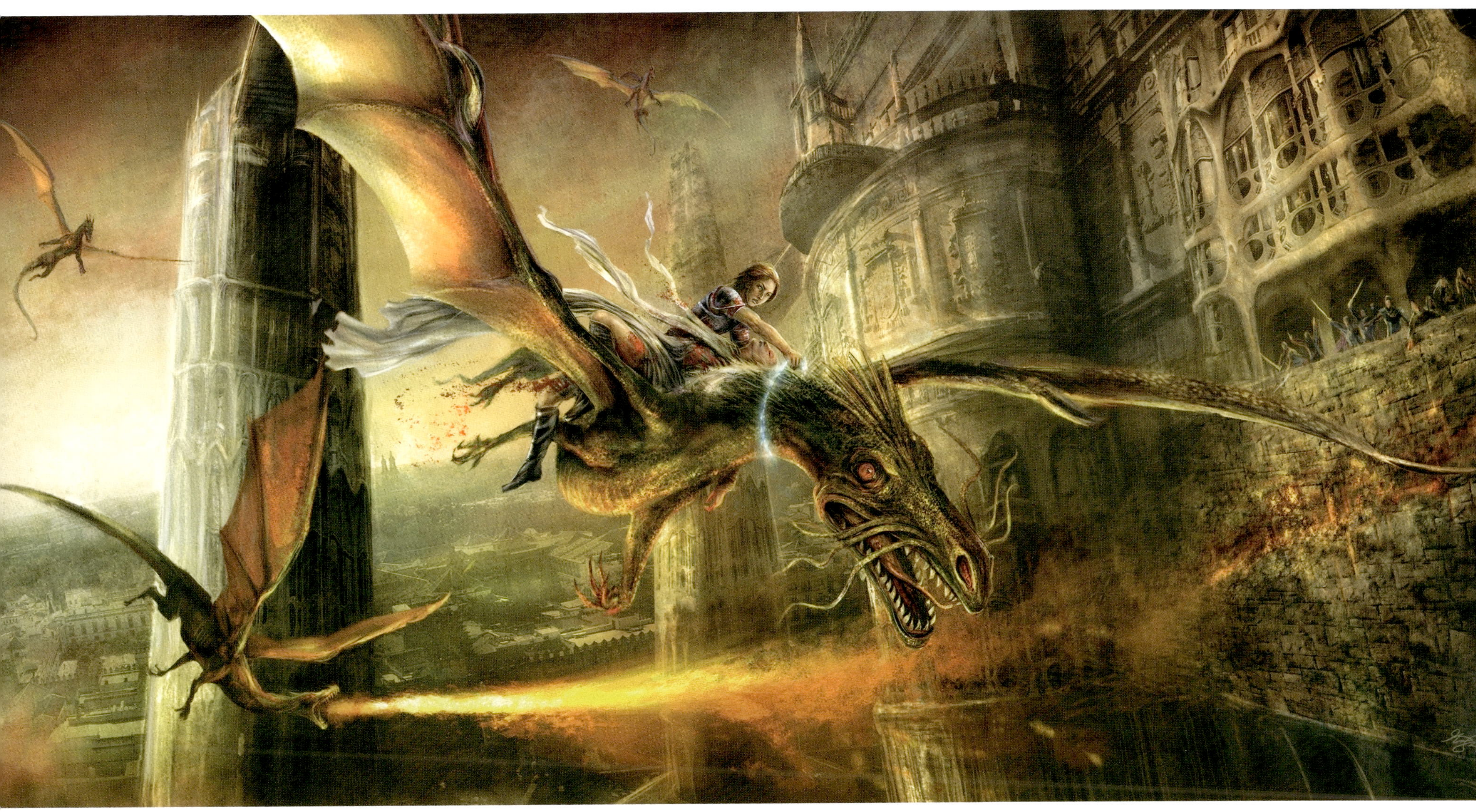

enjoyed creating the comics he had been drawing since he was five – he admits he learned much technique from the discipline of 'proper' painting.

Comic Capers and Cover Creations

Throughout the 1940s, Frazetta worked on a number of comics, mostly of the 'funnies' variety, until he began in the 1950s to work on more adventurous titles, including the Tarzanesque *Thun'da*, the futuristic *Johnny Comet* and covers for *Buck Rogers* comics, which apparently influenced George Lucas's vision for *Star Wars*. During that period, he was also a ghost artist for Al Capp's famous *Li'l Abner* cartoons, for which he was rewarded handsomely.

THE FALLEN EMPIRE by Kirsi Salonen
© Kirsi Salonen 2007 · Digital media: Photoshop
An illustration for the artist's personal book project 'Ordera'.
The young emperor of Ah'Are is badly wounded but rescued from the blades of his own minions.
www.kirsisalonen.com

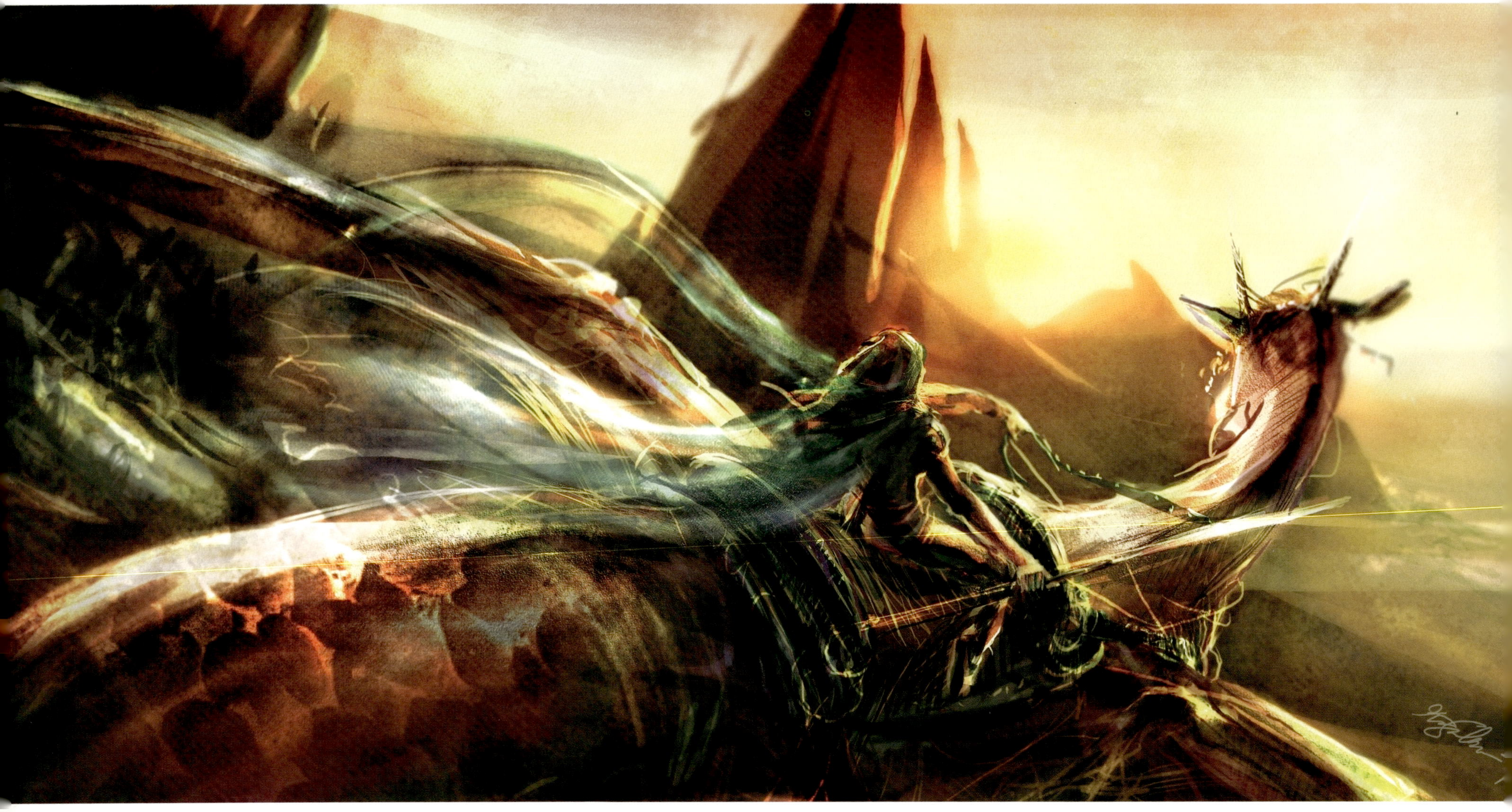

In the 1960s, Frazetta was introduced to the world of paperback novel covers. In 1963, he illustrated his first cover, a very striking and powerful painting for Edgar Rice Burroughs' *Tarzan of the Apes*, much to the pleasure of the reading public. He also soon found himself creating posters for films, including *What's New Pussycat*.

If that was not enough to seal his place in the minds of artists worldwide, his series of covers for Robert E. Howard's *Conan* book series for Lancer publishing in the late 1960s blew the doors off. Perhaps they might not have been to the taste of the more writerly – the action on Frazetta's Conan covers rarely reflected anything written in the book itself – but the images themselves were so overwhelming and powerful that his work helped the publisher shift significant volumes. Frazetta's covers and illustrations for horror comics *Creepy* and *Eerie* were equally well received.

SIRAD NOX by Kirsi Salonen
© Kirsi Salonen 2007 · Digital media: Photoshop
An illustration for the artist's personal book project 'Ordera'.
Sirad Nox is a massive fortress that rises from the ground and sucks even the sunlight around it.
www.kirsisalonen.com

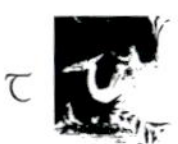

Detractors Dealt a Blow

Similarly striking is his character, Death Dealer. According to Frazetta's website, he came up with the character in response to an industry-wide rumour that he had 'lost it'. So he came up with his mysterious, horn-helmeted, hatchet-wielding destroyer. The character, soon to become a role-play game in its own right, was accompanied by Silver Warrior, both of which easily quashed detractors instantly. Similar, too, is his personal work, 'Cat Girl'.

SUNRIDER by Kirsi Salonen
© Kirsi Salonen 2007 · Digital media: Photoshop
A speedpainting.
www.kirsisalonen.com

It is simple to describe just what it is about Frank Frazetta that creates such a stir. According to artist Alan Lathwell, 'Growing up I used to go to comic shops. I must have been in my mid teens when I first came across Frazetta. The power of his work just jumps off the pages. There's like an adrenalin-fuelled high

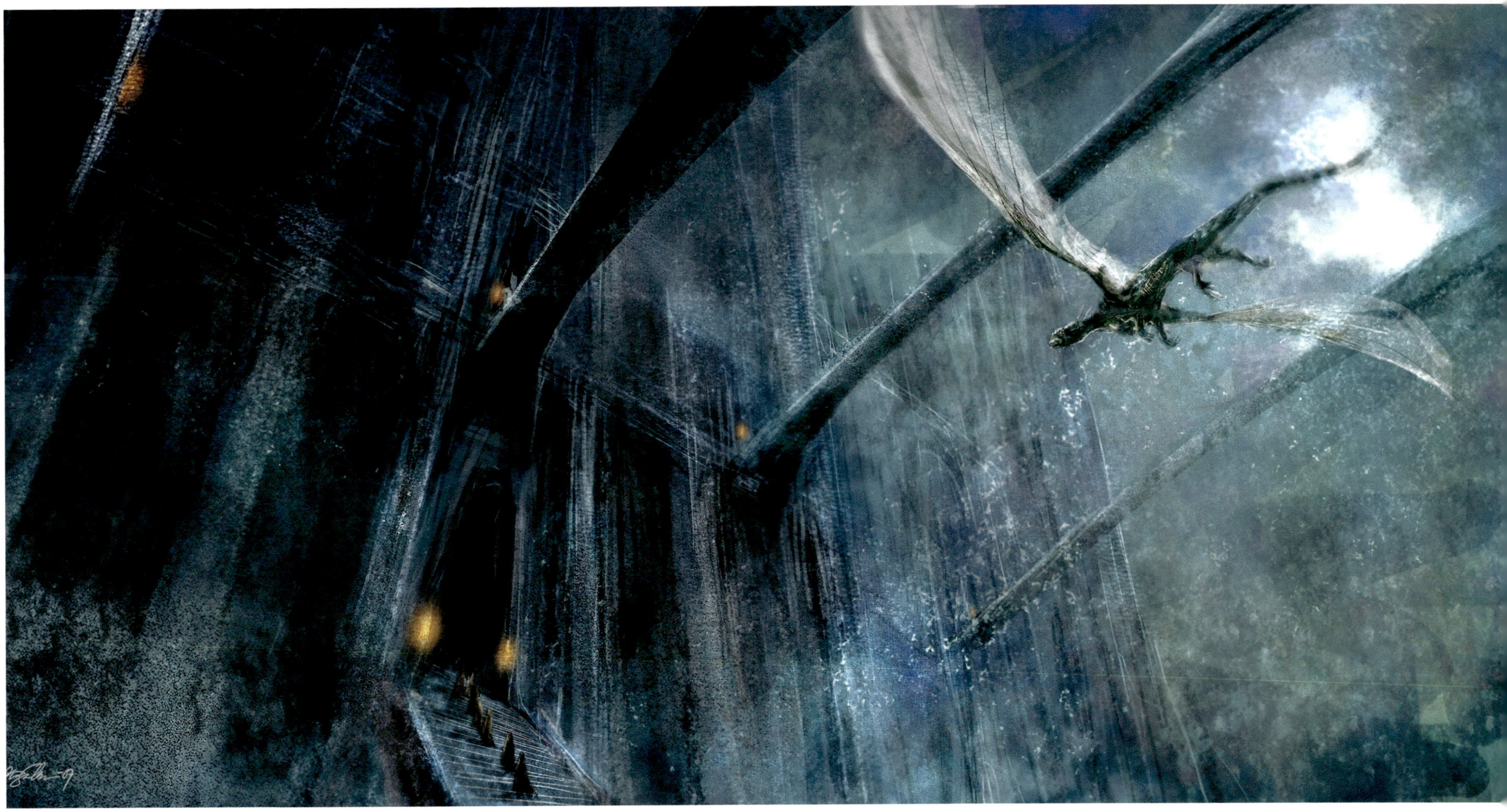

Eversor by Kirsi Salonen

© Kirsi Salonen 2008; Digital media: Photoshop; A speedpainting; www.kirsisalonen.com

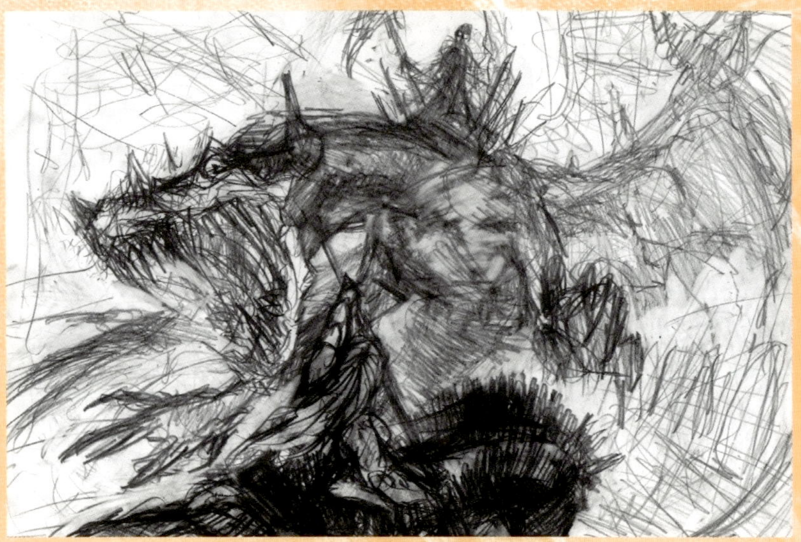

SAMPLE STEP 1. I scanned an early traditional sketch and then brought it into Photoshop. I then took the 'burn' tool and darkened the parts which were closest or which would be in shade, which defines the piece's action and drama.

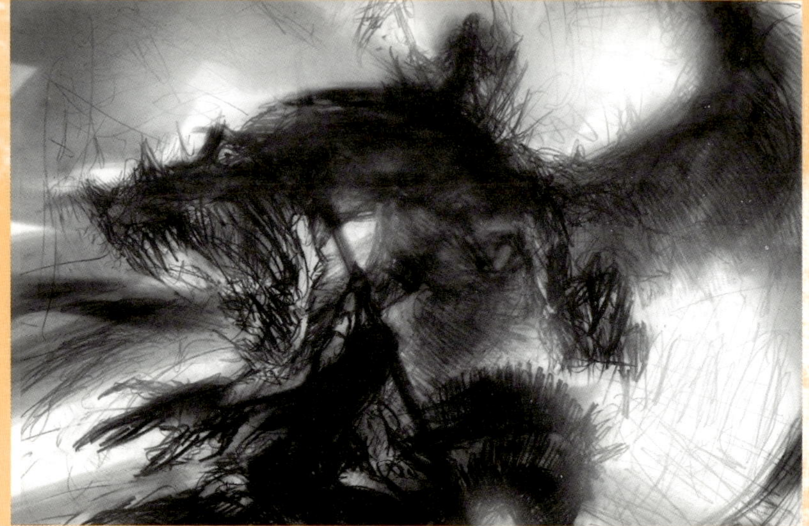

SAMPLE STEP 2. Moving on to black and white to define the painting areas. Here I've constructed and balanced the main light and shadow ranges. I went on to soften and adjust the masses and dark areas to create a feeling of action and space between the figures. This is easiest to figure out in greyscale mode and with gradient tool, before switching to RGB.

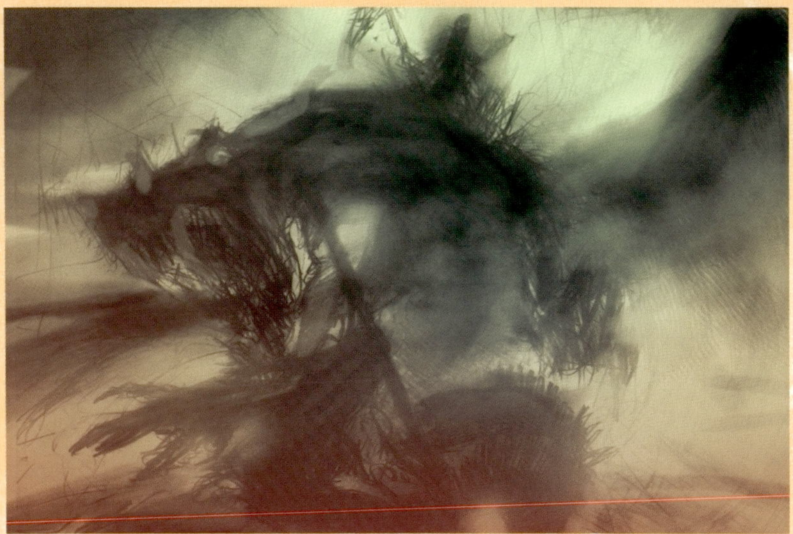

SAMPLE STEP 3. To define the basic colour scheme I used a simple gradient on top and some burn tool and eraser to make certain parts pop out. The paint job takes some time and nerves, but with the right brush and a duel brush you don't have to change those at all while the process continues. I construct the colours of the gradient to shapes and adjust colour levels to make the figures pop out.

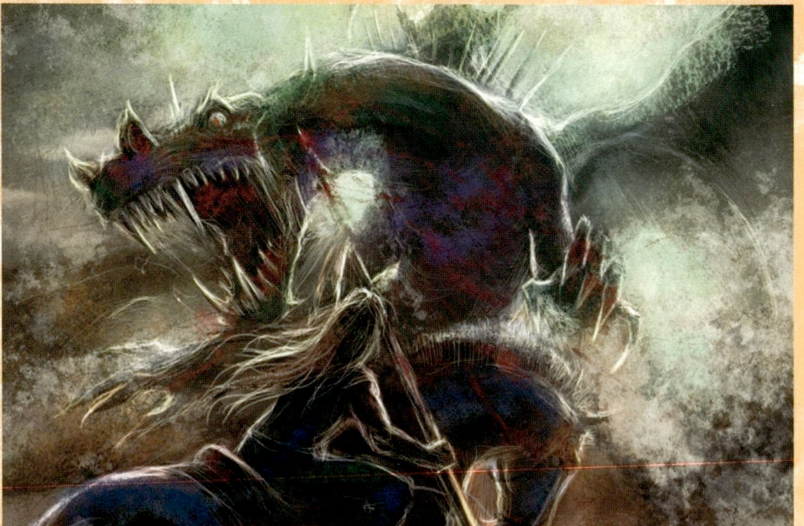

SAMPLE STEP 4. Here I've added some colder-toned traces of shadow and used rougher-looking textured brushes to create the sense of battle and raw power. The distinctive purples and blue hues will be faded and become more transluscent as I make final touches to define the surfaces. I then used the dodge tool to add contrast and more clearly define the structure of the dragon and horse.

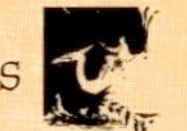

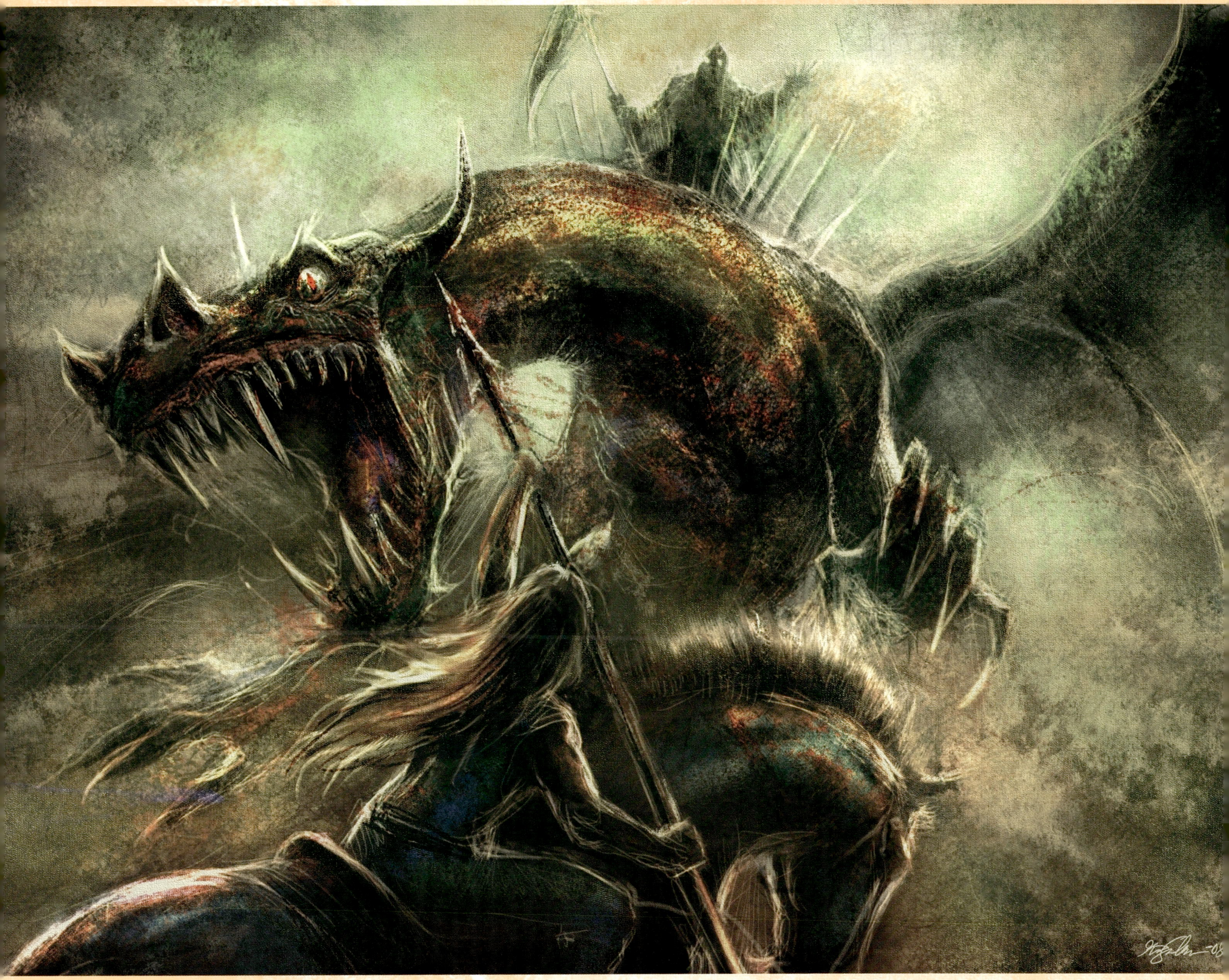

FINISHING TOUCHES. I added the last sprays of blood, details and more colour contrast to emphasize the feel of close battle between the larger beast and weaker man.

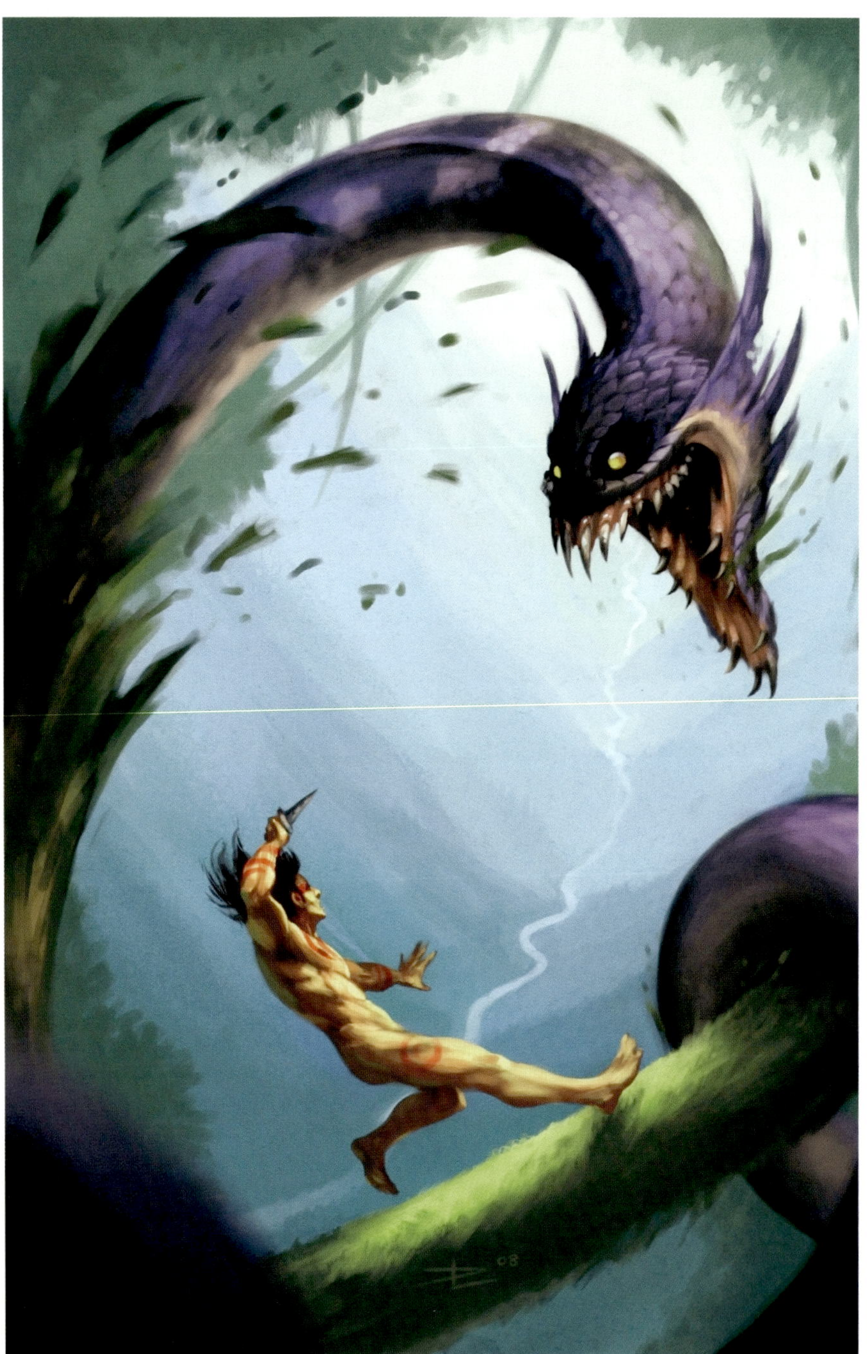

BATTLE by Daniel Lundkvist
© Daniel Lundkvist 2008 · Digital media: Photoshop
Daniel is 20 years of age and is currently working as a production artist in Gothenburg, Sweden.
www.dlart.se

energy. And it does seem to be apart from the rest of fantasy. You can see why it kick-started so many artists. It is raw power, movement, energy – brilliantly executed. [It is] the anatomy, the action, the poses, the colours, everything really.'

Kerem Beyit is similarly impressed. 'Conan has immensely affected me. I guess, by imitating the Conan covers as a child, I was unconsciously taking my first steps into fantasy art. And when you decide to go professional with that kind of a background, the field you're going to choose can't be anything other than fantasy art.'

Bob Eggleton adds, 'Frank Frazetta is a legend in fantasy art. He really paved the way and he made it kind of cool to get into fantasy art. But for me, I see him as somebody who's really a legend, and a man in his own time.'

The Influence of Michael Whelan

Frazetta's figures are very much about muscle and tendon, blood and sweat, triumph and glory; his counterpoint could be said to be the artist Michael Whelan. Whelan's sword and sorcery adheres very closely to the conventional symbols of the genre, with its beasts to be slain and battles to be won, long-haired warriors in big boots and the like, but his figures have an emotional depth that is admired by everyone from high-fantasy enthusiasts to spiritual and fairy tale fantasy artists worldwide. The moral ambiguity, mental stress and inner turmoil of his figures is distinctive and apparent.

THE SECRET SEA DRAGON by Andy Fairhurst
© Andy Fairhurst 2008 · Digital media: Photoshop
Andy is a digital painter currently based in North Wales.
www.wildlifehoodoo.deviantart.com

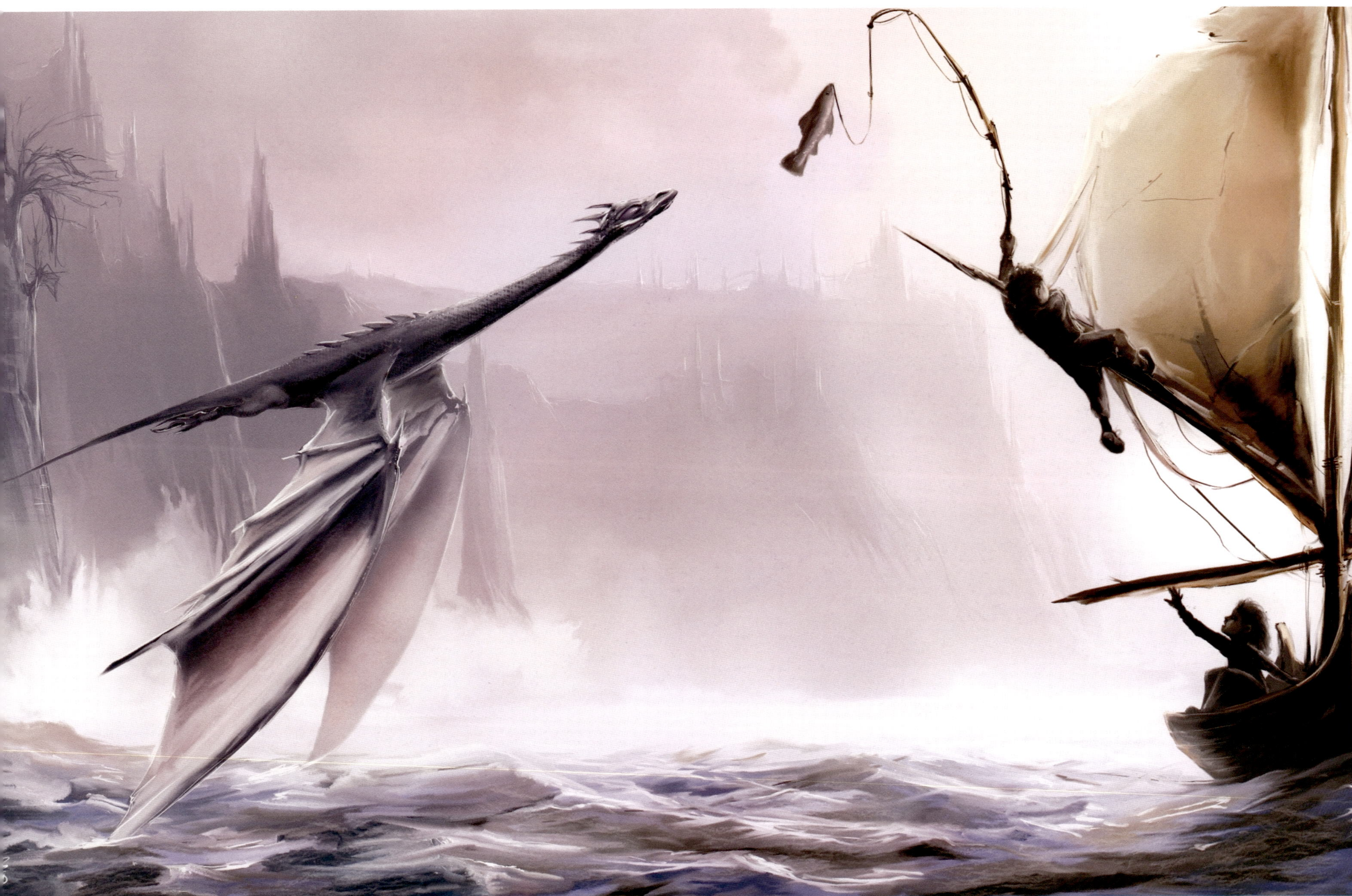

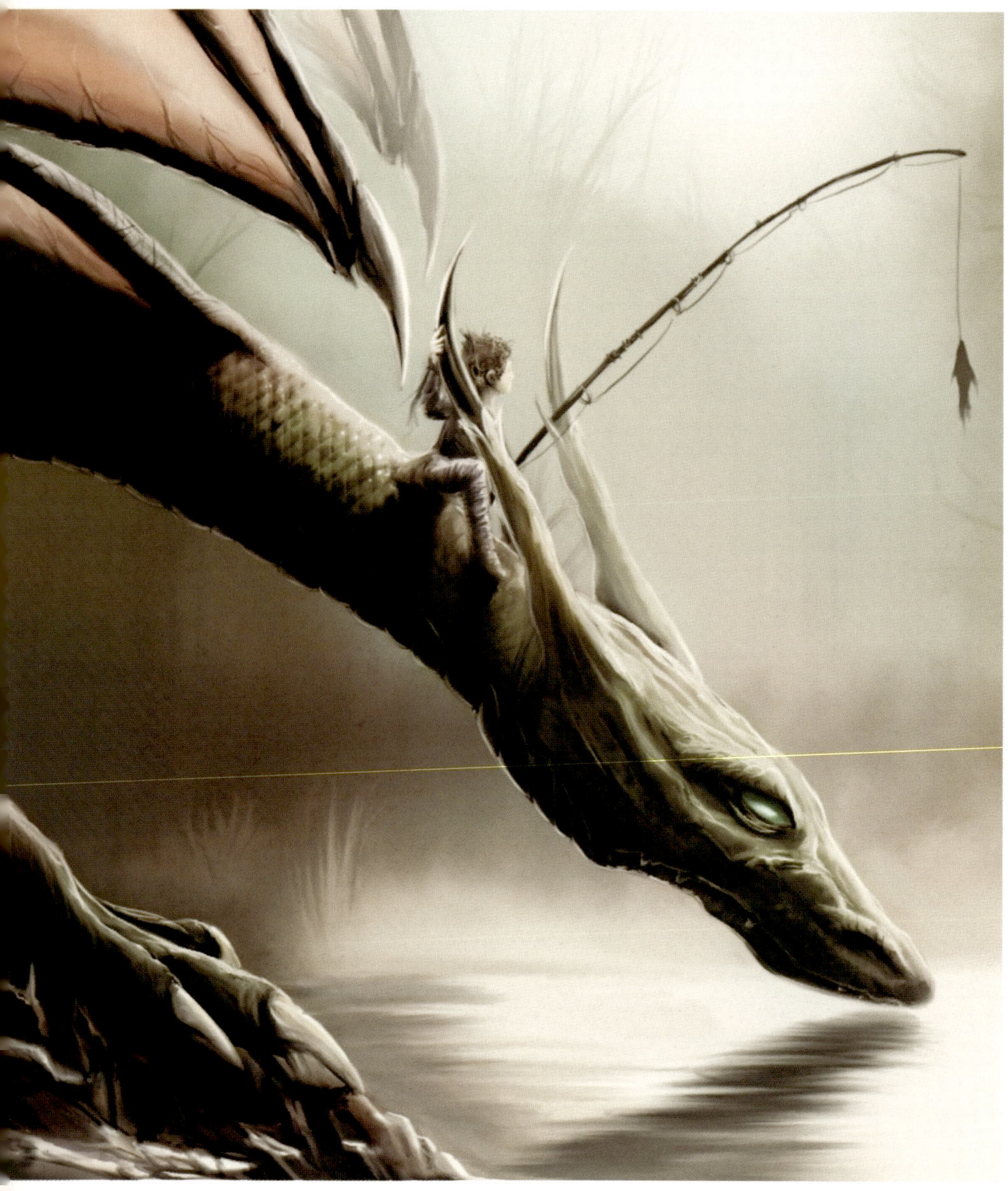

URSULA'S PRIDE by Andy Fairhurst
© Andy Fairhurst 2007 · Digital media: Photoshop
www.wildlifehoodoo.deviantart.com

The Career

Michael Whelan was born in Culver City, California, in 1950. His art education included summers at the Rocky Mountain School of Art in Denver, Colorado, in 1965 and 1966. He graduated from San José State University to study Art and Biological Sciences. He graduated in 1973 as a President's Scholar and received his Bachelor's with Great Distinction. He enrolled at the Art Center College of Design in LA, but left after nine months for his first professional assignment in 1974: a cover for Donald Wollheim of DAW books in New York. Although he was illustrating professionally during the mid-1970s, it was his illustration for Anne McCaffrey's *The White Dragon* in 1979 that was perhaps the turning point of his career. By the next year, he had won his first Hugo award.

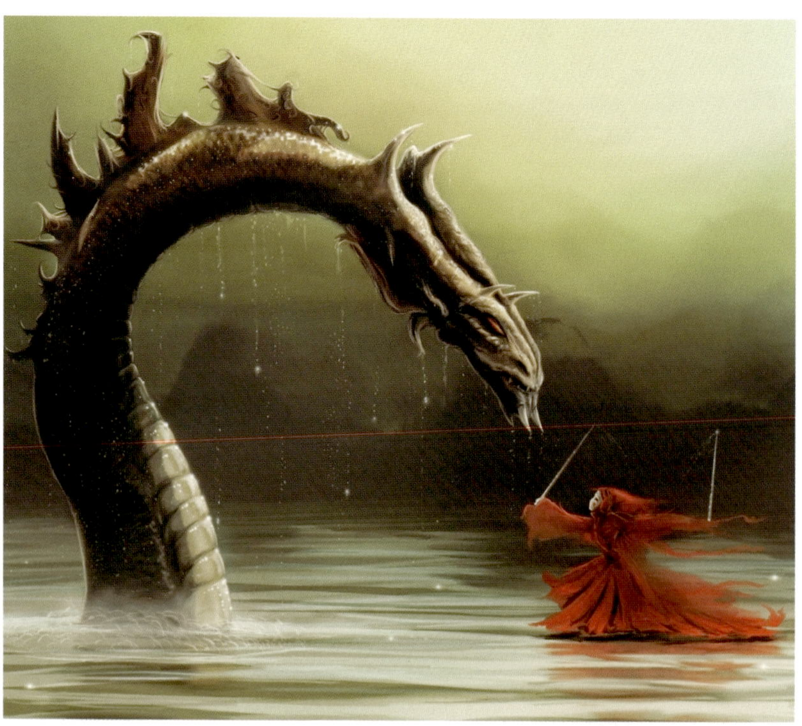

FISHING ON THE DRINKING DRAGON by Andy Fairhurst
© Andy Fairhurst 2008 · Digital media: Photoshop
Andy has been a contributing artist in features for the magazine *Imagine FX* and has had artwork on the cover of *Nowa Fantastyka*.
www.wildlifehoodoo.deviantart.com

THE WYRM AND THE WIZARD by Andy Fairhurst
© Andy Fairhurst 2008 · Digital media: Photoshop
Andy works on projects such as character designs, book covers and general illustrations.
www.wildlifehoodoo.deviantart.com

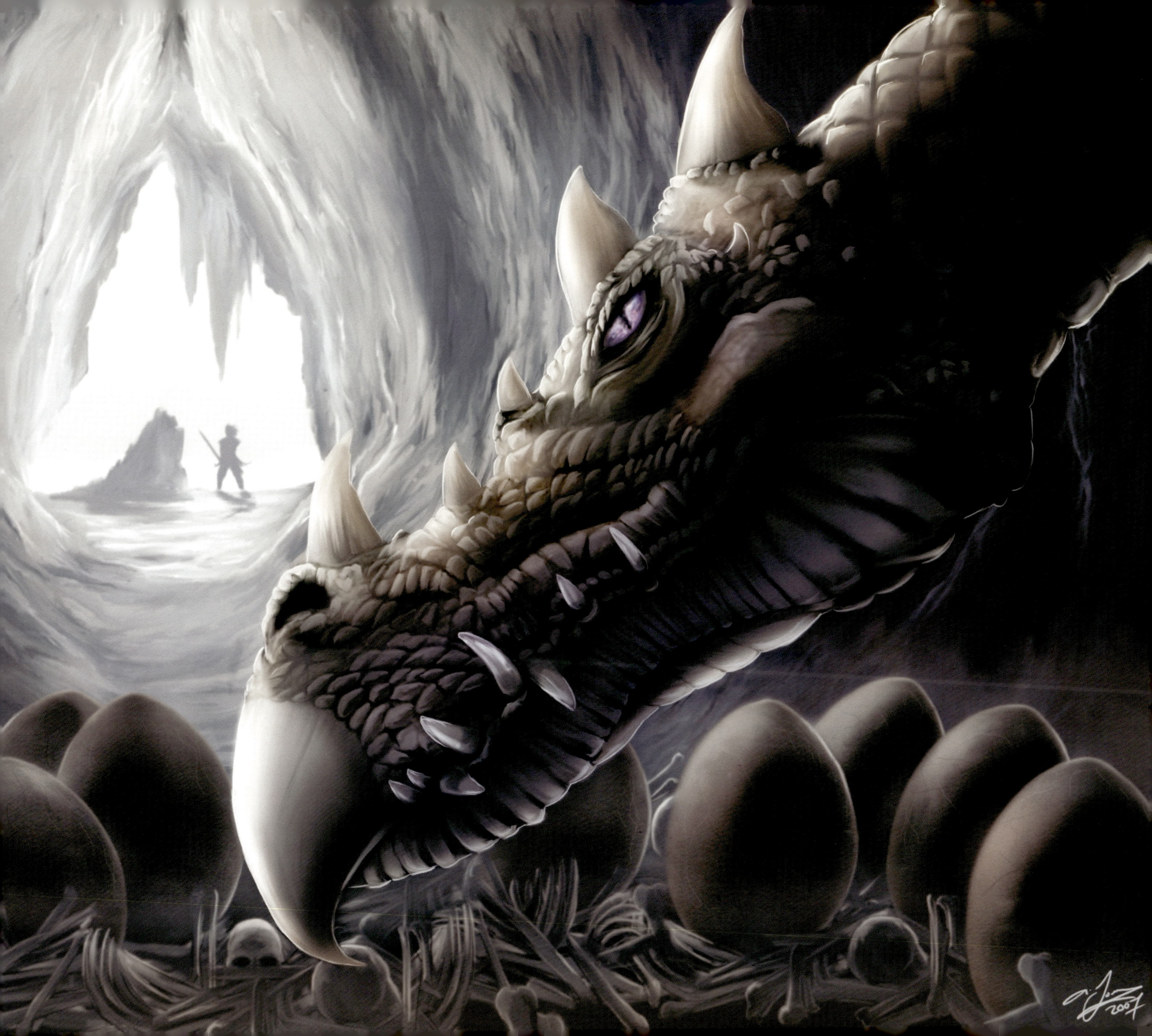

Whelan is not limited to fantasy book covers: he has created plenty of science fiction, horror and album covers too, including covers for work by Isaac Asimov, Ray Bradbury and Stephen King, and albums by the Jacksons and Sepultura.

JHEREG by Kerem Beyit
© Kerem Beyit 2005 · Digital media: Photoshop
Kerem was born in Ankara, Turkey, in 1980 and started drawing in his early childhood, influenced by comic books.
www.theartofkerembeyit.com

The Qualities

Whelan describes his non-commissioned art as 'Imaginative Realism', with an emphasis on symbolism. He also says that he tries his best to suffuse his work with layers of meaning while also maintaining an 'immediate, initial subjective or emotional impression'.

Perhaps it is testament to Whelan's insight and sensitivity that Hicaru Tanaka, writing an introduction to Nippon 2007, or the first Worldcon Japan, said that Whelan was one of the very few – and there were very few – original illustrators whose work was retained for the Japanese translations. According to Tanaka, 'I loved the colour harmonies, delicate tones and sophisticated details of Whelan's paintings. And the brightness of his paintings' base colours, his treatment of the characters in the frames, and the expressions he gave them made me feel positive, as though I were being offered hope about future universes and other worlds. I realized then that I had another hero painter.'

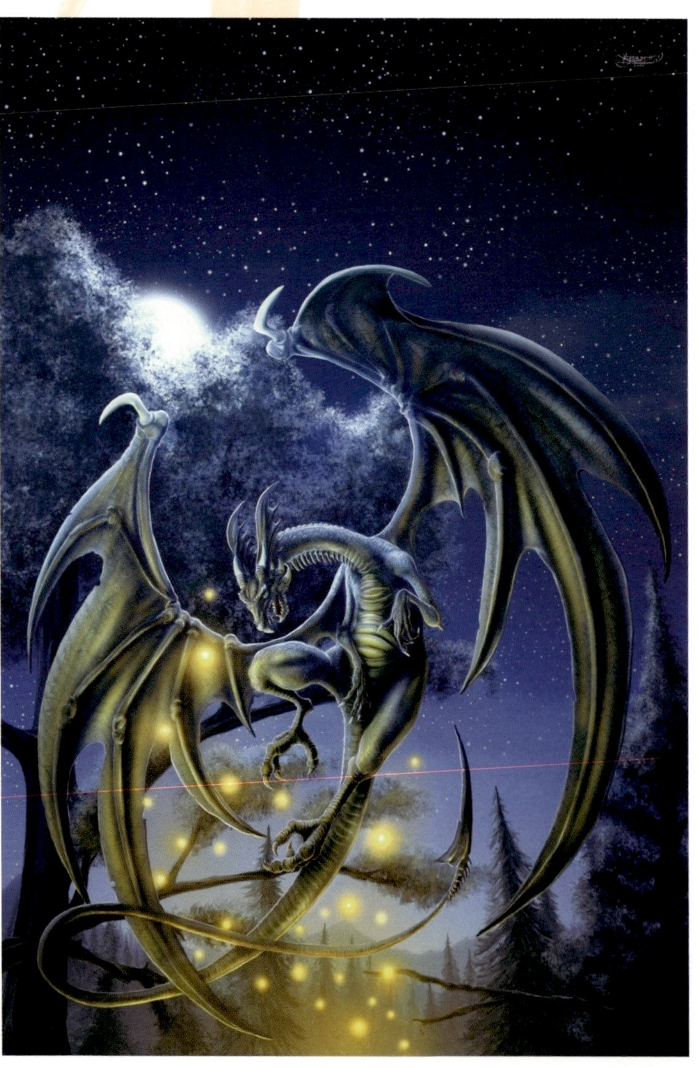

Communication

But Whelan's approach to his covers makes him worthy of added attention, certainly for anyone interested in creating fantasy art. The artist is a simplifier, says Whelan, meaning that he or she must distil the author's central ideas, removing any distracting or auxiliary information to make sure the intended meaning comes through unequivocally. In his own words, 'A good artist is a good communicator. The art form may be written, oral, visual or a host of others, but the resulting creation must convey something to its audience. Therefore, the artist has to skillfully combine craftsmanship and approach so that an idea or feeling is clearly communicated to a significant number of people. In the field of illustration, this concept is complicated further by the illustrator's task of expressing the ideas of another artist: the author.'

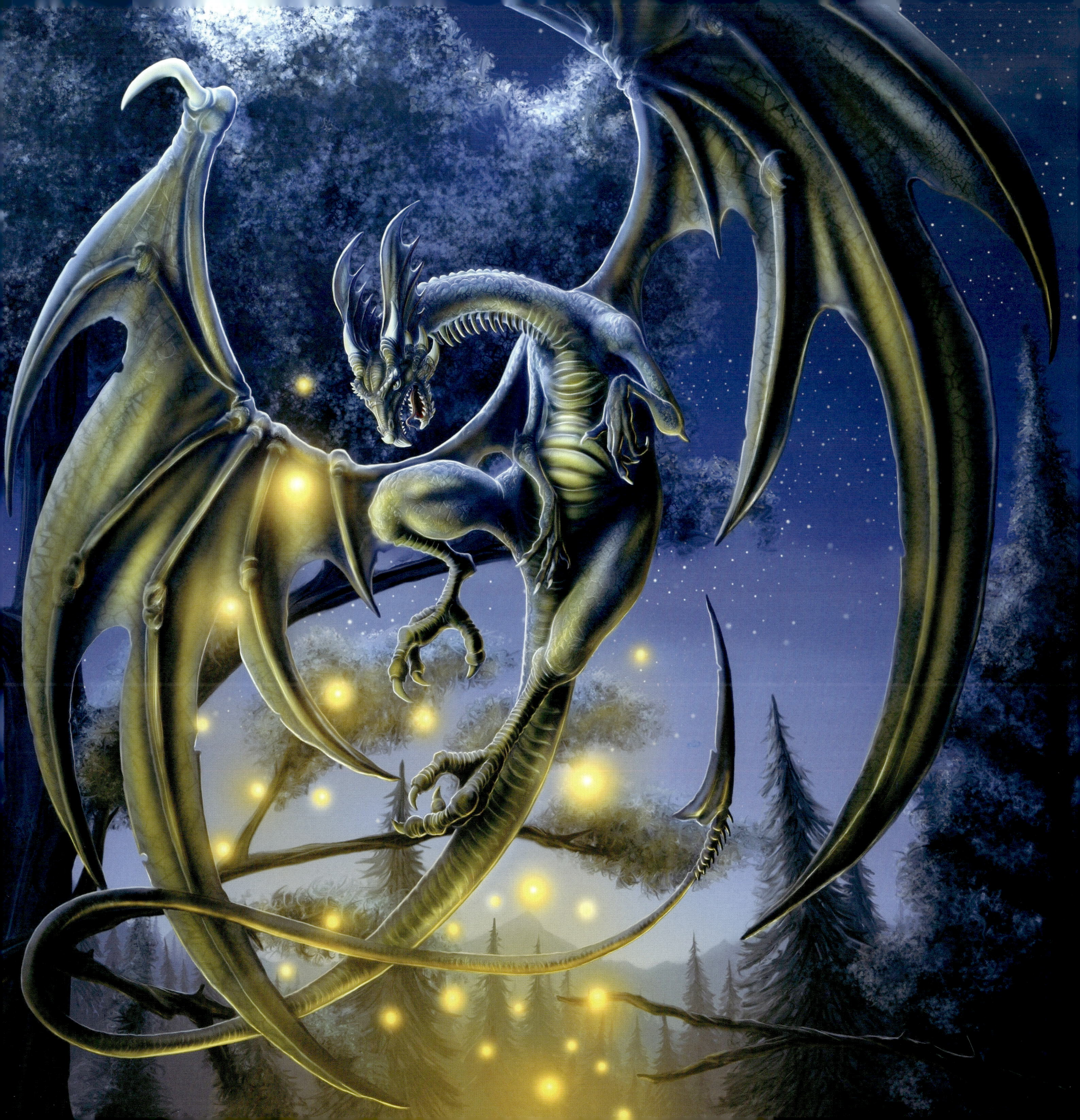

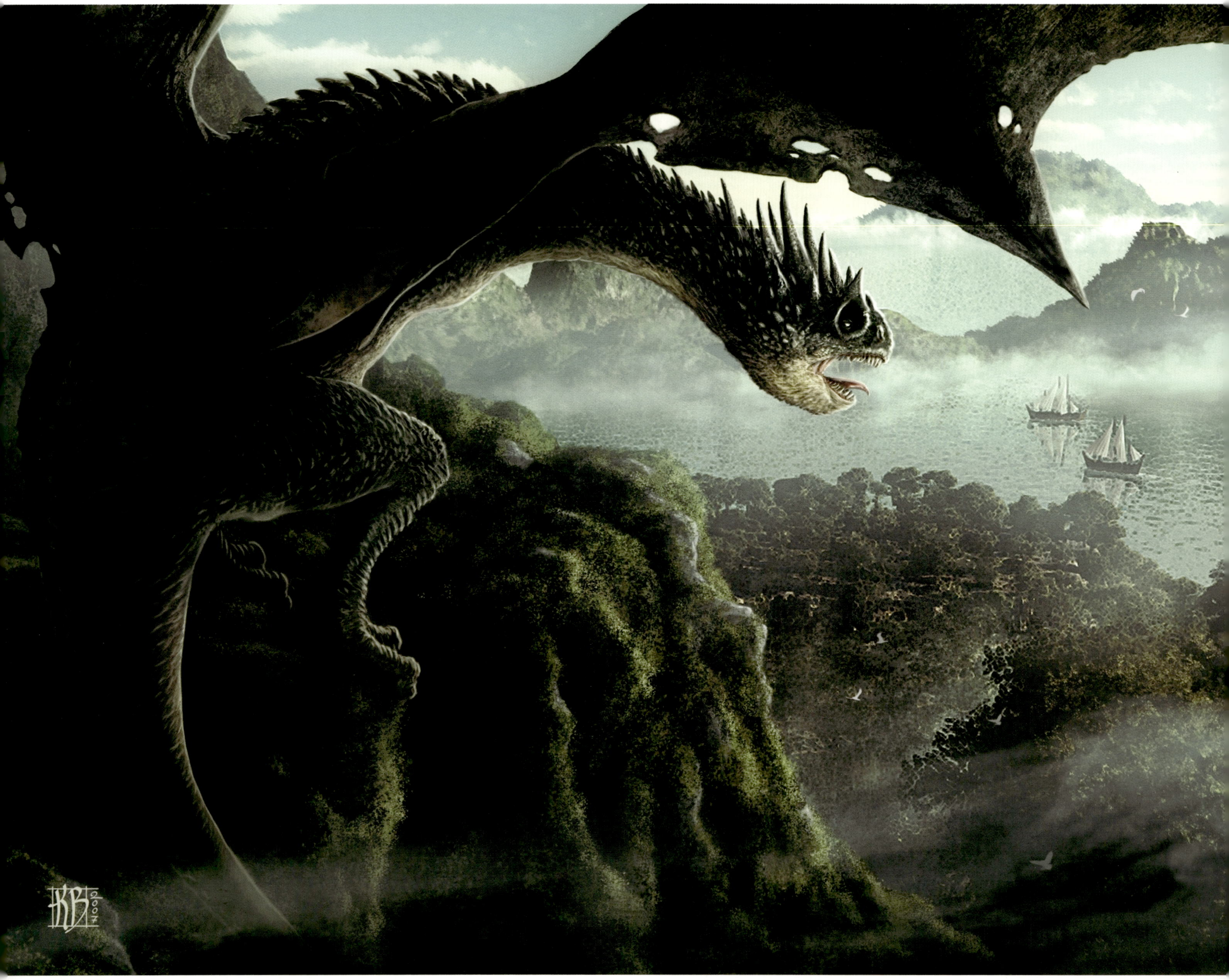

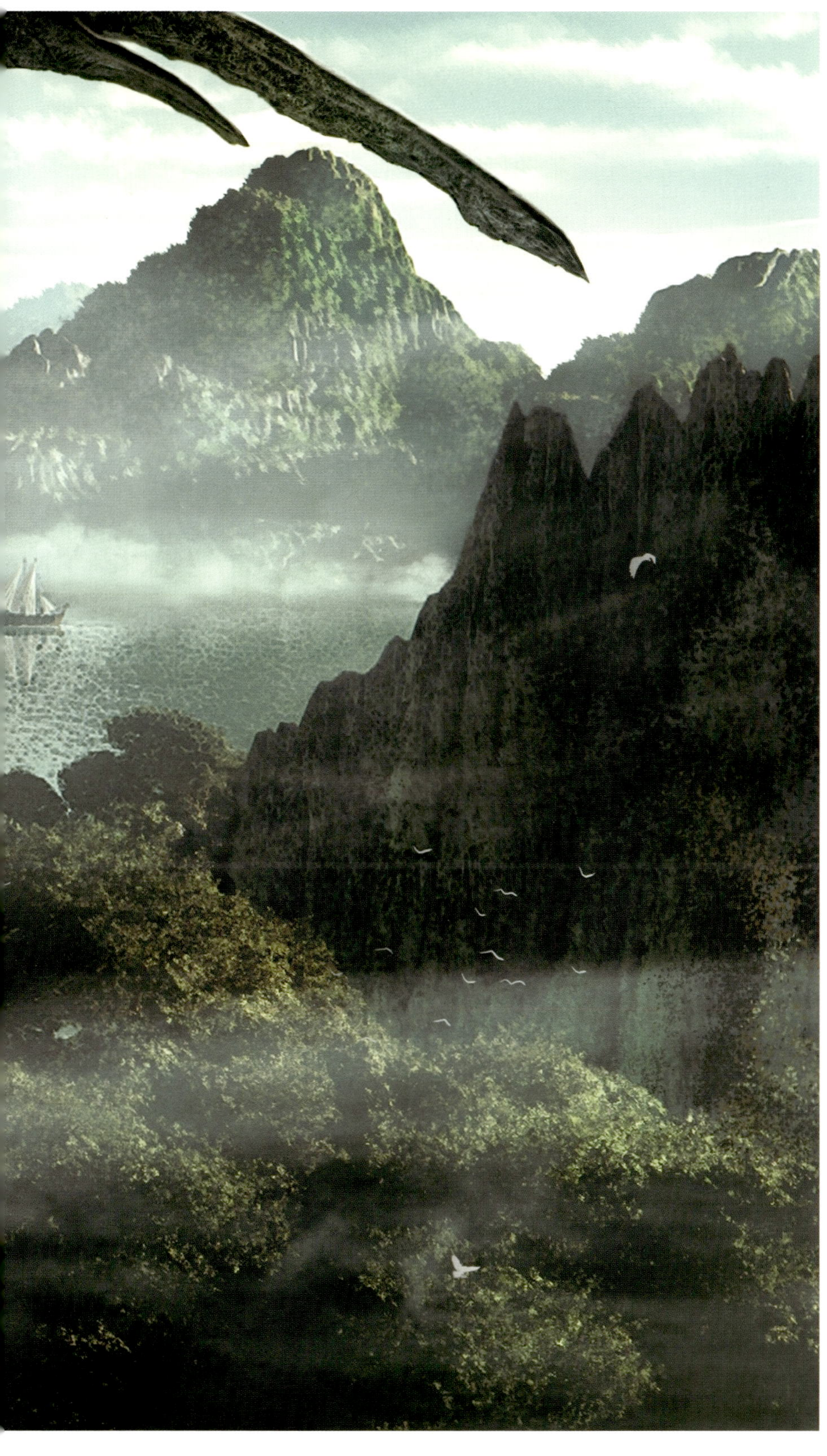

Fidelity

Fantasy author Poul Anderson says of him, 'He *reads*. Remarkably, very few illustrators do. Far too often (with honourable exceptions of course), the pictures they produce bear little or no relationship to what the author was describing. Michael Whelan obviously studies manuscripts with care, then thinks hard, before starting work. I assure you that in everything mentioned above, and surely in most everything else, he has gotten settings and people – including non-human people – exactly right.'

A case in point is Whelan's own account of how he created the illustration for the cover of Michael Moorcock's 1977 novel *Stormbringer*, featuring the albino anti-hero Elric. He recalls grabbing a curtain rail from the wardrobe and running around wild outside, swishing it to and fro in the long grass in order to understand the character's feeling of power. Where he might usually have taken a Polaroid to capture pose, he chose instead to go straight to canvas in order to preserve the immediacy of the idea.

Dragons

Whelan, of course, has plenty of dragon illustration under his belt, but he has an altogether original take on the subject. For instance, there is his cover for Alan Akers's 1976 novel *Renegade*

INTRUDERS by Kerem Beyit
© Kerem Beyit 2007 · Digital media: Photoshop
Kerem studied graphic design at Gazi University for four years. He does not have any formal training for illustration, having trained himself – his influences were the great fantasy artists like Frazetta and Brom.
www.theartofkerembeyit.com

of Kregen for DAW books. The cover features many of the traits of sword and sorcery – the muscle-bound hero, the sword, the immodestly clad woman and the dragon. However, rather than choosing the battle as the point of action, he depicts the couple just after the dragon has been slain. She is back to viewer, holding on to him for support. Both humans stand elevated, with eyes closed, exhausted and pensive in a manner devoid of the triumphalism that one might expect of such a victory. The dragon itself has been entirely robbed of any magic in death, one glazed, dead eye remaining open, a trickle of blood spilling out.

Its vulnerability is miles away from Frazetta's steely Conan, atop a mountain of slain carcasses, shadowy eyes promising plenty more death if required, while his muscular, naked female companion stares back similarly, holding his ankle as if to avoid sliding down the hill of carnage and also to promise Conan, and you the viewer, seriously hot sex.

The White Dragon

Anne McCaffrey, writer of the Dragon Flight series, is definitely a fan. Of his cover for her fantasy novel *The White Dragon*, she said, '[He] has subtly touched the ambivalence of the hero's position, hinted at his strength of character, clearly depicted the dragon's beauty and size, added the darting curiosity of the fire-lizards ... [the] dragon and rider, the rough, harsh landscape of

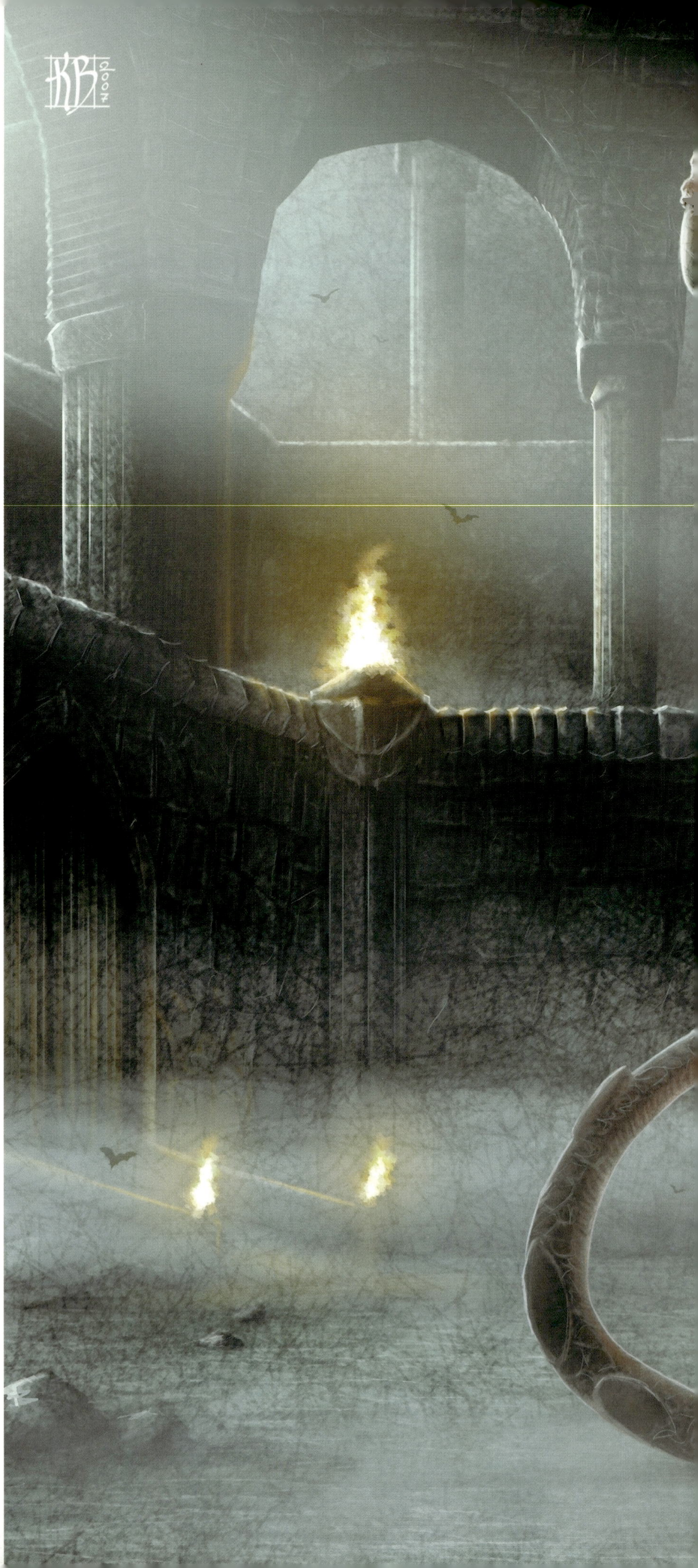

SHERWOOD DUNGEON DRAGON by Kerem Beyit, 2007
 · Digital media: Photoshop
Kerem has worked for a whole range of companies, comics and magazines, doing graphic design and illustration, including book covers.
www.theartofkerembeyit.com

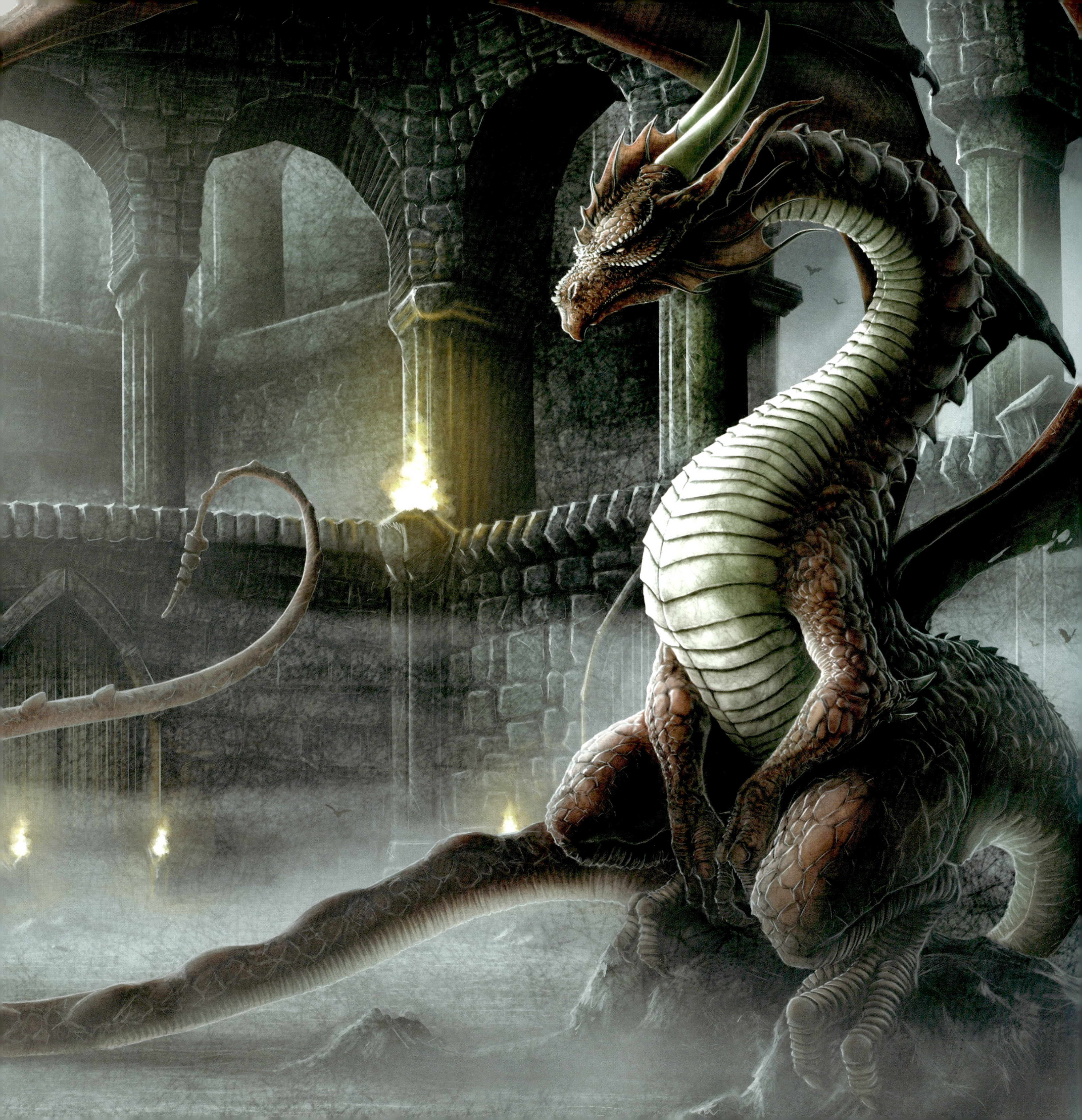

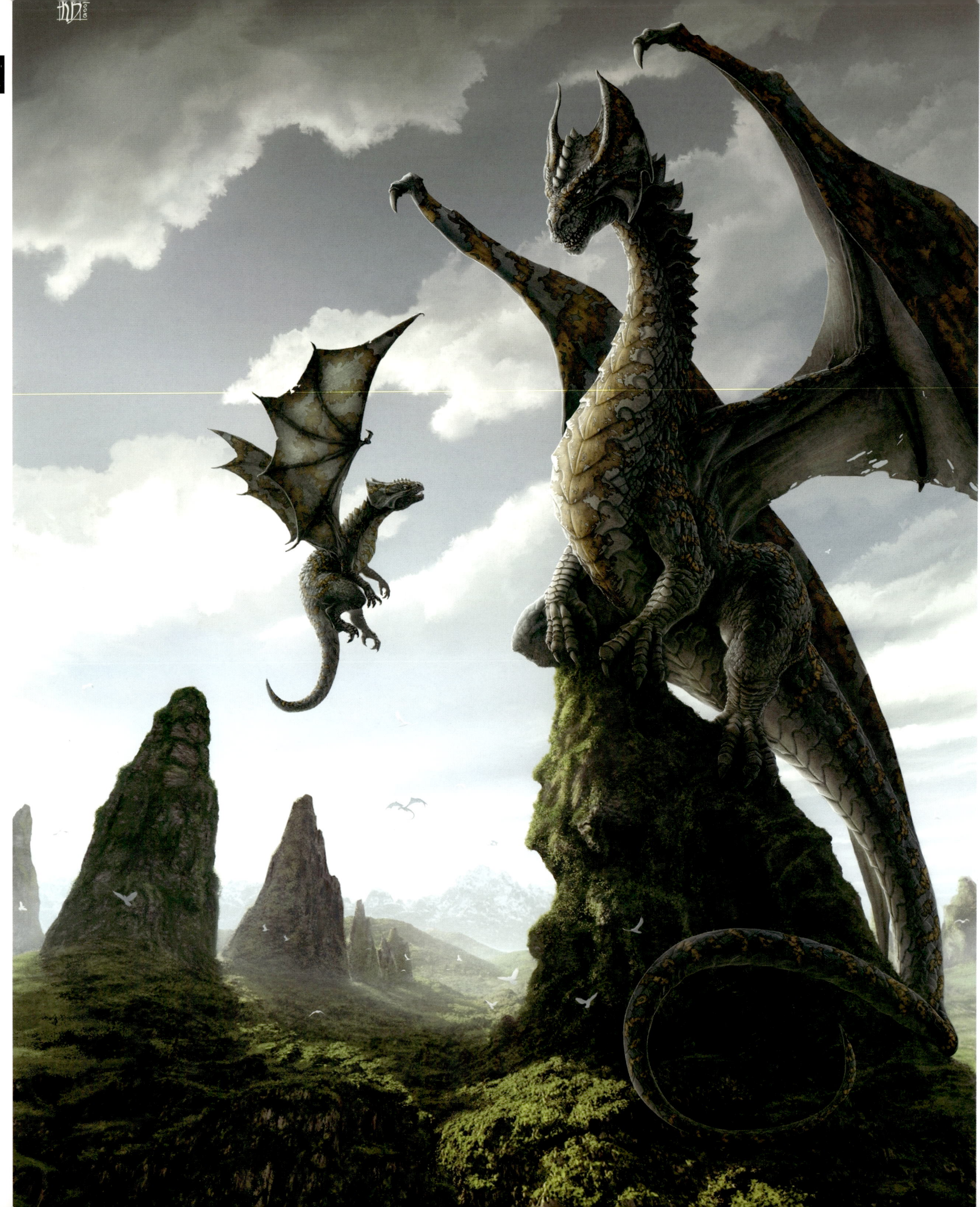

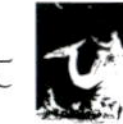

the beleaguered planet Pern, and the significantly distant figures of dragon riders silhouetted against the dreaded Red Star. Fortunate indeed is the author who has Michael Whelan for illustrator.'

Indeed he does avoid the serpentine, scaly, winged lizards McCaffrey was keen to avoid, hinting at something far more magical and fantastic – and narrative, perhaps – than a more standard journey into the world of swords, fire-breathing and dragon slaying.

Contemporaries

According to Todd Lockwood, 'I think he just has a great mind. You can tell that he's put a great deal of thought into his cover concepts. There's nothing slapdash about anything he does. Everything is well thought out and measured. He's sort of the yang to Frazetta's yin. Frazetta is all energy and spontaneity and he's another artist whose work I admire a great deal. But they're like two sides of a coin, and they barely meet around the edge. Both astounding, but it's that thoughtfulness that Michael Whelan puts into everything that really drives me to his work.'

FIRST LESSON by Kerem Beyit
© Kerem Beyit 2008 · Digital media: Photoshop
Kerem has been working in the digital arena for four years and has done many book covers.
www.theartofkerembeyit.com

Whelan's versatility means that his influence extends beyond those keen to depict that timeless showdown between hero and dragon in a storm of fire and shadow. Artist Tracy Trowbridge says, 'There was this one particular piece that he did called *Filed Teeth*. That painting was, I think, the first I saw of his work, and it just blew me away. It's the level of detail. I remember reading his description of that piece in an interview, and he was talking about all the scales he painted on that dragon. That's one of the things that I've always been fascinated with, the amount of detail that artists put into their work; I'd have to say that that was probably the most inspiring of it. From that I just started experimenting.'

A Host of Influences

While the names of Whelan and Frazetta will appear frequently in conversations with fantasy artists about their influences, there are plenty of others, unsurprisingly. Some appear frequently, while others are a bit more specialist.

Brom

American artist, illustrator, writer of wry tales and self-confessed army brat, Brom crops up relatively frequently in discussion as influential and highly regarded.

Of Brom, Turkish artist Kerem Beyit says, 'The characters Brom creates and the poses he places them in have always impressed me a great deal. I always pay full attention to the pose, more than anything else, while doing character designs. For me, a picture is done when I see line-art that works. Texturing and colouring are, to me, the icing on the cake; no matter how much you work on rendering an 'off' pose, the result will not be pleasant.'

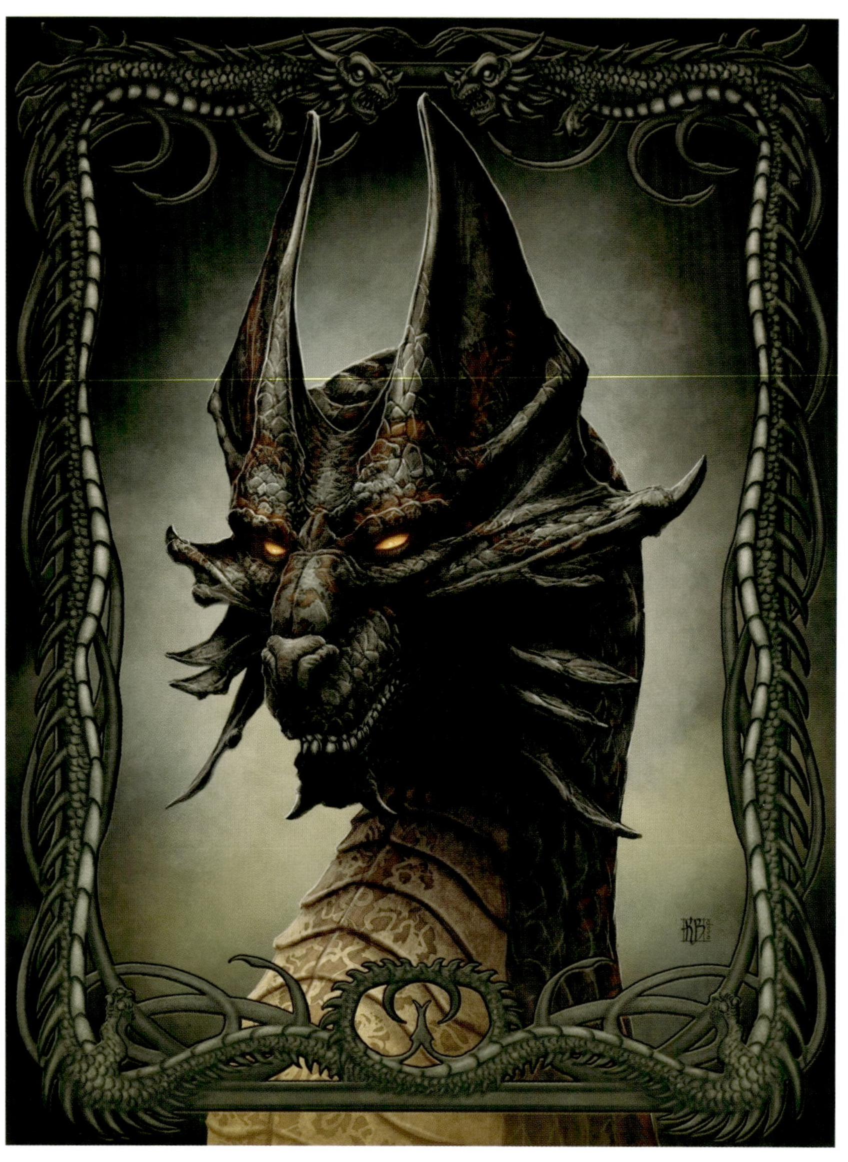

BLACK by Kerem Beyit
© Kerem Beyit 2008 · Digital media: Photoshop
Kerem has received awards from CGSociety, CGChannel, Gfxartist, CGGallery, 3DTotal and CGArena.
www.theartofkerembeyit.com

Art All Around

Bob Eggleton takes inspiration from many artists. 'Stylistically, I find myself gravitating to these great museums and galleries because that's really where my influences come from. It's looking at the work of Thomas Cole, Fredric Edwin Church, people like that. And John Martin: he created some really apocalyptic visions. While not directly considered fantasy, they certainly have fantastical elements in them, and that's what makes them really worthy of study.'

Bob continues, 'My feeling is when artists are looking to get a style that's their very own, the worst thing in the world is copying another person's style that's current, like a peer. The best thing in the world is to go back and look at these great classic master artists in museums. That way you get a real overview of what was going on then, and you get a more fresh approach because you're sort of interpreting it in a modern way, and then it becomes your original idea.'

Jeff Easley

The names mentioned so far are by no means the only influential modern artists around. There is Jeff Easley, for example. Together with Larry Elmore in the 1980s, Easley was a pace-setter at TSR, maker of *Dungeons & Dragons*. Together they designed many of the characters and creatures that seduced and hooked role-play-game fanatics.

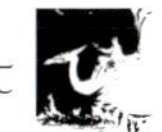

Of him, Todd Lockwood says, 'There is never a static place in any of his paintings. Everything serves a purpose. It all has an energy and life. That's the thing I admire about his work.'

From Park to Giger

Tracy Trowbridge is very much a fan of American fantasy artist Michael Park, for instance. For Kerem Beyit, Swiss surrealist H.R. Giger has had just as marked an effect. He recalls, 'I met Giger in my college years, a period when I didn't have a specific plan about my future and the profession I was to choose. But Giger is one of the reasons I started drawing again,.I remember being impressed mostly with his use of the airbrush; smooth tones and render in his works create a very photorealistic effect, while his themes and drawing technique are completely surreal. I think that contrast was what had an impact on me the most.'

Comic Fans

Beyit also calls Marvel illustrator John Buscema 'one of the best comic artists I had ever known, very few people can be as good as him when it comes to panel action. I learned a lot from him about anatomy and stylized anatomy. May he rest in peace.'

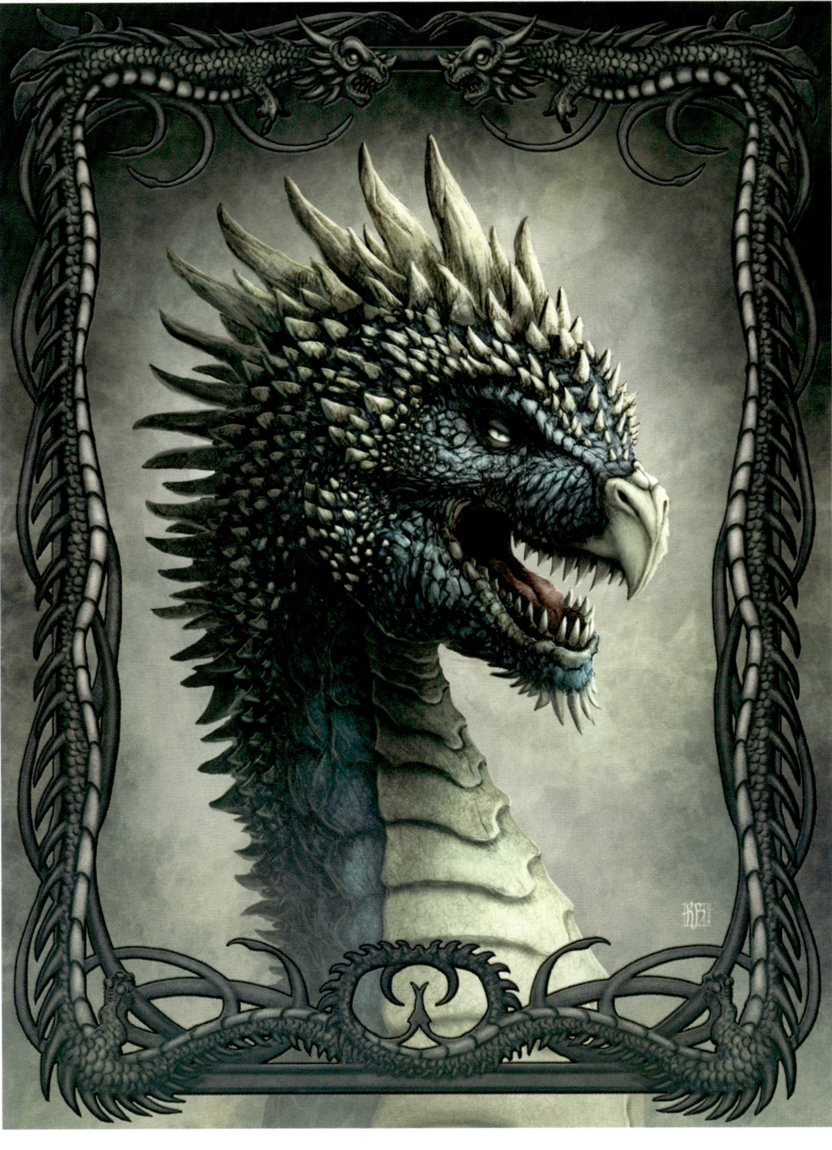

BLUE by Kerem Beyit
© Kerem Beyit 2008 · Digital media: Photoshop
Kerem's works have also been selected for inclusion in the Ballistic Publishing albums *Expose* and *Exotique*.
www.theartofkerembeyit.com

John Hodgson is also a comic artist fan. In his case, it is *2000 AD* comic artist and illustrator Simon Bisley. He says, 'I'm of a generation of artists that were really blown away by Simon Bisley. He did these really dynamic, really painterly comics, and it's ... incredible, [with] strong colours, [great] action and so on. That had an impact on me as a teenager, which I'm sure it was designed to do.'

McBride to Pyle

Hodgson is also a stalwart of the art of the late great Angus McBride. He says, 'If I had to pick one favourite artist, I think it would be

Angus McBride. He deals a lot with history. I like fantasy art that has one foot in history. I think his handling of light is just incredible, and he manages to pack a lot of detail and focus into illustrations whilst still being quite painterly. He's a painter for definite and it really appeals.'

Janny Wurts was influenced as a child by early-twentieth-century American children's illustrator Howard Pyle. She remembers, 'I grew up very near to the Brandywine River, [in the area where he founded the style and artists colony of the] Brandywine school. He ran a school there and he wrote and also illustrated books. So from a very early age we took a school field trip to the Delaware art museum where a lot of his originals were hanging. The Brandywine River museum has a lot of his students' work hanging, and a few Howard Pyles also. So I was exposed very young to the actual paintings. (Of course Maxfield Parrish also was from that area.) [Hence] the idea of [being] a writer-illustrator: from a very young age I said it could be done, and no one could convince me otherwise because there was all that history right in front of my eyes.'

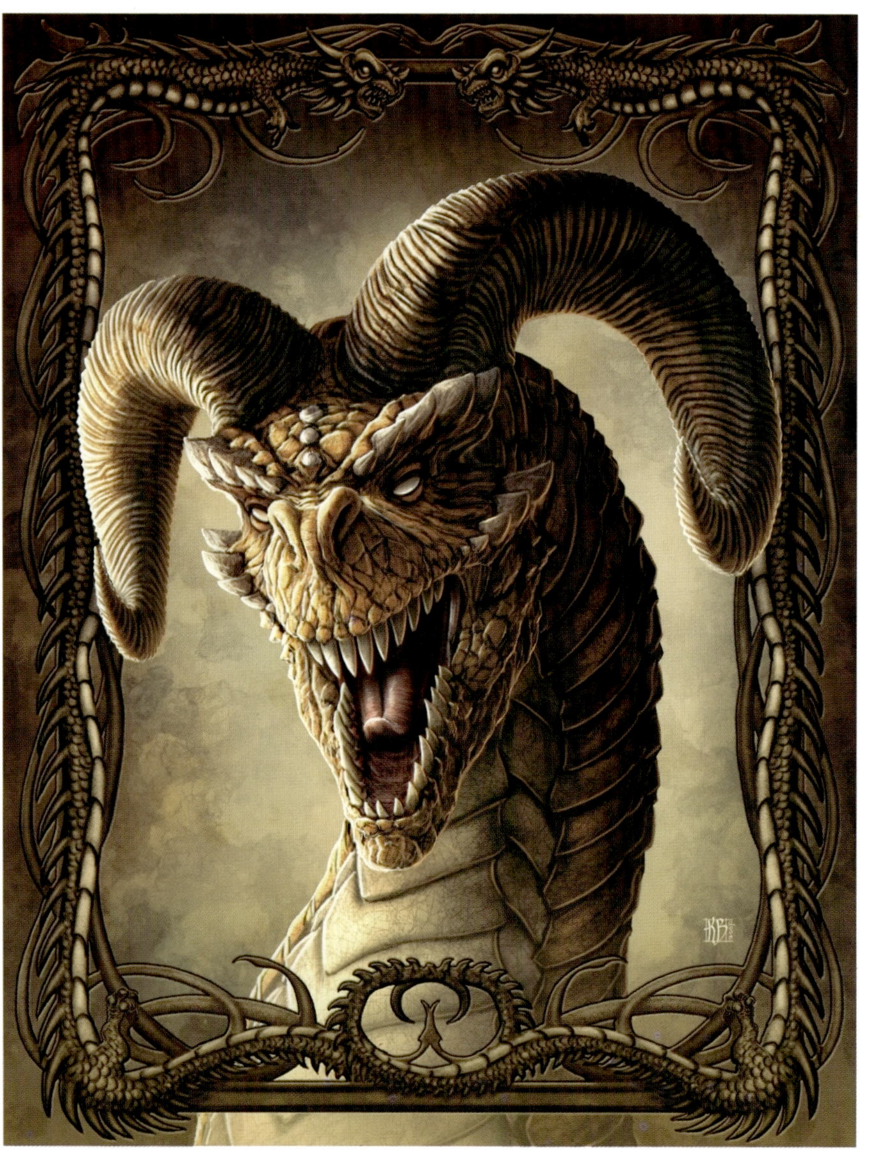

The Temptation of Imitation

In all art forms, there is a tendency to wish to be 'like' either your favourite artist, or be part of a contemporary style. However, influences, while worthy of study and understanding, should remain influences and not become blueprints for a bad pastiche.

As Bob Eggleton points out, 'There's a million Frazetta clones. Everybody wanted to be Frank Frazetta when they were younger but there's only one Frank Frazetta. It's the same thing with Michael Whelan. There should only be one Michael Whelan. My stuff really drastically became my own when I started looking at the masters of art [throughout history]. That was when things really started shining. If someone would say to me, do me a Frank Frazetta, my feeling would be, well go get Frank Frazetta.'

BRASS by Kerem Beyit
© Kerem Beyit 2008 · Digital media: Photoshop
Kerem currently works as a freelance artist.
www.theartofkerembeyit.com

The Attraction of Fantasy Art

Fantasy art is not really a choice: it is a compulsion. Artists cannot always be sure why they are as they are, they merely know that for some inexplicable reason they simply have to create as they do. Whether it is dreams, daydreams or an inescapable urge to get pen and pencil on paper and begin drawing, they simply must put pen to paper and draw. Even Frank Frazetta himself began his career with a comic character called The Snowman that he invented when he was a mere five-and-a-half years old.

Daydreaming

Artist and writer Janny Wurts has a particularly interesting story. As a young girl, her busy household and access to wide open spaces made it easy for her to run freely through fields, developing her imagination in the form of daydreams.

She says, 'School came as a terrible shock. Running wild outdoors I never separated what was going on in my imagination with what other people could see and feel and hear. So my first grade report card came back and I had failed attentiveness, and I passed everything else with flying colours but literally failed attentiveness and you don't fail a subject or attitude in school without being talked to by your parents.' Much to her chagrin, she was informed that the rest of the world was not able to see her daydreams. She recalls, 'I had never seen the difference. It was awful. I suddenly had to figure out what was real to me and what was real to everybody else, and that they were two different worlds.'

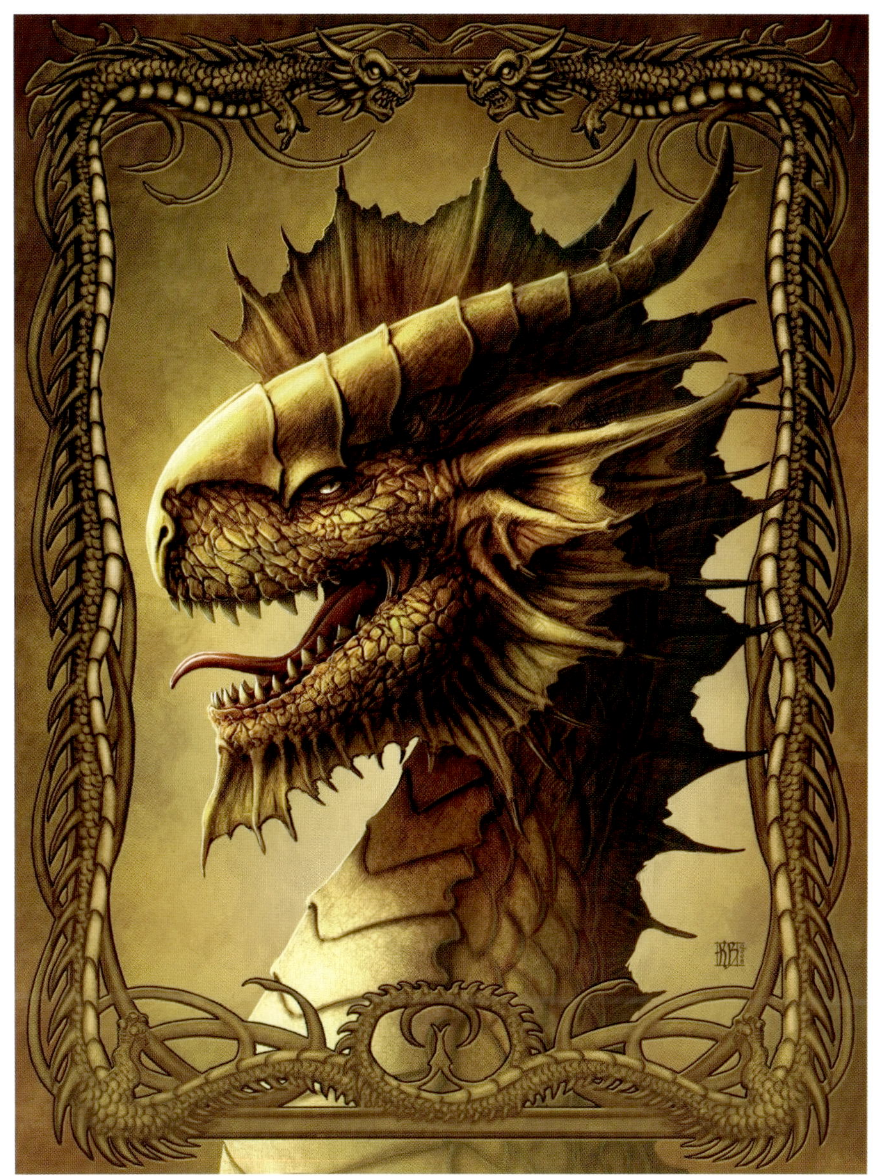

GOLD by Kerem Beyit
© Kerem Beyit 2008 · Digital media: Photoshop
www.theartofkerembeyit.com

Bronze by Kerem Beyit

© Kerem Beyit 2008; Digital media: Photoshop; www.theartofkerembeyit.com

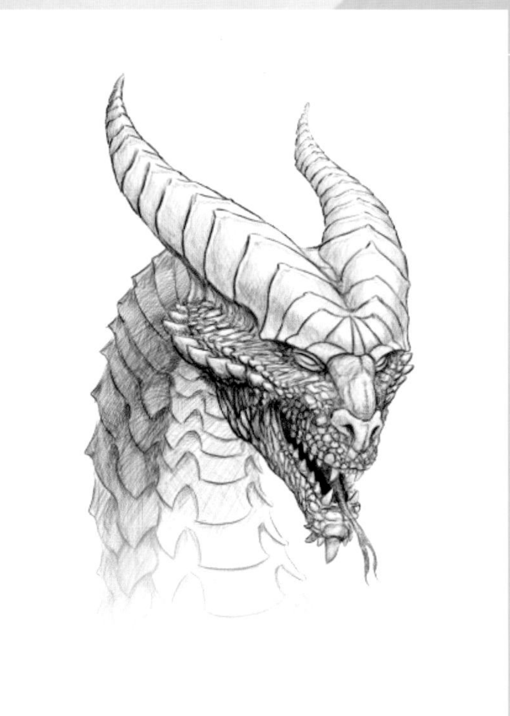

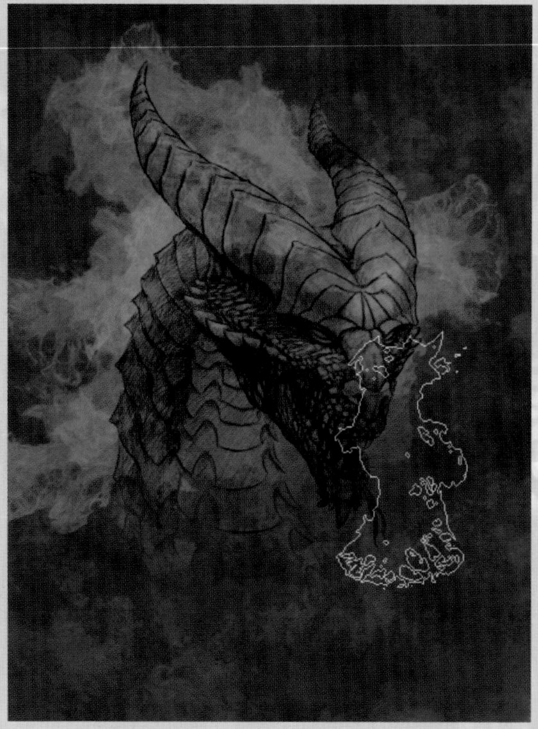

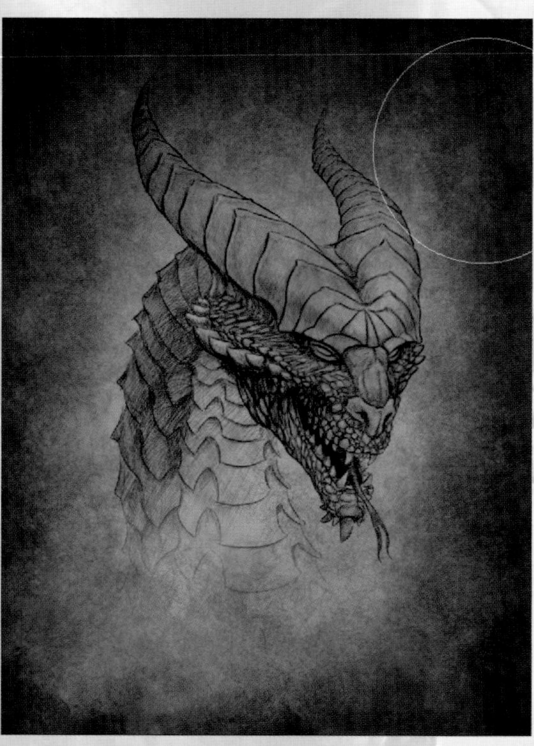

SAMPLE STEP 1. It's impossible to make a good painting without a good sketch. If your drawing is not as strong as you'd like, you should buy a sketchbook before taking up Photoshop or a tablet.

SAMPLE STEP 2. Here, I create the background with my flame brush; the drawing is in the multiply layer. First I form a dark background and then lighten the parts around the portrait with the same brush, this will help us see the figure clearer in the future.

SAMPLE STEP 3. Using my texture brushes, I apply texture to the background, though I am careful not to apply at the same intensity around the figure. The best way is to open a new layer and apply as much texture as you want, then erase the parts that are too much.

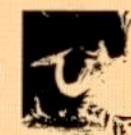

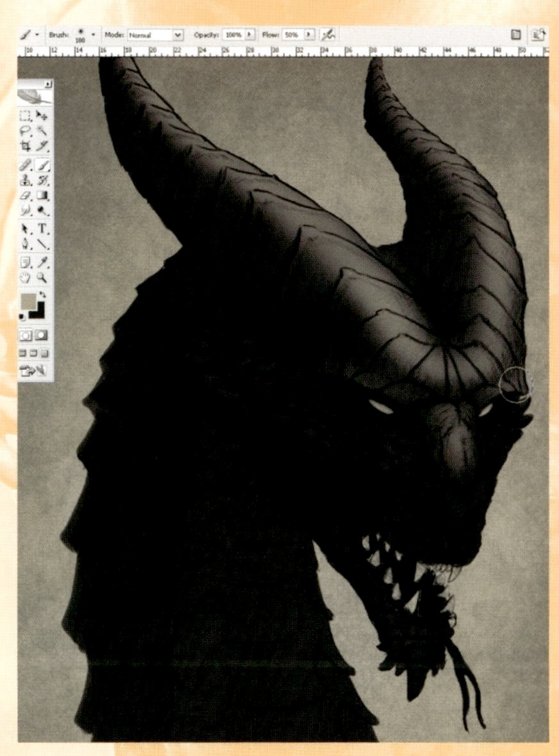

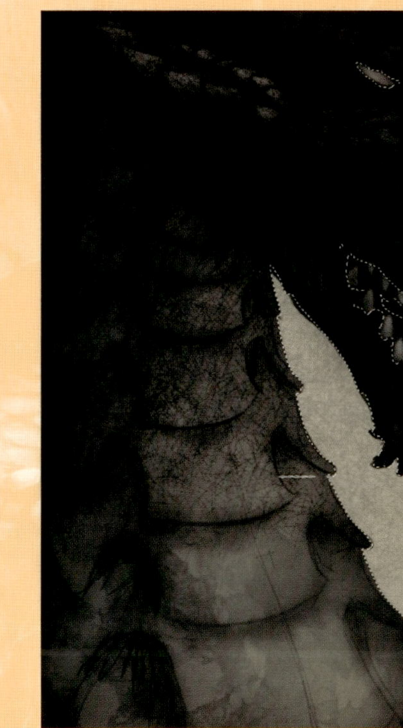

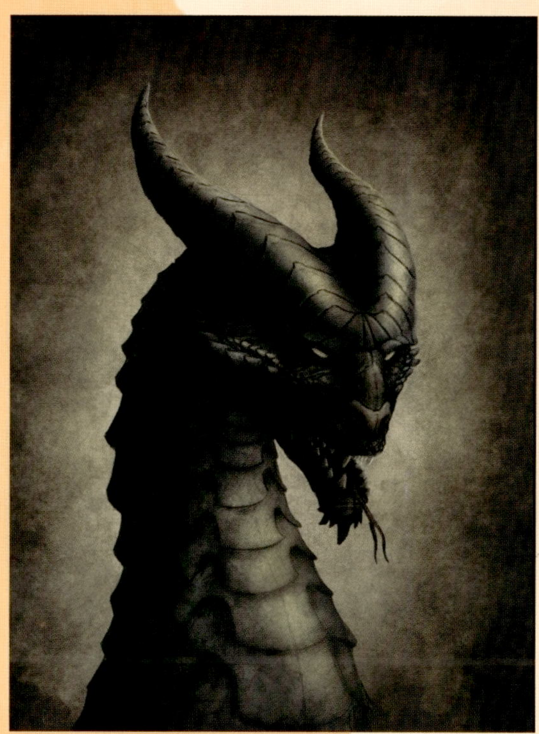

SAMPLE STEP 4. I start filling inside the figure very roughly, first I apply base colours and create highlights with lighter volumes of the base colours.

SAMPLE STEP 5. After painting the figure completely, I apply texture on it and erase the parts I don't like by using the borders of the figure's layers which I select by clicking 'load selection'.

SAMPLE STEP 6. The texturing stage is over after merging the layers. I then apply 'dodge' – the dodge tool should be used wisely, I advise you to work it by making light touches.

Bronze by Kerem Beyit (Continued)

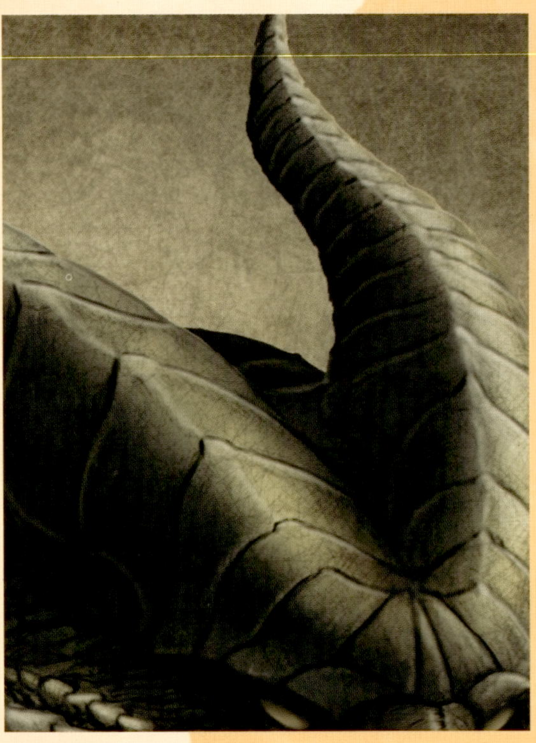

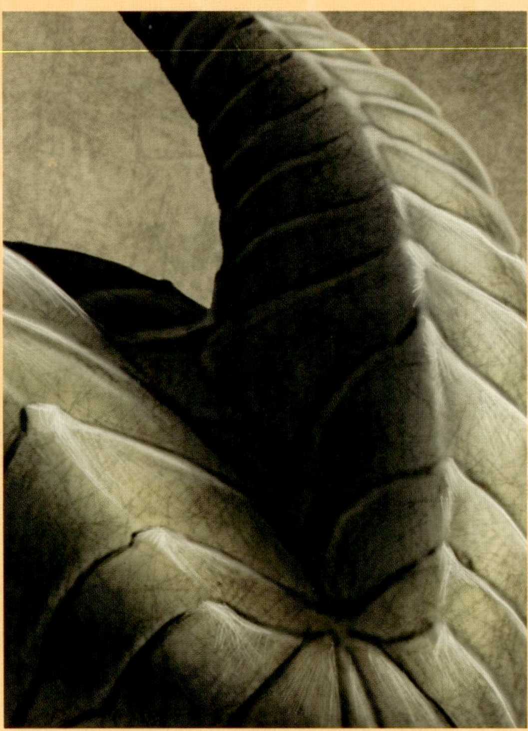

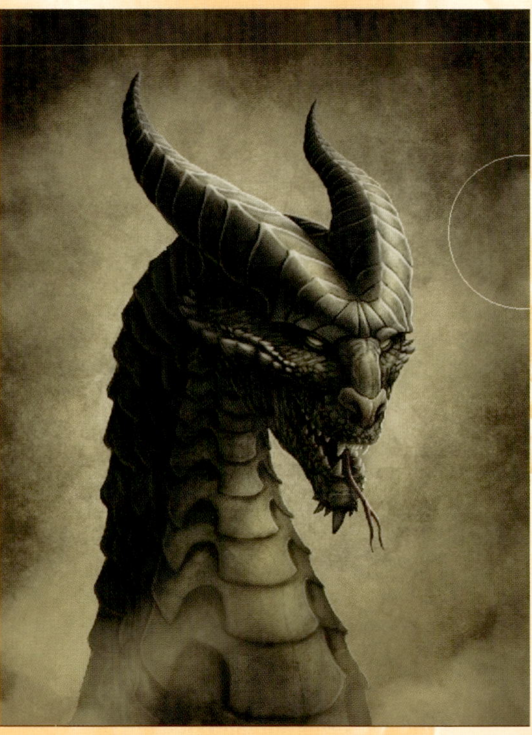

SAMPLE STEP 7. Now we can use highlights, first I paint the big parts that should get light with a small soft round airbrush. You don't have to choose a very light colour, you can always go back and use the dodge tool to increase the light volumes.

SAMPLE STEP 8. Now I paint the sharper parts with a thin hard round brush and a lighter volume.

SAMPLE STEP 9. I then apply fog in front of and behind the figure, this will fix the attention only on the face and will help you not waste time with lower parts of the painting.

FINISHING TOUCHES (RIGHT). Lastly, I use the dodge tool to shine up the highlights' brightness values, I play with contrast and colour values, lighten the background a bit more with my fire brush and since the creature's neck seems too bulky, I finish the illustration by making it more curled.

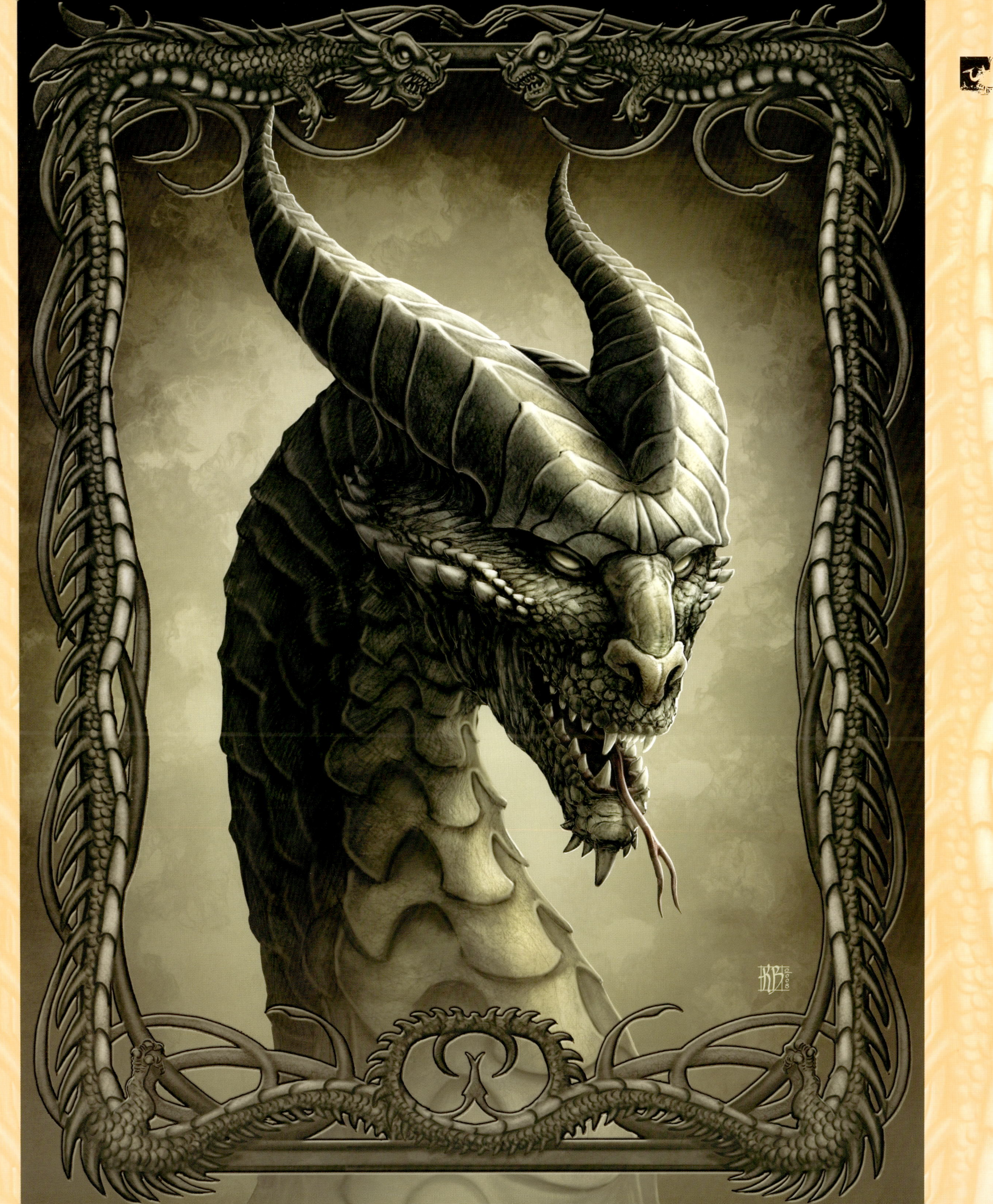

Holding on to Imagination

Janny describes a rebellious streak in her that caused her to read obsessively and make sure she retained her heightened sense of imagination. She speculates, 'I suppose I kept it alive far longer than many people do. A lot of people give up on their imaginations and they're taught that it's for children and you're supposed to give up on it. For me, our imagination is our most powerful tool. It tells us where we're going, it tells us where not to go, it looks at the past, it looks at the present, it recombines solutions all the time in ways no person has thought of. Without that, really, we have no ability to pull in anything new.'

Alan Lathwell echoes the sentiment. 'It's more than a job,' he begins. 'I would paint fantasy if I didn't earn my living from it. When you're a child, you live in a world of imagination. Some people seem to grow out of it and move on to other things. For other people it seems to live within them and they nurture it and nourish it. So I would say I'm lucky enough to be one of those people.'

Tracy Trowbridge describes her art as a 'window' into her incredibly vivid and detailed dreams. 'I just like to be able to create those places and the different odd-looking creatures – I kind of pull them out of my imagination. It's hard to explain. I have this kind of spiritual connection with those places. Each piece that I create has a story in itself.'

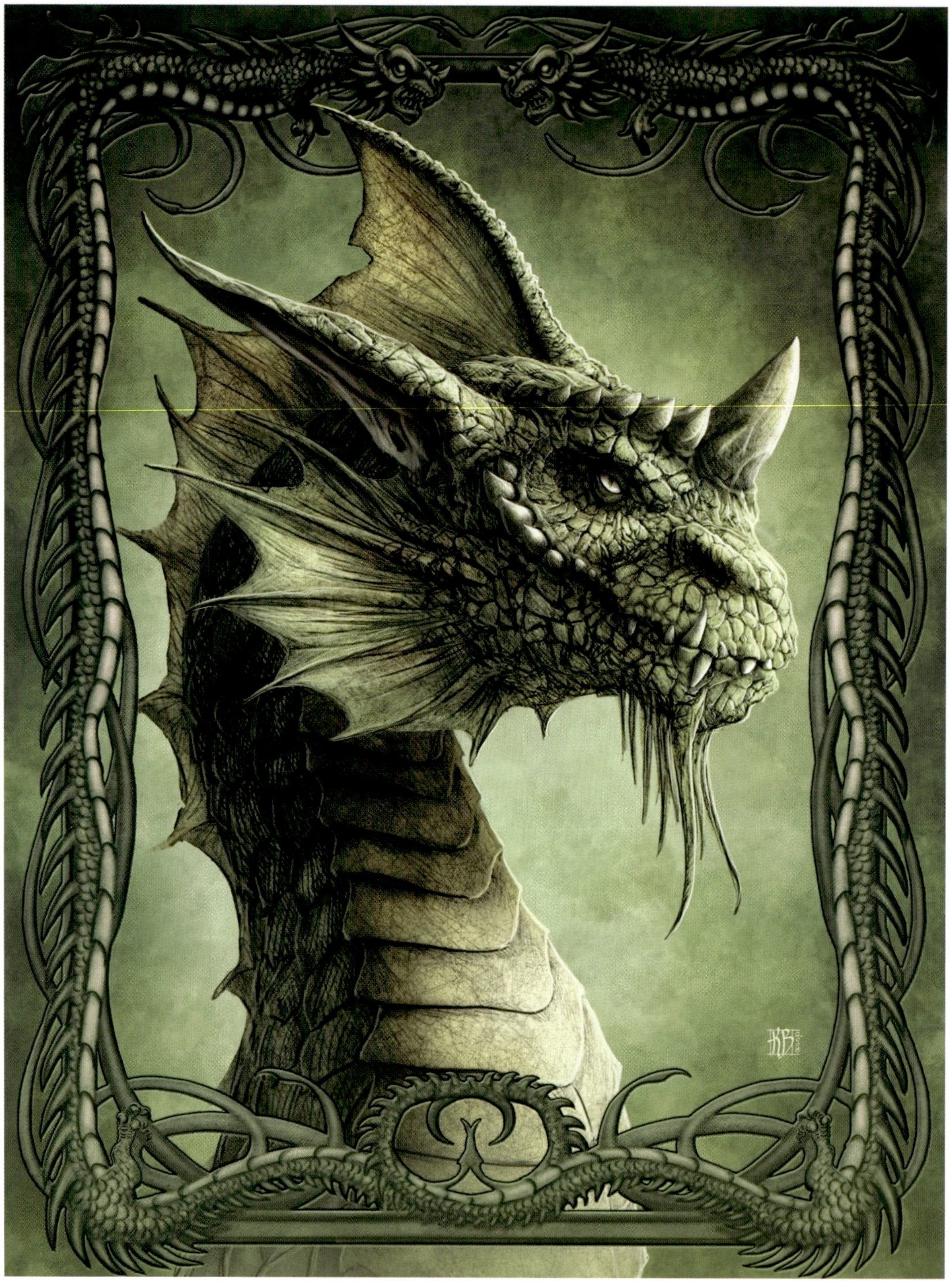

GREEN by Kerem Beyit
© Kerem Beyit 2008 · Digital media: Photoshop
www.theartofkerembeyit.com

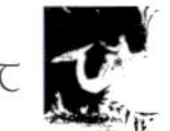

Science Fiction and Fantasy Art

There is an undeniable link between fantasy art and science fiction. Both genres are, perhaps, 'fantastical', simultaneously tapping into the artist's (or writer's) wildest imagination while trying to add an element of plausibility and possibility. It is a sense of 'this could be' or perhaps, 'it could have been this way' or, 'this could be, but in another dimension'. Many fantasy artists also work on science fiction imagery; many read or were raised reading science fiction and draw fantasy, for whatever reason.

Real World v. Inner World

Artist Todd Lockwood says, 'Someone once said to me that science fiction tends to be about the real world, often metaphor for things that are happening in society or government, whereas fantasy is about the inner world, emotions and mythology, or religious experiences. I think that crosses over in the art to a degree. I grew up on science fiction. That was my first love, the hard science, and of course it was during the era of the race to the moon and it was one of the important languages of my childhood. So I do think that my approach to fantasy art is to treat it as if it was real and to try to make the nuts and bolts of it make sense from the perspective of feasibility.'

By way of illustration, he adds, 'For example, I like to invent armour, but I like for it to look like it would function. I don't like to see a painting of a girl in chainmail bikini with little runway model stick arms hoisting a sword that's longer than she is, that she couldn't possibly lift with a winch! I just can't bring myself to go there. It's just childish to me.'

POLAR by Kerem Beyit
© Kerem Beyit 2008 · Digital media: Photoshop
www.theartofkerembeyit.com

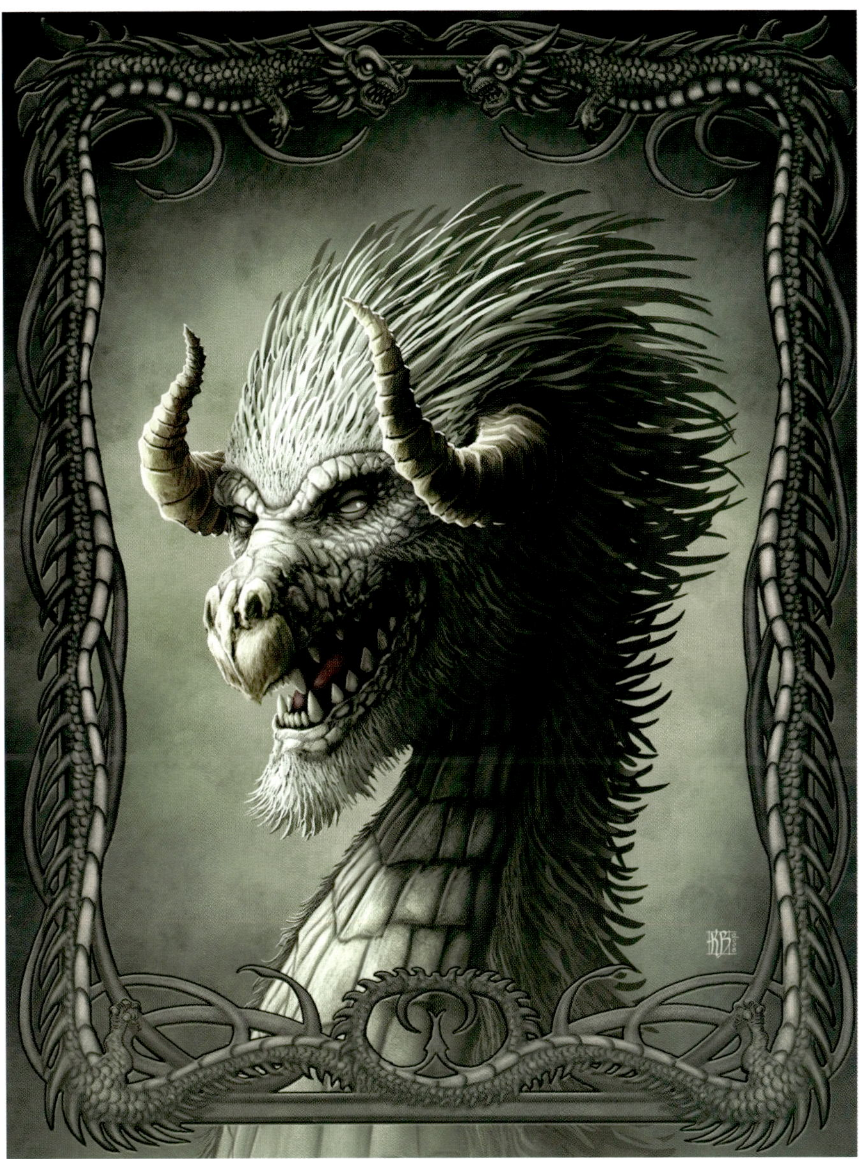

Janny Wurts says, 'I think science fiction is more involved with the concrete, what can be measured. Fantasy steps beyond that, so I see fantasy as a bigger bubble.'

Boundaries

There is something else about science fiction. It can be more visually limiting than fantasy art. That is not to say that there is not some amazing, striking science fiction art out there, but great sci-fi imagery has to work so much harder for the connection with the viewer. Many of the markers of science fiction in art include robots, space suits, dunes and a large Jupiter-like planet in the background. Of course, there is more to it than that, but these are frequently appearing memes in science fiction art. But it is not as immediate as an image of a fire-breathing dragon! We are, perhaps, so imbued with the idea of legends, fairy tales and fables from such a young age that we have a more immediate connection with imagery of familiar mythical creatures and settings. Images of ancient sword-wielding warriors in the midst of battle barely need an explanation; they stand on their own.

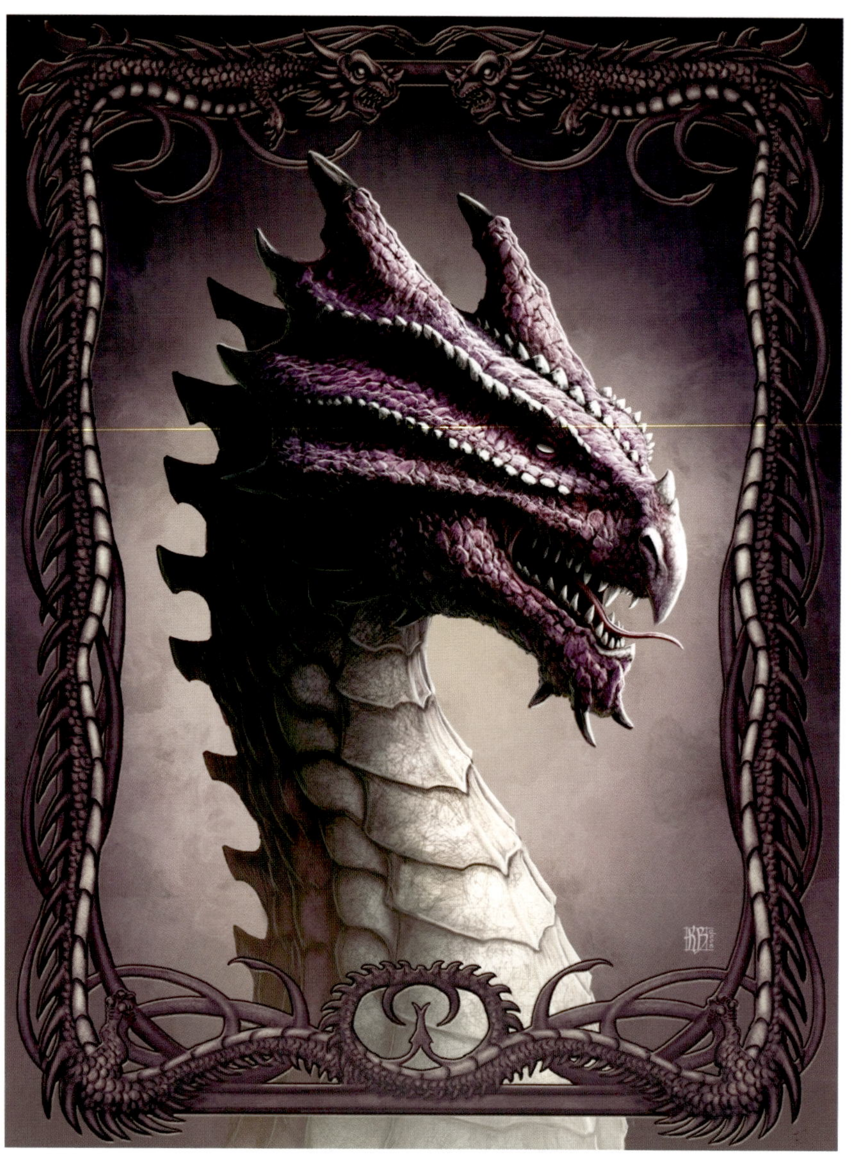

PURPLE by Kerem Beyit
© Kerem Beyit 2008 · Digital media: Photoshop
www.theartofkerembeyit.com

The Joy of Dragons

The limitless potential and more visceral experience of fantasy art in comparison to science fiction helps to explain why, in turn, dragons are so attractive for so many fantasy artists. They do not really need a lot of explanation. You paint a dragon and everyone has an idea of its capabilities (such as that it can fly and it can breathe fire). They are also universal: most cultures on earth can identify with dragons in some way or shape. Dragons are also very pliable. They allow the artist to give them plenty of personality. They can be mean and evil, they can be enigmatic, crafty, vain, amiable or benevolent. We usually accept something magical and ancient about them too, so they add a mythical, sometimes mystical element to an artwork.

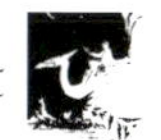

In his book *Myth and Magic: The Art of John Howe*, Howe puts the attraction of dragons succinctly: 'They are absolutely bristling with claws, fangs, horns and the like. They have bats' wings the size of a 747's, glistening scales to render and, even better, many of them breathe fire.'

Elemental Beings

In one form, they are formidable forces of nature; from *The Lord of the Rings* to *Reign of Fire*, the dragons are the natural world's unstoppable death machines. They are practically unbeatable. They fly, so they always have the advantage of elevation, they are enormous and they are usually impervious to standard weaponry. If an artist aims to represent terror and fear, how better than to pit a subject against a dragon? For us as viewers, that image connects with us at a very deep level.

Says Todd Lockwood, 'They're almost manifestations of part of our id. We respond to them in different ways. In some ways they're combinations of things we've always been fearful of. They're lizards and bats and snakes all rolled into one creature.'

Creatures of Wisdom and Character

In other cases, they represent a wisdom, protection or understanding that enchants the viewer, or they add a sort of *deus ex machina* to a narrative. For an artist, it adds a challenge: imbue this beast with personality.

Alan Lathwell explains, 'They don't just have to be chaos-loving destroyers. They can be wise. You try to express that on their faces, the wisdom, give them a character. You wouldn't say that you would give a *dinosaur* wisdom. There is something unique about dragons. You can give them their own presence.'

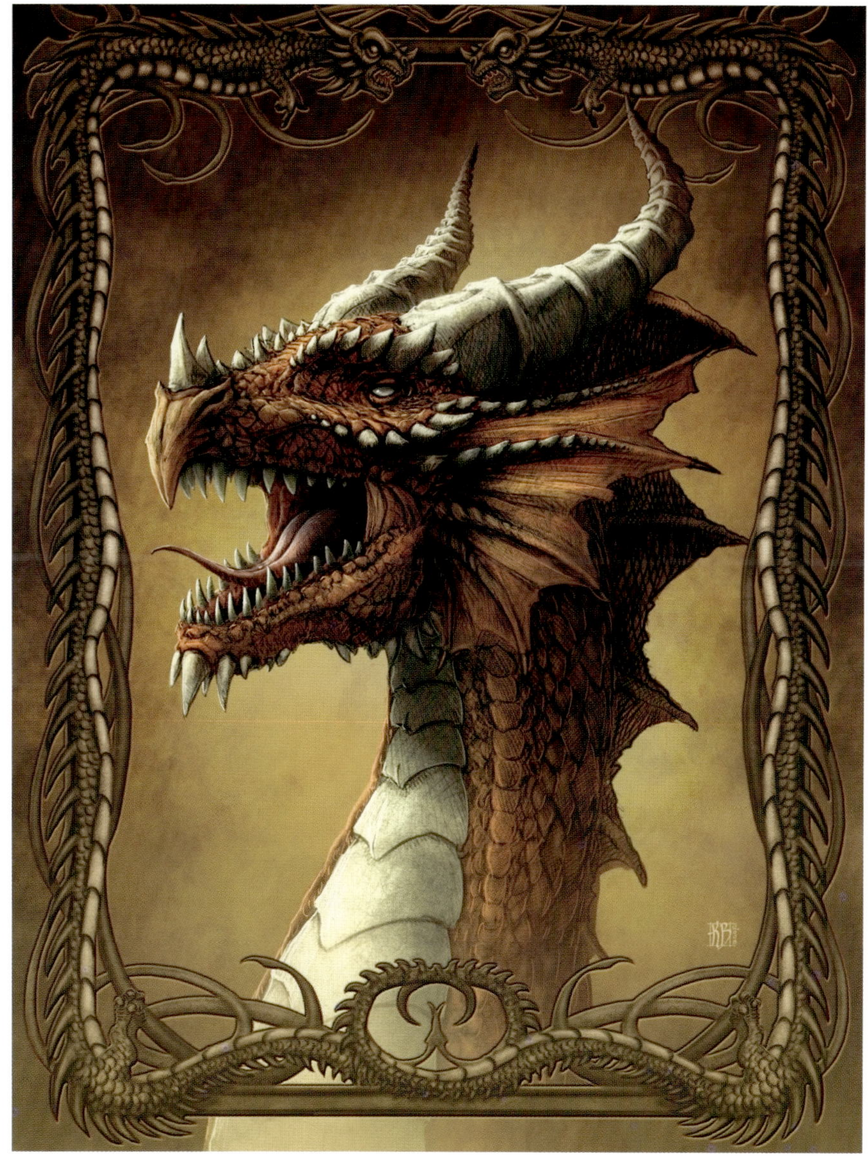

RED by Kerem Beyit
© Kerem Beyit 2008 · Digital media: Photoshop
www.theartofkerembeyit.com

Endless Possibilities

But no matter how you dress it up, dragons are enjoyable to create. They can embody so much variation while still being recognizable as dragons, which is attractive for artists. Alan Lathwell explains, 'Given my choice, I would paint more dragons because they're great; basically I love dragons. You get such a wide range of reality with a dragon. From sea serpents to wyverns to griffins – you could class them as dragons – you can give them horns, gills, fur: the possibilities are endless. Even the colours – I've got wyverns that are orange, and I've got another one that's green. You can give them stripes – from an artistic point of view, dragons are great fun to create.'

Dragons beguile and enchant artists for a number of reasons. For Ciruelo, it has been a passion of the past two decades. He says, 'I have been drawing fantastic characters since I was a kid. But I specialized in dragons since 1989 when I created *The Book of the Dragon*. I am amazed about the fact that many different ancient cultures, distant in time and space from each other, have the figure of the dragon in their myths, and since I've always been fascinated by the mysteries of this world it was natural to be attracted by dragons.'

Kerem Beyit makes sure he keeps his output mixed and as such he is not hooked on dragons. But, he readily admits, 'I started making dragon artworks after I went into digital art. The reason for that is 1), they're pretty cool creatures and, 2), they don't actually exist and therefore, they give you the liberty to play with their anatomy, with no one to step up and say: "That's not what a dragon looks like!" You have to play inside certain limits of course. They're strong, powerful and proud, and they can fly!'

SILVER by Kerem Beyit
© Kerem Beyit 2008 · Digital media: Photoshop
www.theartofkerembeyit.com

DRAGON by Krzysztof Madej
© Krzysztof Madej 2005 · Digital media: Photoshop
http://digitalart.org/azakiel

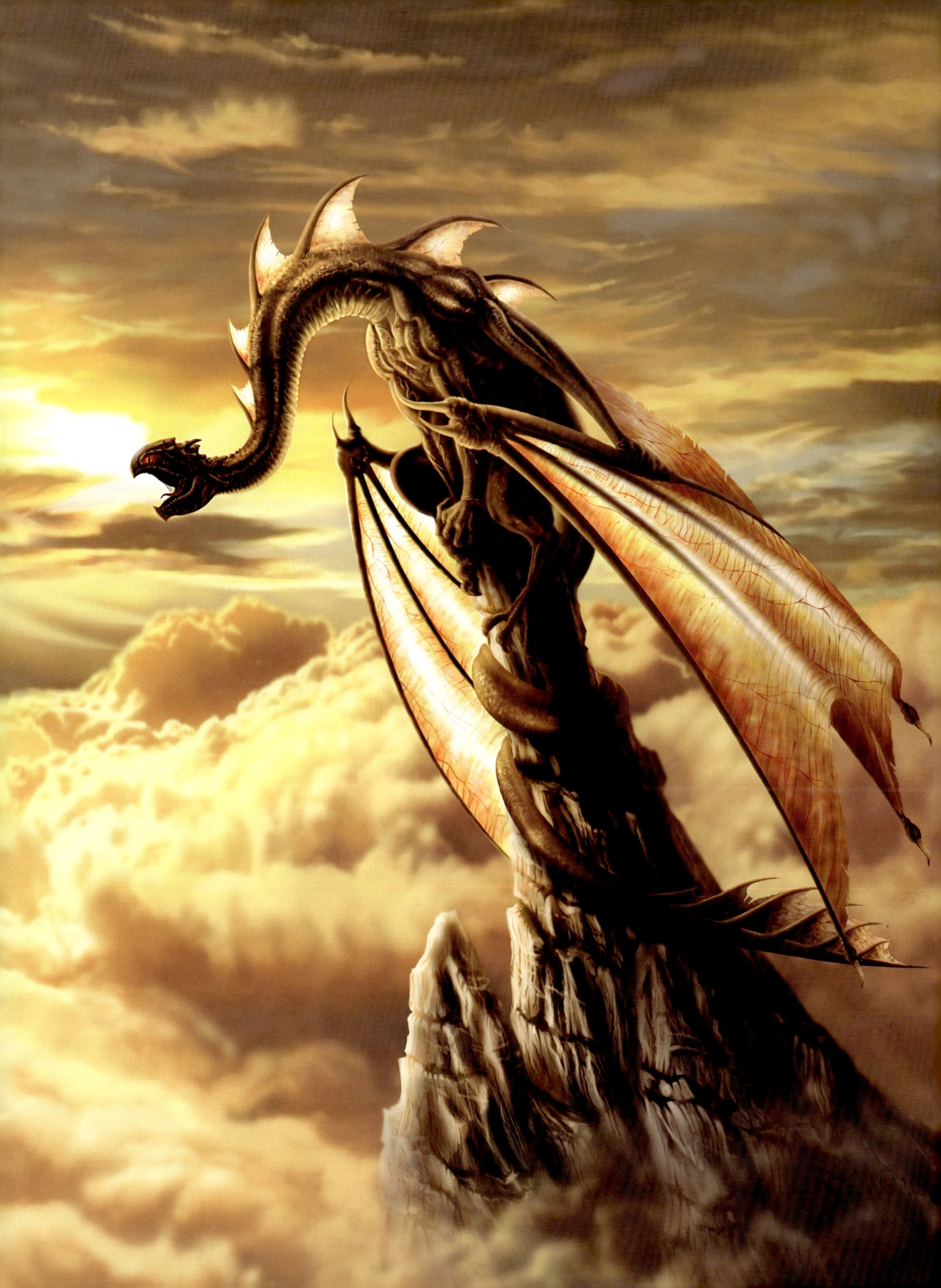

The Guardian of the Lake by Engin Deniz Erbas

© Engin Deniz Erbas 2008; Digital media: Photoshop; From the series entitled 'Five Guardians', created during the concept development process of the comic project *Anhatol Legends*; www.edeart.net

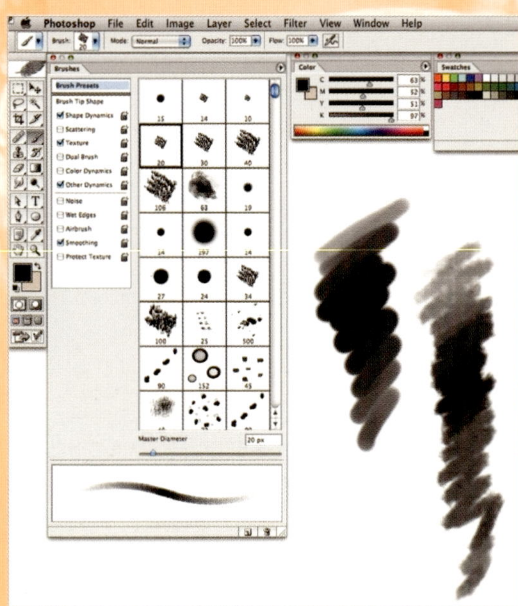

SAMPLE STEP 1. I started with selecting my two favourite brushes to make sketches in Photoshop.

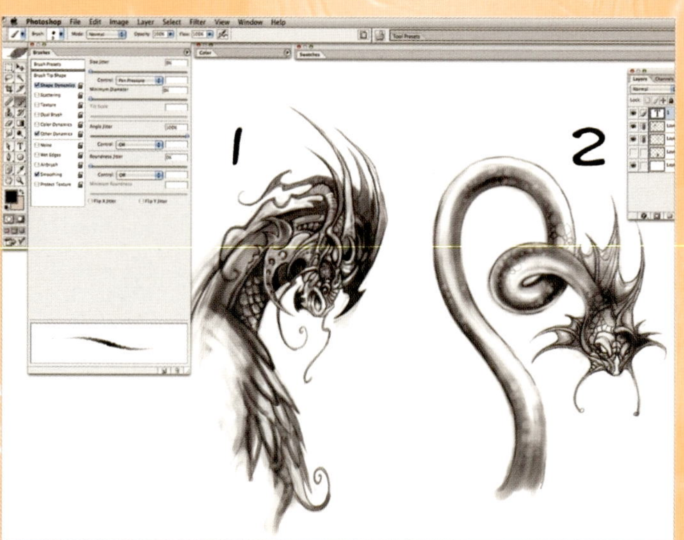

SAMPLE STEP 2. After sketching designs for the character, I started sketching the dragon. This was more challenging. It took me a few sketches to decide how to proceed. In fact, the sketch I decided to go forward with also transformed while I was painting it.

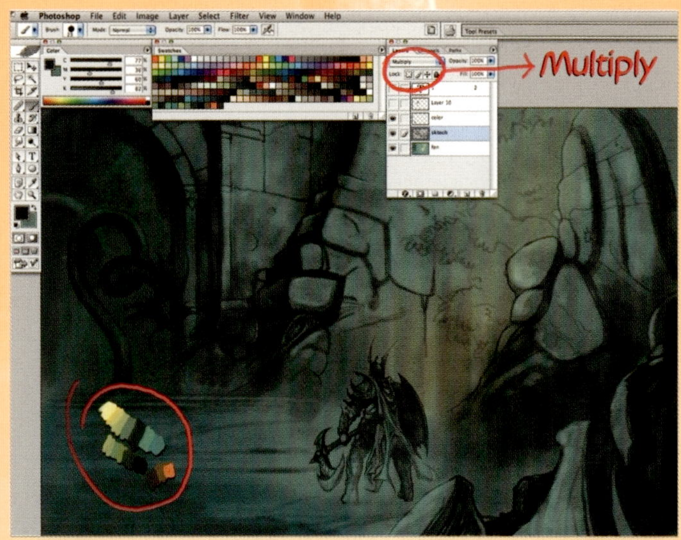

SAMPLE STEP 3. Then, I selected another brush to shade the background as I developed the general composition. I created a background layer behind the sketch and roughly coloured it. Then, I used the multiply effect to the layer of the sketch and created the colour palette I wanted to use for the illustration. I wanted the scene to have depth.

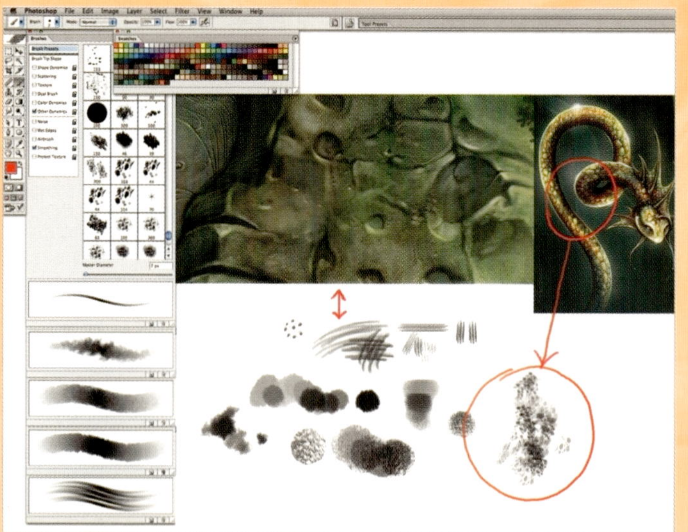

SAMPLE STEP 4. These are examples of the brushes I used for painting the textures. As it took me quite some time to complete this work, a number of differences occurred between the initial sketches and the final product. When you change one thing, everything changes.

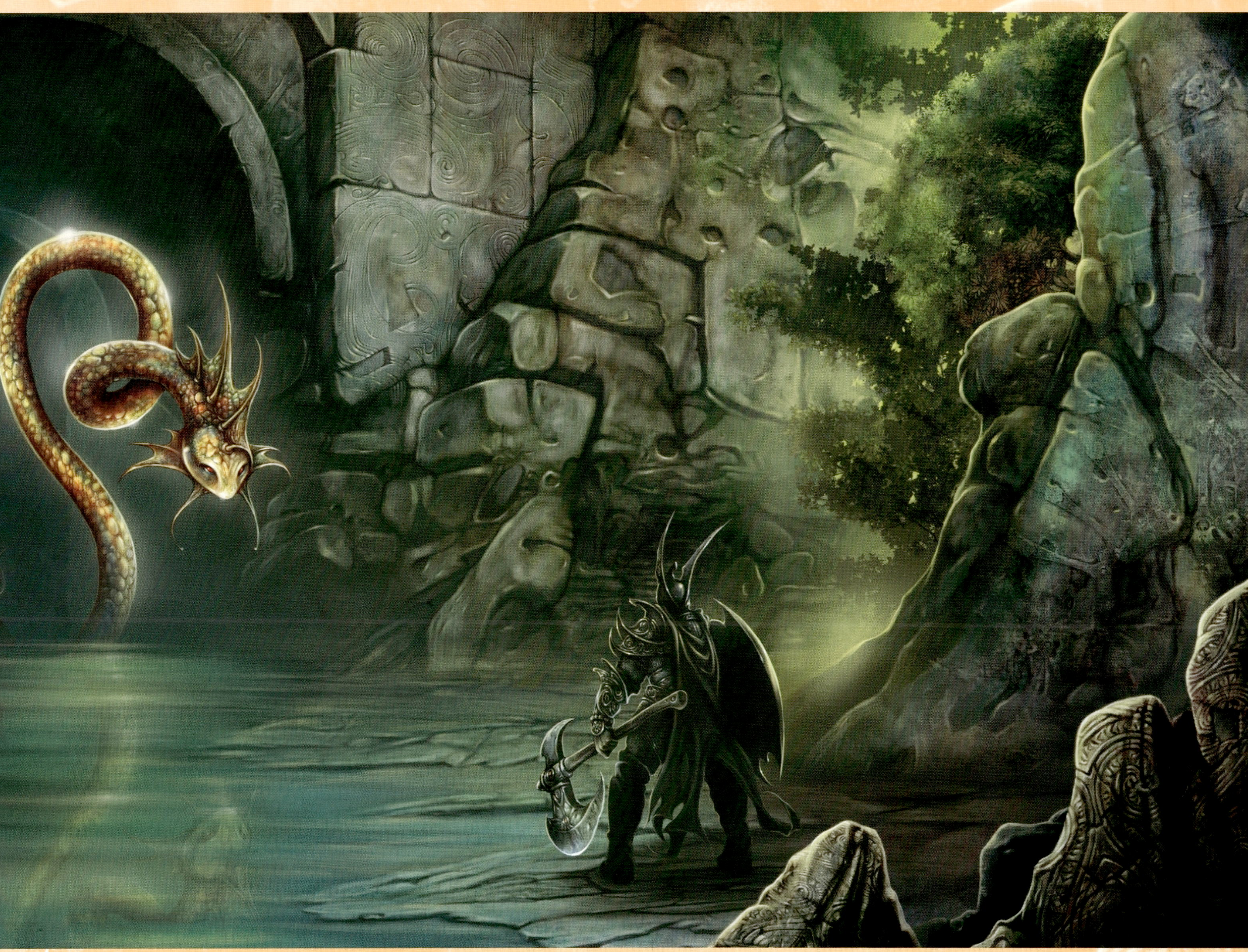

FINISHING TOUCHES. After 50 hours of work, the result is *The Guardian of the Lake.* I hope you like it.

UNLEASHED by Minna Sundberg
© Minna Sundberg 2006 · Digital media: Paint Shop Pro
Minna was born in 1990 and is an art student in Finland.
http://shadowumbre.deviantart.com

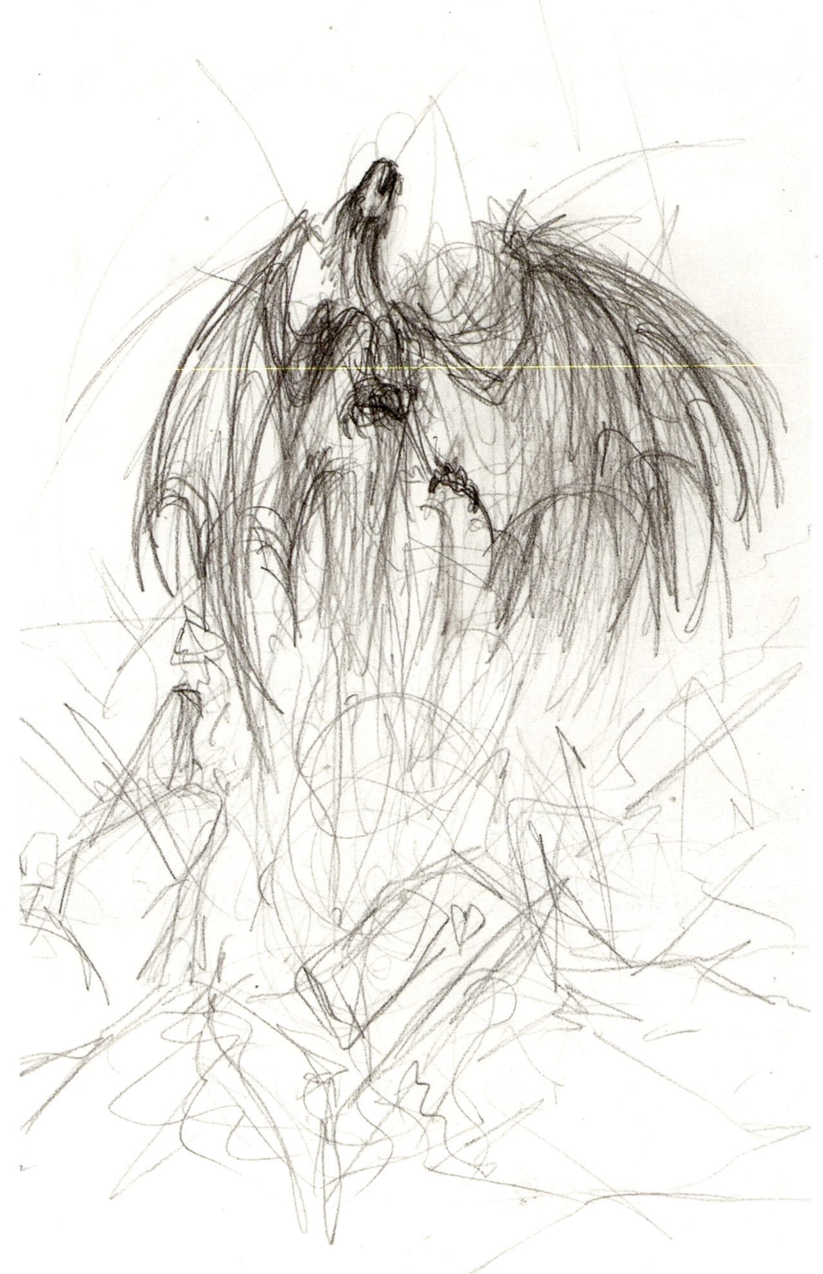

Michele-lee Phelan has strong spiritual beliefs, and this is one of the major influences for her art. She says, 'Dragons are one of my totem energies. My earliest dreams were of dragons, of flying with them, and of talking to them. To me, they are akin to angels, which is why I have never depicted a dragon doing harm, or being harmed. They are creatures of immense wisdom and power, and yes, capable of harm, but more benevolent than dangerous.'

The Influence of Tolkien

To return to the idea of journeys, one of the greatest influences on fantasy artists of certain leanings – especially those concerned with quests and epic journeys – is the work of J.R.R. Tolkien.

John Ronald Reuel Tolkien was born 16 April 1892 in Bloemfontein, South Africa, to Arthur and Mabel Tolkien, who had emigrated from England not very long before. Mrs Tolkien was far from enamoured with the climate and conditions of their new home, however and, while 'Ronald', as she called him, and his brother Hilary were very young, the three returned to England, to live just outside Moseley in Sarehole, an area that has now become part of Greater Birmingham, and awaited the return of Arthur after he finished up his affairs at the Bank of Africa where he worked. However, Arthur fell ill with rheumatic fever and, while he nearly recovered, he was overcome and died in 1896.

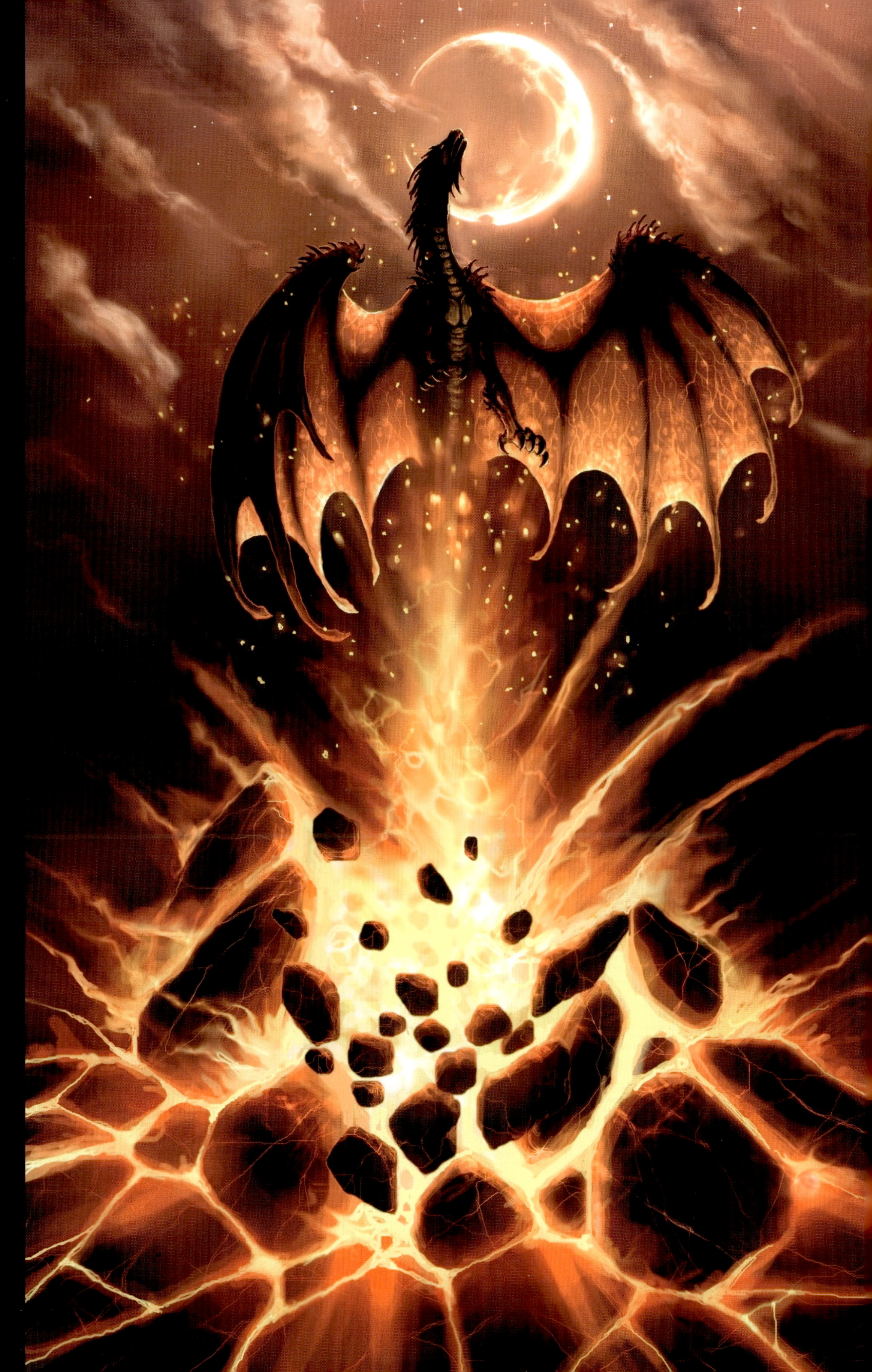

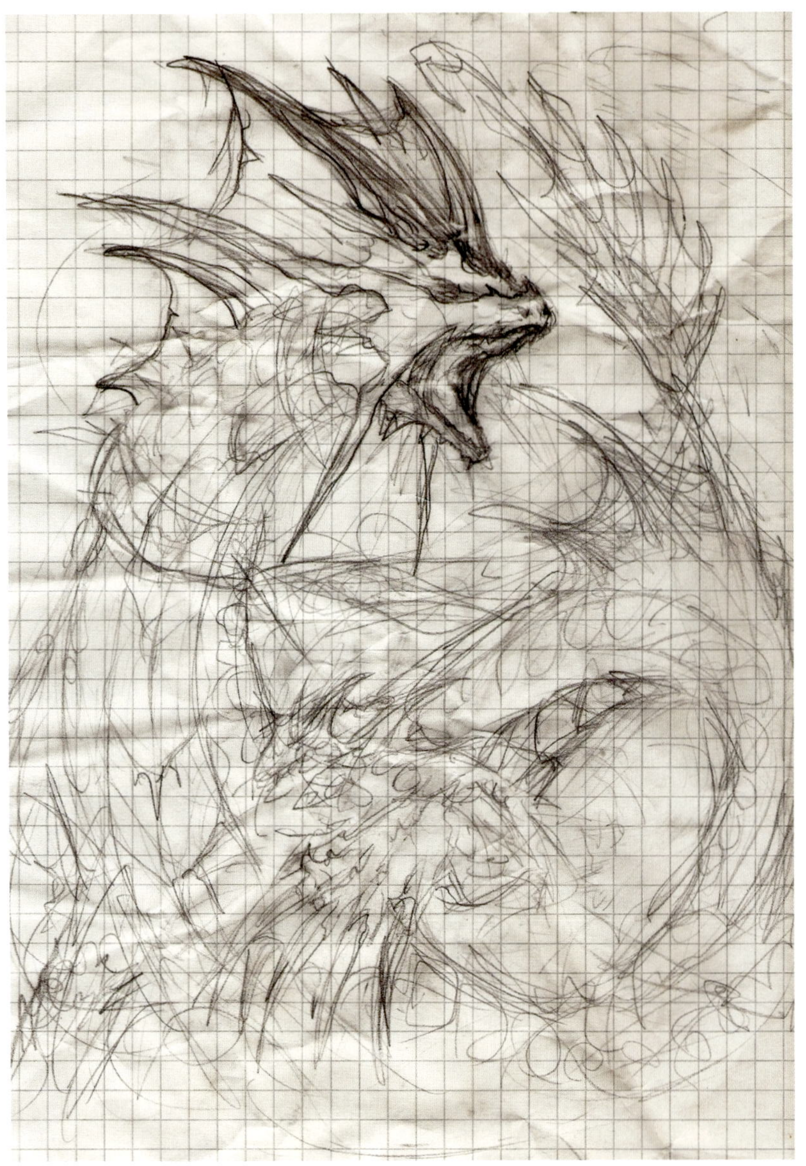

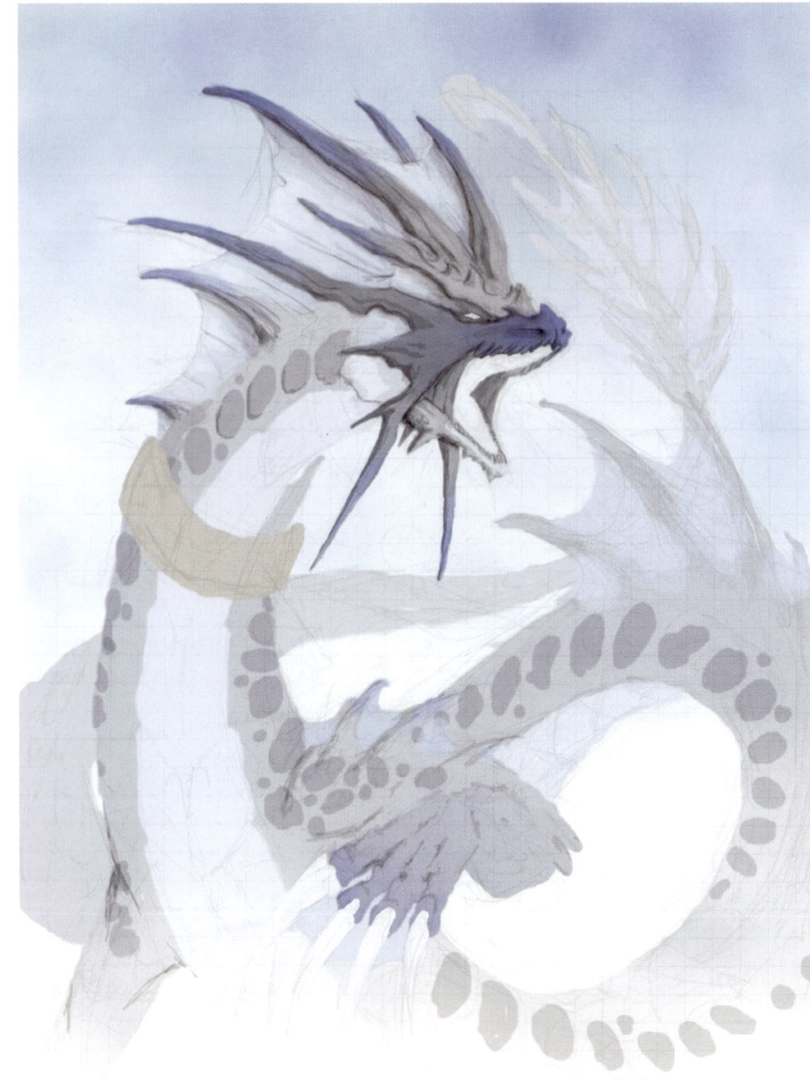

And So it Begins

Mabel was thus widowed with two sons. She chose to home school her sons, and Tolkien developed a firm interest in various fairy tales, calligraphy, Latin and German. He was also keen on botany. His interest in dragons was fired by reading the Sigurd stories at a very young age in *The Red Fairy Book*. His outdoor play in the rural Worcestershire countryside also cemented a bucolic vision in his mind that would later appear in descriptions of the Hobbits' habitat.

Tolkien was orphaned in his early teenage years, his mother having been diagnosed with type 1 diabetes and dying from its complications. Young Tolkien, under the care of a sympathetic catholic priest, managed to earn a place at Exeter College,

SILVERSTORM by Minna Sundberg, 2007
© Minna Sundberg 2007 · Digital media: Paint Shop Pro
http://shadowumbre.deviantart.com

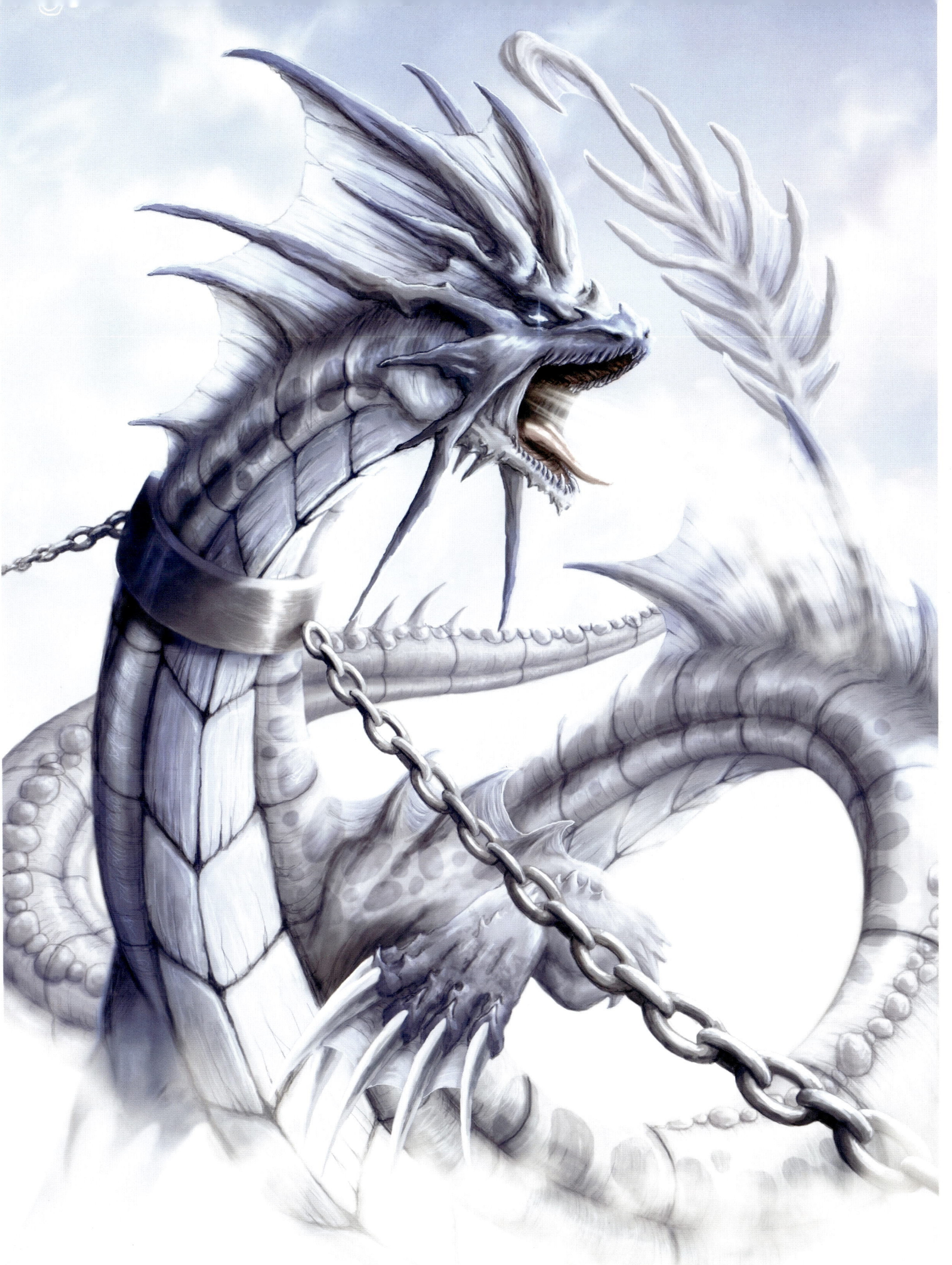

Oxford, along the way developing a love of poetry and prose, much of which was an outlet for his love of fantasy. He joined the army for the First World War, but ill health meant that he was spared much battle on the front lines.

In 1923, he began a book called *The Book Of Lost Tales*, which was later to become *The Silmarillion*. Between this time and the middle of the 1930s, he wrote plenty of poetry and children's stories, worked as assistant lexicographer for the precursor to the Oxford English Dictionary and taught at Oxford as an expert in Old English literature, including *Beowulf*.

Birth of The Hobbit

In the early 1930s, on a family outing, it appears he wrote the immortal line 'In a hole in the ground, there lived a Hobbit', but he could not really explain why. The book *The Hobbit* was ready for publication in September 1937 in the UK, and the following year in the United States.

This famous children's novel concerns the journey of a small, humanoid creature, a hobbit, called Bilbo Baggins, who journeys from his comfortable home at the behest of the wizard Gandalf to help a dwarf kingdom retrieve a hoard of treasure stolen from them long ago by a dragon called Smaug. Along the way, Bilbo finds a ring that enables him to become invisible, and this, along

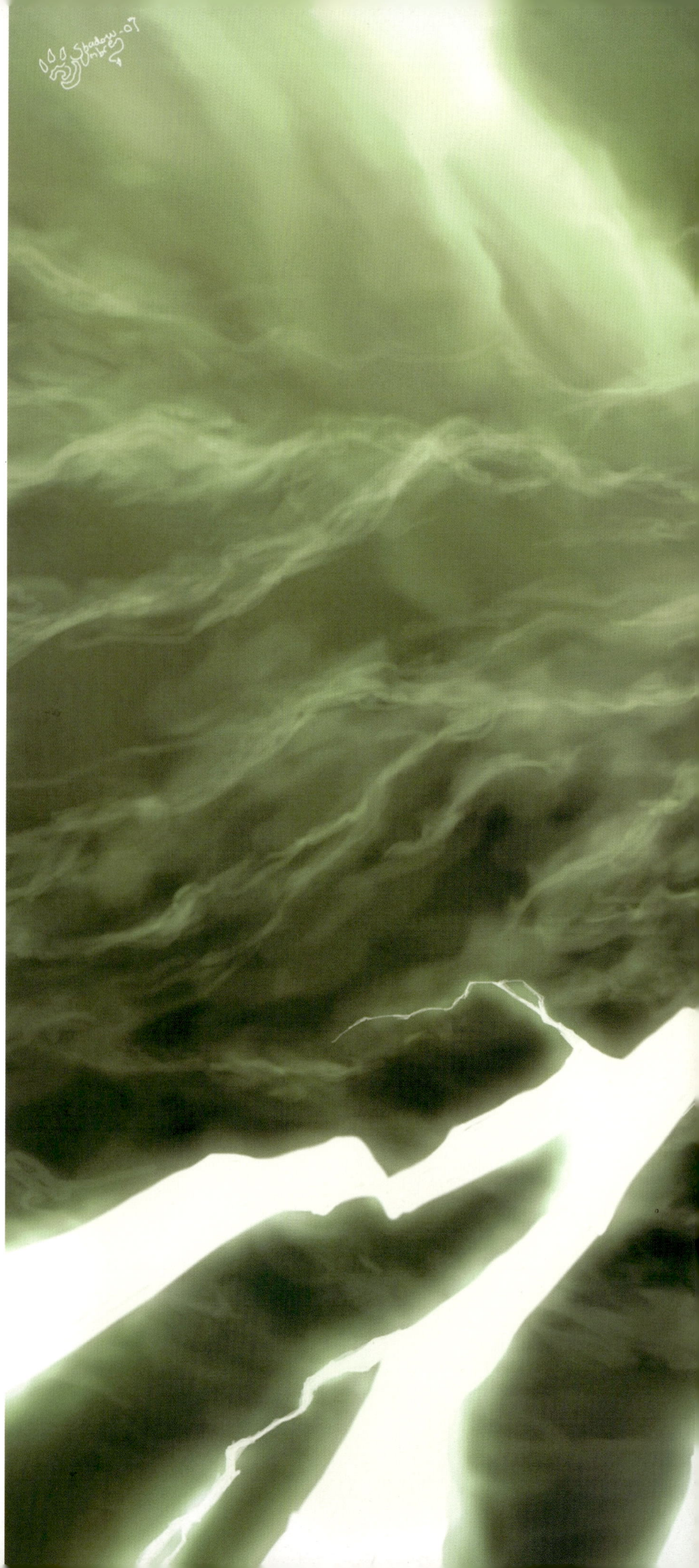

SHOCKWAVE FRONT by Minna Sundberg, 2007
© Minna Sundberg 2007 · Digital media: Photoshop
http://shadowumbre.deviantart.com

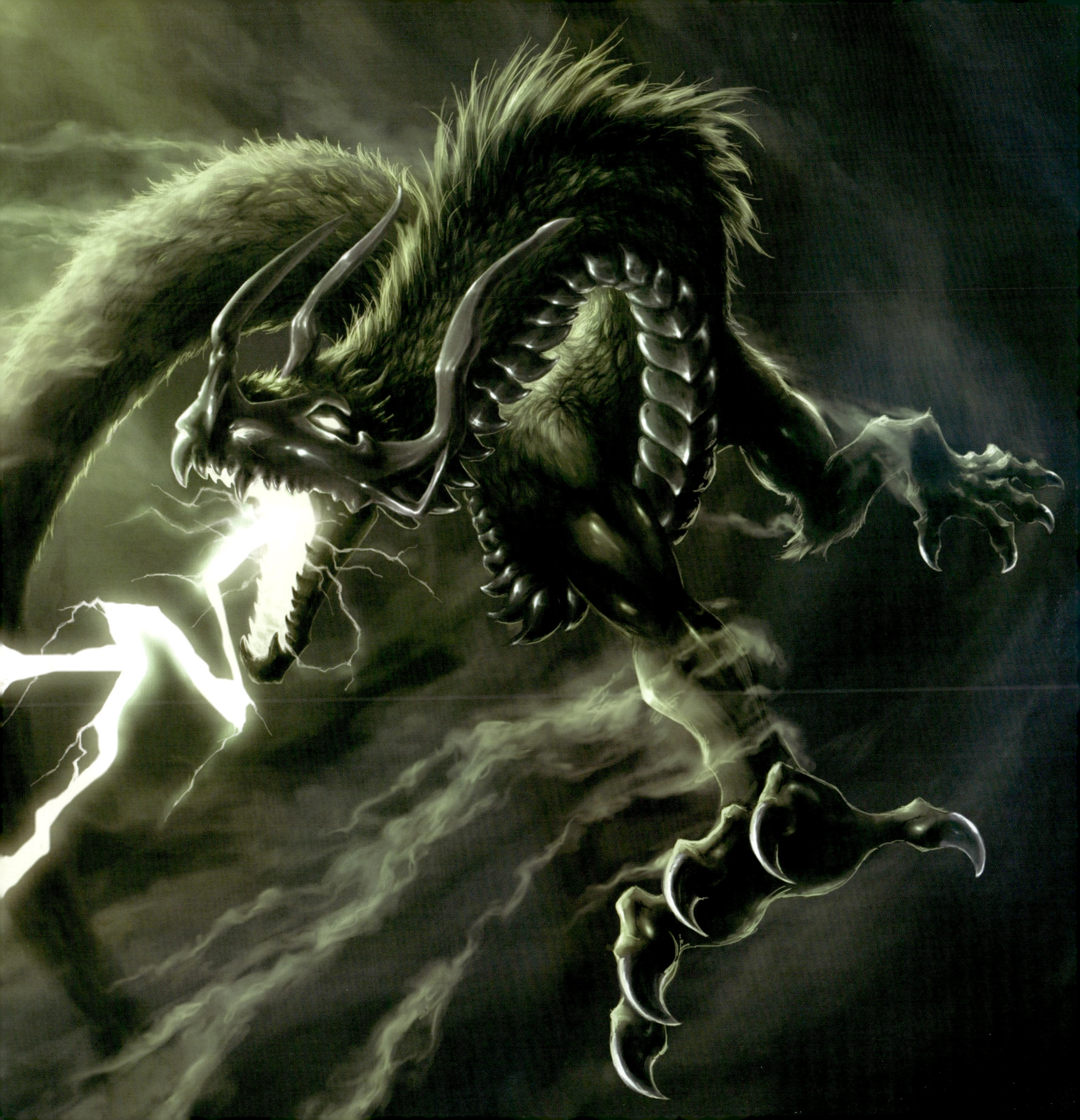

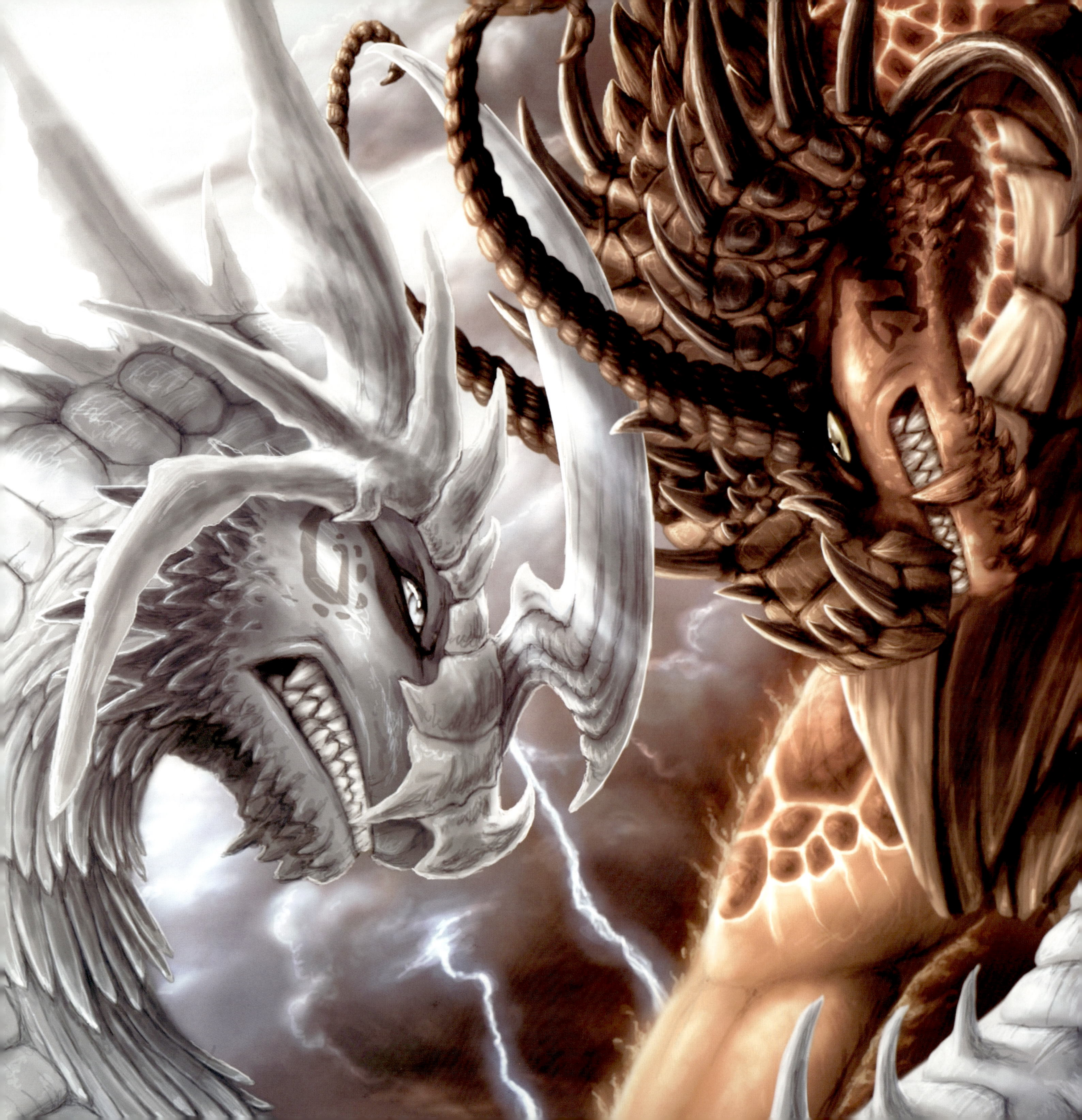

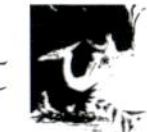

with cunning, guile and co-operation, enables him and his companions to defeat the dragon, recover the gold and return home.

The Lord of the Rings

Following publication, Tolkien was faced with a dilemma. The book was very well received and the publishers were keen for a sequel. However, the book ended with the Hobbit protagonist, Bilbo Baggins, living out his days at home, with no more adventure.

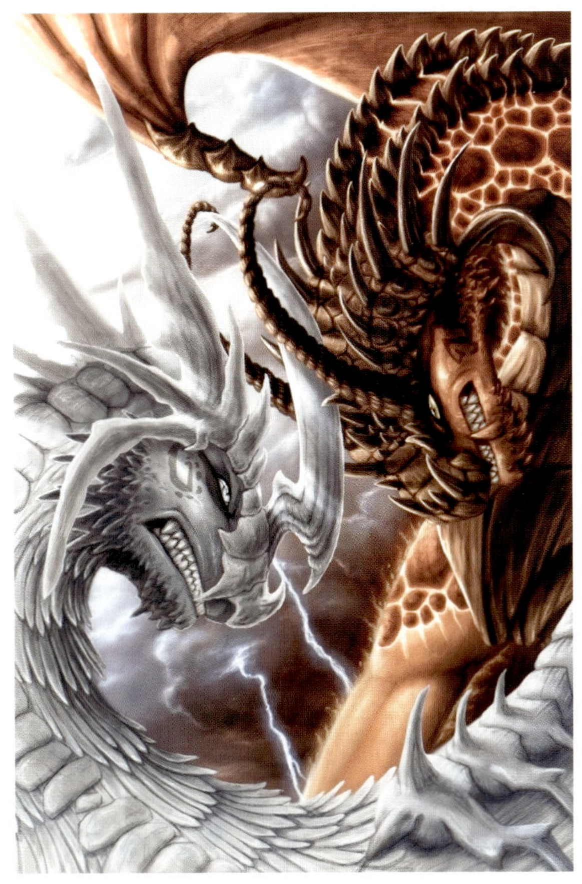

Tolkien got around the problem by introducing a nephew, initially called Bingo, who would have to destroy the ring at Mount Doom, as its power was a potential threat to the safe existence of the Tolkien-created land of Middle Earth. *The Lord of the Rings* is a trilogy of books published between 1954 and 1955 about the journey of Frodo, his hobbit companions Sam Gamgee, Merry and Pippin, and other characters representing each of the free peoples in Middle Earth, all of whom combine to form the Fellowship of the Ring.

The Father of Modern Fantasy

Tolkien died in 1973. He has since become viewed as the father of modern fantasy, a touchstone across sub-genres, from fairy-based fantasy to sword and sorcery, even with hints of horror. His legacy was cemented by the epic film adaptations of the trilogy by Peter Jackson between 2001 and 2003.

Todd Lockwood notes of *The Lord of the Rings*, 'I was a teenager, and I think that was probably the first fantasy novel I had read, or least it was the first that I remember reading. I had resisted it because a friend told me it's got elves and dwarves in it, and I thought, elves and dwarves? I don't want to read that! But it was the depth of the emotion in the story perhaps more than anything. [It is clear just how much it] sucked me in [when I recall the part with] Gandalf telling Frodo about the story of the ring, in his little front chamber [...] as Frodo looks up and realizes that it's going from daylight to darkness back to daylight, I realized I'd done the same thing. It connected on a lot of levels, personal and mythical. It appealed to that inner sense I think we all have of that larger mystery or ominous sense of purpose in the universe.'

Janny Wurts adds, 'He did a phenomenal job. He wrote a wonderful classical story. And it has a lot of reverberations [reflecting] what happens to people when they hold power and they can't bear to let it go. It's just an astonishing piece of work.'

TERRITORY DISAGREEMENT by Minna Sundberg, 2007
© Minna Sundberg 2007 · Digital media: Paint Shop Pro
http://shadowumbre.deviantart.com

The Influence of Robert E. Howard

If Tolkien wrote the rulebook when it comes to all things mythological and mystical, the master of sword and sorcery is an entirely different matter.

The sword-wielding warrior is one of fantasy art's most recognizable motifs, and the writer who inspired much of the imagery is Robert E. Howard. His characters, King Krull and Conan, with a little bit of help from Frank Frazetta, set the standard for the image of the warrior in fantasy art. In fact, fellow fantasy writer Fritz Leiber said, 'The best pulp sword-and-sorcery writer was Robert E. Howard, 1906–36. He grew out of Jack London, Sax Rohmer and Edgar Rice Burroughs.'

Growing Up

Oddly enough, the landscape and people Howard described in his books were shaped significantly by the environment in which he was raised. Howard was born in Peaster, a small town outside Fort Worth, Texas, in 1906. The Howards moved around Texas during Robert's early years, through areas that did not have a great reputation for law and order. It was still frontier land essentially, with plenty of fighting, shooting and desolation.

As a boy, Howard was very bookish and, as such, was ribbed and bullied. To counter taunts, he embarked on a regime of fitness and bodybuilding, and as a man he cut quite a robust figure, nearly six feet tall and rippling with muscle. Yet he maintained his interest in books, avidly consuming works by the likes of Edgar Rice Burroughs, Edgar Allen Poe, Sir Walter Scott, Omar Khayyam and his favourite, Jack London.

Weird Tales

Importantly, as the nineteenth century was drawing to a close, technology like the linotype machine and advances in lithography drove down the cost of publishing, leading to a flourishing of magazines in the early twentieth century. Of these, it was *Weird Tales* that was particularly significant in the life of Robert E. Howard and, as we have seen, was in fact highly significant in the story of fantasy fiction.

The brainchild of Jacob Clark Henneberger, *Weird Tales* was established in 1923 in order to provide a platform for what was essentially offbeat, non-'slick' mainstream writing. *Weird Tales* and others would take submissions from various writers and pay them per word.

H.P. Lovecraft

If we can digress, it is this movement that brought another of fantasy's 'founding fathers', H.P. Lovecraft, to light. Howard Philips Lovecraft was born in East Providence, Rhode Island in

WHERE CLOUDS ARE BORN by Minna Sundberg, 2007
© Minna Sundberg 2007 · Digital media: Photoshop
http://shadowumbre.deviantart.com

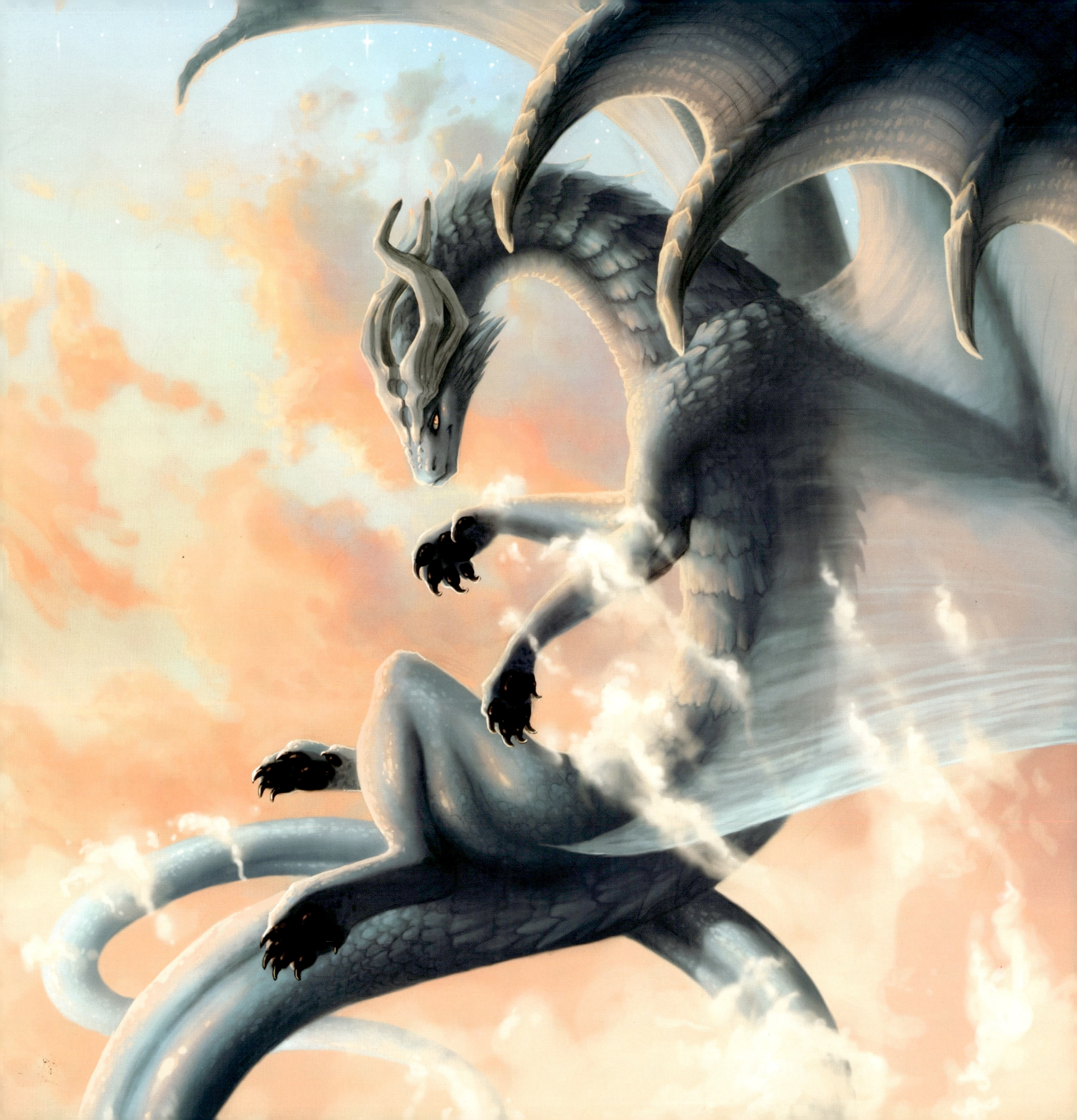

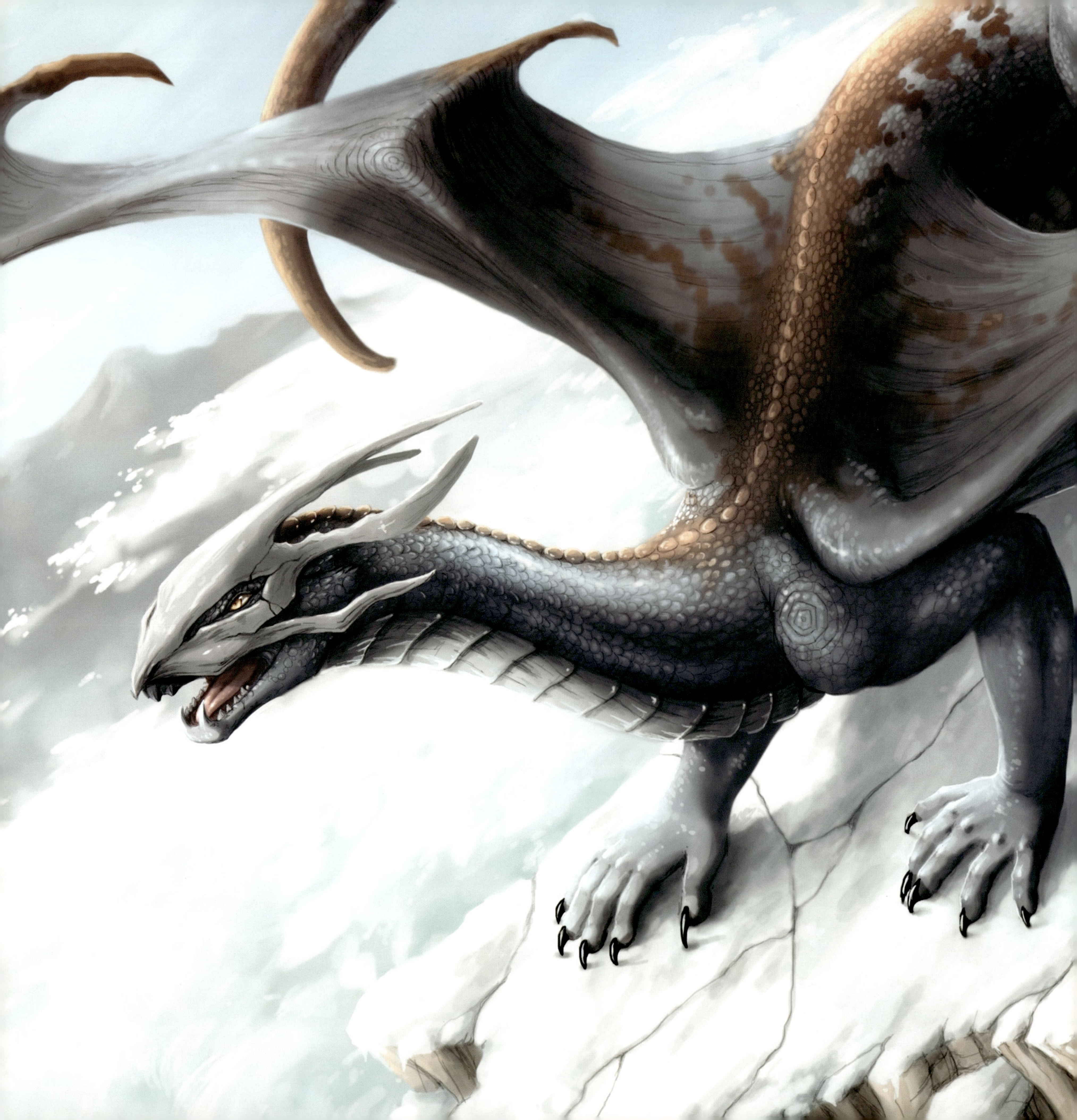

 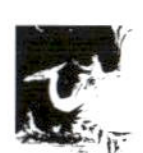

August 1890 to what he considered to be quite aristocratic stock. Like Robert E. Howard, he was also a voracious reader in his youth, and quite academic, but he suffered a terrible nervous breakdown in 1908, just before he was due to graduate high school and matriculate into Brown University.

This led to young Lovecraft becoming a complete recluse for around five years, living at home with his mother. (His father had suffered a mental breakdown and died many years earlier, and his mother would also suffer nervous collapse later in Lovecraft's life.) During his time in seclusion, Lovecraft would buy the new, cheap magazines, including *Argosy* and *Popular Magazine* among others, for their strange mix of fantasy, mystery and horror. The magazines also had popular letters pages and would publish column inches of reader feedback. As a prickly youth, he also frequently contributed letters to these magazines, criticizing or praising stories and writers as he saw fit, and it is one of these letters that changed the course of Lovecraft's life.

Lovecraft Earns a Reputation

Lovecraft gained some infamy among the publishing staff and regular readers of the magazine stable of publisher Frank Munsey. In 1914, he took exception to the sentimental work of writer Fred Jackson and set about him in letter form in Munsey publication *Argosy*. However, Jackson was quite

AVALANCHE by Minna Sundberg, 2007
© Minna Sundberg 2007 · Photoshop
http://shadowumbre.deviantart.com

Dragon's Den by Kris Eggleston

 Digital media: Photoshop; www.kriseggleston.com

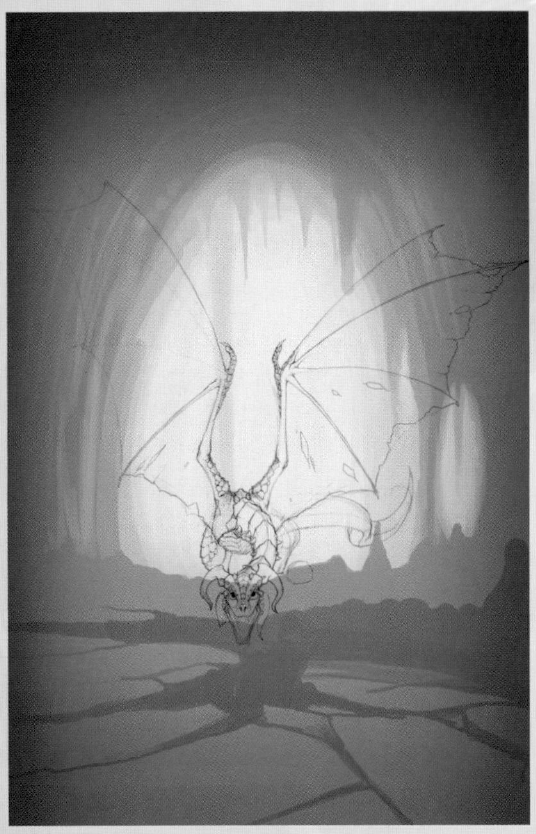

SAMPLE STEP 1. The first step is roughing in the background. A hard brush and monochromatic tones are used. Once the background rough-in is completed, the dragon is sketched in place on a separate layer.

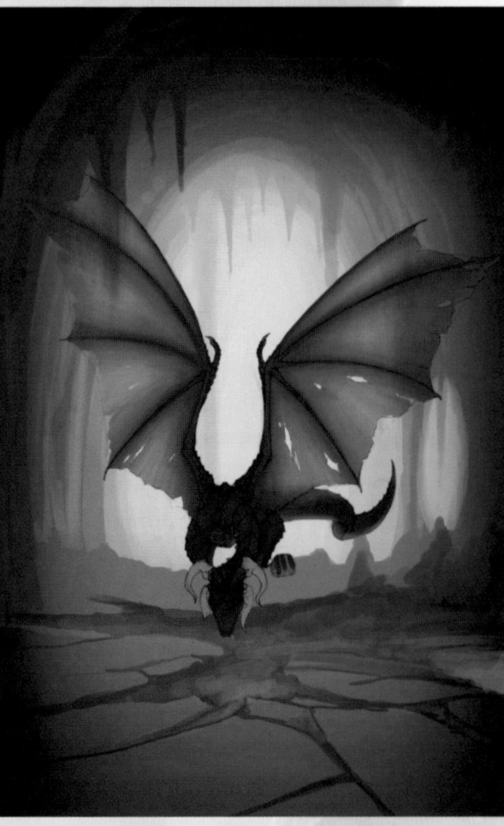

SAMPLE STEP 2. The next step is colourizing the background layer, in this case blue to complement all of the warm tones to be used later for the fire. At the same time, the dragon is filled and given its base colours.

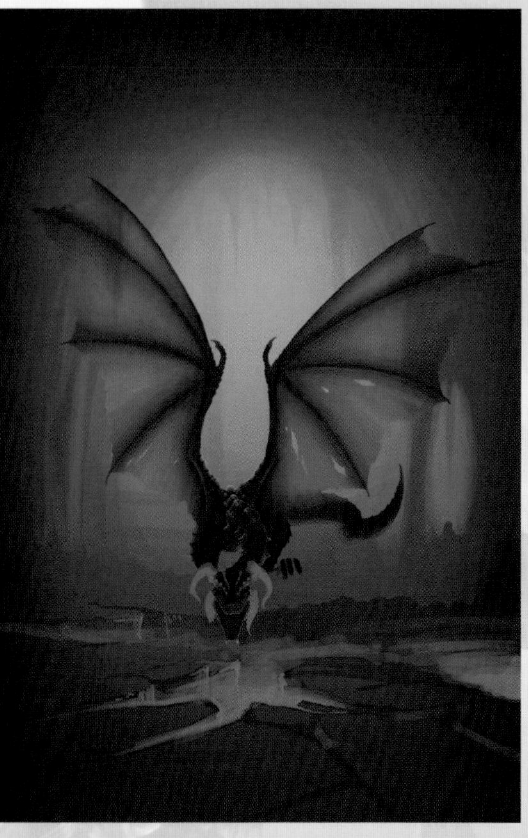

SAMPLE STEP 3. The background is given more atmosphere by blending some warmer foreground tones into the cooler colours used in the background. The dragon is given some first pass key and backlighting.

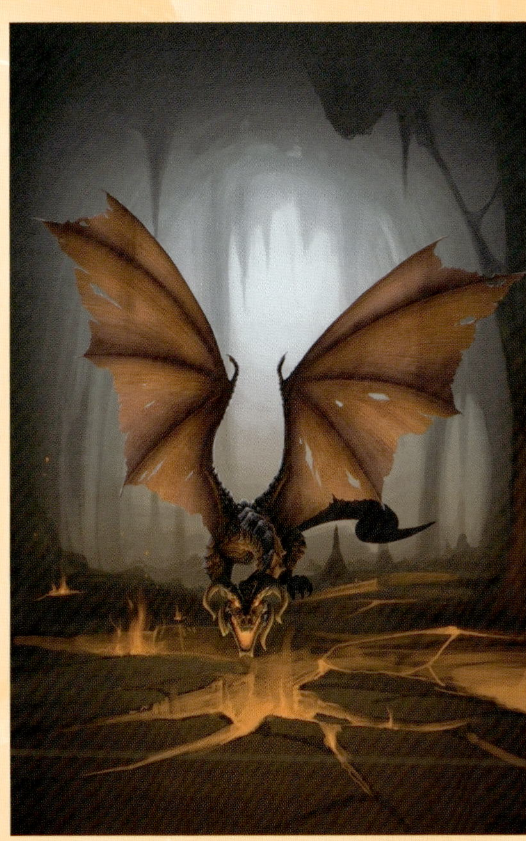

Sample Step 4. Lighting in the background and on the dragon is defined further. Texture is added to the cavern in the foreground and the fire detailing begins.

Finishing Touches. The blues in the background have some orange added to them which warms up the entire scene nicely. The fire is given more heat by adding bright yellow to the centres and saturated orange glows around it. The dragon's lighting is completed and the horns and other details on the head are redesigned to give the dragon a more streamlined appearance.

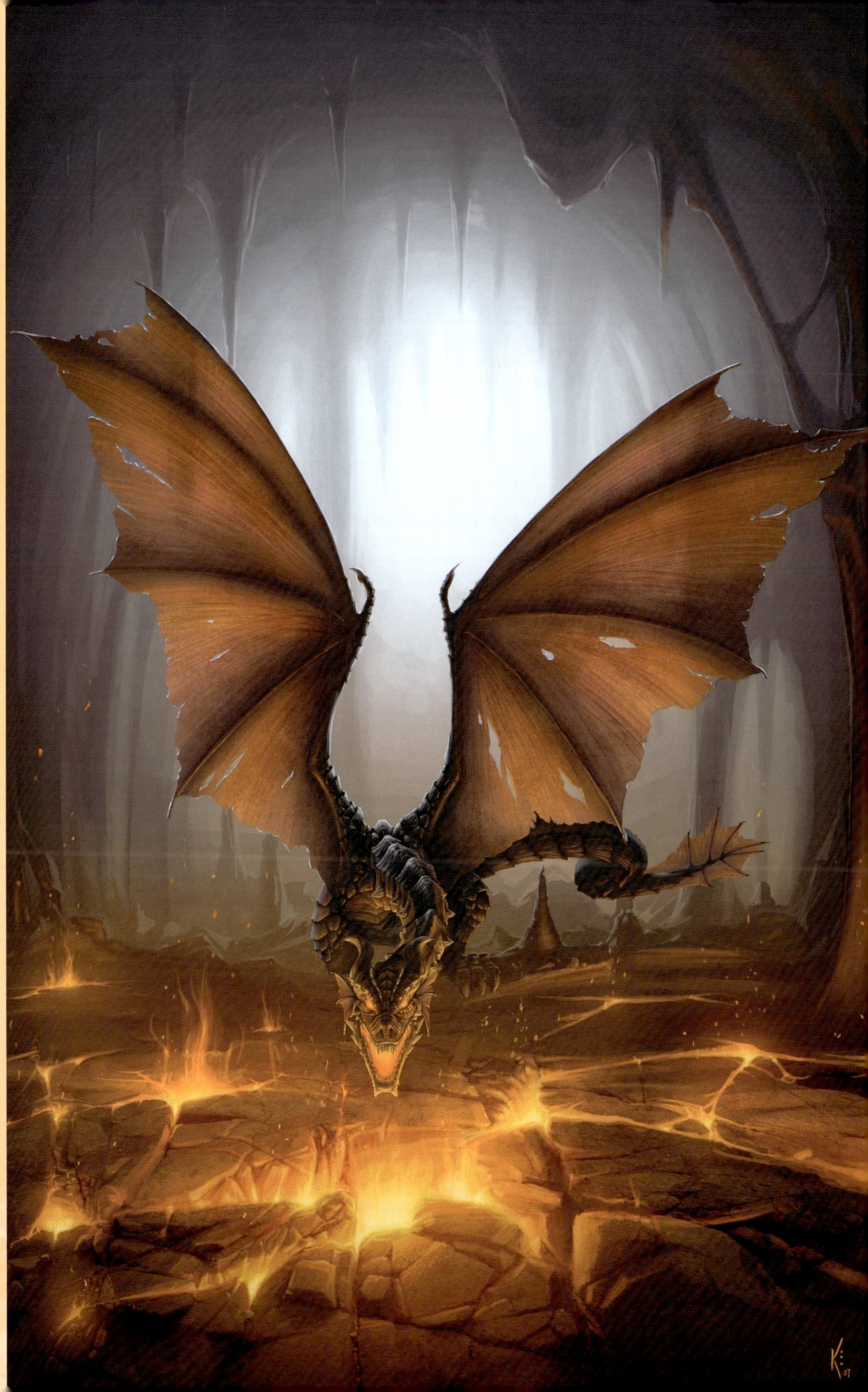

DRAGON SLAYER by Kris Eggleston
© Kris Eggleston 2007 · Digital media: Photoshop
Kris has been working as a professional artist for around 12 years. He is currently employed as a 3D Modeller, Texture Artist and Concept Artist in Ottawa, Canada.
www.kriseggleston.com

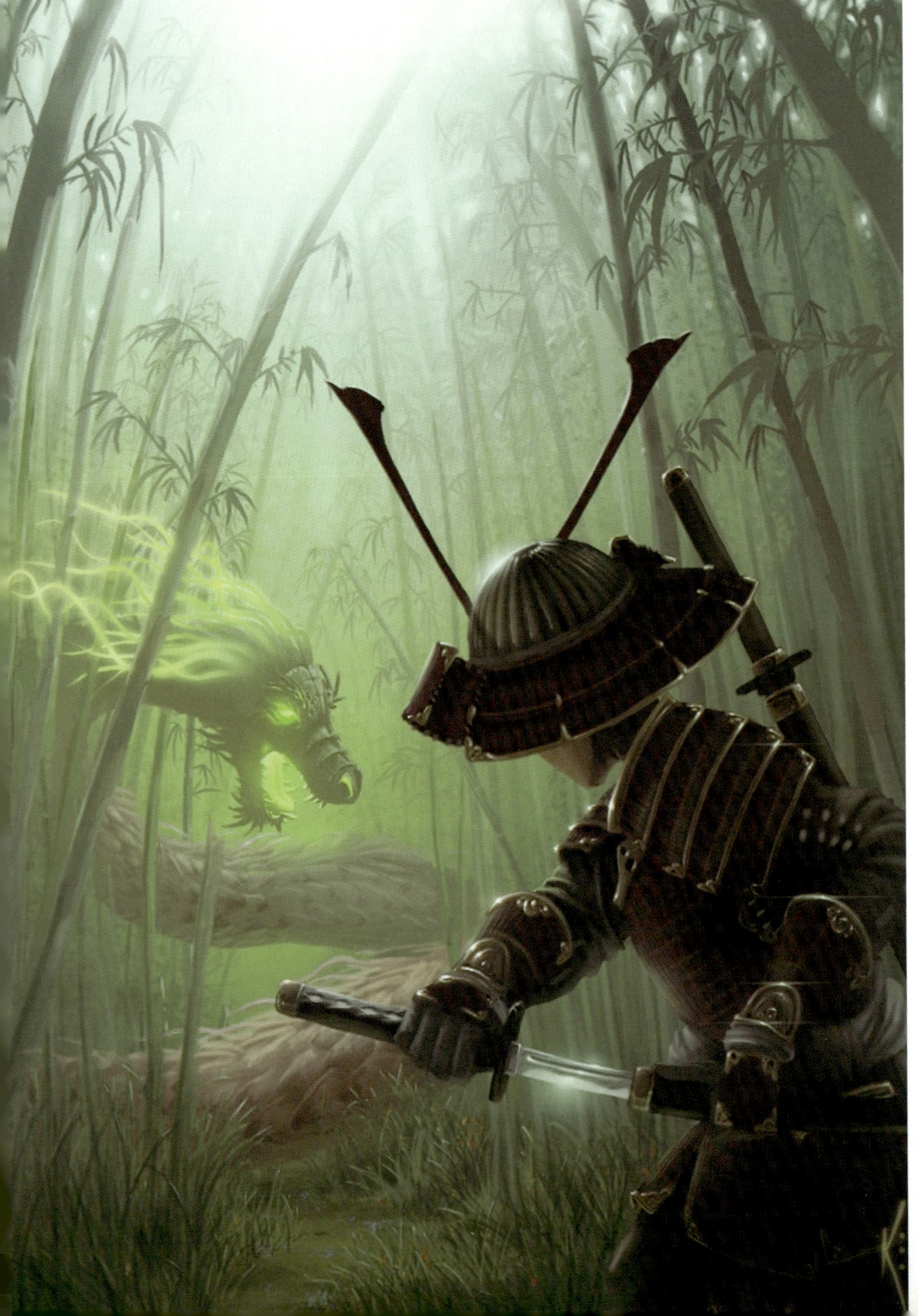

popular among the readership, and others wrote in criticizing Lovecraft's criticism, with one response written as a short poem. Lovecraft responded himself in verse, and what we might in this day and age consider a bizarre flame war ensued, with both detractors and supporters of Lovecraft all chipping in. By the close of the year, the letters page had become something of a feature in itself and, at the beckoning of the magazine, the campaign was brought to a close. However, Edward F. Daas, editor with the United Amateur Press Association, had been following proceedings and invited Lovecraft to join in 1914.

This gave the young recluse a purpose in life once more and ended his period of seclusion. It also rekindled his childhood love of bizarre storytelling, and would eventually lead to close correspondence with young Robert E. Howard.

A Host of Characters

In 1925, a 19-year-old Robert Howard made his first successful submission to *Weird Tales* – just one of the titles which were springing up in this growing industry of popular cheap magazines – an industry that gave him his avenue to pursue writing. It was a prehistory-set tale called *Spear and Fang*. His stories regularly appeared in the publication for the rest of his life.

LUNAR MAGIC by Anne Stokes
© Anne Stokes 2008 · Digital media: Photoshop
Commissioned by Enchanted Tree for the 'Here be Dragons' set of greetings cards.
www.annestokes.com

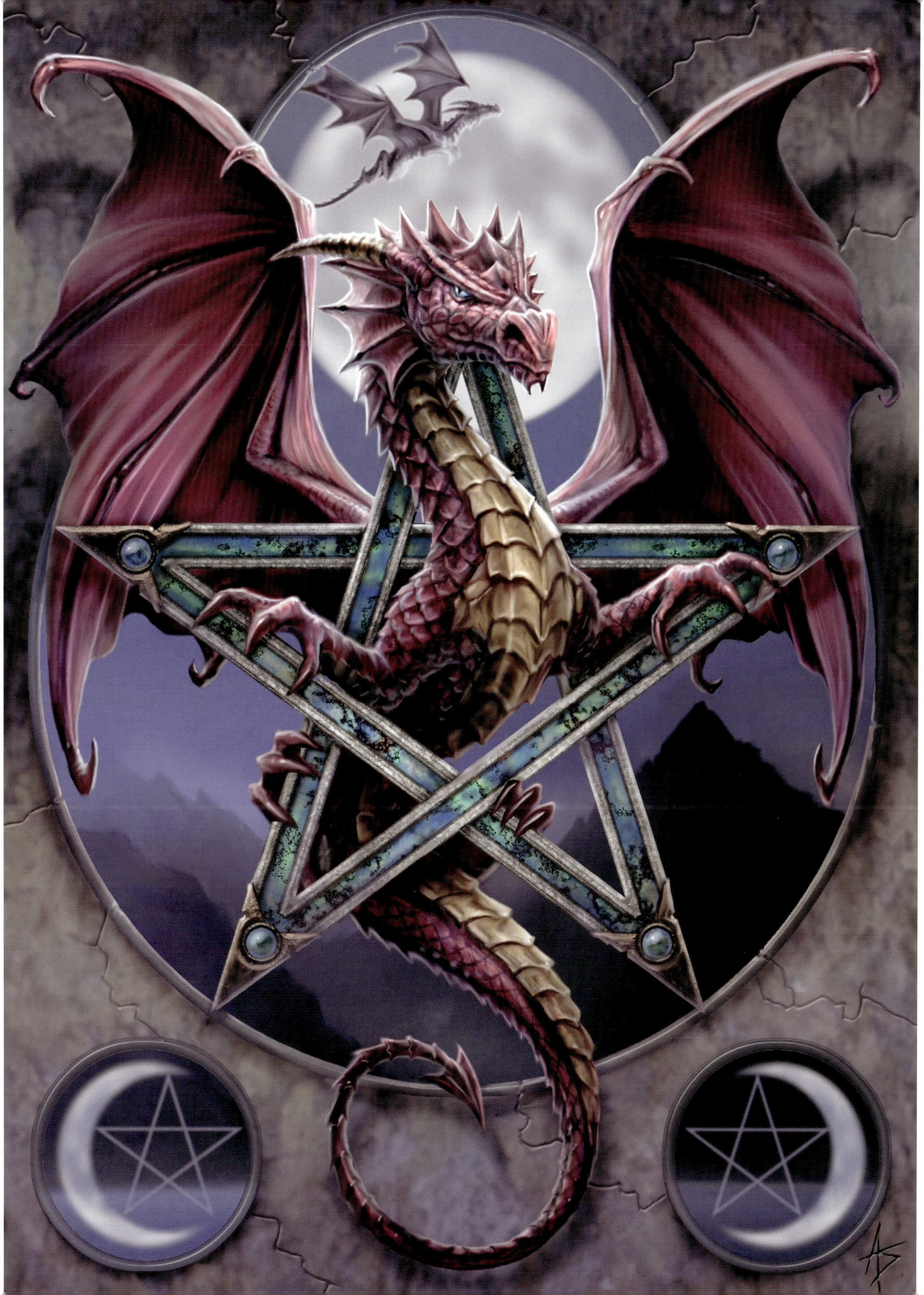

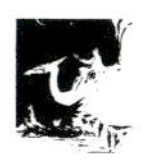

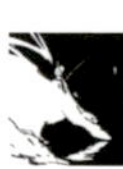

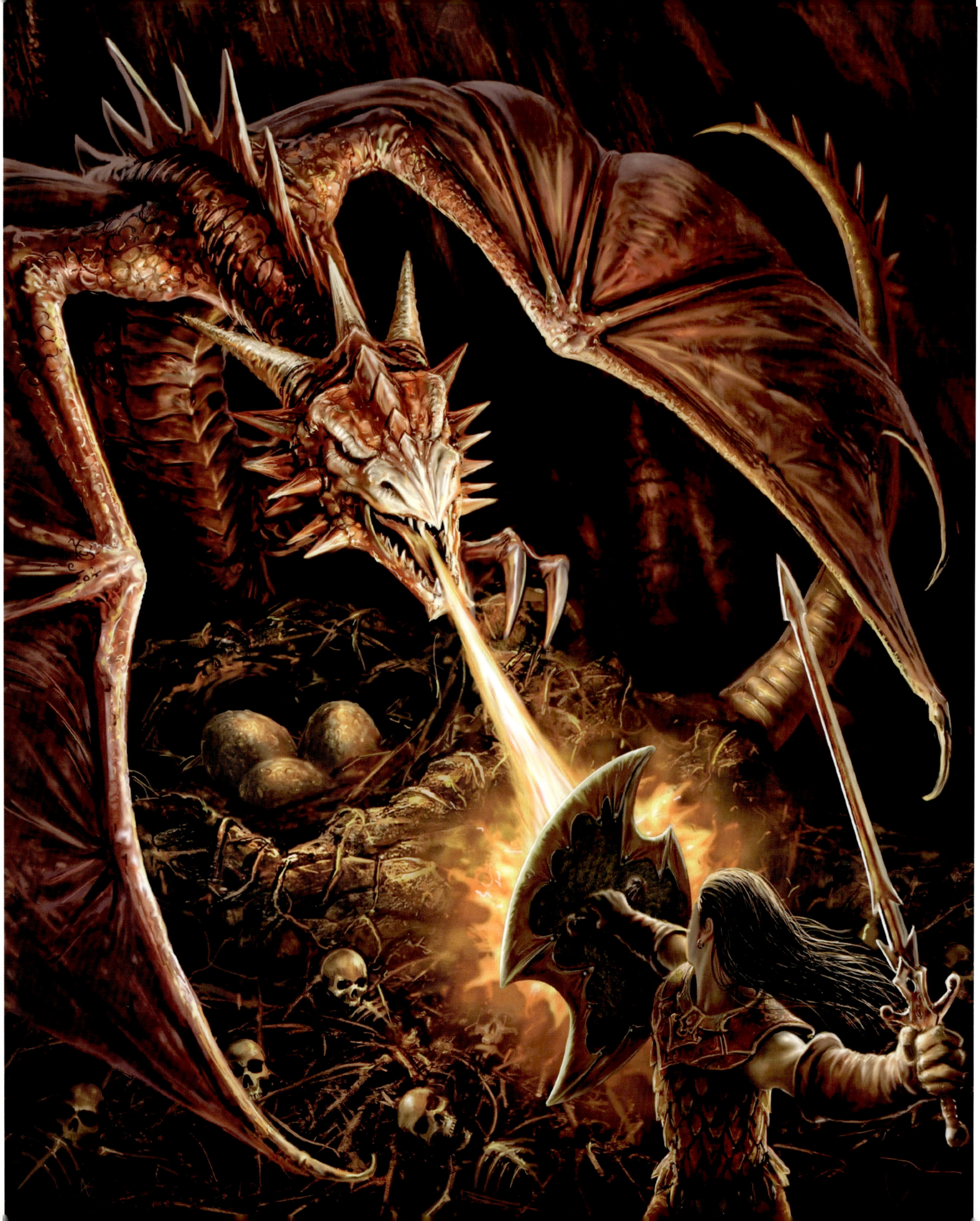

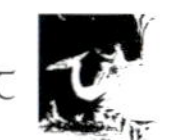

DRAGON'S NEST by Anne Stokes
© Anne Stokes 2006 · Digital media: Photoshop
The painting was originally commissioned for a t-shirt by Spiral and has since appeared on a variety of products including card sleeves by Max Protection Deck Armor.
www.annestokes.com

He created plenty of other characters: the Pictish king Bran Mak Morn, Elizabethan swashbuckler Solomon Kane, and King Kull (not to be confused with the DC Comics character of the same name; Howard's character was also known as Kull of Atlantis or Kull the Conqueror), the central character in what many consider a true work of sword and sorcery, *The Shadow Kingdom* of 1929. While Kull is full of the carnage that is associated with or expected of the genre, complete with the setting on an Earth that may have been, Kull is also quite an introspective character. His stories are regarded as a high point of Howard's writing, but many of the Kull stories did not actually make it to publication.

The Birth of Conan

Circa 1932, Howard rewrote a Kull tale, *By This Axe I Rule!*, to feature the imaginary world of Cimmeria, with its central character, a barbarian called Conan. The story, re-christened as *The Phoenix On The Sword*, was the first ever Conan story and it appeared in *Weird Tales* in December 1932.

FIRE BREATHER by Anne Stokes
© Anne Stokes 2007 · Digital media: Photoshop
This painting was originally commissioned by Max Protection Deck Armor.
www.annestokes.com

Rusty Burke quotes Howard in a letter, saying of Conan, 'While I don't go so far as to believe that stories are inspired by actually existent spirits or powers (though I am rather opposed to flatly denying anything) I have sometimes wondered if it were possible that unrecognized forces of the past or present – or even the future – work through the thoughts and actions of living men. This occurred to me when I was writing the first stories of the

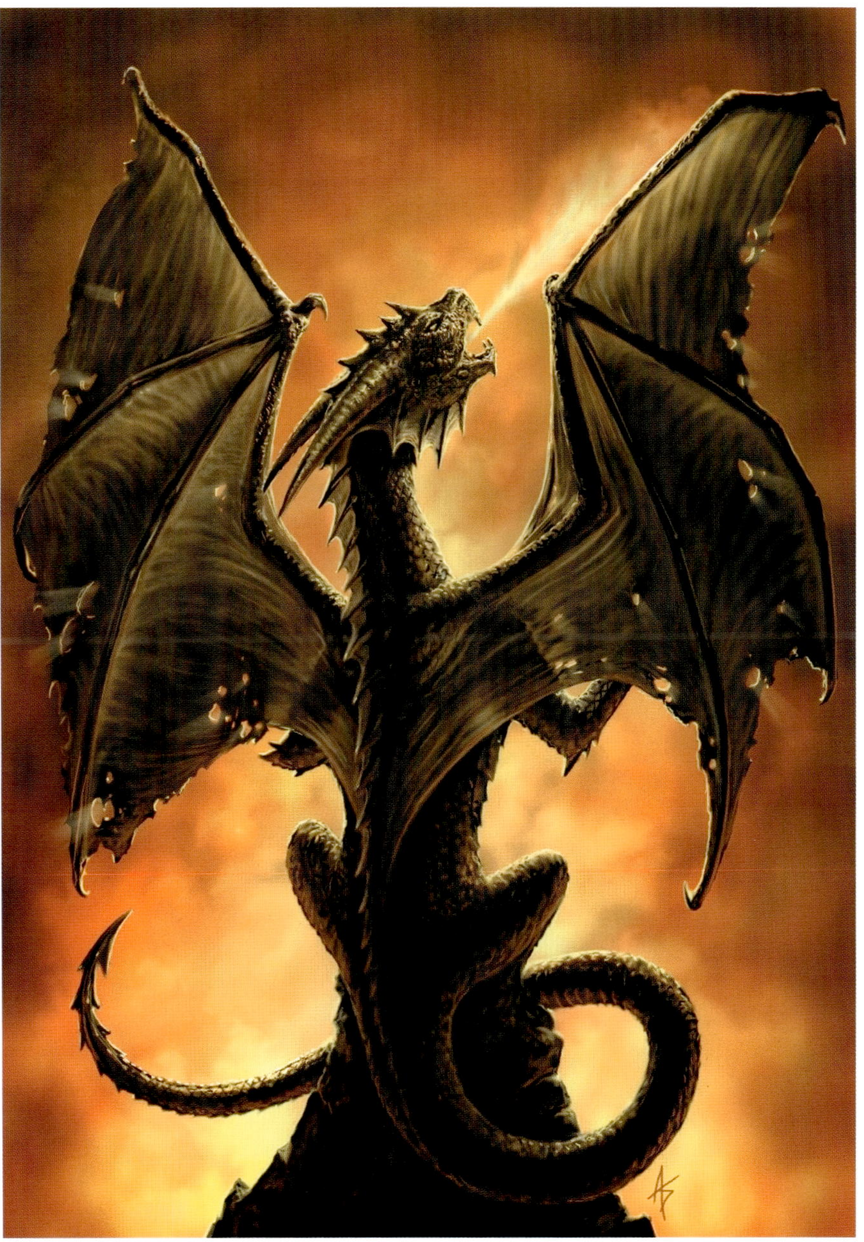

Blue Dragon by Anne Stokes

© Anne Stokes 2006; Digital media: Photoshop; Commissioned by US gaming company Wizards of the Coast for an internal illustration in one of their *Dungeons and Dragons* rulebooks; www.annestokes.com

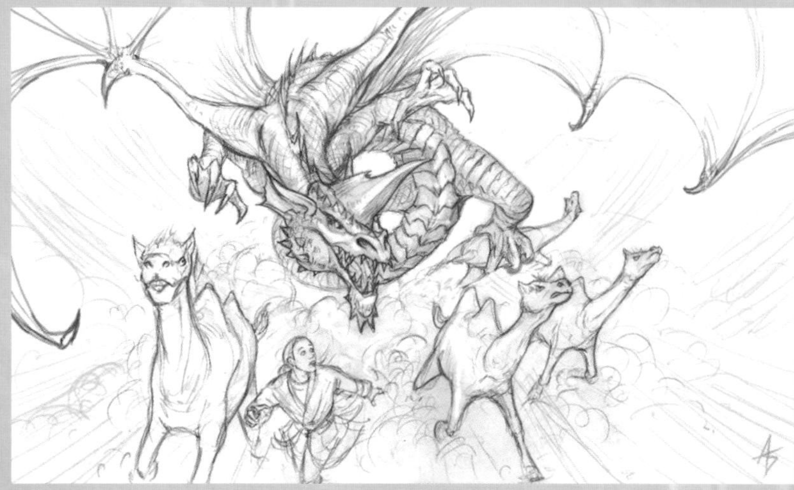

SAMPLE STEP 1. With the brief in mind I produced a pencil sketch to show the art director. Once this had been approved I scanned it into my computer to paint digitally using Photoshop and a Wacom graphic tablet and pen.

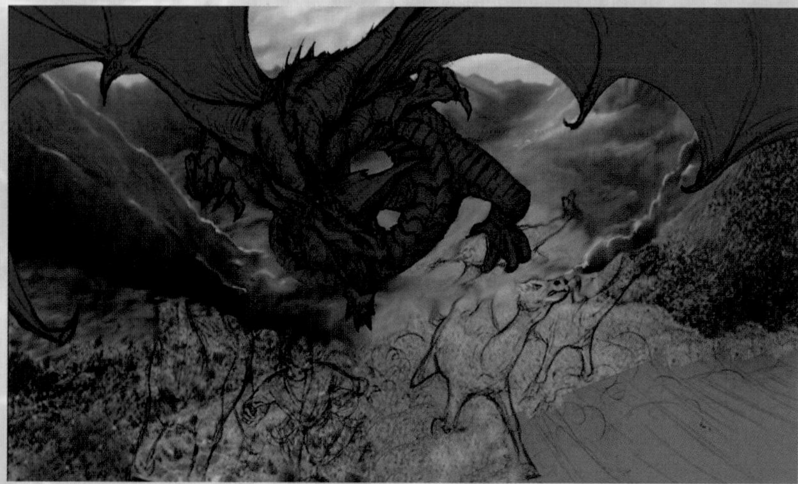

SAMPLE STEP 2. I work on different layers so that they can be easily altered and moved independently of each other. In the first stage of the painting, I blocked in the dark blue colour of the dragon and began to colour the background.

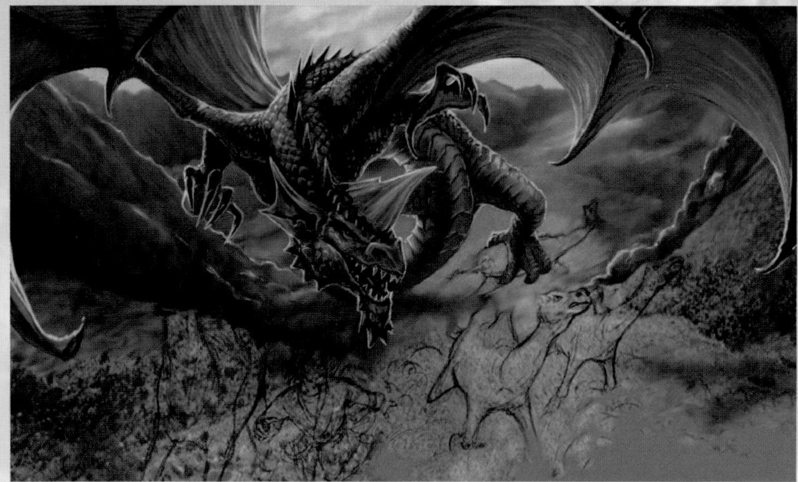

SAMPLE STEP 3. Once the basic colours were established I moved on to adding more details to the dragon.

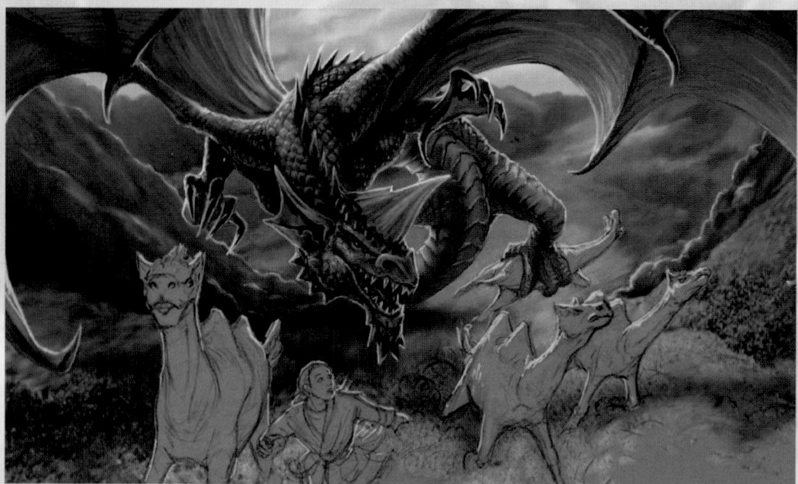

SAMPLE STEP 4. I then began on the foreground layer of the camels and fleeing figure.

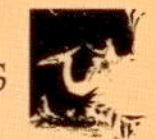

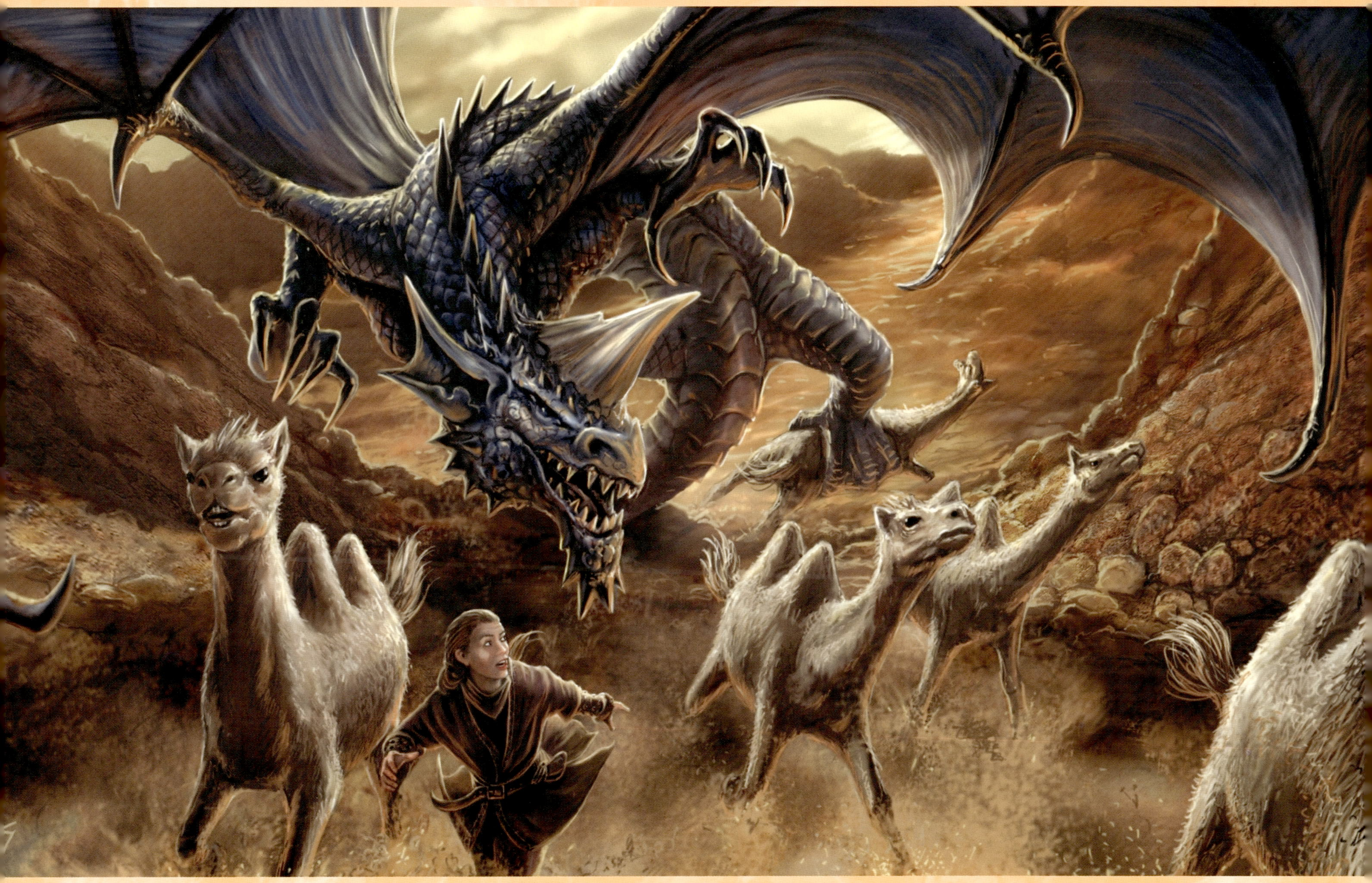

FINISHING TOUCHES. The final image has the details finished off and some sand being kicked up. I also decided to add one more camel on the right – although you can only see part of its body I felt that it added to the sense of the subjects moving towards the viewer and therefore the drama of the scene.

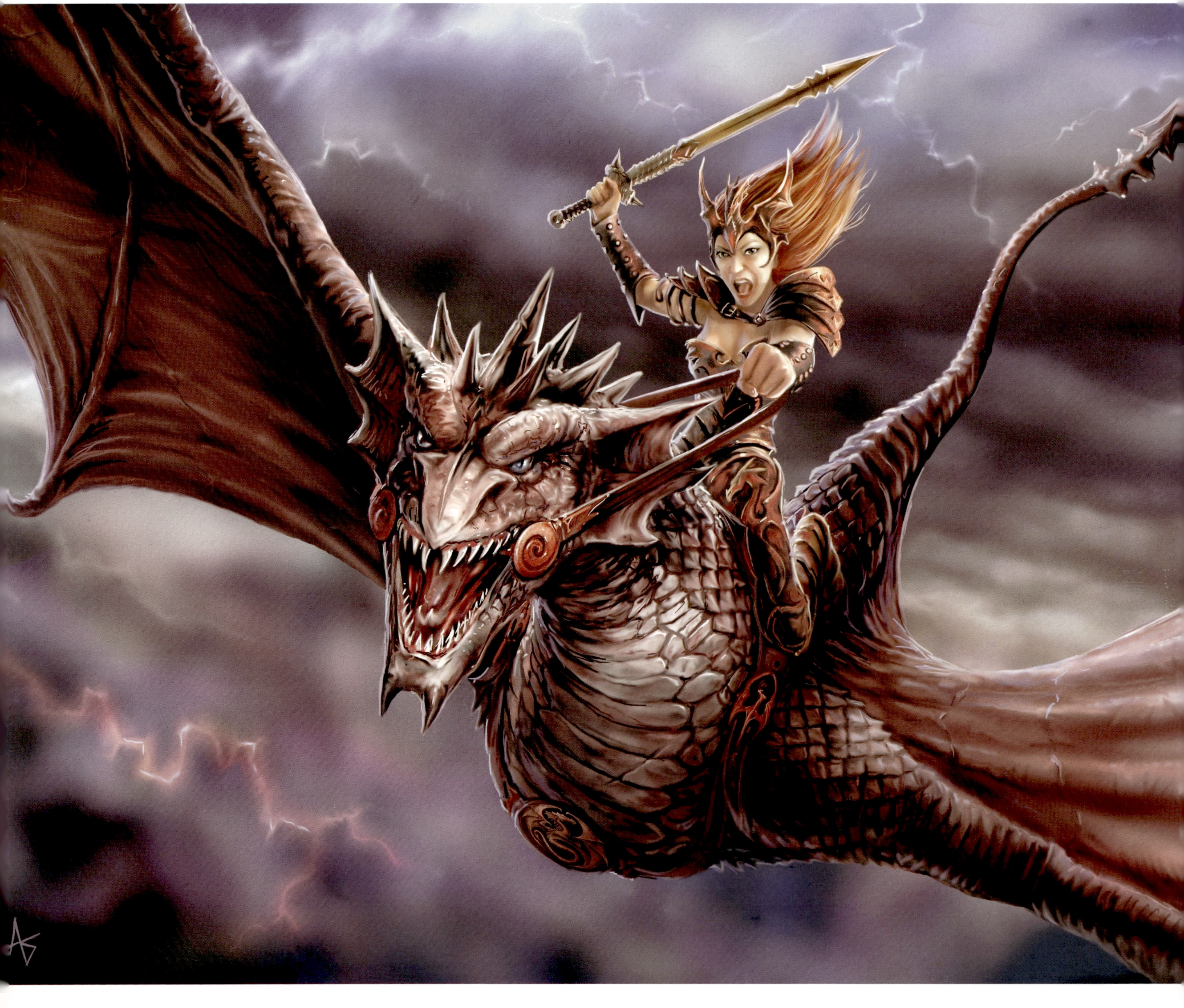

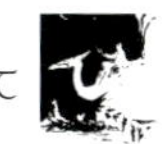

Conan series especially. I know that for months I had been unable to work up anything sellable. Then the man Conan seemed suddenly to grow up in my mind without much labour on my part and immediately a stream of stories flowed off my pen – or rather, off my typewriter – almost without effort on my part. I did not seem to be creating, but rather relating events that had occurred. Episode crowded on episode so fast that I could scarcely keep up with them. For weeks I did nothing but write of the adventures of Conan. The character took complete possession of my mind and crowded out everything else in the way of story-writing.'

There was much Conan to come, including *Conan The Conqueror* in 1935, which was a full-length tale that fleshed out the land of Cimmeria in more detail, in his mythical Hyborian age, as Howard imagined it.

Howard's mother slid into an irreversible coma in 1936, and the 30-year-old writer decided it was a good time to act on a promise he had made previously not to outlive her. He went into his car and shot himself in the head, dying some eight hours later.

Influential Dragons of Literature & Legend

It is an exaggeration to claim that Tolkien wrote the rulebook on fantasy fiction, but both *The Hobbit* and *The Lord Of The Rings* set the standard. It is not so much the action that takes place as it is the scenes the author sets up that enthrall and engross. And it is Smaug, the arch enemy of all that is good and decent in the world, that is perhaps the dragon of all dragons.

The Formidable Smaug

Smaug is a dastardly creature, introduced in the text as 'a most special greedy, strong and wicked worm'. He has driven the dwarves from Lonely Mountain and stolen their gold, ruling the area with evil for nearly two centuries before the action takes place. His personality is painstakingly constructed, with the reader really getting to grips with just how terrifying he is. Smaug says of himself, 'I kill where I wish and none dare resist. I laid low the warriors of old and their like is not in the world today.' He adds, 'My armour is like tenfold shields, my teeth are swords, my claws spears, the shock of my tail a thunderbolt, my wings a hurricane, and my breath death!'

But Smaug is not invincible. While he has one particular vulnerability, which is exploited by the archer Bard who kills him, it is his arrogance and laziness that are really his undoing. He finds it incomprehensible that the dwarves he has cheated out of their riches might come back for revenge and he is introduced napping on his treasure. He flies into a rage when Bilbo Baggins shows that he might manage to get the better of him. Smaug is simply a masterpiece of fiction.

DRAGON RIDER by Anne Stokes
© Magazine Exchange · Digital media: Photoshop
This painting was commissioned by Magazine Exchange for use on card sleeves.
www.annestokes.com

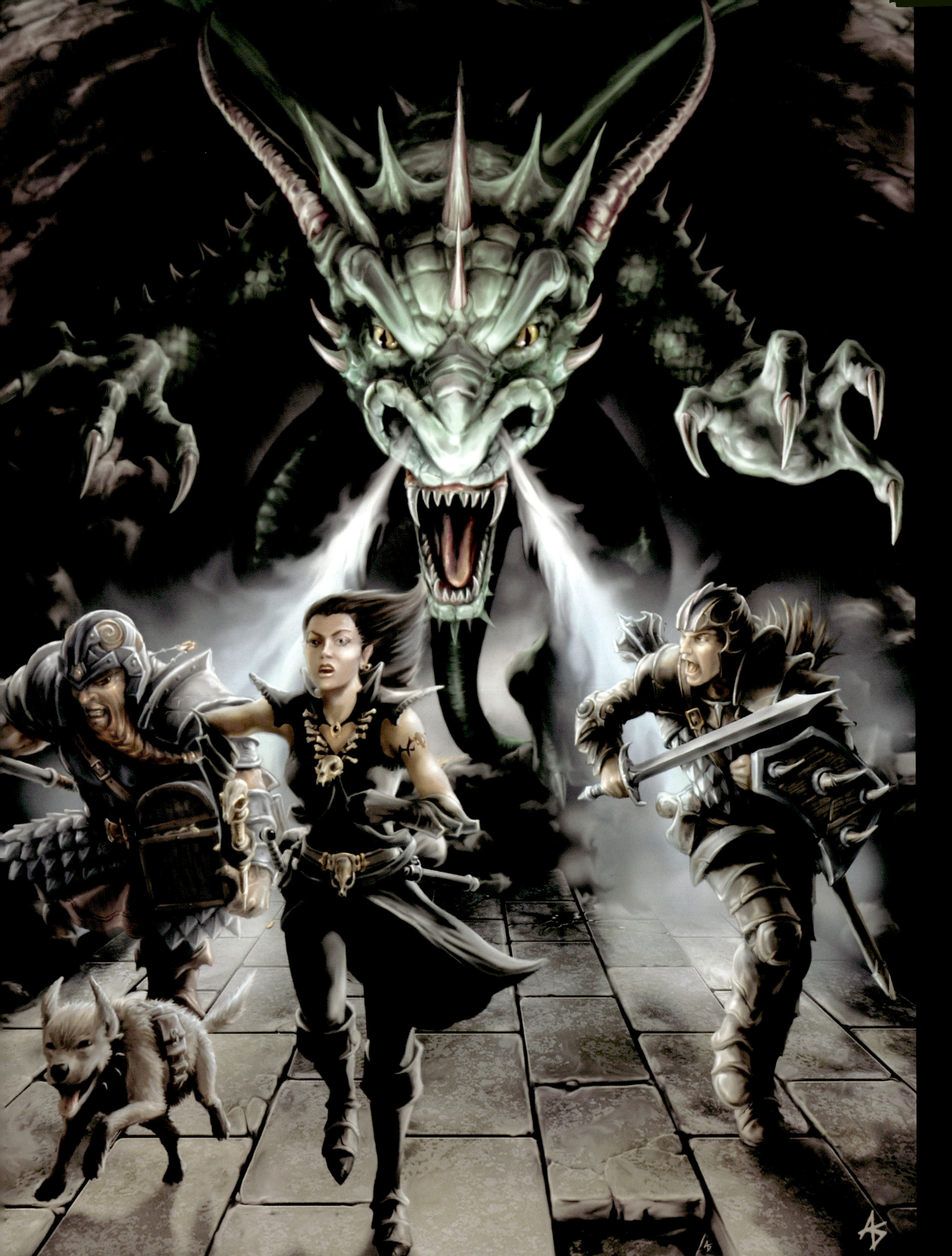

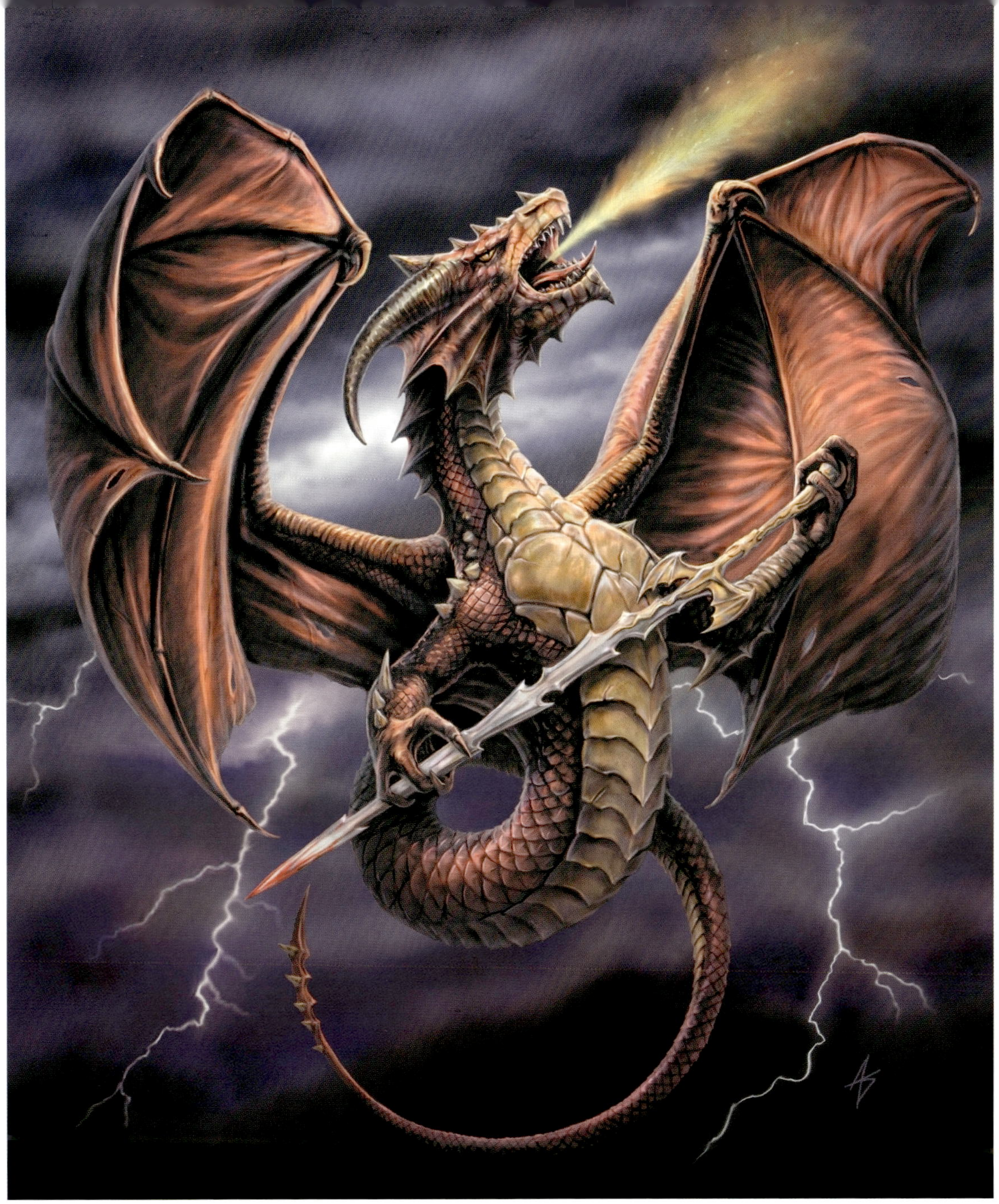

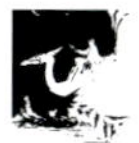

Fafnir: Norse Dragon

Given Tolkien's background, it is not difficult to see the influence of the tales of Sigurd from old Norse mythology – several variations of which formed part of young Ronald's home education – particularly the *Volsunga Saga*, which concerns the reluctant hero Sigurd, who is recruited to rescue a hoard of gold from the evil dragon Fafnir.

Essentially, Sigurd's father Sigmund dies after a misjudged attack on the god Odin. In the throes of death, Sigmund is able to tell his wife Hiordis that she will have a son, and leaves him the fragments of his shattered sword. Hiordis gives birth to Sigurd and marries King Alf. After some time, Hiordis sends Sigurd to the smith Regin, as ward. Regin, however, is something of a disreputable character. He and his brother Fafnir have previously killed their father, Hreidmar, to get their hands on a stash of gold he has plundered from Andvari the dwarf. However, Fafnir has transformed himself into a dragon and kept the gold for himself.

Regin seeks to get his stepson to kill Fafnir so that he may recapture the gold. Sigurd eventually agrees to the task after Regin forges him a mighty sword, which splits an anvil without shattering. Regin has his stepson dig a pit and hide beneath, sword in hand. As Fafnir leaves his cave for water, Sigurd despatches

RUN AWAY! by Anne Stokes
© Anne Stokes 2006 · Digital media: Photoshop
This image has been used on various products and a red version of just the dragon in the tunnel is a t-shirt and card sleeve design under the name Unleashed.
www.annestokes.com

VICTORIOUS by Anne Stokes
© Anne Stokes 2005 · Digital media: Photoshop
This painting is the cover image for the 2009 Dragon calendar that Anne has done with US publisher Llewellyn.
www.annestokes.com

Fafnir by stabbing him from beneath. Regin asks Sigurd to roast the beast's heart. However, when he is cooking the organ, Sigurd checks its condition by sticking a finger in it, and then popping said digit into his mouth. Through this action, he finds he is able to understand the language of birds, whose chirping reveals that the plot is a setup: Regin, his foster father, is planning his death. So the sword is wielded anew, and Regin literally loses his head. Sigurd then takes the treasure and sets off on adventures new.

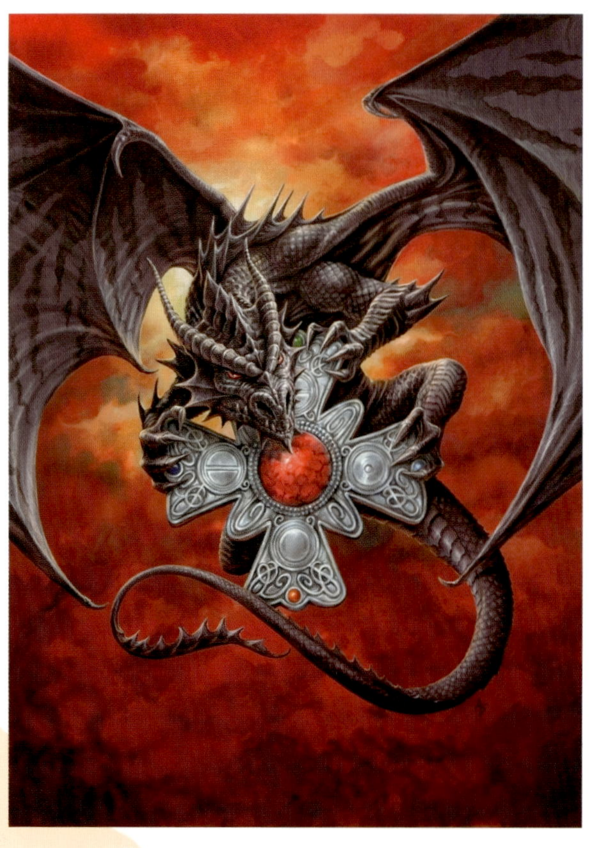

Beowulf's Dragon

Tolkien was, of course, an eminent scholar of such legends, including the legend of Beowulf. And in Beowulf, too, there are echoes of the hobbits' quest. After becoming king of the Geats, Beowulf learns that his kingdom is being terrorized at night by a massive and rather nasty dragon. Beowulf has in his youth slain both the ogre Grendel (by ripping his arm off with his bare hands) and Grendel's vengeful mother. But the Beowulf who takes on the dragon is an old man.

It is revealed that the dragon has been guarding a treasure trove quite peacefully for centuries, but one of Beowulf's subjects has unfortunately enraged it by stealing a single flagon, not unlike an action undertaken by Bilbo Baggins in *The Hobbit*, which sends Smaug into his final paroxysm. Beowulf attempts to take the dragon on by himself, but is mortally wounded. All but one of the retainers flee and hide, with only the young Wiglaf to help him. Wiglaf, with the help of the dying Beowulf, manages to stab the dragon under its jaw, killing it.

St George and the Dragon

It is actually a common motif in Western mythology. There is a dragon, it has gold, it terrifies the locals, a hero is selected to kill it. The dragon lives somewhere remote and so inspires a quest: it is true of Gilgamesh and Enkidu as they seek to slay Humbaba (not necessarily a dragon, but certainly a terrific monster who is described in a not too dissimilar way from Smaug) or Bilbo Baggins. St George's myth is perhaps not quite as much of a quest; in fact, for most of the story, George is not actually there.

According to the legend, St George's dragon is more of a scaly extortionist than a vainglorious and mighty creature. It lives in a marsh on the outskirts of town, controlling access in and out. The dragon breathes noxious vapour that overcomes all who breathe it, and will only desist from spreading its malodorous

CURSE OF ARASTOLD by Anne Stokes
 · Traditional media: acrylic on board
This painting was originally commissioned as a novel cover for *The Curse of Arastold* by Jo Whitemore, published by Llewellyn.
www.annestokes.com

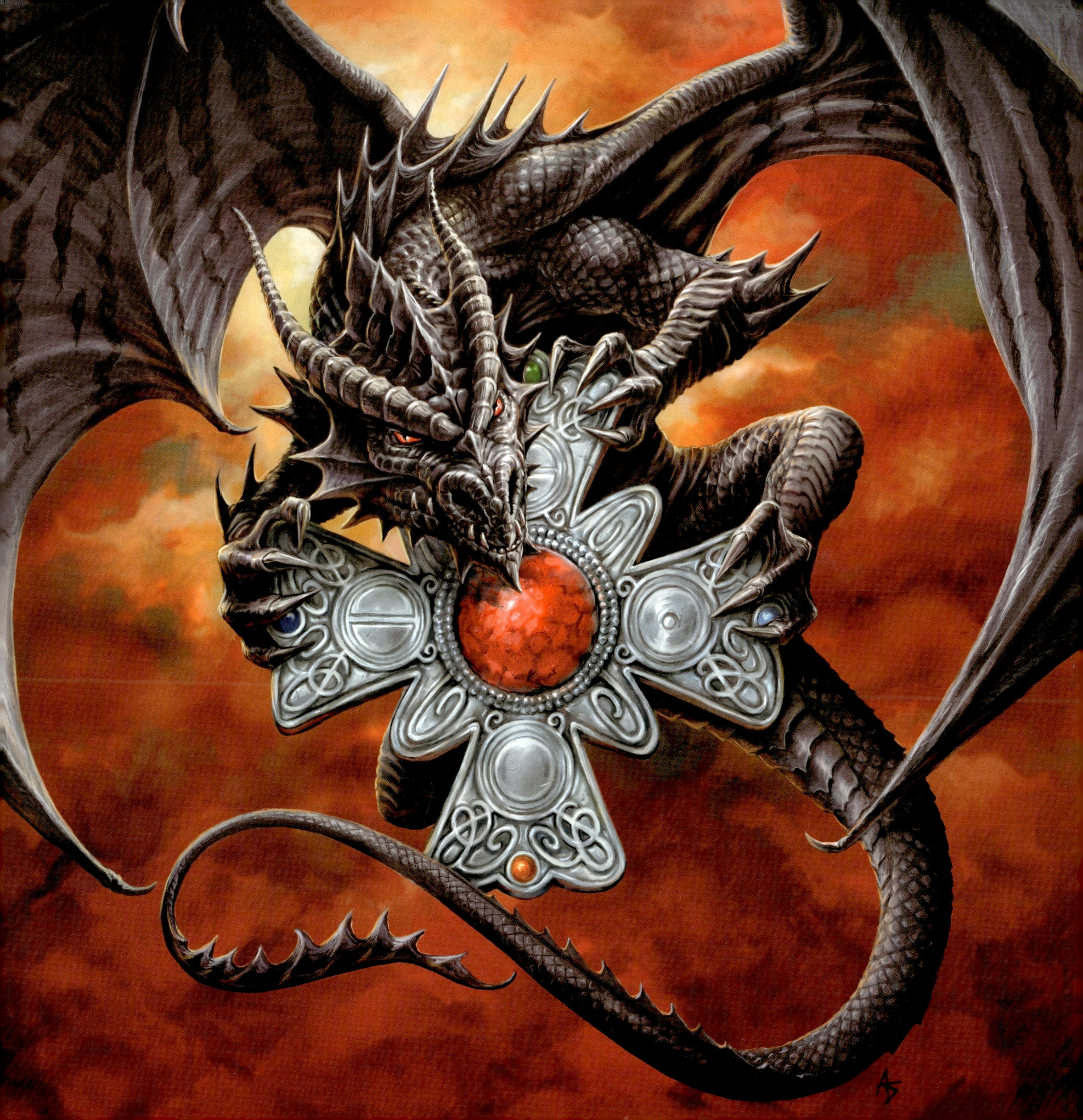

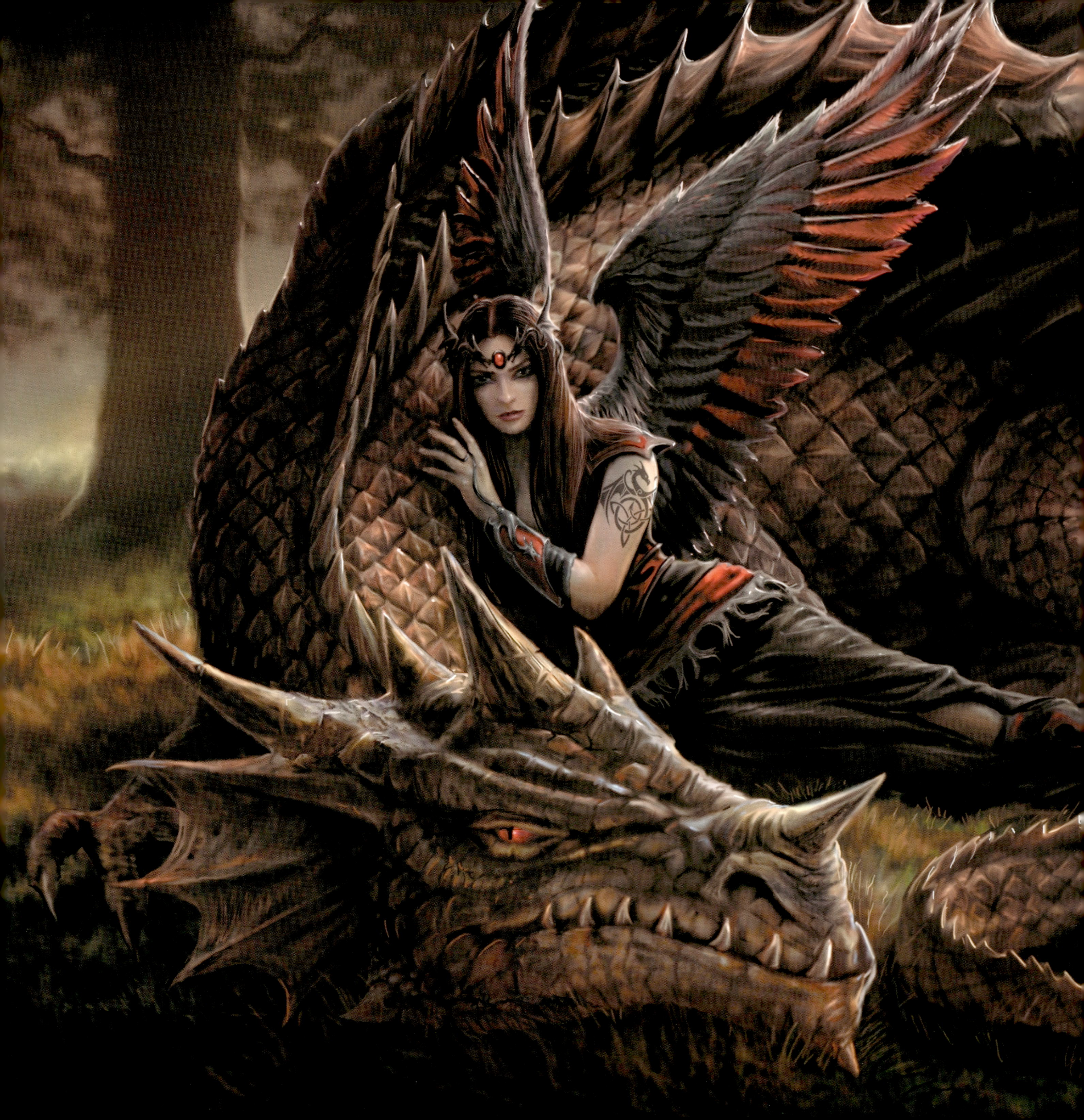

 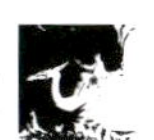

exhalation if it is supplied with a meal of two sheep a day. The king orders that this should be done. Over time, the supply of sheep runs low, and knight after knight volunteers to go and slay the creature; most succumb to the fumes very quickly and expire.

When the sheep finally run out and the town is on the brink of starvation, the king tries to negotiate with the dragon anew. However, the dragon demands a meal of one child a day to leave the town unmolested. So the people cast lots every day to select which child should be left outside the city walls for the dragon to devour. Finally, the day comes when the king's own daughter is selected, a fate which she accepts graciously. It goes without saying that the king's daughter is a very attractive young lady; and, as she is waiting for the dragon, up rides a very noble and attractive knight who decides he cannot simply leave such a beautiful young girl outside the city walls to be devoured by a dragon.

She tells him to leave her to her fate, but he refuses. And then the dragon appears, belching forth its noxious fumes, fire coming from its eyes. The knight engages the dragon for a good long time and, while most other adversaries could not withstand the poisonous breath, this knight, though weary, seems to hold fast through the smoke and fug. So long is the fight, with the knight thrusting his lance uselessly into the iron-plate-like scales, that he notices there is but one spot that the dragon tries to protect, just beneath its left wing. So the knight aims there, finally

WINGED COMPANIONS by Anne Stokes
© Anne Stokes 2008 · Digital media: Photoshop
The scene was a lot of fun to paint. An angel and a dragon relax together in a sunlit glade.
www.annestokes.com

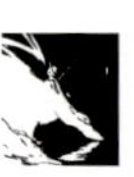

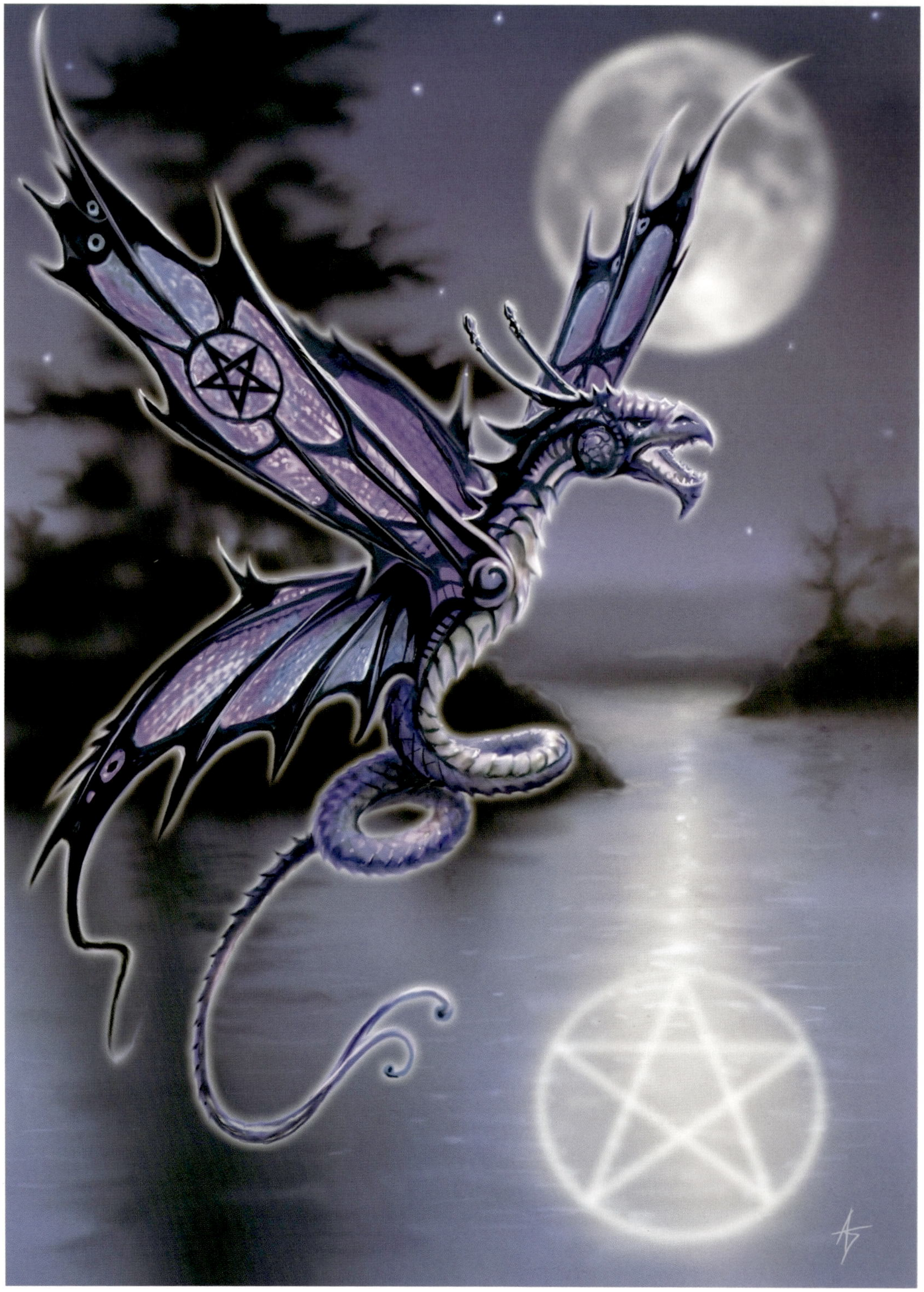

Spiny Woodland Hopper by Anne Stokes
© Anne Stokes 2007 · Digital media: Photoshop
This little dragon makes an appearance in Anne's 2009 Dragon calendar published by Llewellyn and also in Enchanted Tree's 'Here be Dragons' card range.
www.annestokes.com

landing a blow and bringing the dragon down. The dragon is badly wounded but not dead. The knight and the princess lead the dragon back to the town, and the knight kills it for all to see, demanding no other thanks than that the town be baptized in the name of Christ, a task he undertakes himself. That done, he heads on his way.

Sea Dragons

There are also the dragons of the sea. Leviathan is one of the most well known, featuring throughout the Old Testament. The legend of Perseus and Andromeda also features a sea-faring dragon-like figure called Cetus, said to have a canine head, a body like that of a whale, claws and a fan tail.

Dragonfly by Anne Stokes
© Anne Stokes 2007 · Digital media: Photoshop
This version of the picture was painted for Enchanted Tree's 'Here be Dragons' card range.
www.annestokes.com

In this legend, Cassiopeia, Queen of the Ethiopians, has annoyed the gods by comparing her beauty to that of the sea nymph. The enraged deities thus send a monster to attack the coast. To calm the monster down, the king, Cepheus, is advised to leave his daughter, Andromeda, on rocks near the water to be consumed

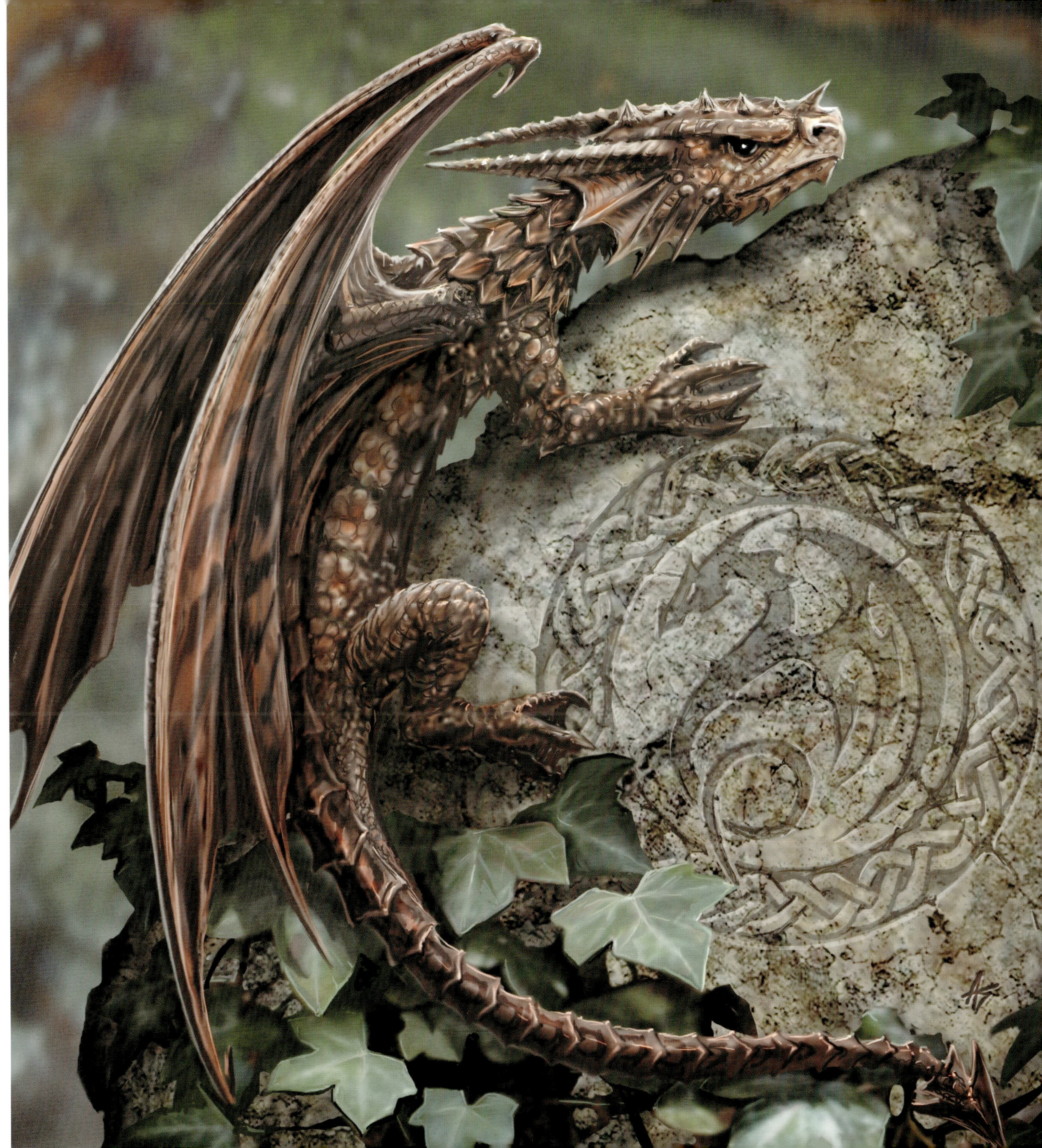

Woodland Guardian by Anne Stokes

© Anne Stokes 2008; Digital media: Photoshop; Commissioned by Enchanted Tree for the 'Here be Dragons' set of greetings cards. Also now on t-shirts and card sleeves in red tones; www.annestokes.com

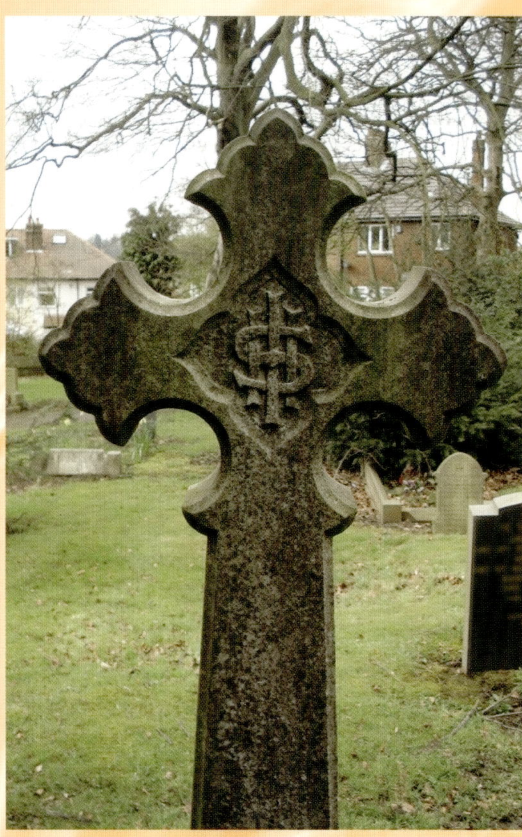

SAMPLE STEP 1. With the brief (a dragon wrapped around celtic cross) in mind I went to my local churchyard and took some photographs of different cross headstones from which to draw inspiration.

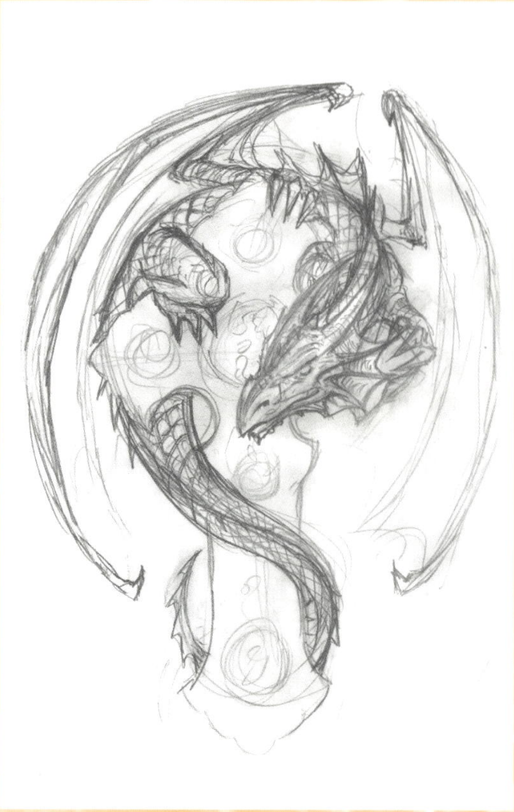

SAMPLE STEP 2. I then sketched a very rough drawing to get the layout established. I scanned this into my computer and began work on the final image. I painted this digitally using Photoshop and a Wacom graphic tablet and pen.

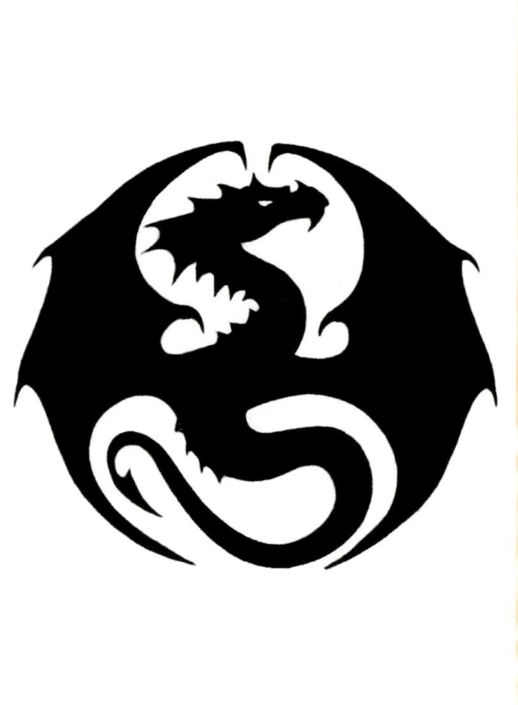

SAMPLE STEP 3. I used the reference photograph as a basis for the design of my cross and added some celtic knotwork and a dragon logo-style image that I had designed for the centre.

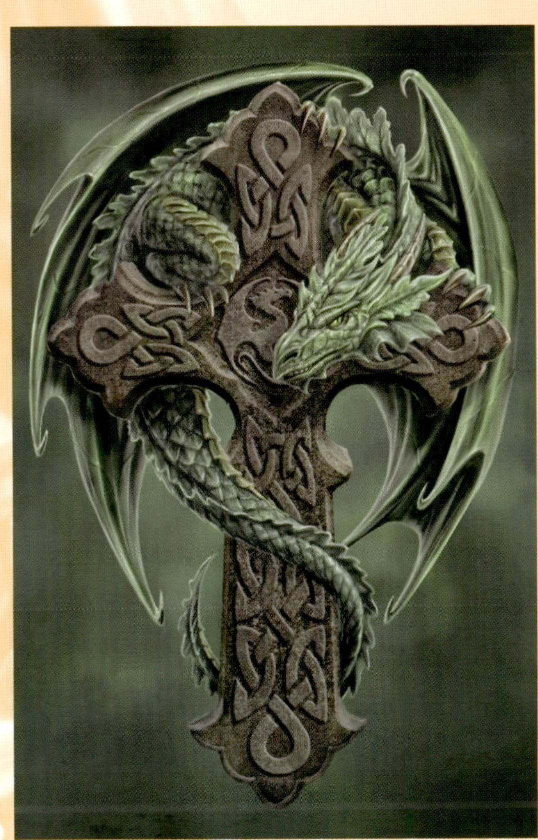

SAMPLE STEP 4. The painting was separated into three layers, the background, the cross and the dragon. I kept the background rather blurred so as to draw all the attention to the main elements of the design. I first painted all the colours and created details on the dragon's scales that would be reminiscent of leaves.

FINISHING TOUCHES. The final stage of the artwork is to add all the highlights and details and bring out more depth.

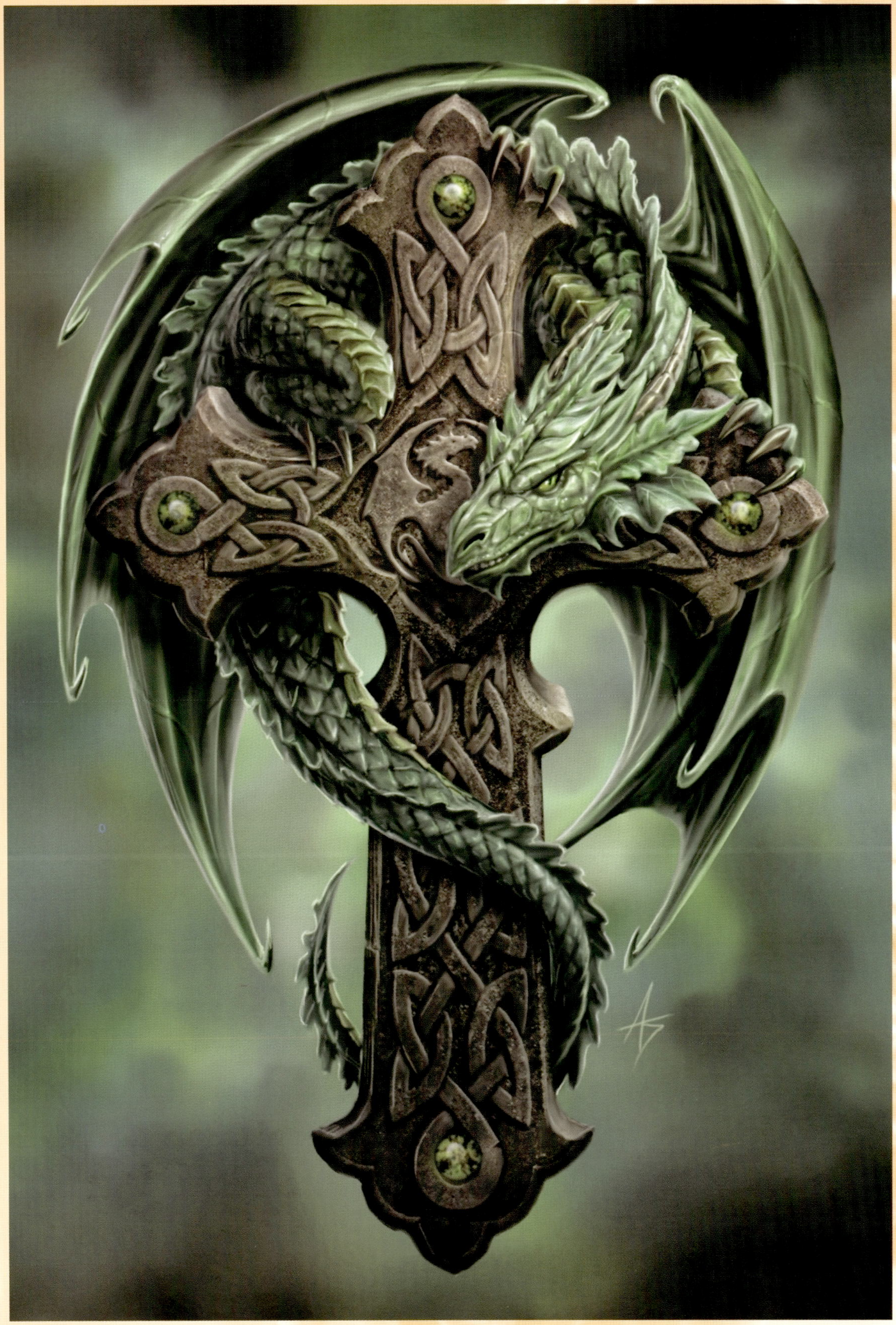

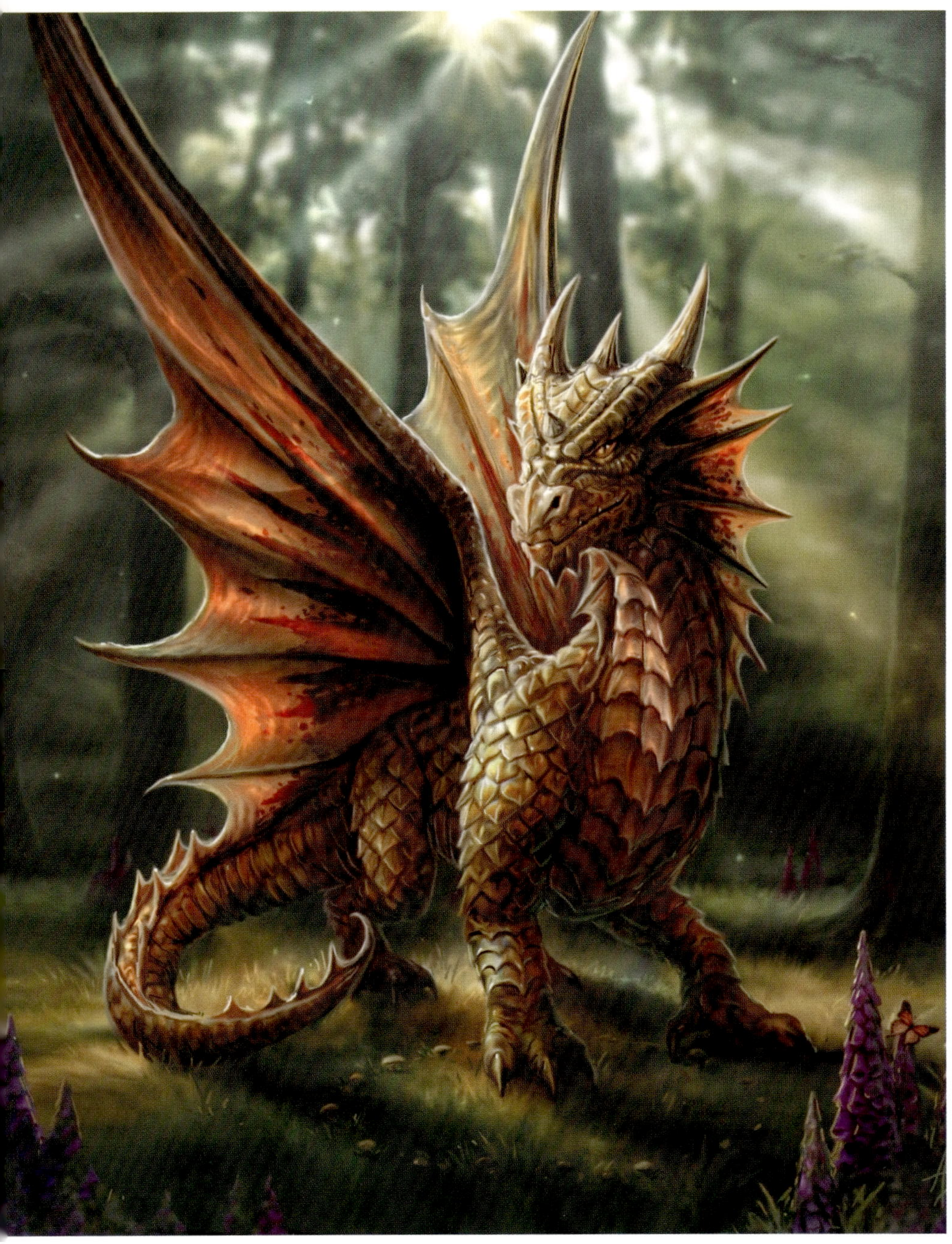

FOREST DRAGON by Anne Stokes
© Anne Stokes 2008 · Digital media: Photoshop
Anne Stokes has been a full-time freelance illustrator for 12 years. She produces artwork for the games industry, and her artworks have been licensed on a wide range of merchandise. · www.annestokes.com

BATTLE FOR THE NIGHT SKIES by Sandra Staple
© Sandra Staple 2008 · Traditional media: coloured pencil
First published in the instructional book by Sandra, *Drawing Dragons: Learn How to Create Fantastic Fire-breathing Dragons*, printed by Ulysses Press, 2008.
www.canadiandragon.com

by the beast. She is chained to the rocks and awaits her fate. Perseus, flying by, sees her there and is enchanted by her motionlessness and her beauty. He asks her why she is chained to the rocks, and she tells him, completing her tale just before the creature appears. The telling of the legend, like so many, varies. In some versions he uses the standard sword-and-stab technique. However, it is worth noting that Perseus has only just finished killing the Gorgon, the woman with a head of snakes, whose stare turns all onlookers to stone. Handily, Perseus has her severed head to hand in some tellings, which he shows to Cetus and turns him to stone before he takes Andromeda.

Dragon as Device

It is not difficult to notice a pattern as regards dragon-slaying texts. The dragon is rather like a magnifying glass to highlight the hero's virtues. He is always a wise and strong warrior who is either the pinnacle of virtue or capable of highly virtuous acts. He is unprepossessing, rarely 'doing it for the money'; honour is usually more important. He may have an eye for the ladies, but he is never rapacious and libidinous.

The dragon is the polar opposite. He is greedy, lazy, vengeful, short-tempered, avaricious, vicious and, rather than merely having

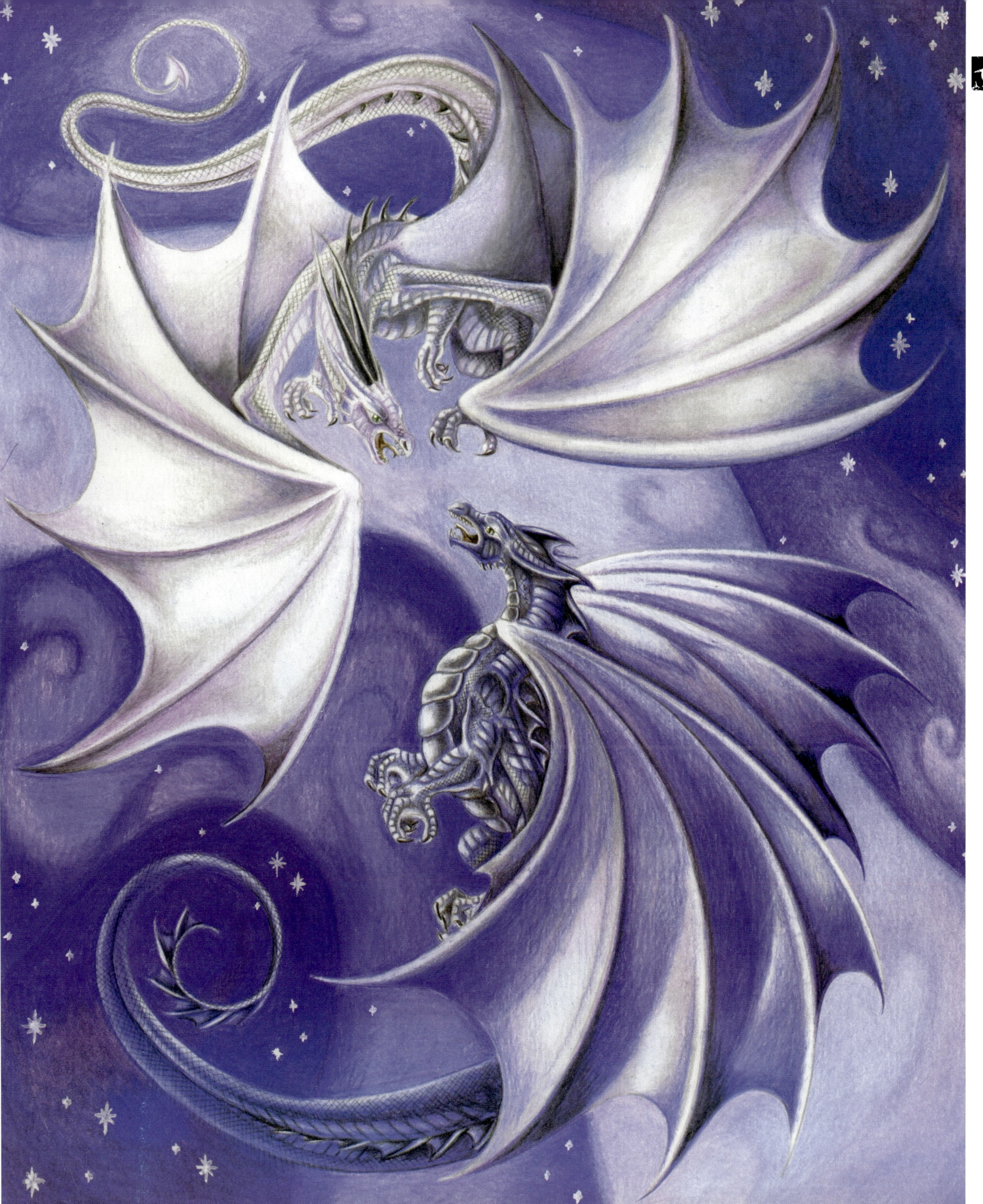

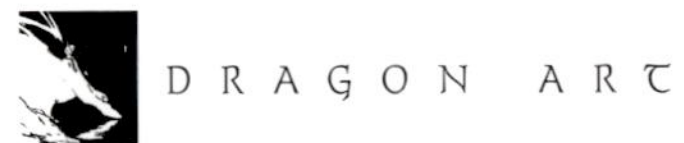

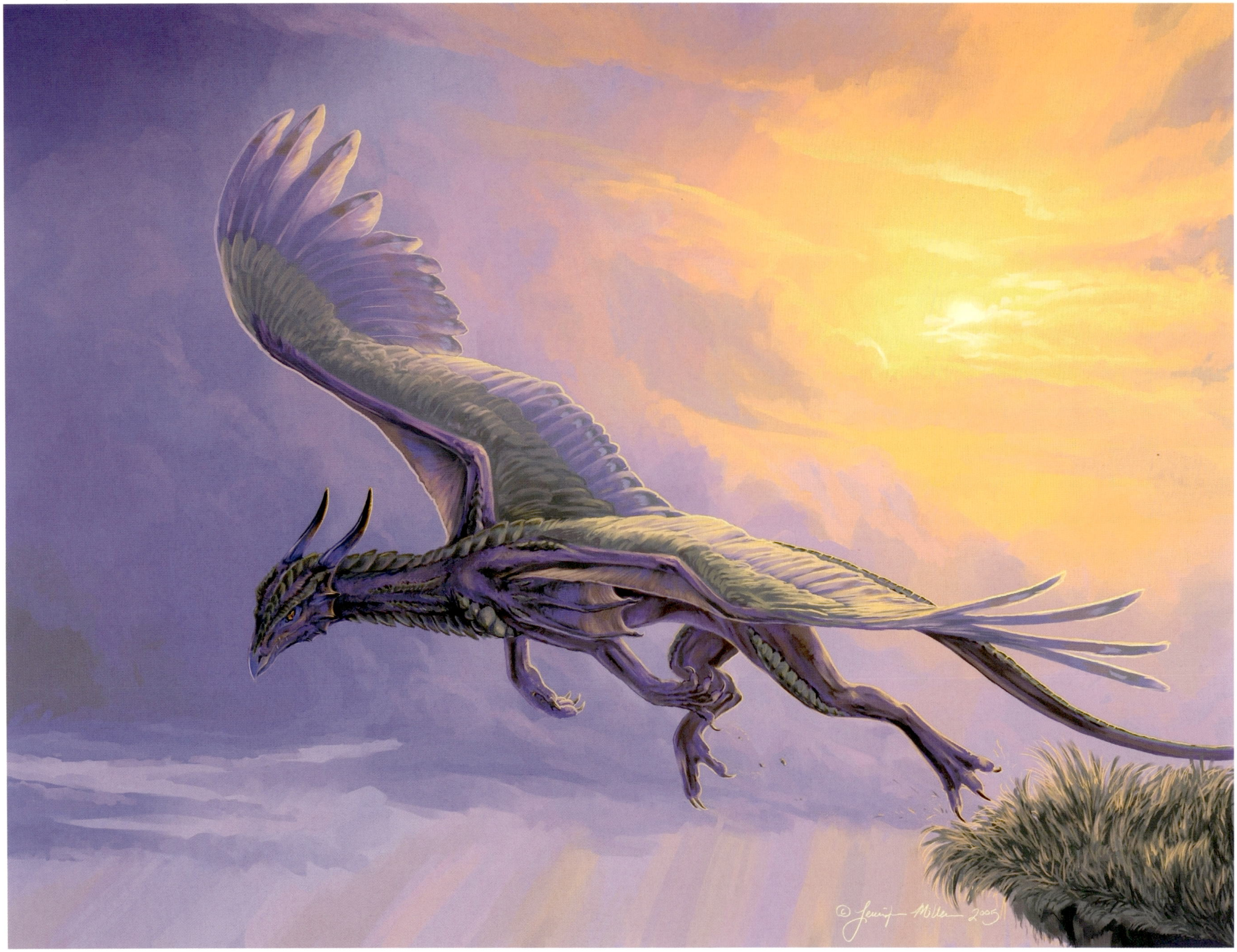

LAYRA by Jennifer Miller (aka 'Nambroth')
© Jennifer Miller 2005; the character 'Layra' is the intellectual property of Laura Douillard. · Digital media: Painter
Jennifer is a professional freelance artist with an emphasis on fantasy, creature design and environments.
www.featherdust.com

a sexual liaison with a maiden, he would rather just eat her up. Furthermore, he is physically more than a match for the hero, whose goodness, God (in the case of St George, and to an extent in Beowulf), virtue and cunning are what set him apart, painting a picture of a mighty warrior, and/or the triumph of righteousness over evil.

In some cases, the dragon could arguably be construed as the embodiment of natural phenomena. In the case of St George, the dragon also lives in the marshes and is characterized by toxic fumes; given that diseases associated with swampland, including

CLOUDSKIMMING by Jennifer Miller (aka 'Nambroth')
© Jennifer Miller 2006 · Digital media: Painter
www.featherdust.com

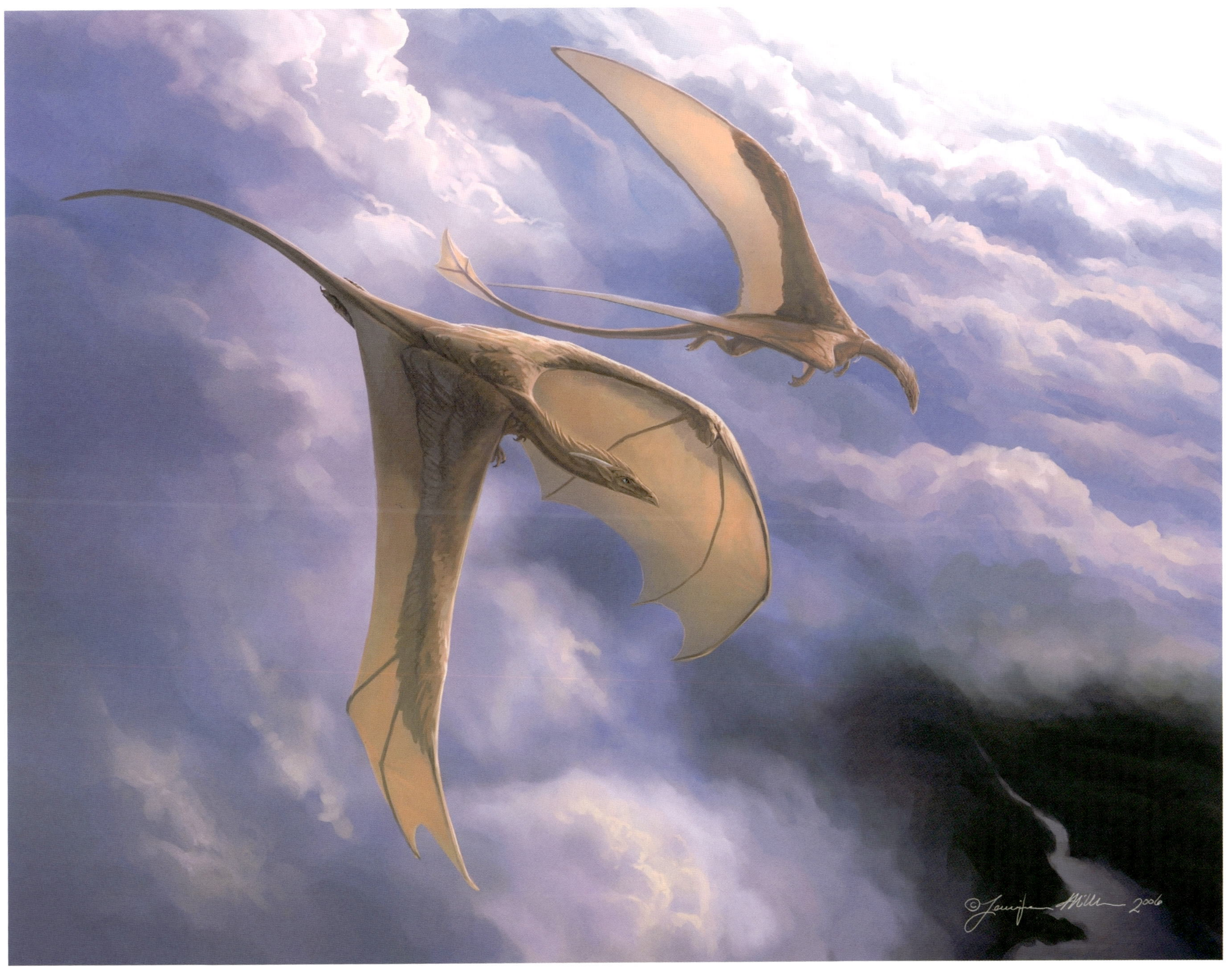

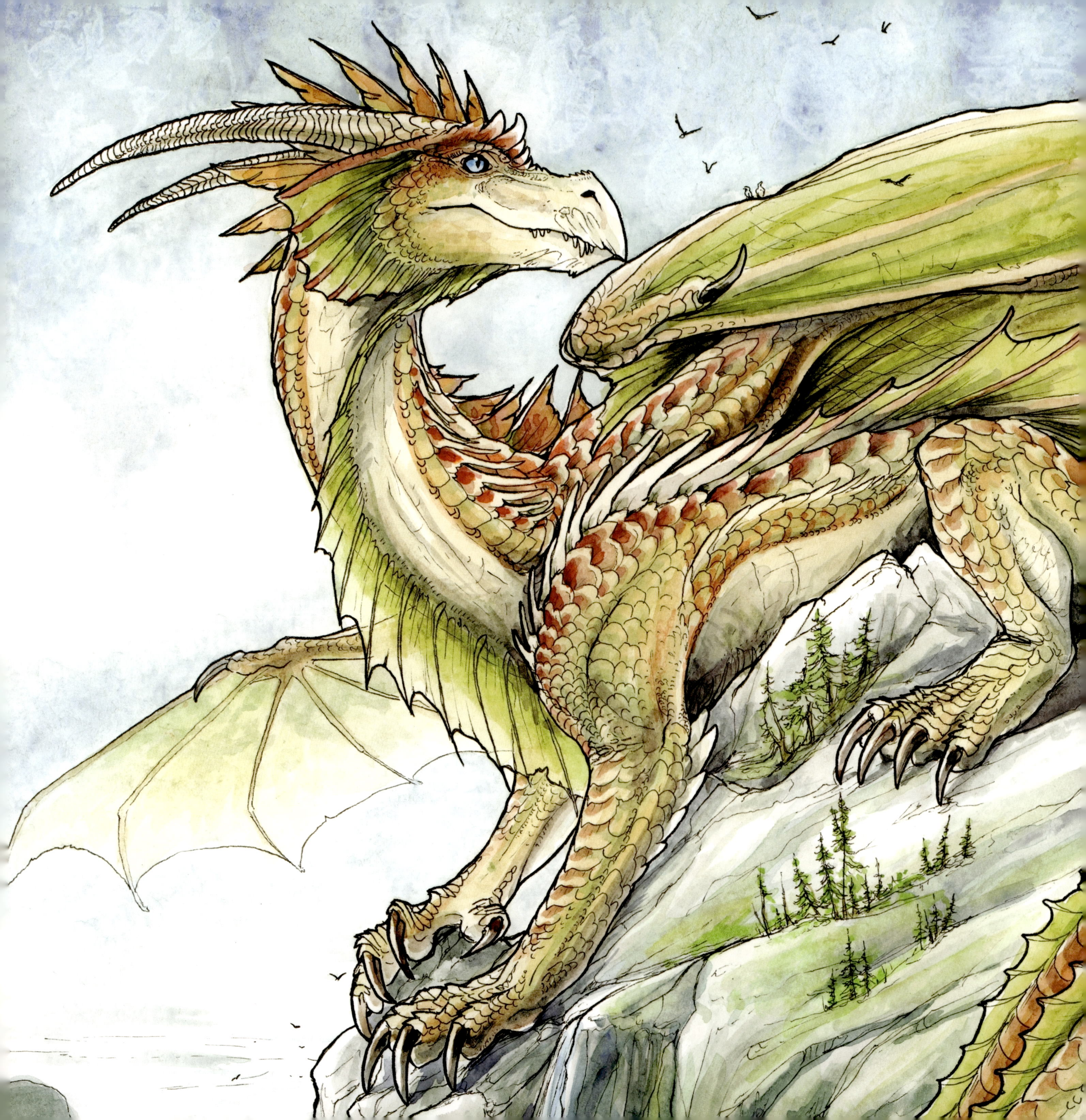

 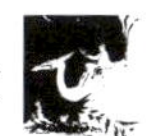

malaria, were common in Europe at the time, the dragon could certainly be seen as a representation of the disease. Perseus's sea monster could also be said to be the living embodiment of the sorts of storms that can make coastal living so arduous.

A MOMENTARY PERCH by Jennifer Miller (aka 'Nambroth')
© Jennifer Miller 2008
Traditional media: ink and watercolour on cold press paper
www.featherdust.com

Eastern Dragons

It is not true that all dragons across the world are seen as so evil. In Asia, dragons are actually seen as holders of great wisdom. In China, the imperial dragon, or Lung, is considered to be one of the four benevolent creatures, alongside the tortoise, the phoenix and the unicorn.

The Lung

The Lung have long, serpentine, scaly bodies and claws. The scales are not merely decoration: they symbolize the yin and yang of the creature and consequently its disposition and ability to act for good or for evil. Additionally, the Lung always have five toes on each foot.

There are a number of types of Lung: tien-lung (the celestial dragon), shen-lung (the spiritual dragon), ti-lung (the earth dragon), and futs-lung (the underworld dragon). Each of these has specific tasks or duties. Tien-lung protects the dwellings of the gods, shen-lung controls the rain and wind, ti-lung controls the rivers and other bodies of water, and futs-lung looks after the minerals and precious metals in the ground.

The Nagas

The Lung may be related to the Nagas, mysterious creatures of legend from the northwestern regions of the Indian subcontinent, the people of which are also known as Naga. They are semi-divine creatures with human heads and the bodies of serpents that are responsible for looking after various earthbound elements and natural phenomena. Their descriptions vary according to location. In Thailand, the Nagas are said to resemble a five-headed dragon that is also protector of temples. In Malaysia, the Nagas are sea dragons that scare sailors and fishermen. In Burma, the Nagas have similar tasks, but look more like a cross between snakes and crocodiles, bestowing jewels upon the favoured.

They appear throughout religious lore and legend, in particular where a great proportion of Buddhism is practised. It is said that the Buddha himself was protected by a Naga king called Muchalinda. Nagas have also permeated Hinduism, as some practitioners of the religion believe that the Naga king Karkotaka controls rainfall, which is a particularly powerful ability in a vastly agricultural society.

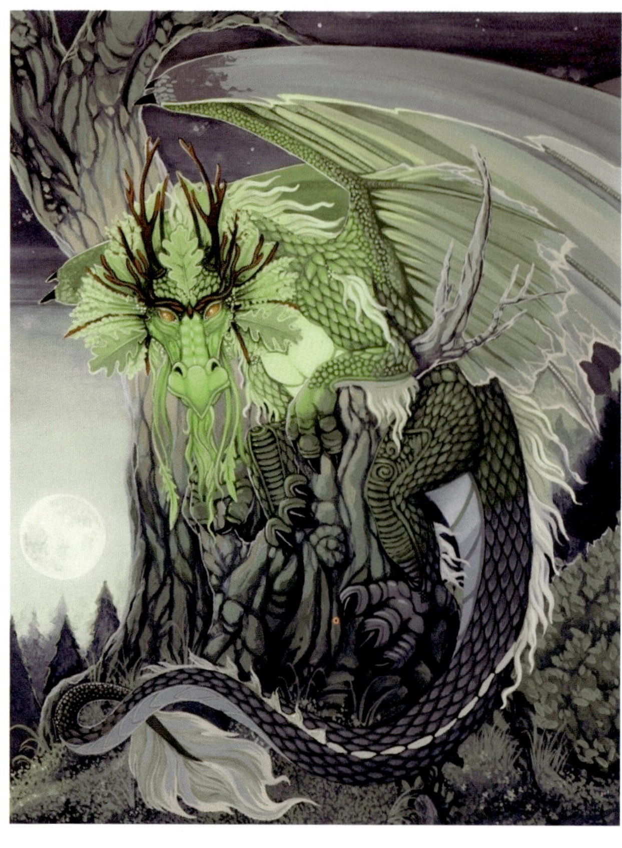

One thing is certain, though: to the Chinese, the dragon is far more than a frightful, fire-breathing menace that kills indiscriminately and waits to devour maidens. In fact, the Chinese Blue, or Azure, Dragon is an essential part of the practice of feng shui. The Blue Dragon symbolizes high places, such as the hills or mountains. Its yang is balanced by the white tiger's yin, responsible for valleys and other low-lying areas. For practitioners of feng shui, it is essential to understand the implications of both before large-scale construction projects get underway.

The Chinese Zodiac

Of course it is worth noting, if we can return to China, that the dragon is so venerated that it has its own zodiacal sign. Unlike the West, all signs of the Chinese zodiac are taken from existing animals, except for the dragon. People who are born in the year of the dragon (which include 1952, 1964, 1976, 1988, 2000 and 2012) are said to be born leaders, no matter their discipline: politics, sport or art. However, while they are powerful, decisive and stubborn, they are also said to be very just and fair and, as such, they tend to be found attractive and will often garner much sexual admiration, according to the legend.

The year of the dragon is also characterized by bluster and largeness. In short, it is seen as lucky and an auspicious time for new ventures, whether that be starting a family or starting a new business. However, in the year of the dragon, when things go well, they go very well; when they go wrong, they are absolutely awful.

Asia Pacific

There are dragon myths throughout Asia Pacific. The Javans have the Anantaboga, the dragon-king who lives in the Underworld with the dead.

Native Australians have their fair share of serpent creatures, too, including the Good Hoop, the serpentine Tasmanian version of the Native Australian Bunyip. The Bunyip possess magical powers and live in billabongs, swamps and other inland waters where they pose a terrible menace to human beings.

CERNUNNOS by Michele-Lee Phelan
© Michele-Lee Phelan 2007 · Traditional media: acrylics, coloured pencil
www.dreamsofgaia.com

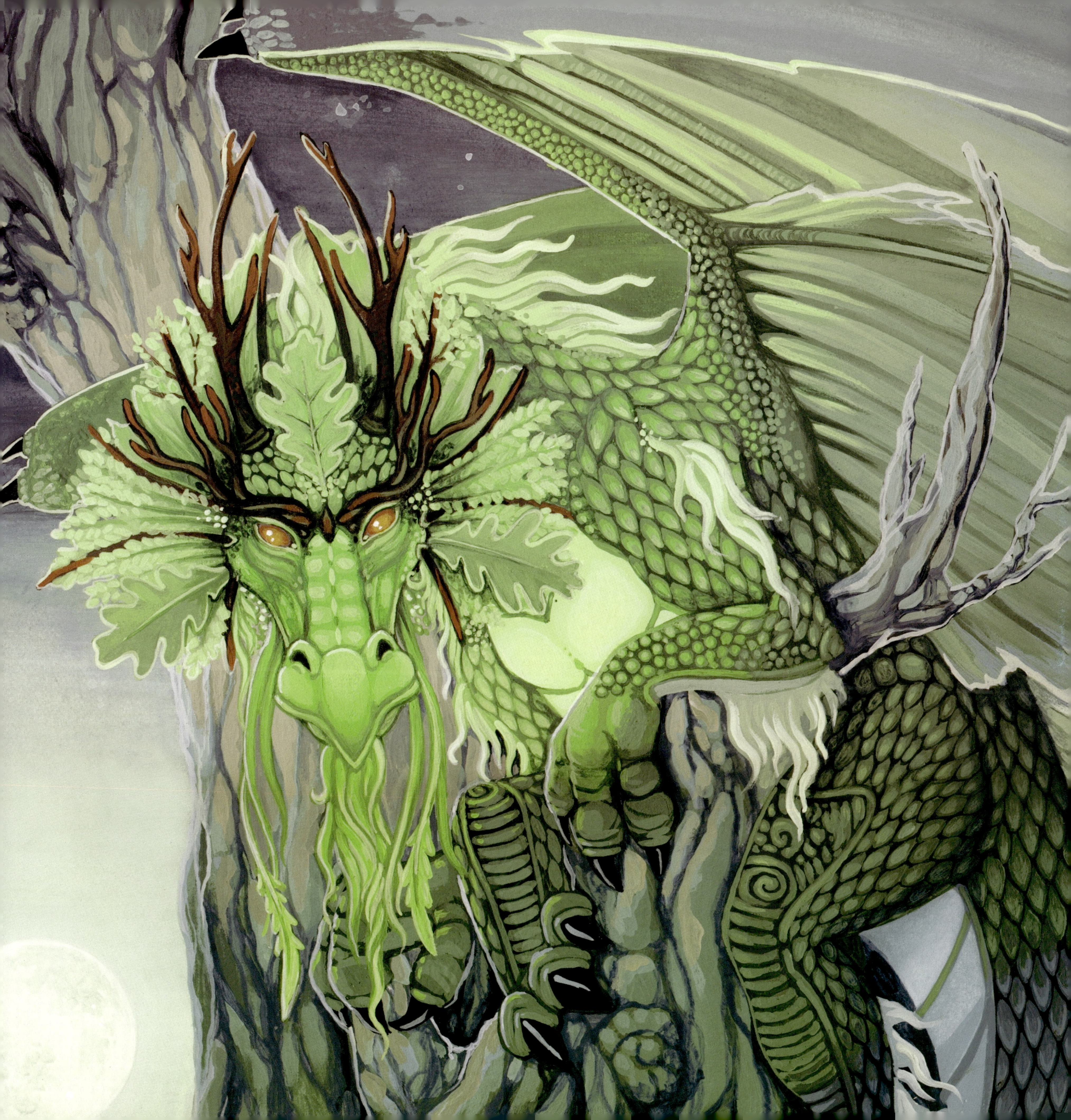

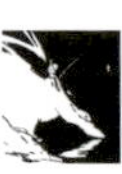

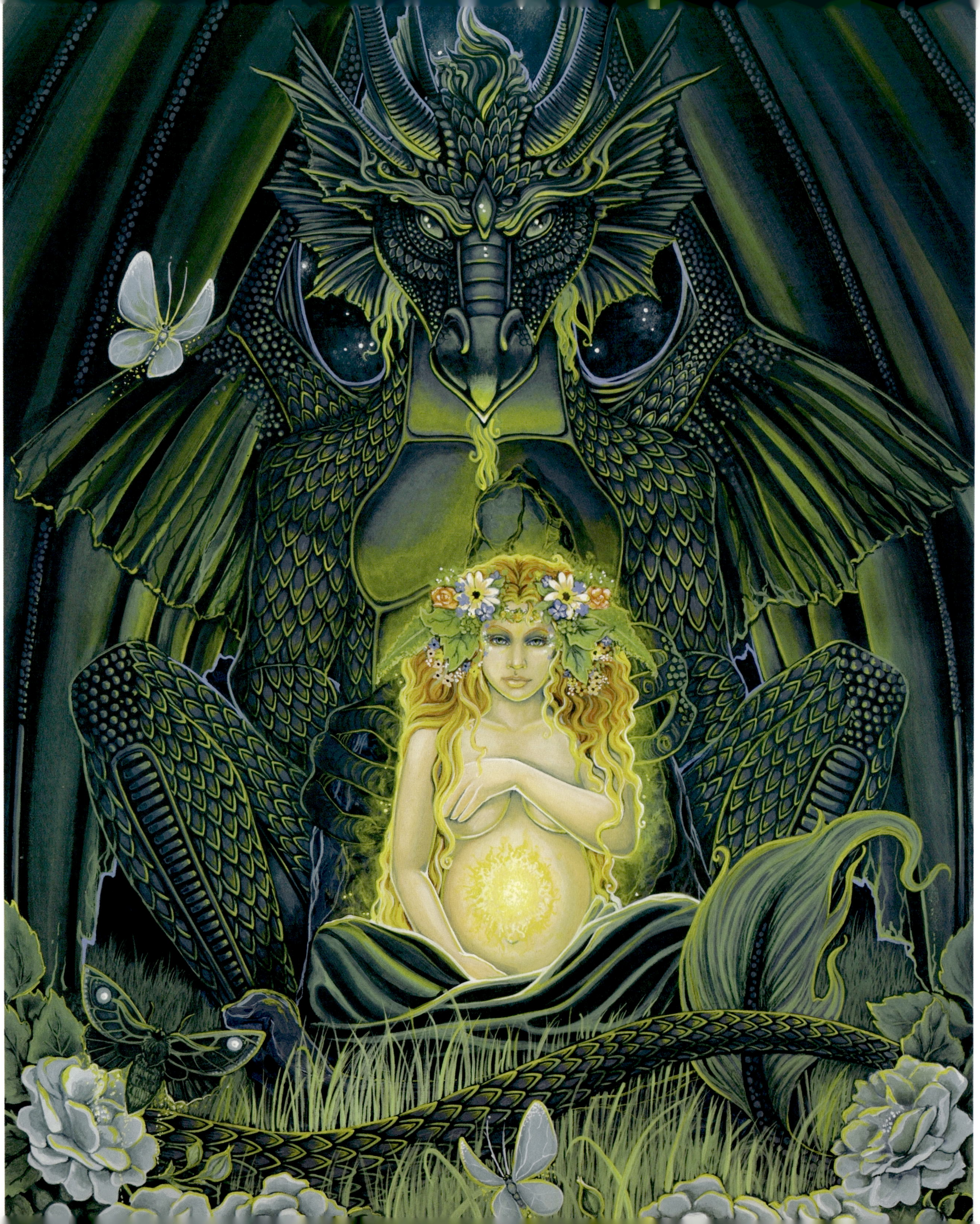

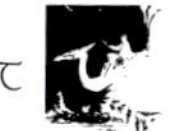

Dragons of The New World

GAIA'S DRAGON by Michele-Lee Phelan
© Michele-Lee Phelan 2006 · Traditional media: acrylic, coloured pencil
www.dreamsofgaia.com

There are also dragons to be found in the New World. Ancient civilizations that flourished in South and Central America feature plenty of mythology about serpents and dragons, feathered, scaled, fire-breathing and flying.

The Aztecs and the Mayans

Mexico, for example, is home to a large pyramid of the feathered serpent from the ancient city of Teotihuacan, believed to be a major conurbation that began life somewhere around 200 BC and was at its peak in AD 600. It is difficult to say exactly what the significance of the feathered serpent is, but the pyramid has been discovered to be a substantial burial ground by various excavations.

The feathered serpent represents the god Quetzalcoatl, who also appeared in human form as a light-skinned, bearded man, who did not hurt conquistador Hernán Cortez when he arrived in the region in 1519. Quetzalcoatl, both as human and feathered serpent, is very important to Mesoamerican cultures, including the Aztecs and the Mayans, although he was known by a number of different names during the period. The Mayans associate Quetzalcoatl strongly with Cihuacoatl, a snake goddess, who helped Quetzalcoatl create human beings.

For the Mayans, serpents were an essential part of the workings of the heavens, enabling the stars to move through the sky, and with their skins serving as a great symbol of renewal. Chac is a Mayan dragon that controls rain; in order to do so, he requires a sacrifice, but is generous with his gifts. According to artefacts, Chac has a long, serpentine body and a tapered snout that appears to have whiskers. He has a crocodile's head sporting stag horns and the ears of a deer. He can also create lightning and is often depicted holding the axe with which he makes this happen.

North America

North America is also awash with dragon myths. For example, there is Amhuluk, a great sea serpent legend from Oregon. The two-horned beast is to be feared, supposedly impaling

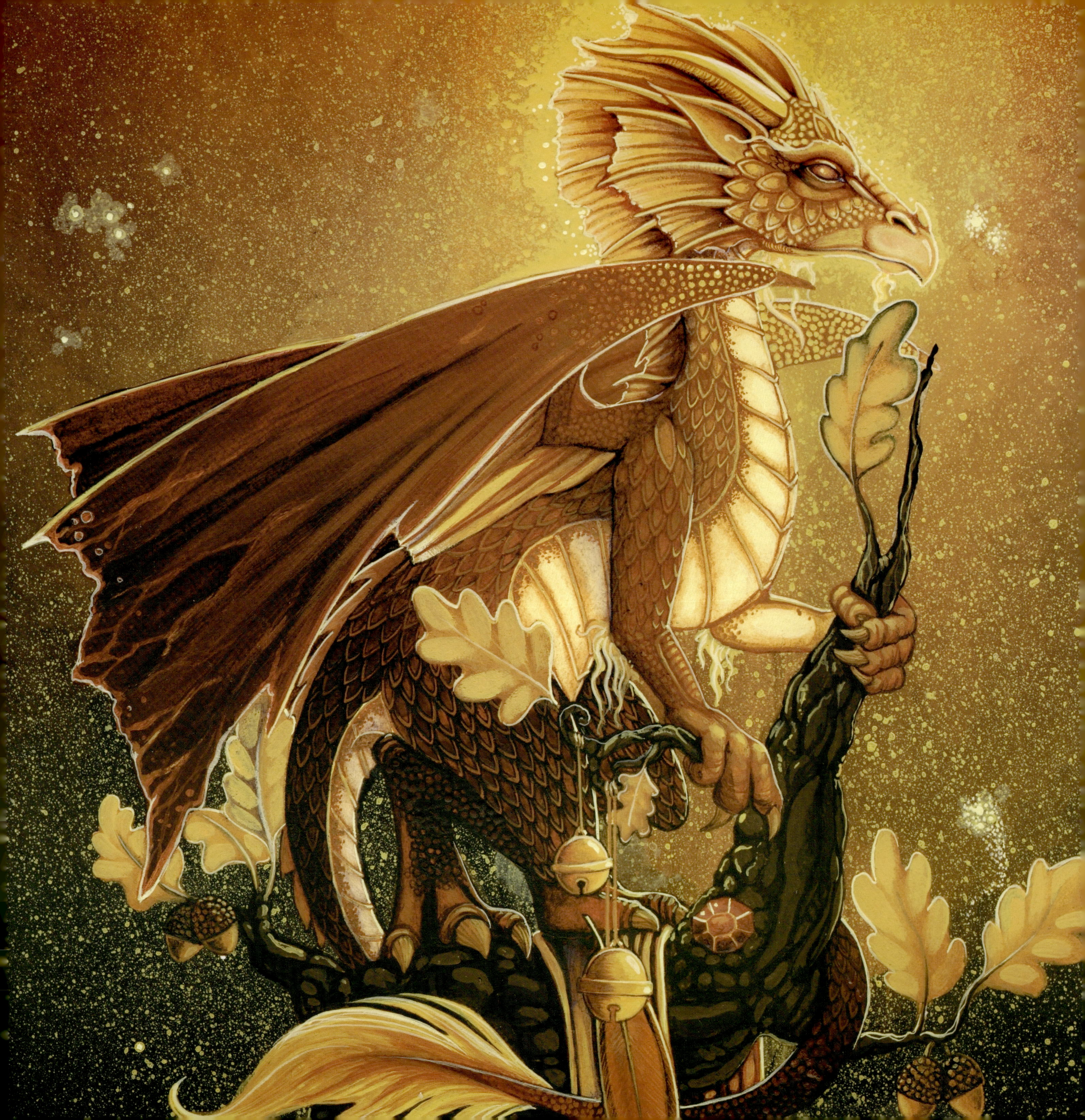

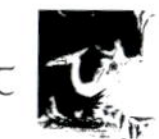

children on its horns and carrying them to the murky depths. Another is Ogopogo, a sea serpent said to live in Lake Okanagan, Canada. It is supposed to have a horse-like head and fins running along its 70-foot-long body.

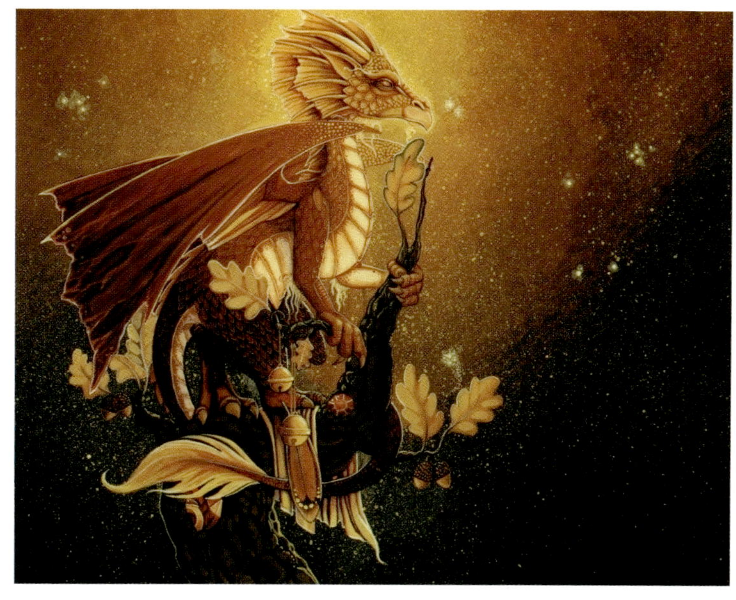

The Huron and the Iroquois legend has it that a Fire Dragon was responsible for the birth of the human race. According to its story, Ataentsic was a beautiful woman who was desired by the 'Chief Of All The Earth'. After subjecting her to a number of tasks of worthiness, she was taken up to heaven. When she fell pregnant, the chief became distrustful of her and suspected the Fire Dragon as Ataentsic's lover. He cast her down to earth where, with the guidance of the creatures living there, her children were the progenitors of all humanity.

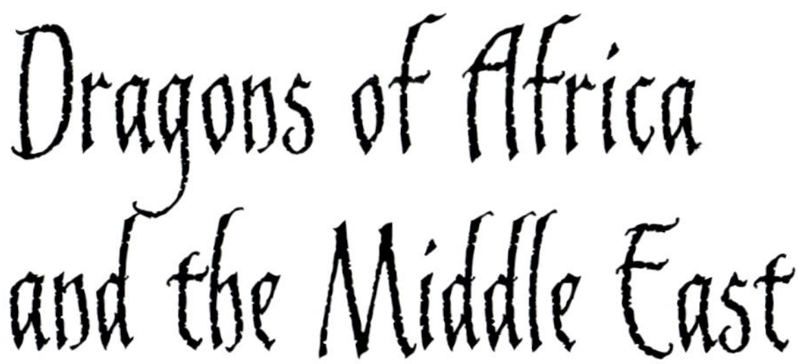

Dragons of Africa and the Middle East

Dragons around the world appear in many different forms, as we have seen. To carry on the tour: in Africa, there are also serpent creatures that are integral to the workings of the world. For instance, in Benin, there is the rainbow serpent, Aido Hwedo or Aido Wedo, who apparently is coiled up beneath the sea and holds the world up, not unlike Atlas. Aido Hwedo is able to carry out this magnificent feat by consuming vast quantities of iron. According to legend, when the iron runs out, Aido Hwedo will eat his tail, and the world will sink into the sea. Aido Hwedo also features in Haitian folklore as Ayida.

There is also the ancient Bida serpent from Ouagadou, roughly corresponding to the ancient kingdom of Ghana. Bida was both protector of the kingdom and killer of sacrificial young girls. When one girl, called Sia, was to be sacrificed to the Bida, her fiancé Amadou Sefedokote decided to kill it. He went to the serpent's cave and hid behind a tree in waiting. Upon the animal's arrival, Sefedokote decapitated it, but the head simply grew back. According to the legend, it takes the fiancé seven attempts to finally kill the creature. However, the loss of its protection over the kingdom of Ghana meant that the country went to rack and ruin, its people becoming nomads.

In the former Jiundu region of southern Africa, where now lies the country of Zambia, there is a legend of a peculiar flying creature called Kongamato, or the Overwhelmer of Boats. And reportedly, the Kalahari Kung people have painted animals that resemble dinosaurs.

DIA GRIENE by Michele-Lee Phelan
© Michele-Lee Phelan 2006 · Traditional media: acrylic, coloured pencil
www.dreamsofgaia.com

Egypt

In Egyptian folklore, there is Aapep, also known as Apopis, Apep or Apop. This creature is sometimes depicted as crocodilian or serpentine with a human face or as just a generally terrifying reptile. Aapep is said to embody all the world's dark forces; he is responsible for life's less pleasant phenomena such as storms or night or death from his lair deep in the River Nile. According to the legend, Aapep moves more like a caterpillar or earthworm than a snake and will shoot out of the murky depths and carry the unsuspecting into the depths of non-existence. A co-conspirator of Set, the god of evil, Aapep is not averse to taking on a deity. Aapep is said to have carried out a daily ritual of lying in wait to take the sun god Ra to the murky depths to consume him. However, Ra had the protection of the serpent Mehen, and always made it across the sky. Now and then, Aapep would get hold of Ra and almost carry him away, but would always be forced to spit him out again, resulting in an eclipse. According to the mythology, Aapep met his match when the mighty god Osiris chopped him to pieces.

Persia and Sumer

Another well-known dragon is Asdeev, the dragon slain in the ancient Persian story of Rustam. Asdeev is similar to European dragons in appearance, but he is white. Rustam is a Persian version of Hercules, and killing Asdeev is one of his tasks in many versions of the tale. Similarly, among Persian Zoroastrians, there is the legend of Dahak, a particularly nasty dragon. Dahak is so mighty that the legendary hero Thraetona cannot kill him. Instead he chains him under a mountain for all eternity.

Ancient Sumerians had to contend with Gandareva, a dragon-like monster so big that, when it reared up out of the ocean, its head reached up to the sky. It wreaked havoc on land as well as at sea, and was defeated by the heroic Keresapa. Keresapa endured a battle with Gandareva that saw the would-be dragon-slayer go blind, lose 15 horses and have his wife and children abducted by the beast. However, Keresapa eventually prevailed, of course.

PROTECTOR OF THE MAGICKS by Michele-Lee Phelan
 · Traditional media: acrylic, coloured pencil
www.dreamsofgaia.com

Good Dragons of the West

It should be said that, despite the prevalence of legend depicting dragons as fearsome and loathsome, European dragons are not always bad. In fact, much of dragons' bad press came about as Christianity took hold, and the creatures became associated with the 'Devil'. In fact, as the countless coats of arms, flags and standards can testify, in much Celtic folklore, dragons are protectors.

The Welsh Dragon

Y Ddraig Goch is the red dragon that adorns the Welsh flag. In the original legend, an invading Saxon army tried to conquer Wales, and its king, Vortigern, tried to build a large fortress atop

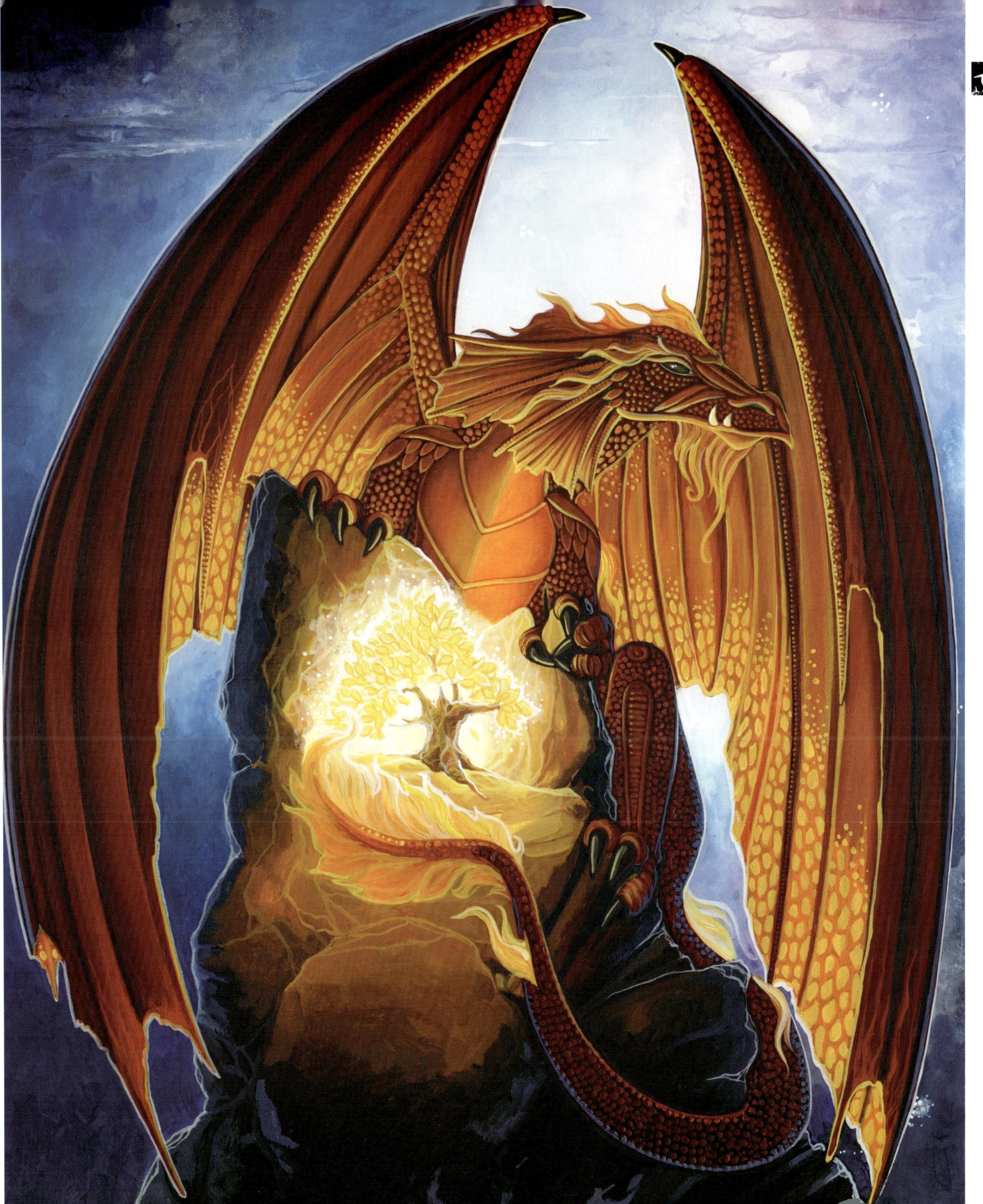

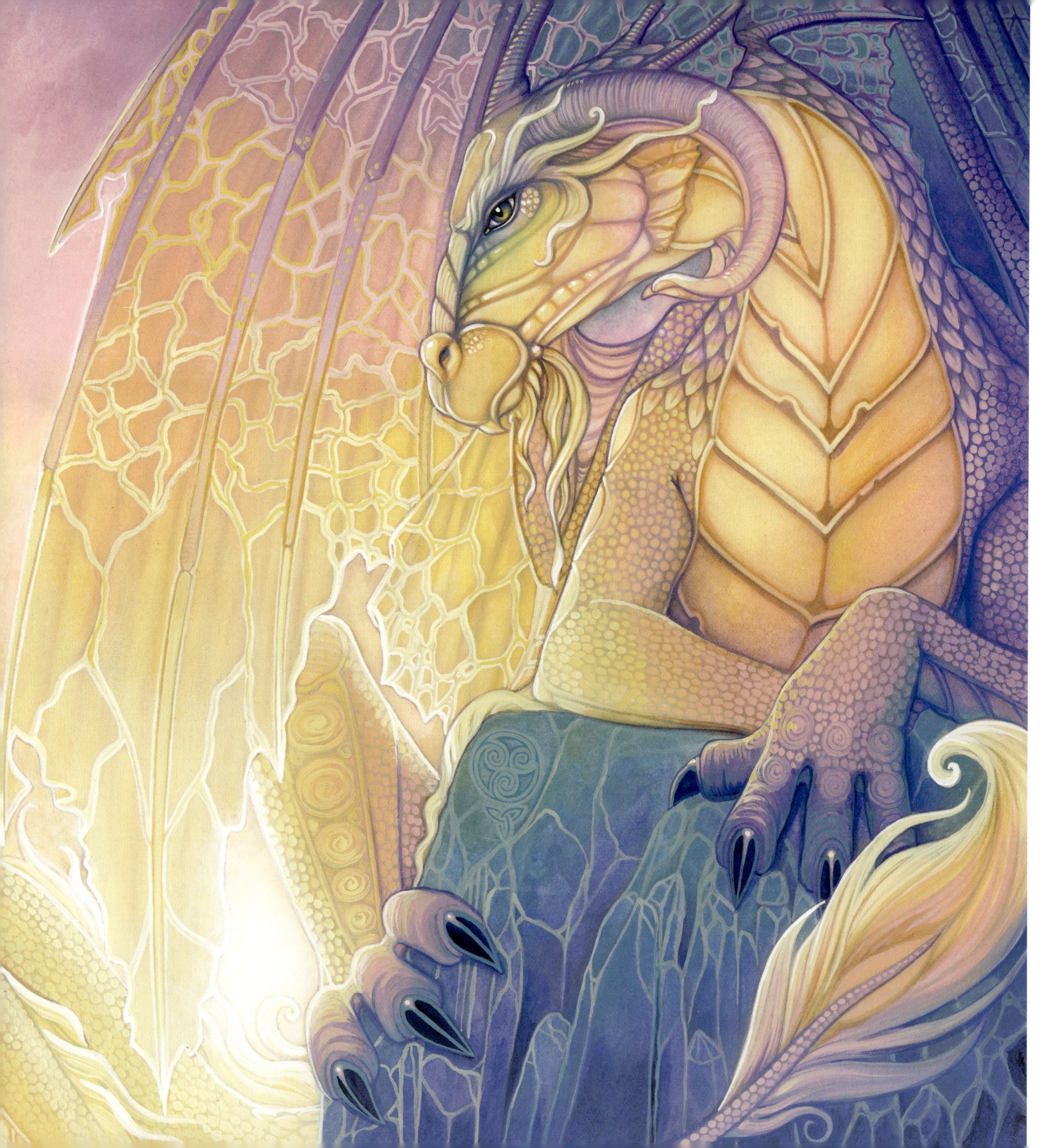

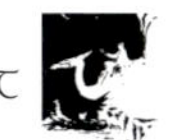

Snowdonia. However, all his building stones would vanish in the night. He was advised that the only solution to the problem was the sacrifice of a fatherless boy. A suitable boy was found in the form of Emrys, or Ambrose, who told Vortigern and his men the real problem was a pair of subterranean dragons. A party dug a shaft into the ground below and discovered the dragons, the white one called Gwiber and the red one, Y Ddraig Goch. Disturbed, the two became locked in mortal combat, in which the red emerged victorious. Ambrose interpreted this to mean that the Welsh, represented by Y Ddraig Goch, would defeat the Saxons, represented by Gwiber, and drive them out of the land.

It should be noted, however, that the legend was rewritten by Geoffrey of Monmouth to include Merlin the wizard as the fatherless boy. The protective might of the dragon is behind the name Pendragon, assigned to King Arthur's father Uther. Some believe that Oxfordshire's famous hillside image of chalk, the Uffington White Horse, is really a dragon, and that it may be a final resting place of Pendragon...

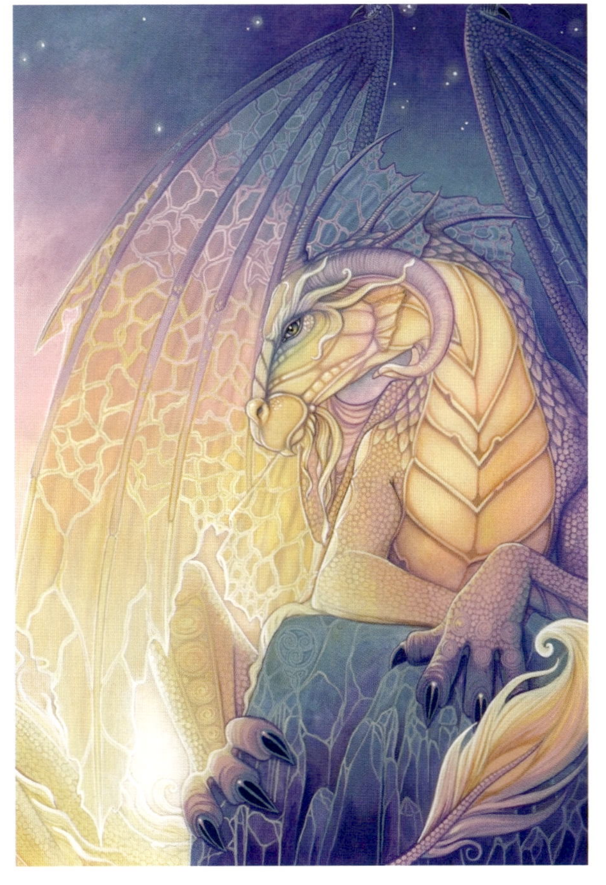

THE FIRST by Michele-Lee Phelan
© Michele-Lee Phelan 2008
Traditional media: watercolours, acrylic, coloured pencil
www.dreamsofgaia.com

Influential Dragons on Film

The allure of dragons has seen them represented in countless films, from fairy tale and mythical epics to modern-day visions and apocalyptic imaginings. Some achieve mainstream success while others have more unique appeal and are inspirational to artists in their innovative creations.

Reign of Fire

Far from a staggering success at the box office, *Reign of Fire* is a modern take on the dragon tale, with a hint of science fiction thrown in. Helmed by *X-Files* director Rob Bowman, it is set in a future where dragons come to life and are in charge. The plot is simple: a tunnelling project accidentally arouses a nest of dragons who have been in hibernation for millions of years. They come to life and wreak havoc on earth; it transpires that their voracity was responsible for the death of the dinosaurs. The dragons feed from the ash created in their incinerating exhalations.

It is an ambitious film, mixing old mythology with Hollywood glitz and a shoot-'em-up sensibility. It is set in a Britain of the near future, following an encampment of humans in Northumberland hiding away from the dragons in an old castle.

They are led by Quinn, who discovered the dragons' den as a boy, and they furrow out a bare existence involving avoiding the terrifying beasts from above while merely trying to go about their days. One day, they are happened upon by a crew of special-ops American military personnel who have established a long-winded scientific, action-packed approach to killing dragons. It transpires that all the dragons are female, and that there is one male that fertilizes the eggs. Eliminate him and eliminate the problem. So they set off on a quest to the nest Quinn originally discovered as a child.

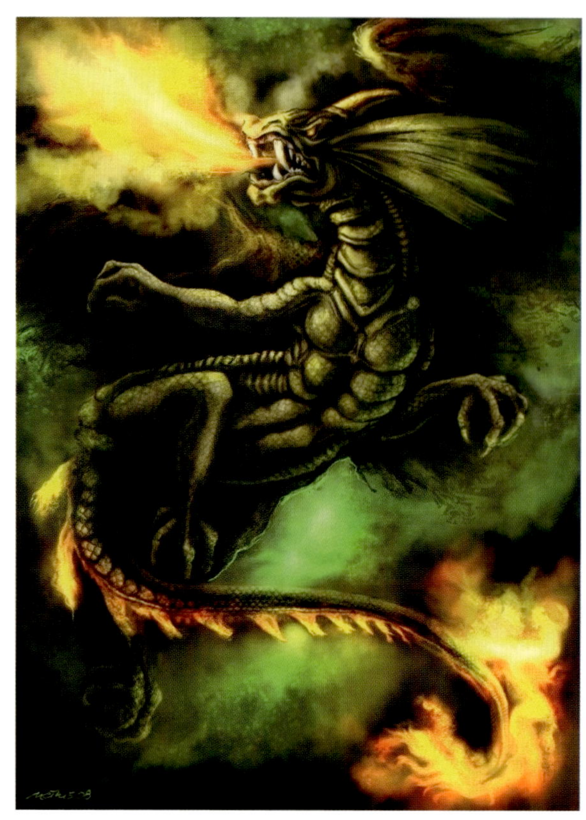

The dragons were the work of visual effects supervisors Richard Hoover and Dan DeLeeuw as well as computer animators at the now-defunct Disney Secret Lab. Alan Lathwell particularly enjoys the portrayal of the dragons and the bleak tone of the film. He says, 'They have the power to lay waste to the entire planet. They're unstoppable. I suppose that's why I like those dragons. They're realistic. They're unstoppable beasts and they would fill you with dread if dragons were real.'

CGI Reigns

As a film, *Reign of Fire* is actually riddled with holes throughout the plot. However, what is particularly attractive about the film is its depiction of the dragons. For those who love nothing more than to see the dragons tear stuff up and breath fire, it is a gem. The CGI is well executed, giving the dragons, designed as fire-breathing, serpentine, scaly red bats with dinosaur heads, a frightening air of realism. Some of the detail afforded the dragons also enhances the effect. For instance, the dragons' wings are given a buzzing noise that adds to the sense of terror. Because the setting is so contemporary, there is also a sense of just how powerful the dragons are. Purists will note that the creatures depicted are more specifically wyverns, having just two legs in addition to their wings.

Dragonheart

Dragonheart sees actor Sean Connery voice Draco, one of the best-loved dragons ever committed to celluloid. The 1996 film, directed by Rob Cohen, stars Dennis Quaid as the mighty knight Bowen, who starts out as teacher and mentor to Einon, the son of a tyrannical king. Bowen tries to instil the 'old knights' code' into Einon, about values like truth, justice and valour, as well as teaching him how to fight. However, Einon becomes involved in one of the king's suppression campaigns. The king is killed and Einon suffers a wound through the heart. The queen takes the dying boy to a cave, where a dragon promises to save his life. The dragon replaces part of the boy's heart with his own.

FIRE DRAGON by Nathie
© Nathie 2008 · Digital media: Photoshop
www.creationwarrior.net

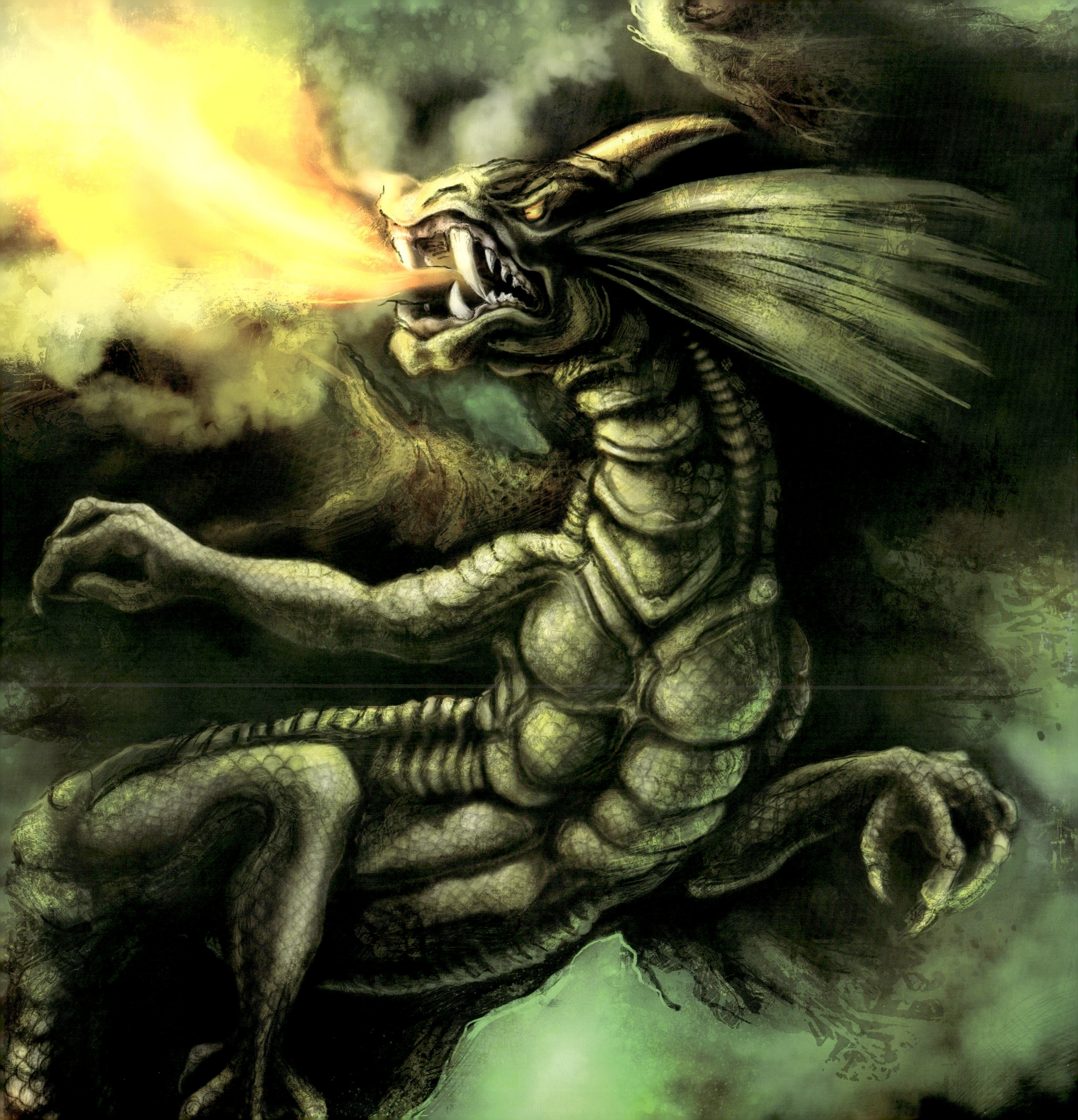

Beyond Bounds by Varony Chay

 Digital media: Painter; Created for one of the inside covers for Varony's comic *Dispar*; http://neioworks.deviantart.com

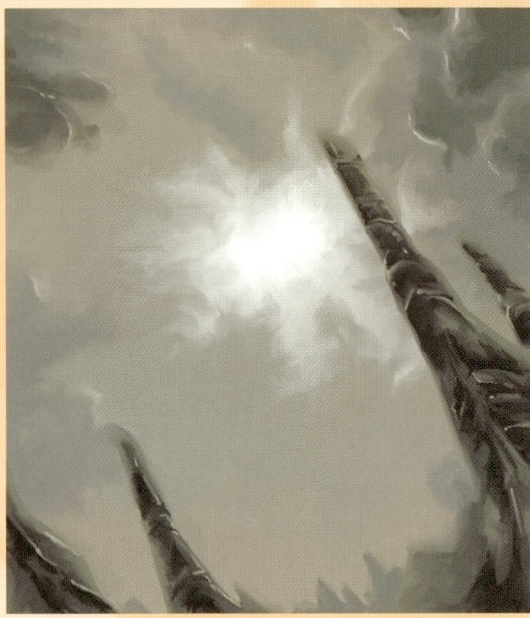

SAMPLE STEP 1. To start off I used an acrylic brush and started to paint the background. I have the light source coming from the back.

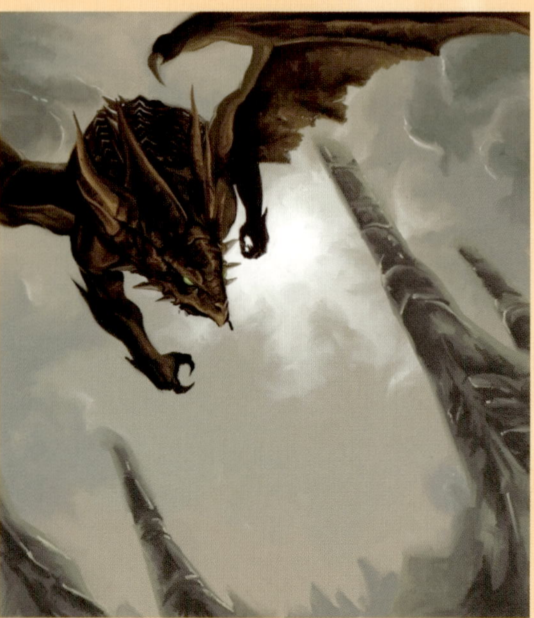

SAMPLE STEP 2. Creating a new layer, I then painted the image of the dragon using acrylic brush again, and the blender brush to blend the colours together, adding fine detail last.

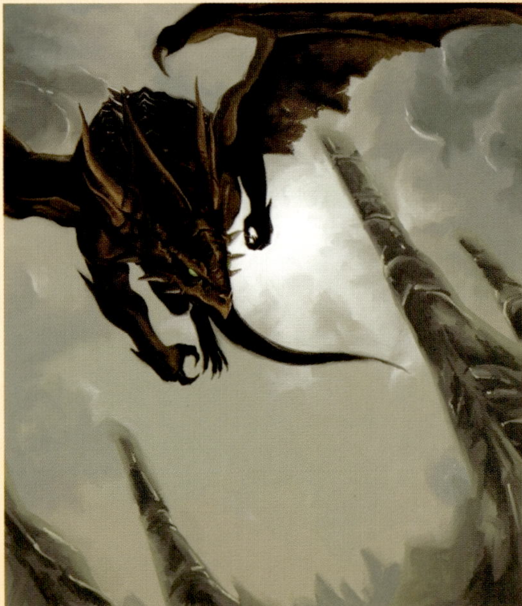

SAMPLE STEP 3. The back limbs are painted on a separate layer because I wanted to give them a more distant and less focused effect.

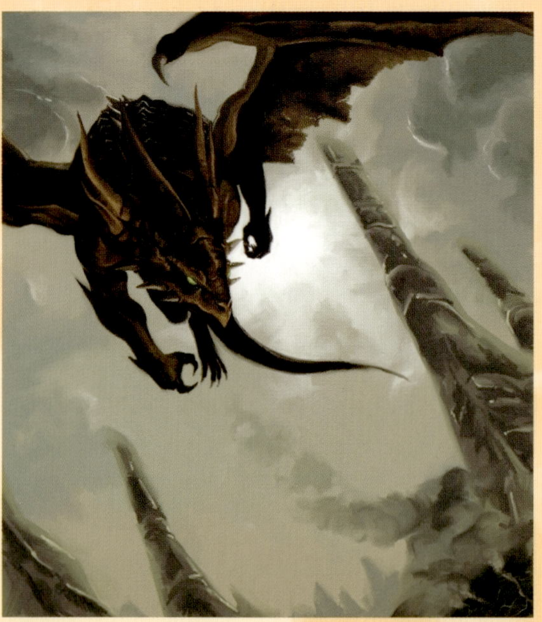

SAMPLE STEP 4. Lastly, I added the final detail to the background, giving a look of an eruption coming from the ground.

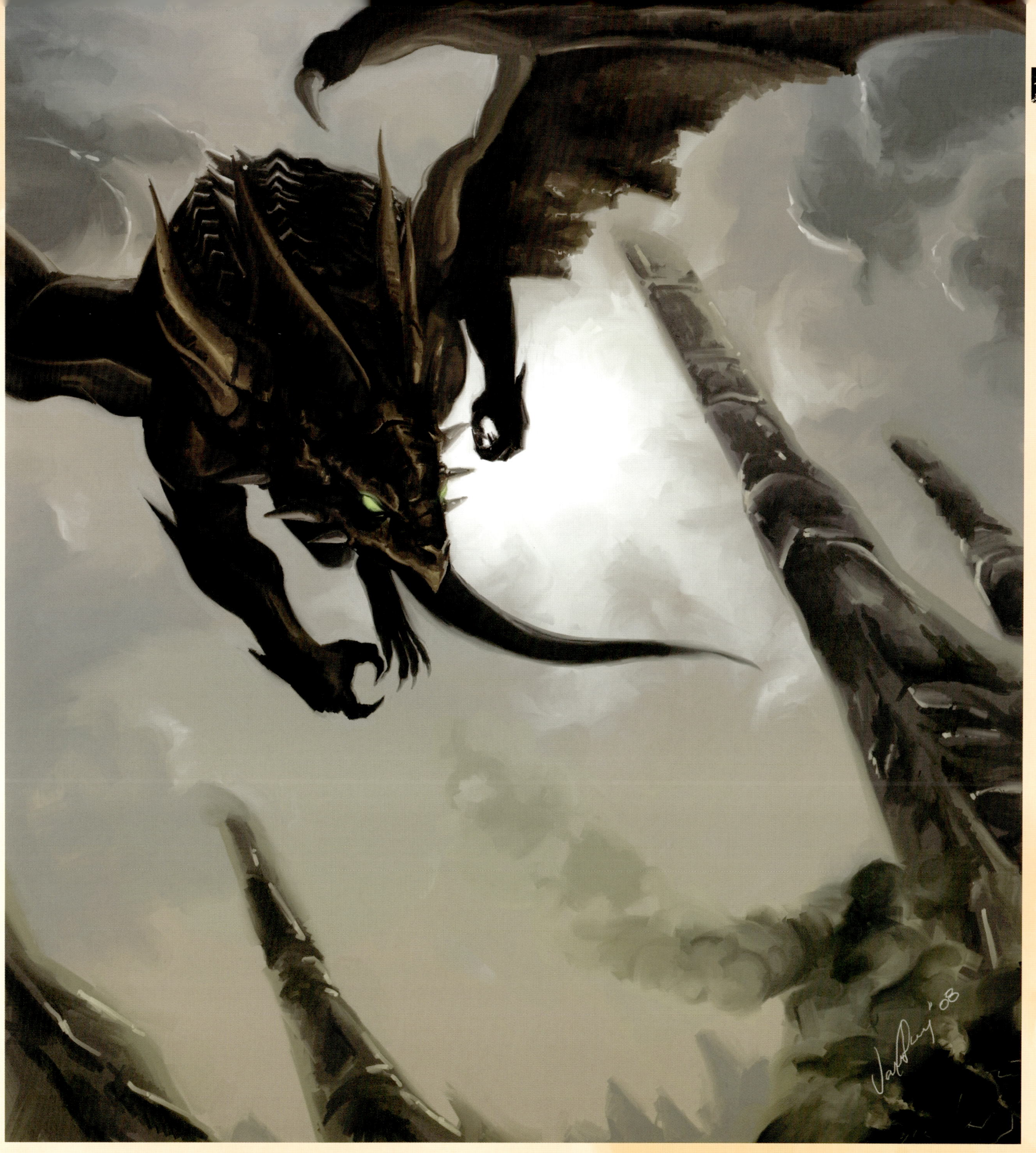

Finishing Touches. I then played around with colour and lighting to get the final image.

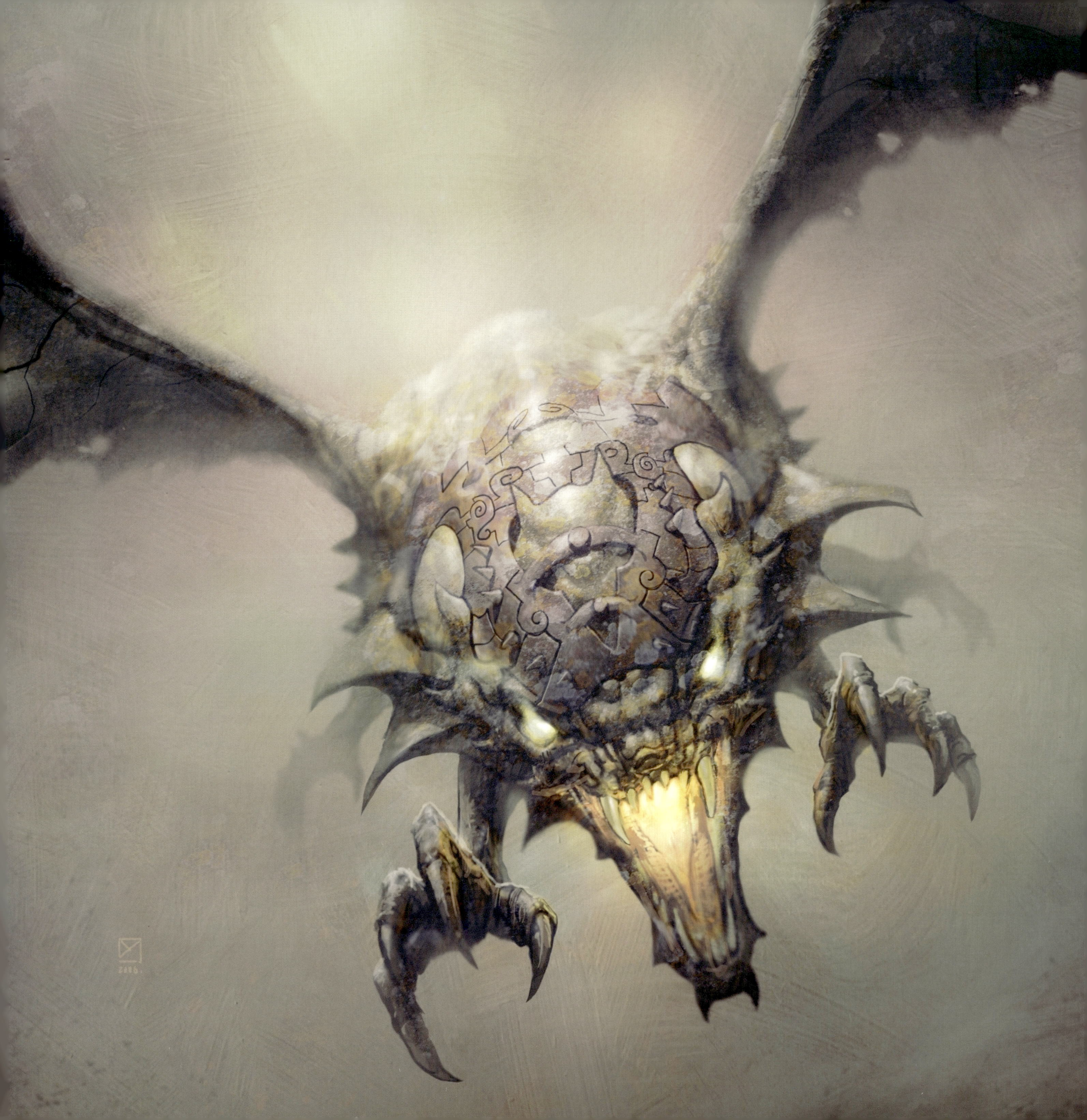

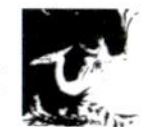

It transpires that Einon grows up to be a more brutal king than his father, and Bowen believes it is the dragon's heart that has tainted his former ward. Thus he vows to kill all dragons for ruining the boy's life. He is nearly completely successful at this task, although his wilderness years have turned him into a cynic and a conman. When he comes across Draco, the long fight leads to a standoff in which they both agree to help one another. Bowen and Draco travel the countryside, the former accepting money to kill the dragon, the latter faking his own death.

However, the daughter of the king who was killed in cold blood by Einon in the previously mentioned rebellion wishes to avenge her father's death and leads a fresh uprising. She asks Bowen and Draco to join her. Draco reveals to Bowen that he was the dragon who donated half a heart to Einon, and that only by being guardians to humans can dragons' souls ascend to their final resting place in the Draco constellation. His donation to Einon was, he believed at the time, his salvation, but Einon's truly dark nature had nullified the gesture. In the end, Draco and Bowen join in the uprising.

Dragonheart's Dragon of Honour

What sets this film apart is its treatment of the dragon. Draco is a wisecracking, sometimes slapstick character who plays it for laughs a great deal of the time. But it explains that dragons are only aggressive to humans if they are harmed first, that they follow an Arthurian code of honour and that they are sworn protectors of humankind. Industrial Light and Magic pull off startling effects work in the animation of Draco, which is impressive given that the CGI would have been arduous to execute in 1996.

Dragonslayer

Many regard the 1981 film *Dragonslayer* as something of a hidden gem. Directed by Matthew Robbins, it is a dramatization of standard dragon-slayer mythology. A medieval king, when faced with an evil and voracious dragon called Vermithrax, offers it virgins chosen by biannual lottery. A party sets out to find someone who can rid them of the blight, and finds a wizard called Ulrich who is murdered in a dare with one of the film's villains. Ulrich's apprentice decides to go and help the town with its problem, with limited success initially, but coming through in the end with a little bit of help from an enchanted spear and his resurrected former master.

Made for a whopping $18 million at a time when that was a lot of money for a movie, it was a co-operative effort between Walt Disney Pictures and Paramount Pictures, and featured special effects work, again from Industrial Light and Magic. Pre-CGI, the Vermithrax is a mix of puppetry and stop-motion animation. As such, there are times when the dragon can be disappointing, especially when judged against today's standards. But Vermithrax is one of the big screen's most terrifying dragon creations, transcending the limitations of the special effects of the time.

YOUNG DRAGON by Johann Bodin (aka 'Yoz')
© Johann Bodin 2007 · Mixed media: pencil on paper, Photoshop
Johann is an award-winning artist, who has created works in many arenas, including the music industry, magazines, books, hobby gaming and video games. The notion of chance is fundamental to Johann's work, leading to new creations.
www.yozartwork.com

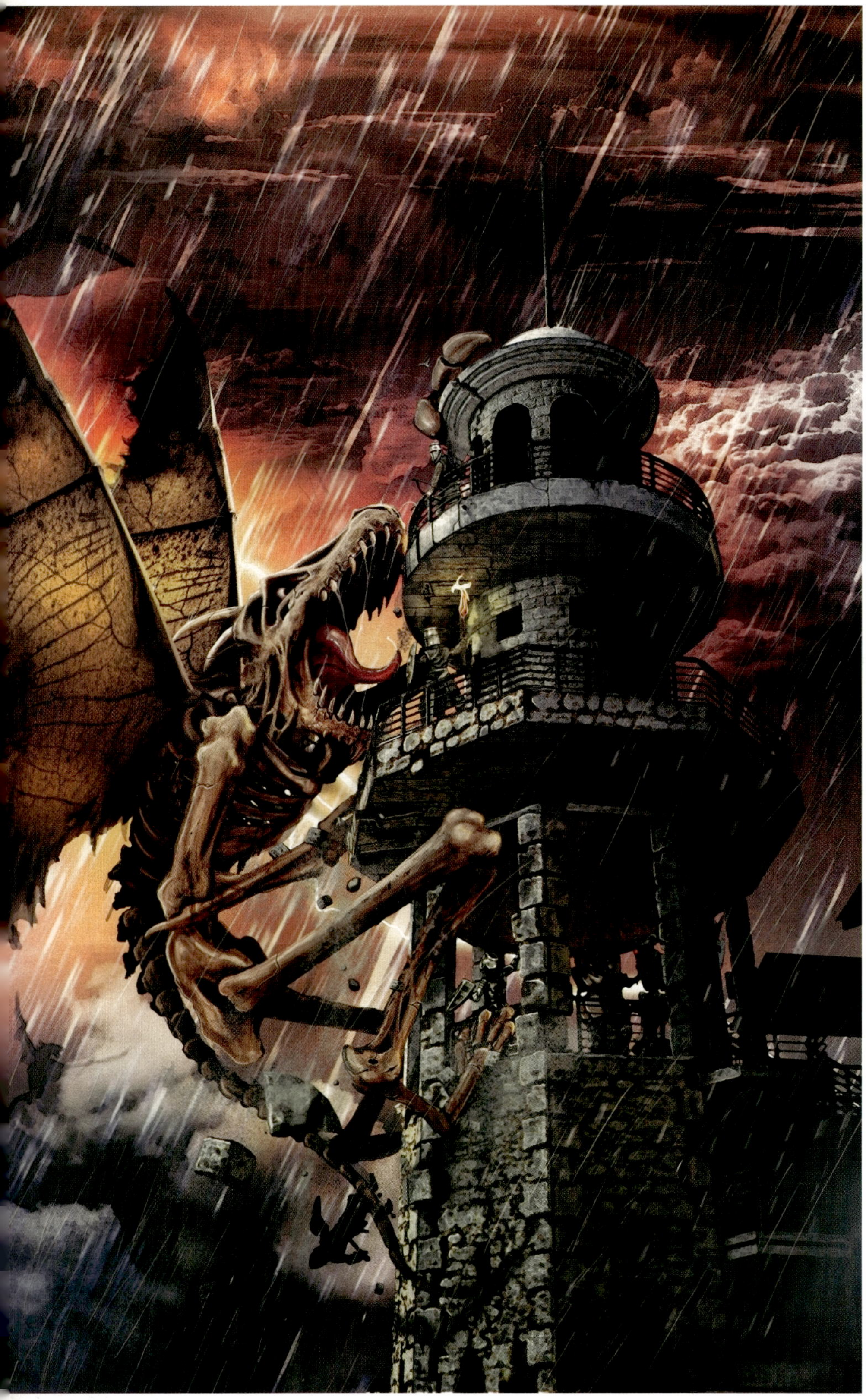

DROLEM – UNDEAD DRAGON by Mario Veltri
© Mario Veltri 2008 · Digital media: Photoshop
Mario is the Art Director for Edizioni Master in Italy, but would like to gain work experience abroad. Mario is blessed with a 'photographic imagination': when someone describes something, he can immediately see it in his mind in all its details.
www.marioveltri.com

The Neverending Story

The Neverending Story (Wolfgang Petersen, 1985) features a dragon of an entirely different cut, who is nonetheless a favourite among fantasy lovers. The Luck Dragon, Falkor, is one of the magical characters that inhabit the land of Fantasia, which is under attack from a mysterious force called The Nothing. However, the viewer follows the action as it is being read by a real world character, Bastian, who is mourning the recent death of his mother and constantly avoiding a trio of bullies at school. It is when fleeing the latter that he stumbles upon the book, entitled *The Neverending Story*, in a bookshop. The owner promises him that if he reads it, he will become even more a part of the story than is usual with other books.

And so, camping out in the school's attic (avoiding trouble for arriving late once again), Bastian sets out to read the tale. He

CALAMITOUS EMOTION by Marissa Rivera (aka 'PearlPhoenix')
© Marissa Rivera 2008 · Digital media: Photoshop
'For most of my life ... I felt I did not have what it took to become [an artist]. It was my hobby, nothing serious. It was frustrating to not have the ability to put my imaginations on paper [...]. I was tired of these frustrations and dedicated myself to becoming the artist I wanted to be.'
www.pearlphoenixsun.com

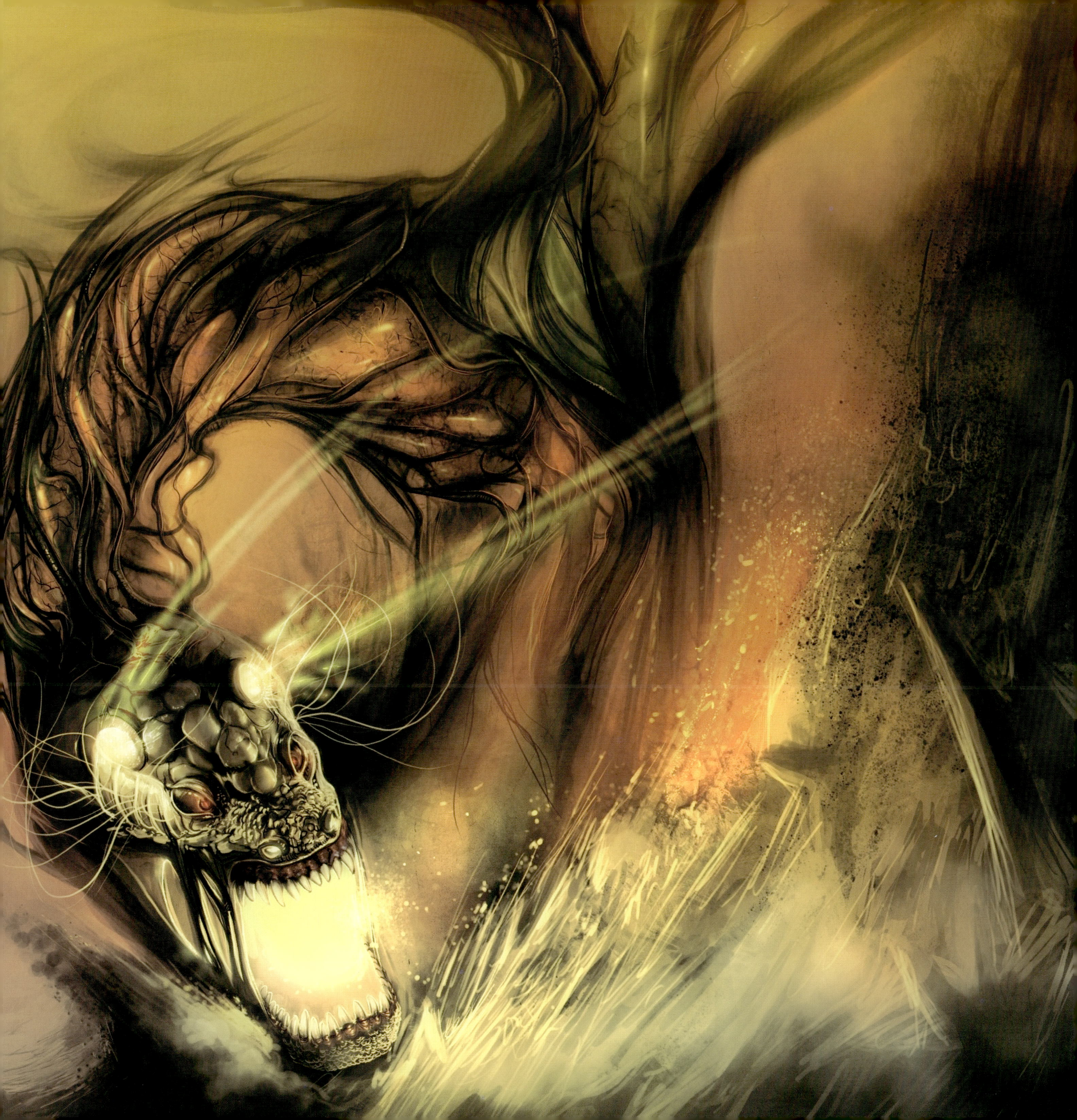

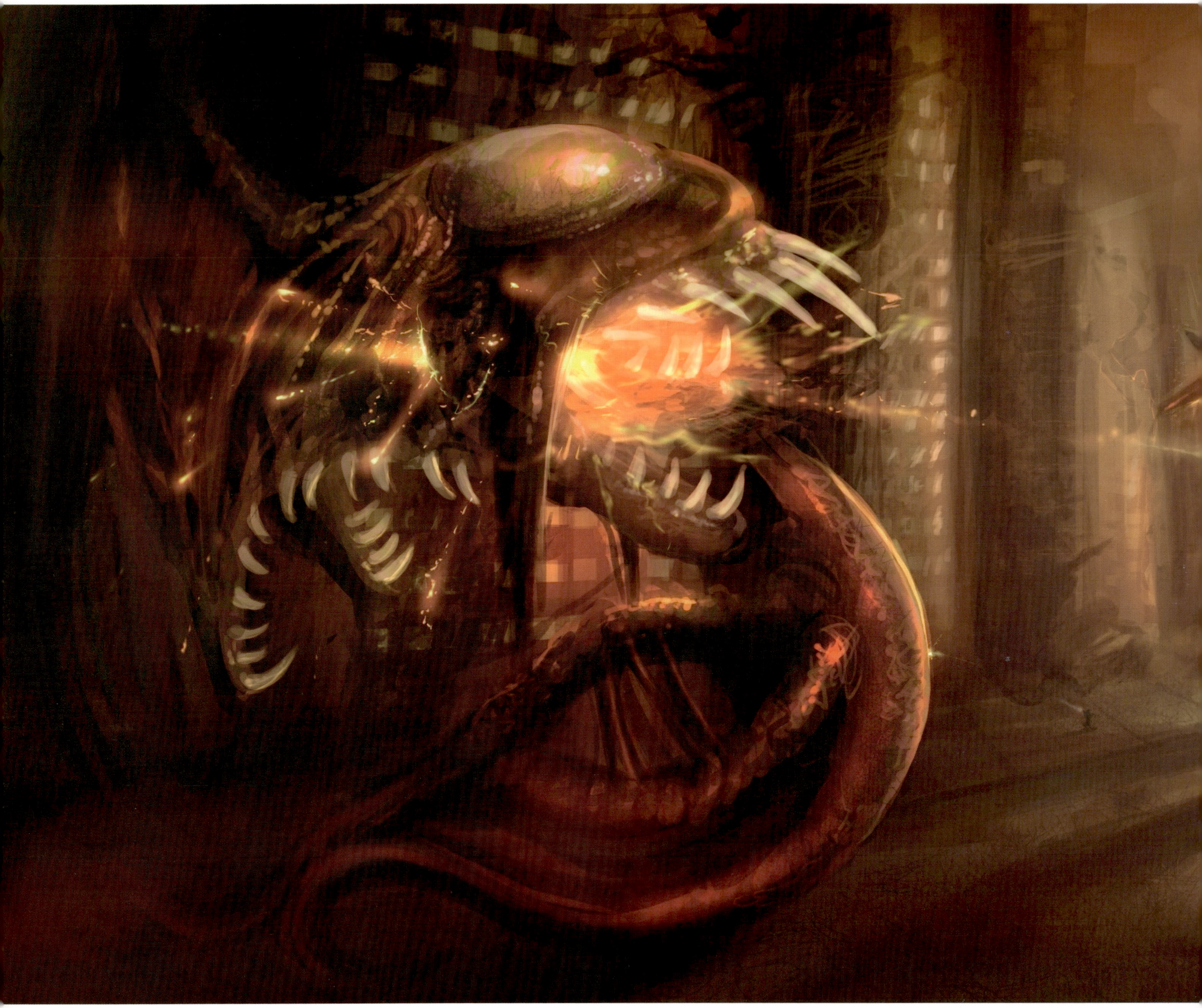

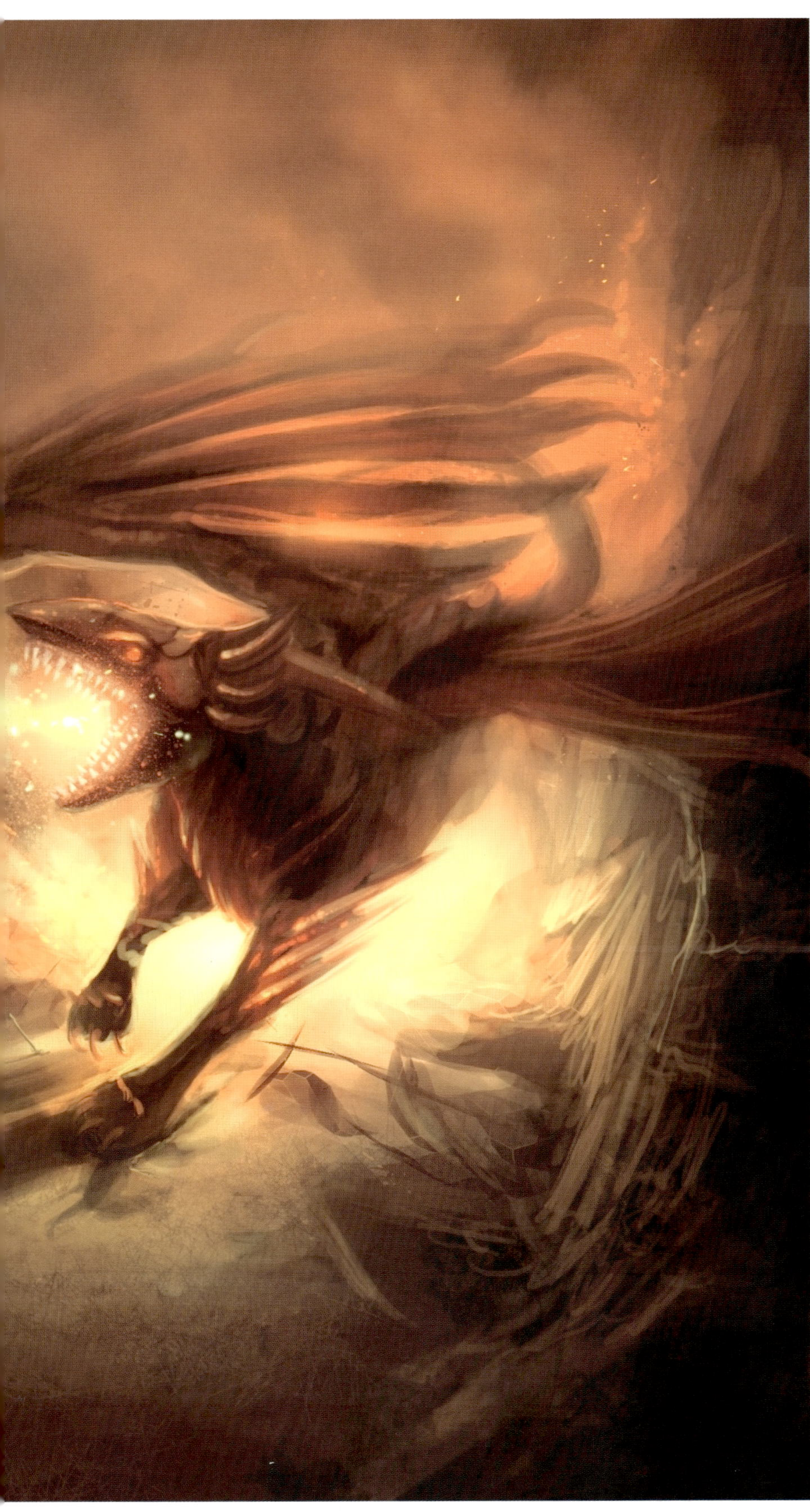

sees various magical creatures – a will-o'-the-wisp, a 'rock biter' and a mad hatter among others – head to a congress of other fairy tale characters at an ivory tower after describing a void that seems to be consuming vast areas of land all around them. They hope the empress who lives there can tell them how to defeat this so-called 'Nothing', but they find she is gravely ill. To save her, and the rest of the land of Fantasia, a warrior called Atreyu is summoned. He is charged with finding a cure and saving the land. Atreyu sets off on his horse and, after finding the first object of his quest, a large existential tortoise called Morla who resides in the Swamp of Sadness, nearly loses his life, but is saved by Falkor, the luck dragon. Morla has told him he needs to travel 10,000 miles to visit the Southern Oracle, who will advise him on what to do. The luck dragon and two gnomes see him back to health and, after surviving two tests, he finds the Southern Oracle, who tells him he must travel to the outer limits of Fantasia to find a human child to rename the flagging empress.

Throughout the action, it becomes more and more apparent to Bastian that he is an integral part of the book's narrative, but he does not understand why or how he is significant. After much more travelling with the friendly Falkor, Atreyu discovers, after a crash landing and an encounter with evil lycanthrope G'mork, that there is no limit to Fantasia. After despatching G'mork and a reunion with Falkor, Atreyu finds the Ivory Tower again, and the Childlike Empress within. She tells Atreyu that if Bastian would just rename her, Fantasia would be saved. Bastian hesitates, having

CONFRONTATION by Marissa Rivera (aka 'PearlPhoenix')
© Marissa Rivera 2007 · Digital media: Photoshop
'Art relaxes me, motivates me, and gets my energy running.
It is my life, how it was meant to be.'
www.pearlphoenixsun.com

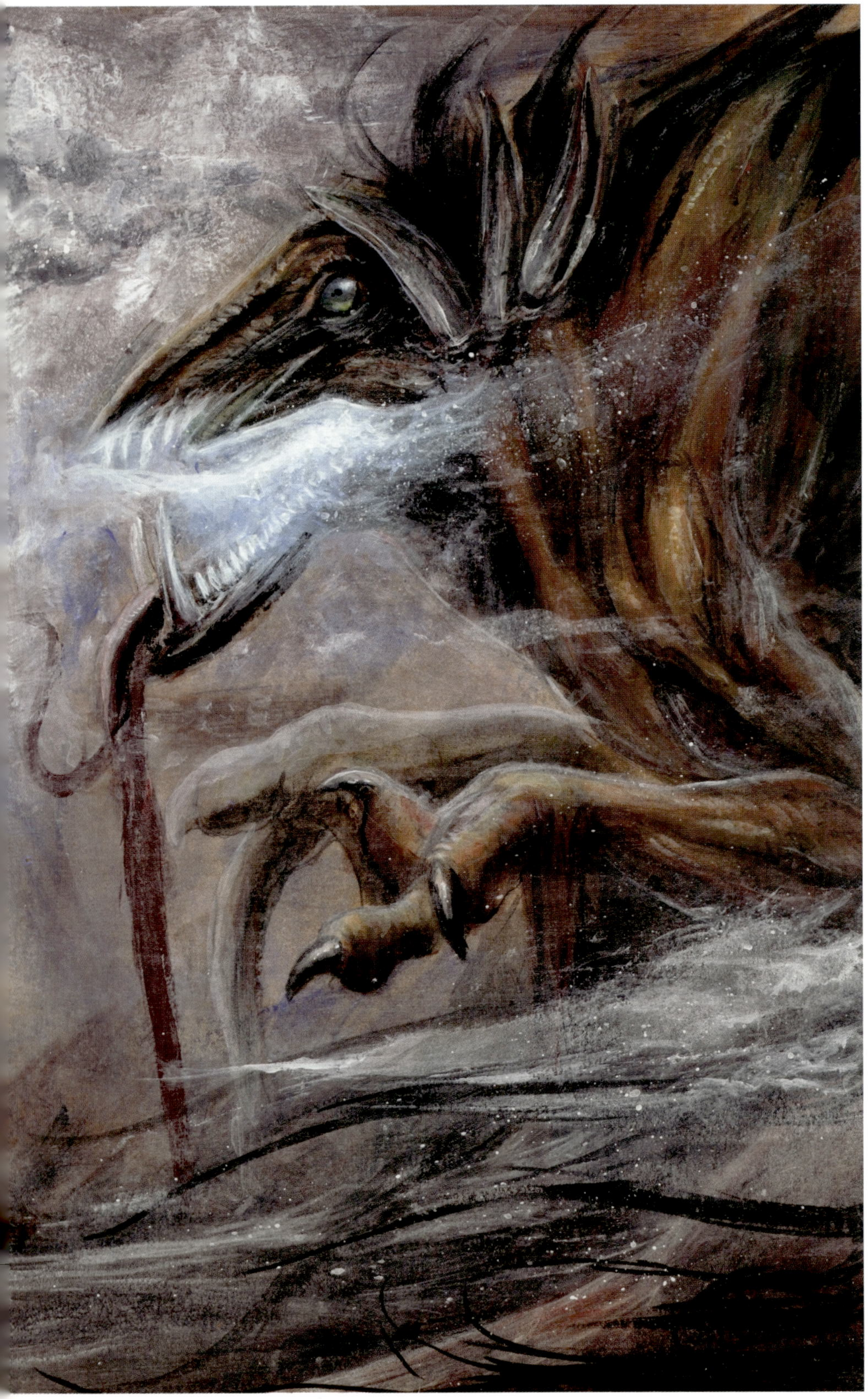

AWAKENING by Marissa Rivera (aka 'PearlPhoenix')
© Marissa Rivera 2007 · Digital media: Photoshop
'I spill my emotions all over [my art]. I genuinely care for others and those who aspire to become artists. It helps me to connect with people and to learn something from them.'
www.pearlphoenixsun.com

been chided earlier by his father for excessive daydreaming. However, just before all is lost, he renames the empress Moon Child and his fate becomes entwined with the story. He finally gets a chance to ride Falkor through Fantasia.

Falkor and the Neverending Influence

Falkor is, perhaps, one of the strangest of the film dragons. He is furry and appears more like a long, white, shaggy dog than a typical dragon. He has no wings and appears to fly as if by magic. He is also incredibly benevolent. Falkor is also very much the product of a pre-CGI era, so, while the effects may look slightly dated, his physical presence makes him a favourite with many fantasy enthusiasts. The film also has a peculiarly strange subtext that sniffs around the edges of existentialism and contemplations on depression, perhaps providing its endurance with adults who first saw it as children. Notably, *The Neverending Story* film is an adaptation of a book by German writer Michael Ende, entitled *Die Unendliche Geschichte*.

A BREATH OF SPIRIT by Marissa Rivera (aka 'PearlPhoenix')
© Marissa Rivera 2008 · Traditional media: pencil and acrylics
'Today, I do not regret my decisions; I only regret holding back for so long. I became an artist for myself and to inspire others.'
www.pearlphoenixsun.com

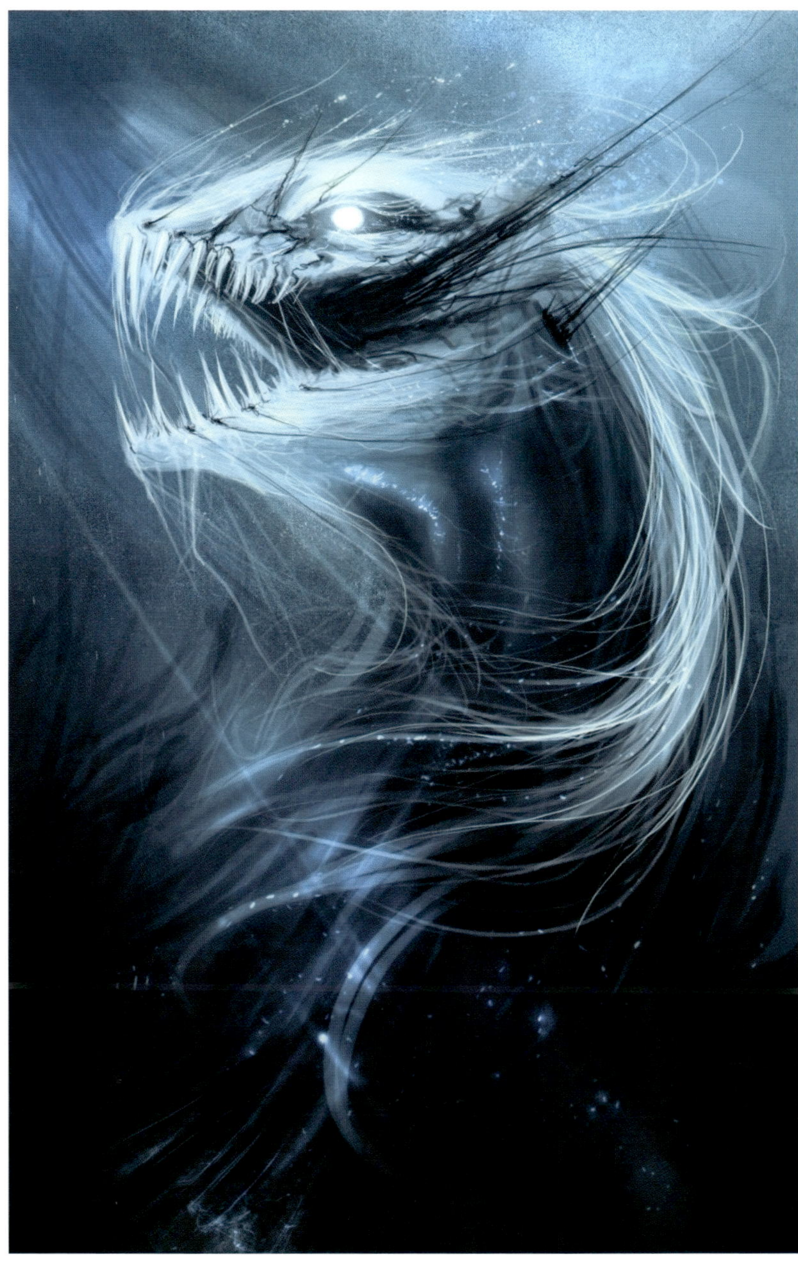

The Open Reality by Marissa Rivera (aka 'PearlPhoenix')
© Marissa Rivera 2008 · Digital media: Photoshop and Painter
'The most rewarding moment is when I am able to inspire and bring a smile to others.'
www.pearlphoenixsun.com

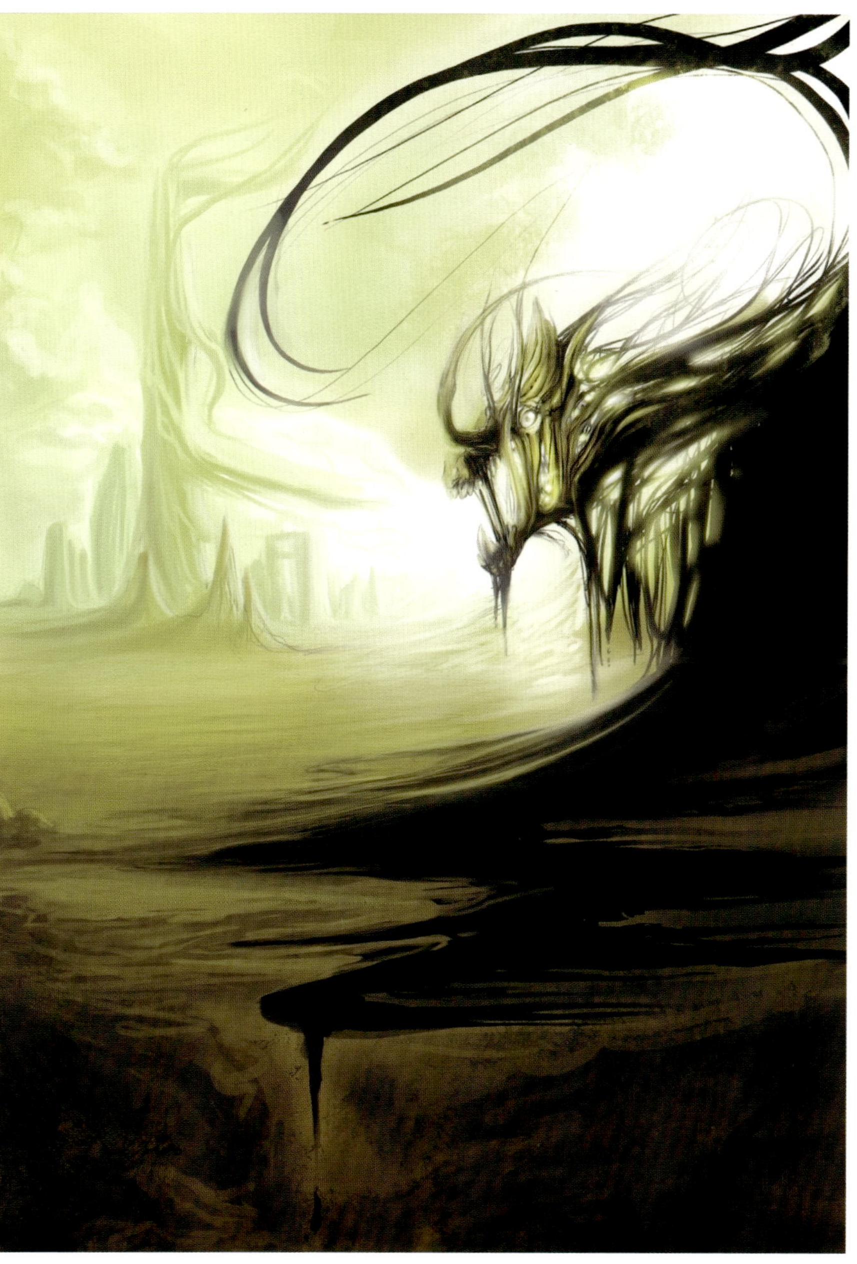

The film certainly had a marked effect on the artist Tracy Trowbridge as an eight- or nine-year-old. She recalls, 'One of the first movies that I saw was the film *The Neverending Story*. It gave me the sense of raw adventure, like not knowing what would happen next on the journey, the unknown dangers that lurk in the darkness. I've always really enjoyed that movie. From that,

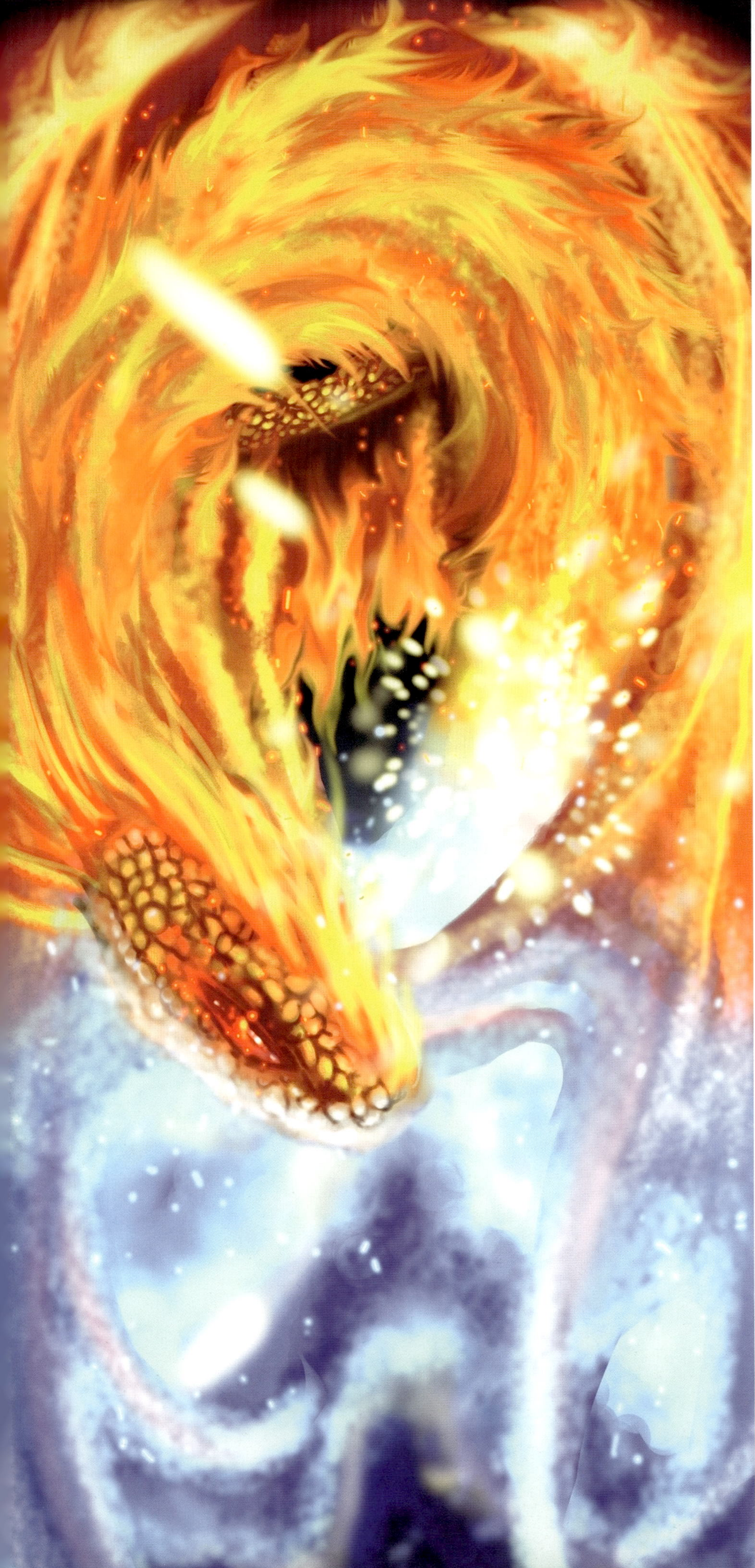

[and] *The Dark Crystal* [...] all those were inspirations. I started out sketching dinosaur-like creatures and they turned into dragons and weird creatures.'

Eragon

Saphira, the dragon featured in *Eragon*, the film adaptation of the Christopher Paolini best seller, is also a favourite. The film tells the story of Eragon, a 15-year-old farm boy and orphan, who finds a mysterious blue stone while out hunting in the wild woods. He takes the stone home and discovers, after it hatches, that it is actually a dragon egg. He keeps the dragon a secret, giving it the name Saphira. It transpires that Saphira is the last of the dragon race, and that Eragon is actually a Dragon Rider, one of an ancient order that once served as protectors of the lands now ruled by the brutal King Galbatorix and his evil wizard Durza.

Eragon goes into hiding, realizing the value of his find, alongside a storyteller named Brom. However, the King is looking for Eragon and Saphira. His agents track them down and Brom is killed, but not before Eragon has befriended a stranger, Murtagh. Brom also reveals, before his death, that he was once a Dragon Rider, and fixed it so that Eragon would find the egg. Eragon, Murtagh and Saphira then set out to find the Varden, a group

TRANSFORMATION, WATER, FIRE by Marissa Rivera (aka 'PearlPhoenix')
© Marissa Rivera 2006 · Digital media: Photoshop
www.pearlphoenixsun.com

I AM THE DEEP by Marissa Rivera (aka 'PearlPhoenix')
© Marissa Rivera 2008 · Traditional media: pencil and acrylics
www.pearlphoenixsun.com

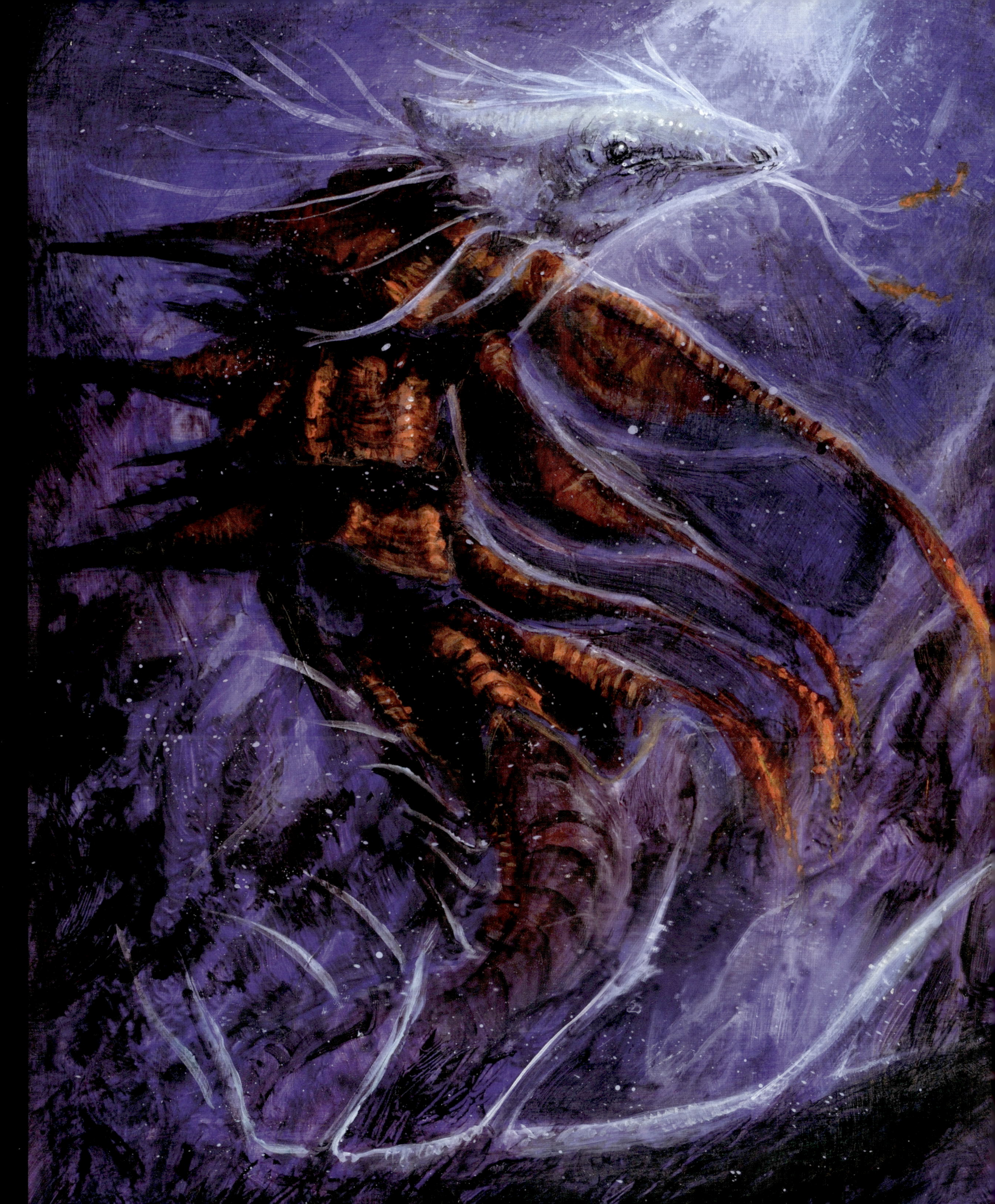

The Conjuration by Tracy Trowbridge (aka 'Machine Guts')

© Tracy Trowbridge 2008; Digital media: Photoshop; An example of Tracy's interest in painting atmosphere and light – 'I utilize these elements to instil a sense of surreal, humid depth'; http://machine-guts.deviantart.com

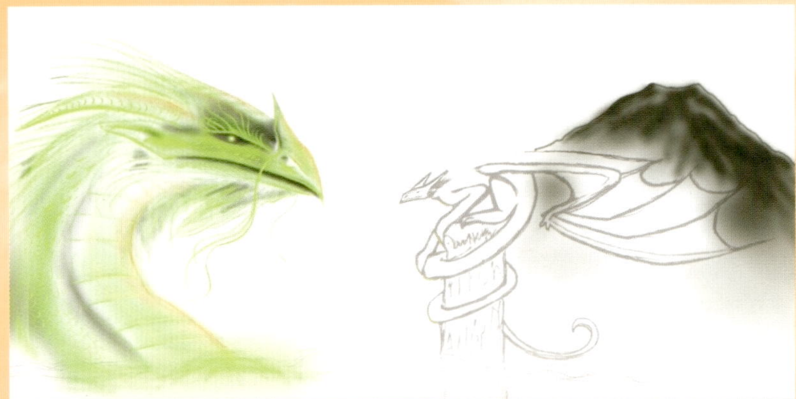

SAMPLE STEP 1. I begin by sketching the basic elements that will appear in my painting. Here I have sketched the two dragons, the water and a shape for the volcano, which unites all of the elements together. Your eye is led from the left, through the middle and to the upper right.

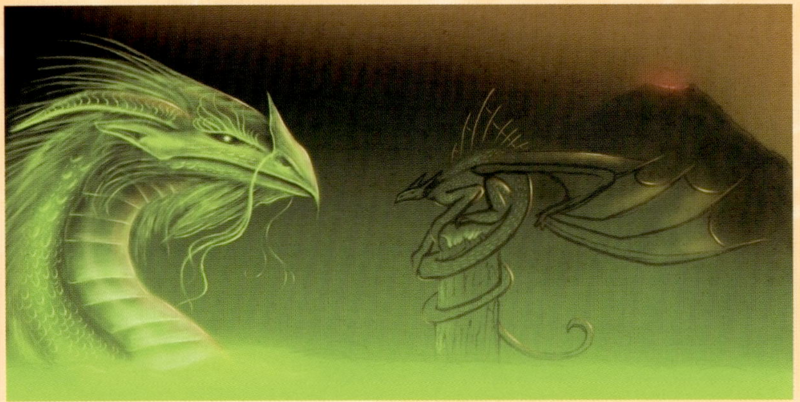

SAMPLE STEP 2. The use of light and shadow is essential to creating a sense of drama in your painting. Here I have loosely painted the colour, which will set the final mood of the piece. I have started painting highlights on the smaller dragon which reflect the colour of the sky. Red hues are then applied to the volcano to suggest a sense of warmth.

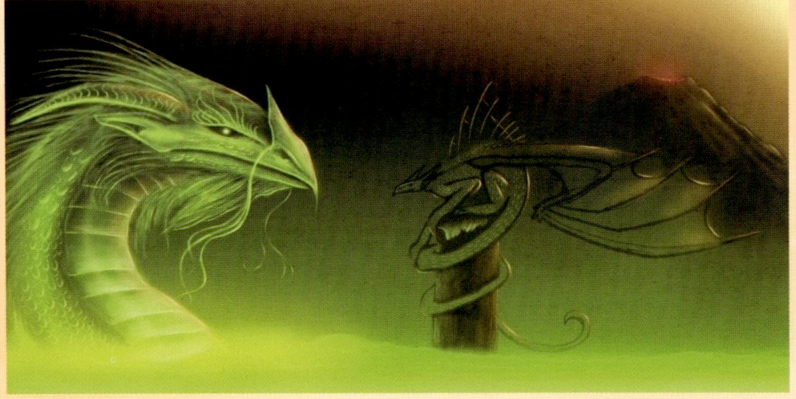

SAMPLE STEP 3. In this stage, I begin adding details and highlights to the volcano and wooden post the dragon is coiled around. The sky has been painted with an additional light source. A glow is also added around the Dragon Spirit, giving it the appearance of an apparition. Loose details are applied to the water.

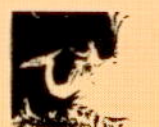

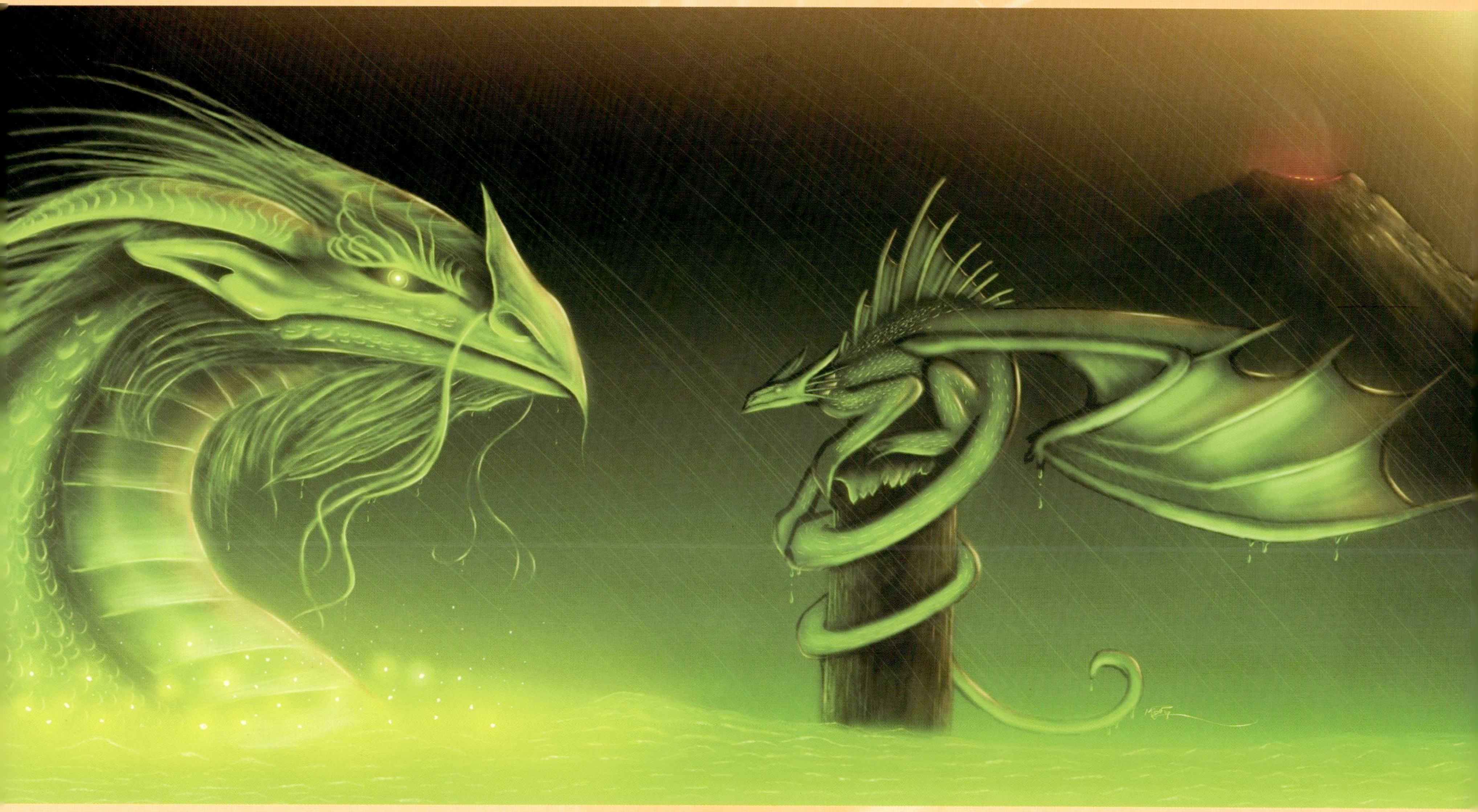

FINISHING TOUCHES. To finish the piece, I create the final colours and details on the small dragon. Glowing sparks are painted at the base of the Dragon Spirit as He emerges from the water. Waves are applied to enhance the illusion that the Dragon Spirit has risen from the depths. As a final touch, rain is added to complete the humid, murky feel of the scene.

of anti-Galbatorix rebels, to help them vanquish the King. Along the way, Eragon meets a mysterious elf girl and has run-ins with various magical, wild and chaotic characters, before they find the Varden and have their final showdown with King.

Christopher Paolini famously wrote *Eragon* as a precocious teenager, having written the first draft aged 15. His parents self-published the first edition in 2001 and it was eventually picked up by Random House imprint Alfred A. Knopf Books For Young Readers, which published its own version in 2003. The 2006 film adaptation, directed by debutant Stefen Fangmeier, brought Saphira to life, voiced by British actress Rachel Weisz. While the film itself was critically mauled, the Saphira has been well received as a screen dragon. Animated by the crew at Industrial Light and Magic, Saphira is additionally interesting in that she has been given feathered – rather than the usual membranous bat-like – wings. As a formidable yet protective, friendly dragon, she is also very popular among those who like their dragons with a bit more personality.

The Lord of the Rings

Of course, with Peter Jackson's *The Lord of the Rings* trilogy film adaptations released between 2001 and 2003, it is inevitable that we return to that film. Much of the design was carried out by John Howe. He recalls the typical days on set, 'It was great.

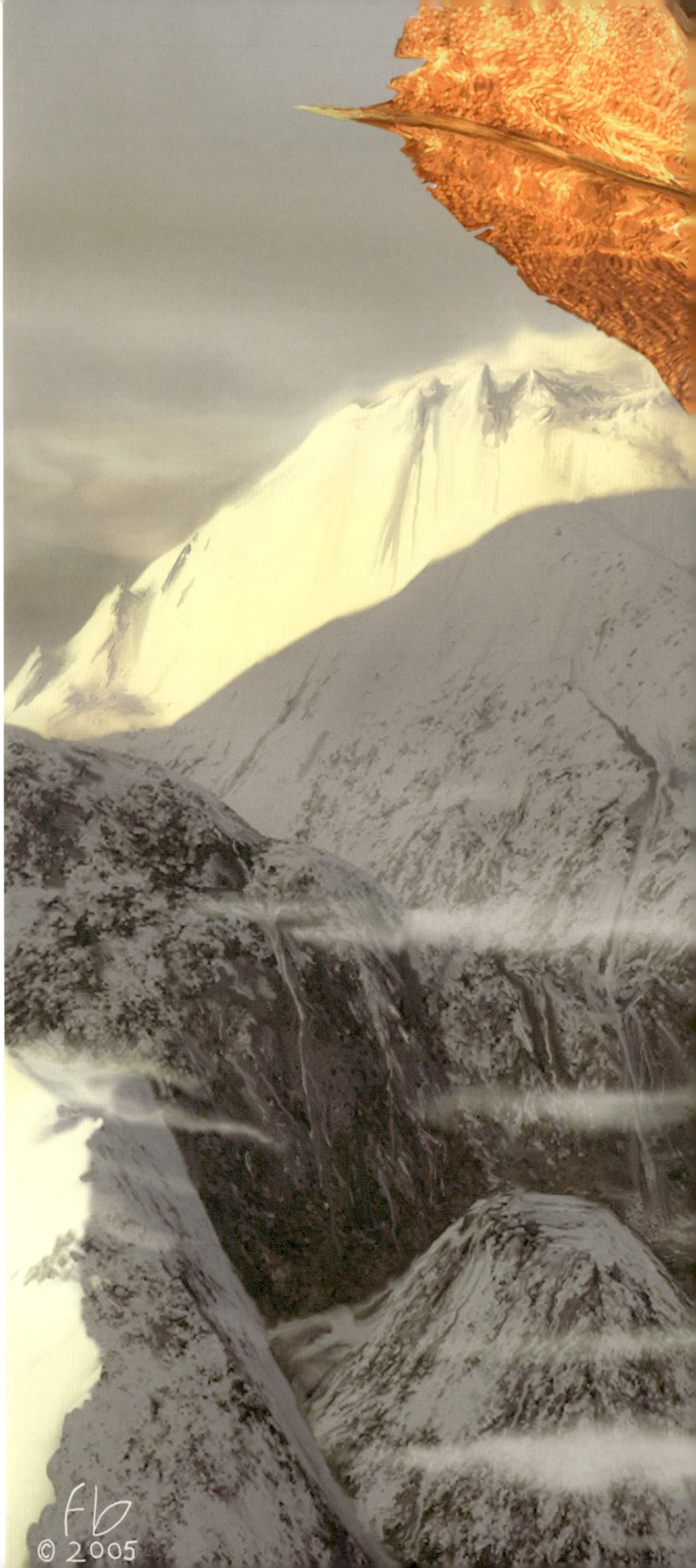

DRAGON FLIGHT by Frank Berger
© Frank Berger 2005 · Digital media: Photoshop
Cover illustration for *One Wizard Place* by D.M. Paul,
published by Outskirts Press.
www.bergergraphics.com

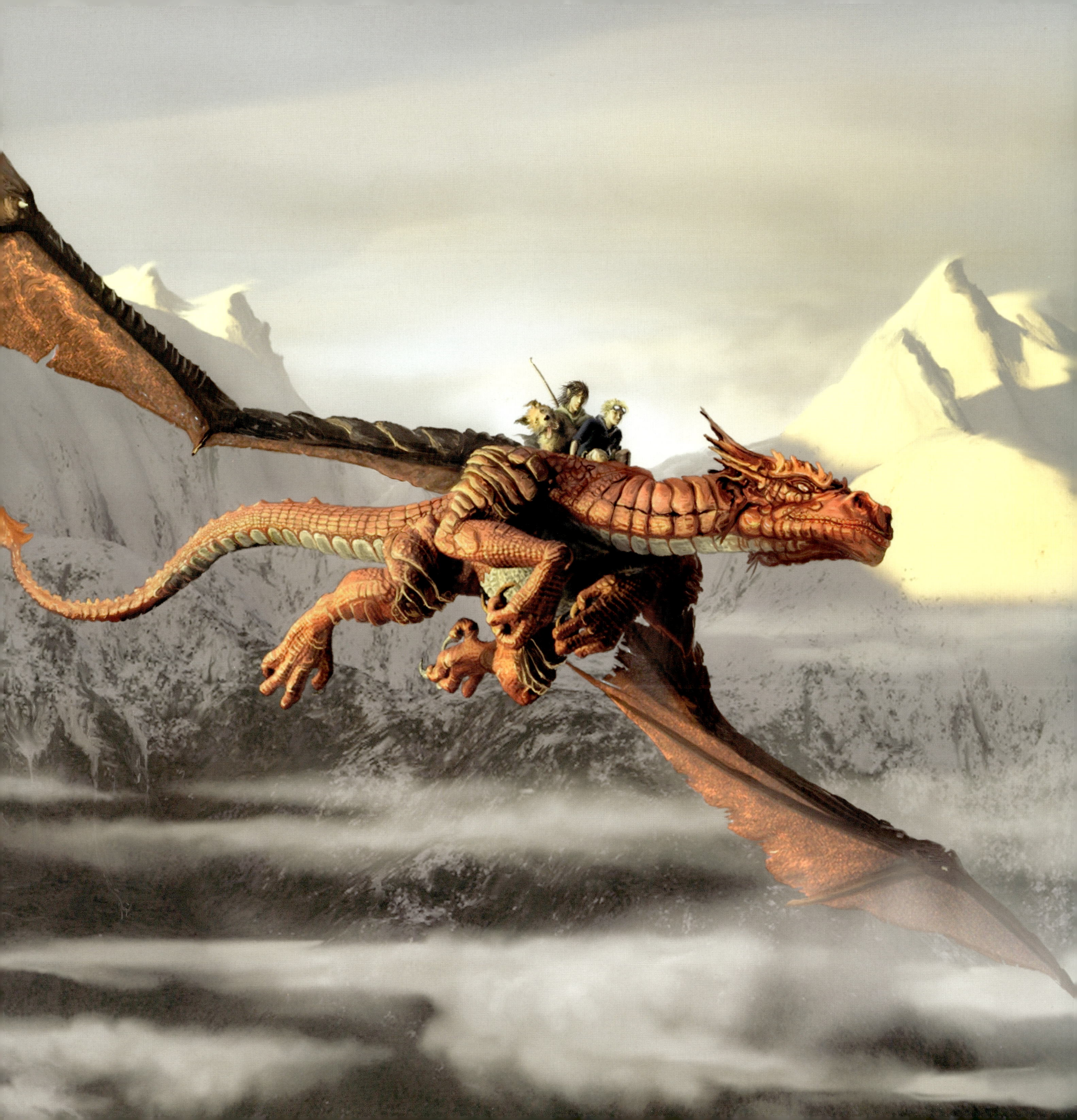

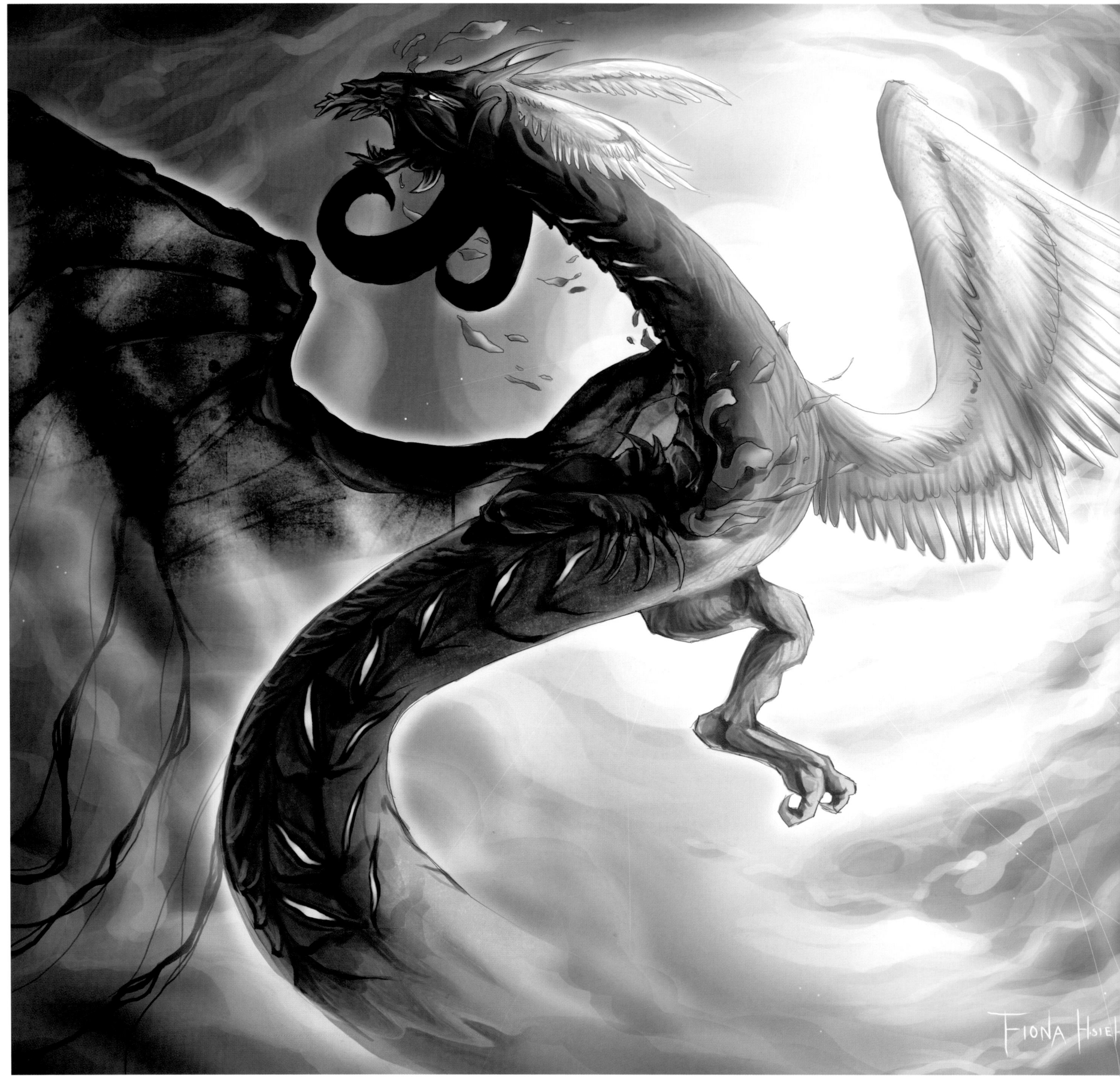
FIONA HSIEH

 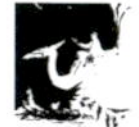

We worked really, really hard, 10 hours a day, five or six days a week, just churning out sketches and sketches. But the fun part was the possibility to be able to go into all these areas you only really touch on when you're doing finished illustration. So we were relieved of the burden of actually doing the director's job. We were just creating the elements, which was really fun because then you can get into the design process, which can be quite intricate.'

He continues, 'On a good day, we'd have a meeting with Peter, who would outline what he saw, and based on that and on the book and on the script, we'd start drawing these locations. When we had enough work to show, we'd have another meeting, and he'd say I like that, I don't care for that, and then we'd go back and draw some more and then they'd build a little 3D maquette and then we'd work up from there. That was just for

IMMORTAL ENTRANCE by Fiona Hsieh
© Fiona Hsieh 2008 · Digital media: Photoshop
Fiona is 15 years old and lives in California.
http://chaoslavawolf.deviantart.com

THE SUMMONER by Kuang Hong
© Kuang Hong 2007 · Digital media: Photoshop
www.zemotion.net/noah

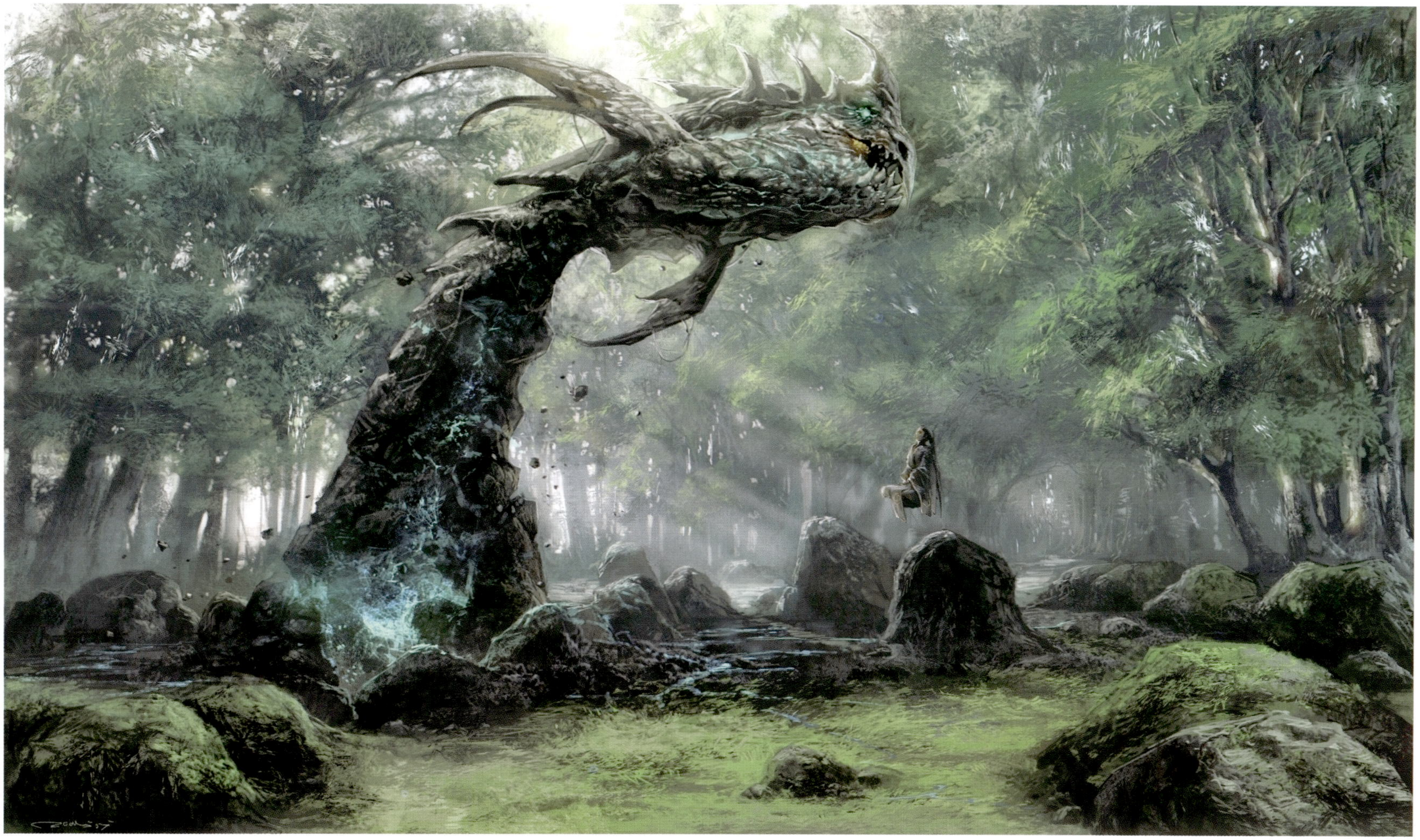

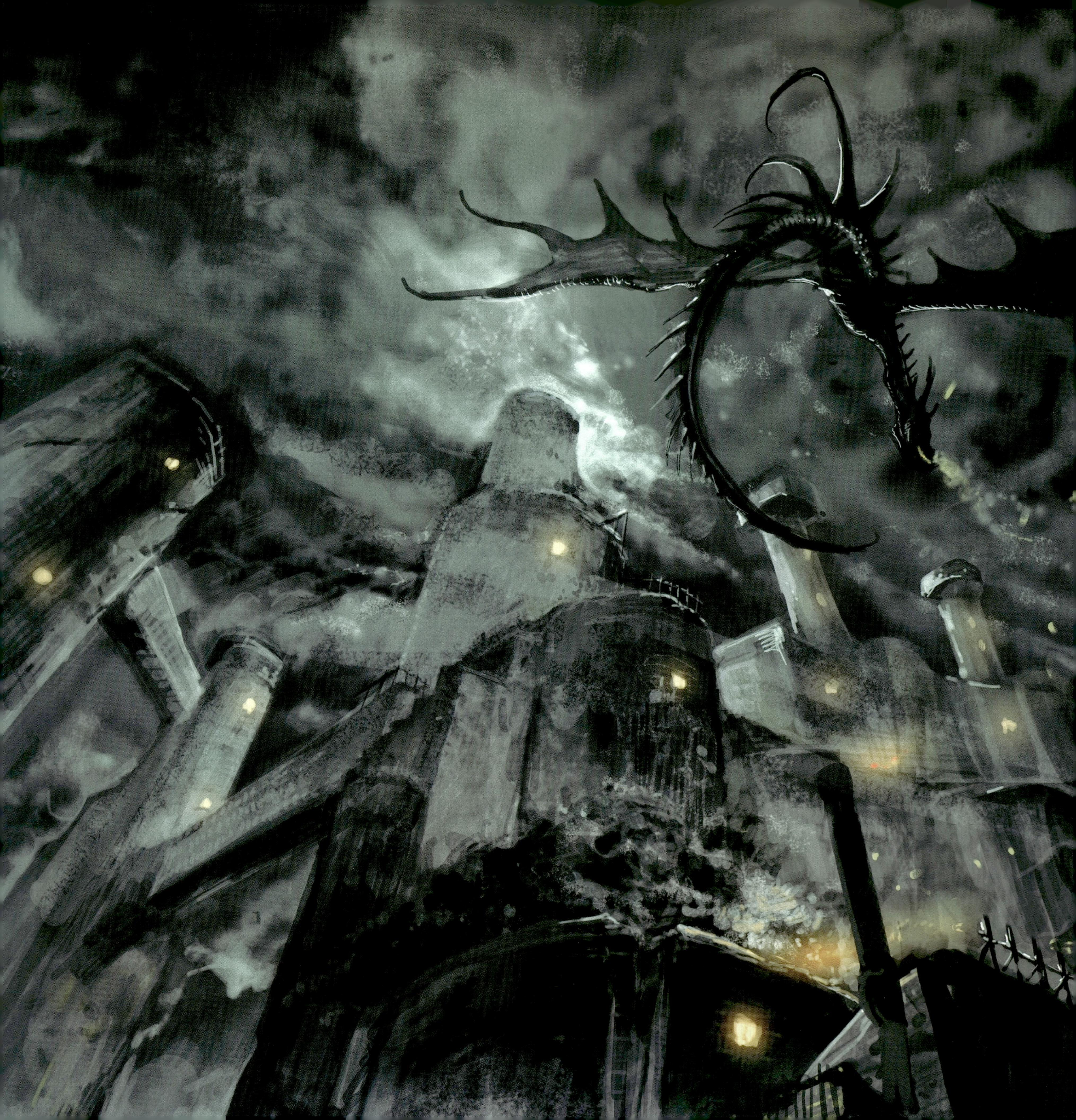

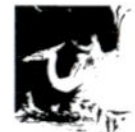

the broader strokes. Then we'd go back and design all the little fiddly bits. But very much a back and forth, symbiotic sort of thing.'

Of course, Howe worked with a team of other illustrators, which included Alan Lee. Howe's input was certainly crucial, however. He recalls, 'The Nazgûl are pretty much how I'd see them, for example. They went very, very quickly into sculpt. Everything was sculpted, and then they would scan the sculpt and then they would build the 3D models from that. So there was always this passage through a physical sculpt. Which I think really anchored it more deeply in reality than you would if you'd gone straight to computer generated. A good sculpture is a very efficient way of pinning something down. It's easier to see, you can walk around it and come back, check it out, and then take that into the 3D computer and stuff made perfect sense. I think it's a more efficient way of doing it.'

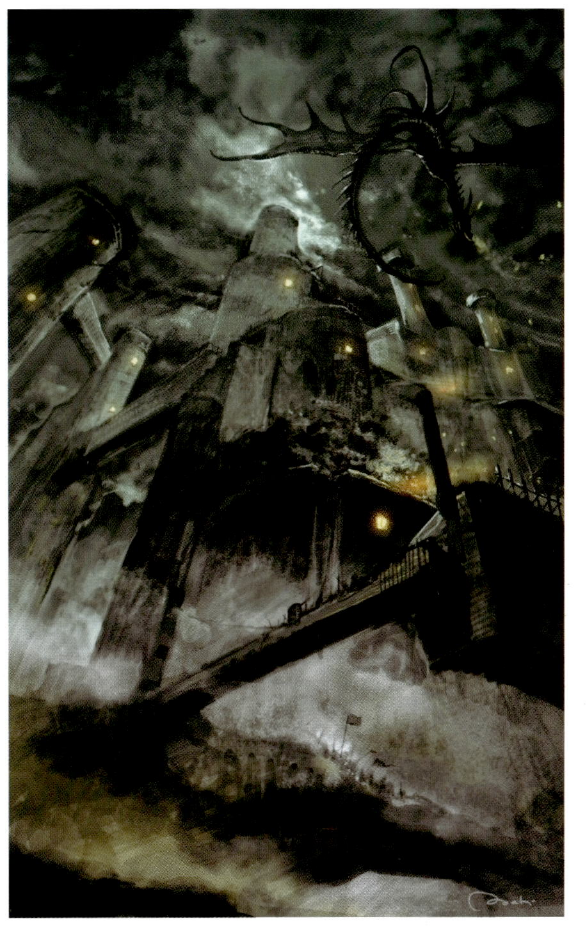

Are They Dragons?

Is Godzilla a dragon? He could be. He has many of the physical attributes of a very reptilian, lizard-dragon and he is a terrible and terrifying fire-breathing monster. In his 1971 outing against pollution monster Hedora, Godzilla even flies. Perhaps when you see him battling three-headed, bi-tailed, bipedal King Ghidorah in the 1991 film he looks less so, but in temperament, his menace and unpredictability give him some of the qualities we have come to expect from dragons in film.

Could the dinosaurs depicted in Steven Spielberg's *Jurassic Park* trilogy be considered dragons? Well, they are certainly 'monsters': they do what monsters do. They frighten the characters in the film with their size and ferociousness, as well as their guile and cunning. What we get in the original film are dinosaurs as dinosaurs: they are big, terrible, terrifying lizards. However, as the trilogy evolves, especially by part III, the velociraptors in particular have become far more 'dragon-like'. The character Billy Brennan steals the velociraptor egg and we discover that a great deal of his misadventure arises as a result of this 'insolence'. It is only resolved once the character Dr Grant makes peace with them. It is more the kind of myth we would associate with dragons. Indeed, Harry Potter guardian Hagrid has a particularly rotten time as the result of coming across a dragon egg that he should not have, in *Harry Potter and The Philosopher's Stone.* So it is not a wild stretch to imagine an element of the 'dragon' in *Jurassic Park.*

LOST CASTLE by Kuang Hong
© Kuang Hong 2005 · Digital media: Photoshop
www.zemotion.net/noah

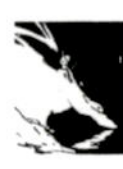

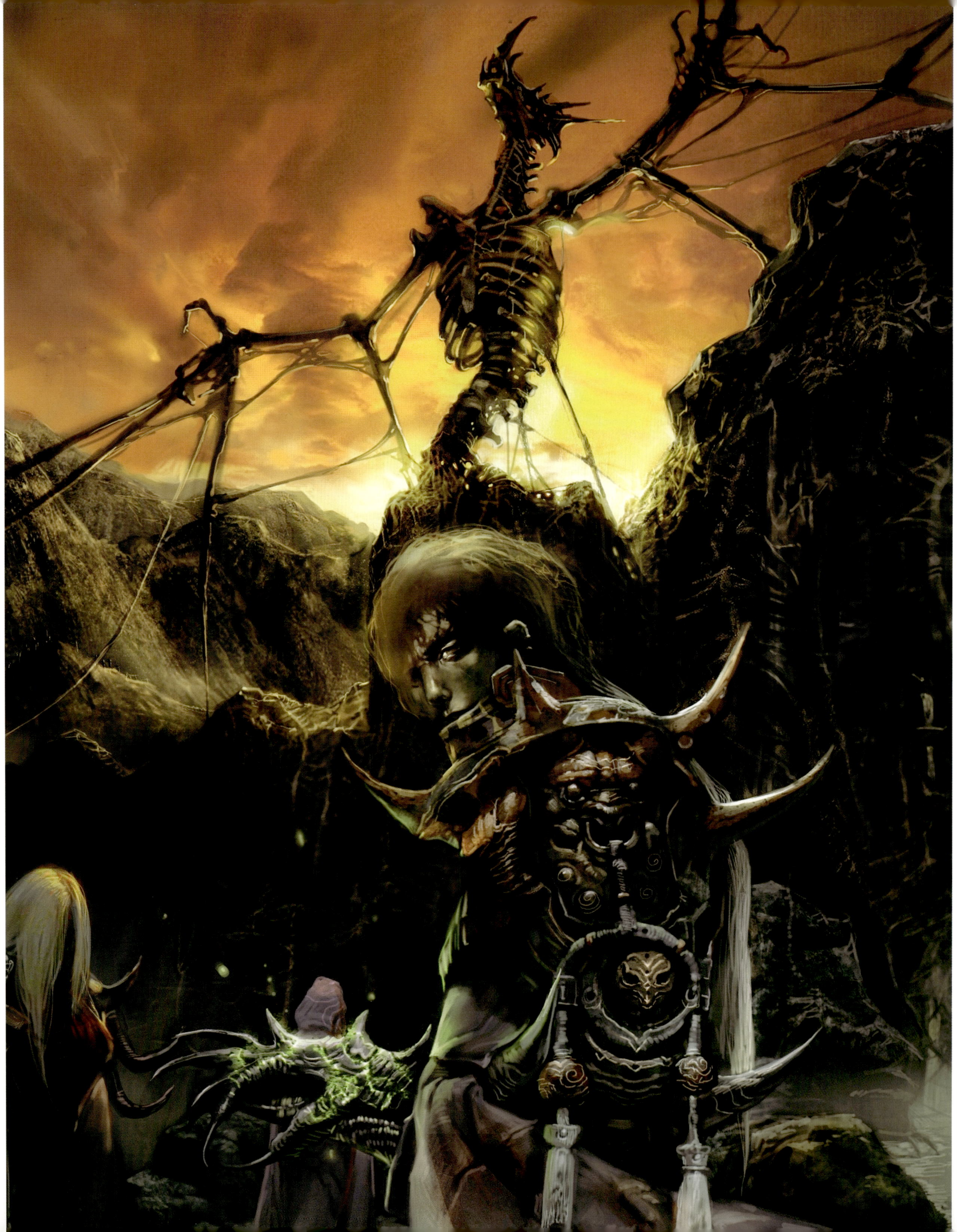

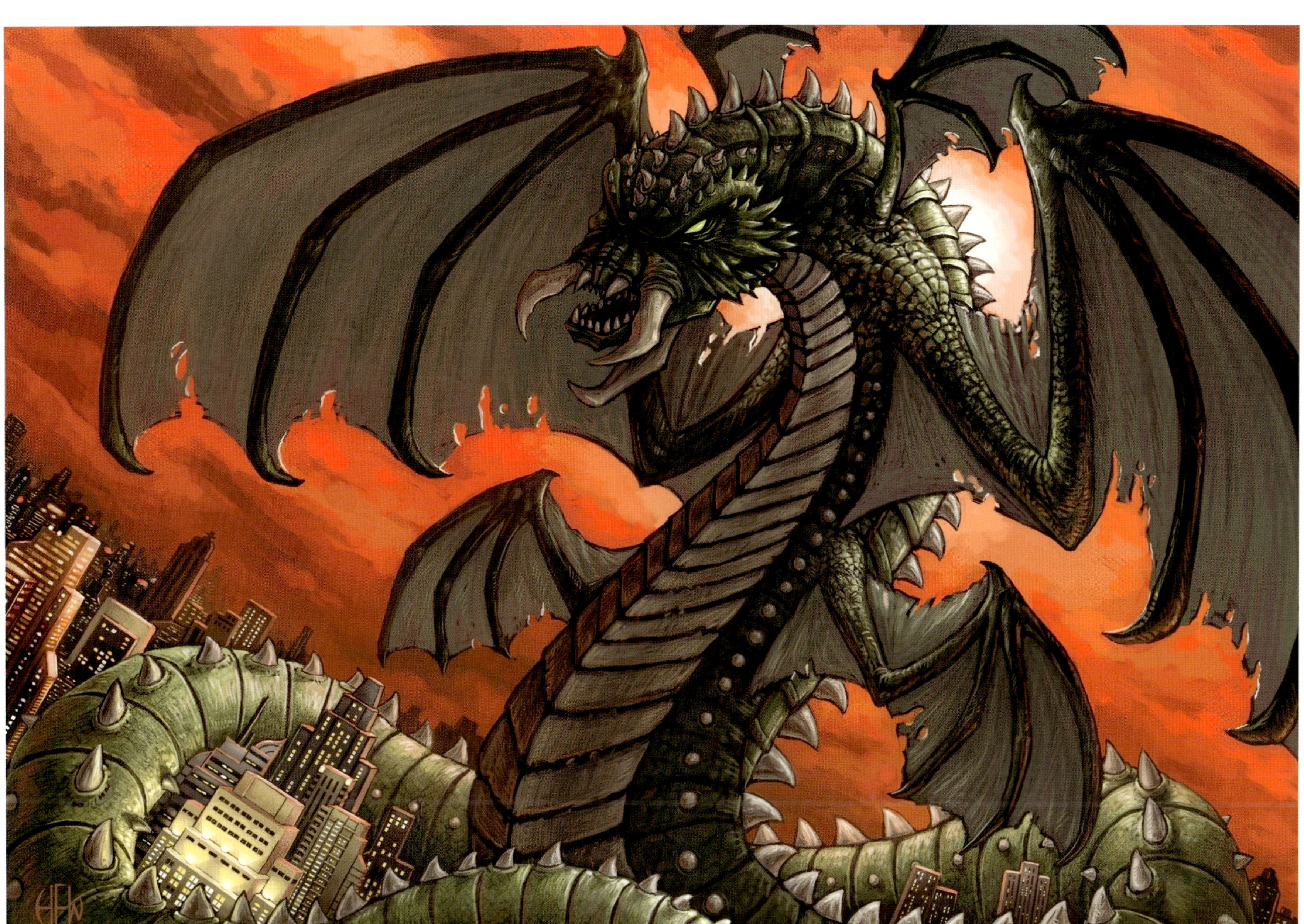

RELIC OF THE DRAGON by Kuang Hong
© Kuang Hong 2007 · Digital media: Photoshop
www.zemotion.net/noah

AWAKENED EVIL by Alvin Hew
© Alvin Hew 2008 · Digital media: Photoshop
www.alvinhew.blogspot.com

And, as Martin Bradbury says, 'Dinosaurs might not be considered 'fantasy' creatures but, for me, they hold as much fascination as any dragon of legend, perhaps more so, as these dragons really did live and breathe.'

There is even something of the dragon in the *Alien* series, particularly parts I and II. Like all good dragons, the alien in the

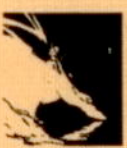

Green Dragon by Julia Tarasenko (aka 'Elfessa')

© Julia Tarasenko 2007; Digital media: Photoshop; Inspired by the books *Dragonriders of Pern* by Anne McCaffrey and the view from Julia's window, when summer sun shines through tree leaves; http://elfessa.deviantart.com

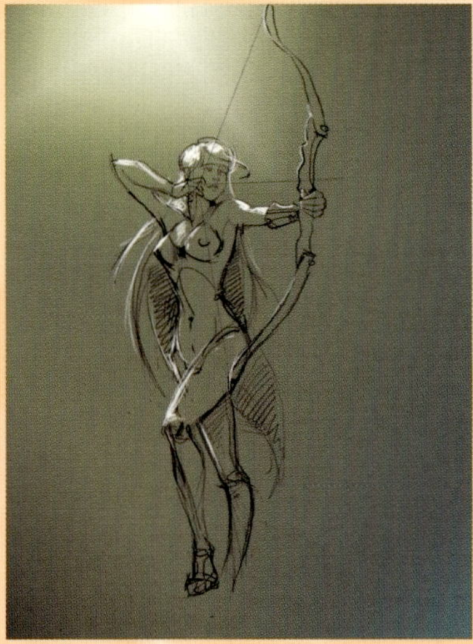

SAMPLE STEP 1. Usually I draw a pencil sketch in the beginning, but for this work I started without it, going straight into Photoshop.

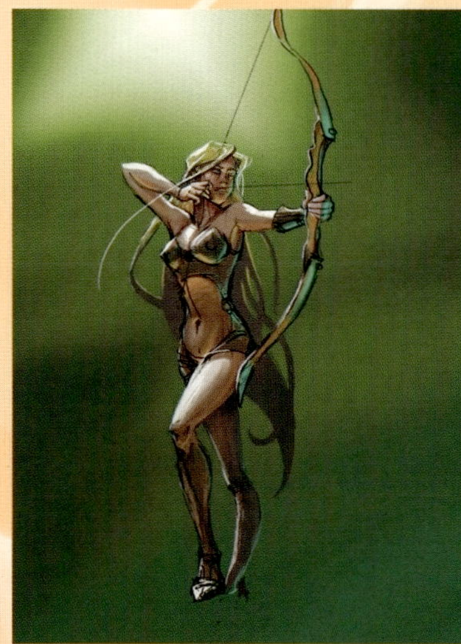

SAMPLE STEP 2. First I drew the figure of the girl, getting her colours and highlights down roughly.

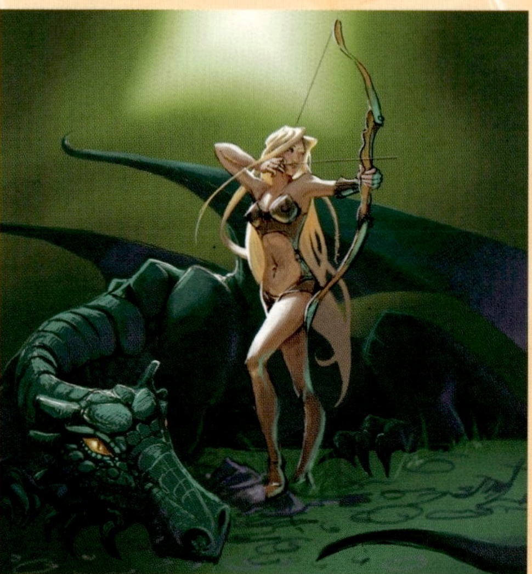

SAMPLE STEP 3. This work entailed numerous corrections in the process. I realized that there was not enough space for the dragon so I increased the width of the canvas.

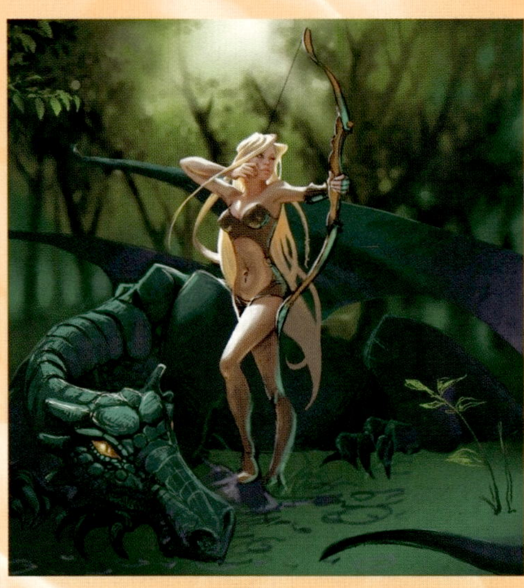

SAMPLE STEP 4. With the background, dragon and girl on different layers I was able to play with the drawing and composition easily.

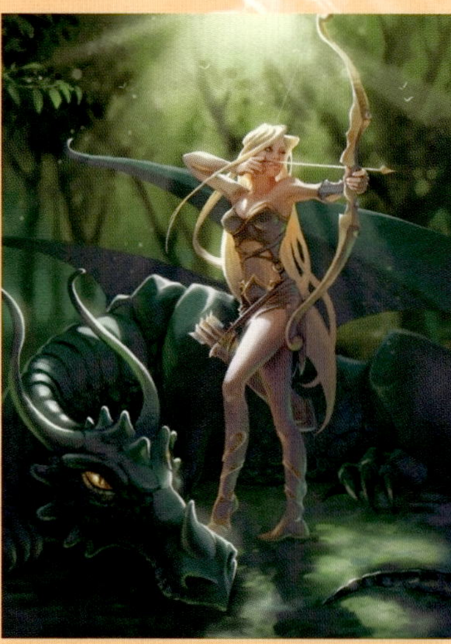

SAMPLE STEP 5. I didn't like the new proportions, so I cropped the picture back. By reflecting the image, I noticed that the dragon's muzzle had the wrong perspective and the girl's leg seemed ungraceful, so I corrected them.

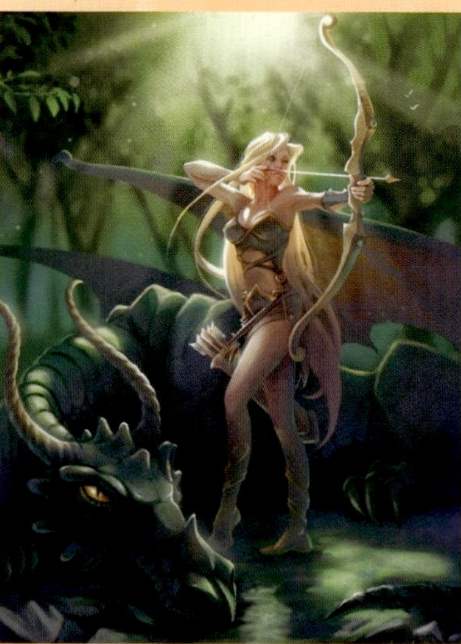

SAMPLE STEP 6. I added more distinctive light rays and flying butterflies.

FINISHING TOUCHES. (RIGHT) At the final stage I added more colours, depth and details.

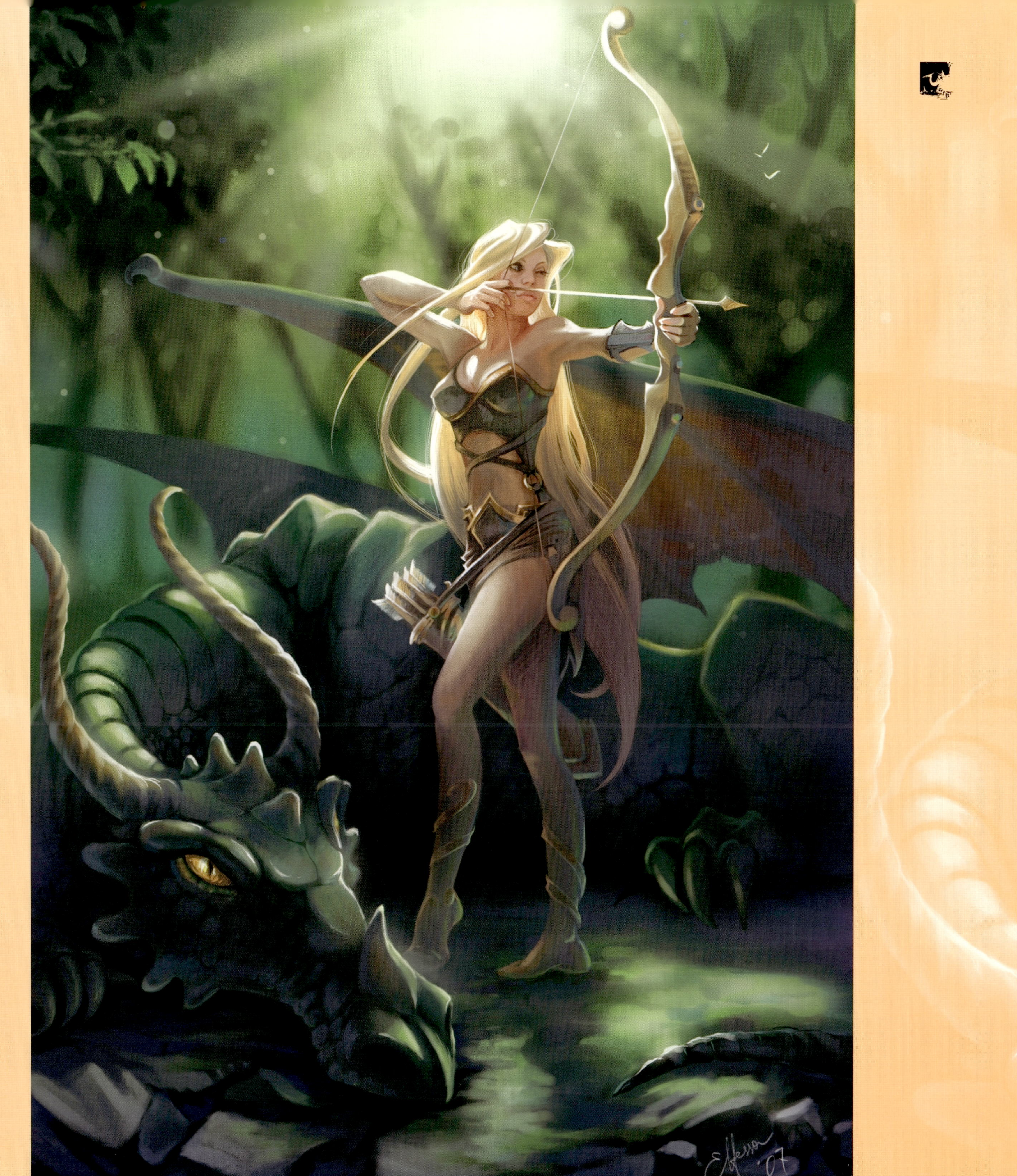

Ridley Scott introduction is practically indestructible and clearly serpentine, although much of the creature's reproductive cycle is based on that of certain insects. It is not to say these creatures are film dragons in themselves, but they do feature elements thereof.

Dragons, Art, Inspiration and Advice

Who would be a fantasy artist? It is a particularly tough profession to choose. In terms of the art 'establishment', it is not one of the more highly regarded disciplines and you have to spend a great deal of time creating abstractions that do not exist and have very little reference in the real world and, as such, require ideas to be completely plucked from the air. Boris Vallejo puts it particularly well: 'In order to create a good illustration, an artist must have a number of attributes: training, good imagination and good narrative among other things. In order to create a good fantasy illustration, the artist also has to be capable of pulling ideas out of thin air, since often they have to paint things that do not exist.'

There is this romantic notion about artists, that they sit in solitary confinement in creative reveries and pluck inspiration from nowhere. Certainly, the talented or inspired artist will have ideas that he or she will be compelled to commit to canvas; but for the working artist, it really is a matter of having to win commission and work to a brief within a set period of time. His or her art will be required to push certain buttons, while also clearly reflecting the artist's own vision – the reason for his or her selection in the first place.

Plausibility

Artists all have different working methods. Some are absolutely certain that you should use reference material. Todd Lockwood is adamant about the morphology of dragons, that those which are supposed to look realistic really do look plausible. He says, 'One of the highlights of my career was getting to design the dragons for *Dungeons and Dragons*. We had a chance to put out a new model for dragons, to sort of dispel some of the things that had always bothered me in terms of dragon art. Things like dragons with a great big potbelly and thunderous thighs, like a T-Rex. But this is an animal that flies. It doesn't need big thunderous thighs, and the potbelly makes no sense.'

CONSTELLATION by Julia Tarasenko (aka 'Elfessa')
© Julia Tarasenko 2007 · Digital media: Illustrator
This piece represents the constellation of Virgo. The dragon represents the star's passions and intrigues.
http://elfessa.deviantart.com

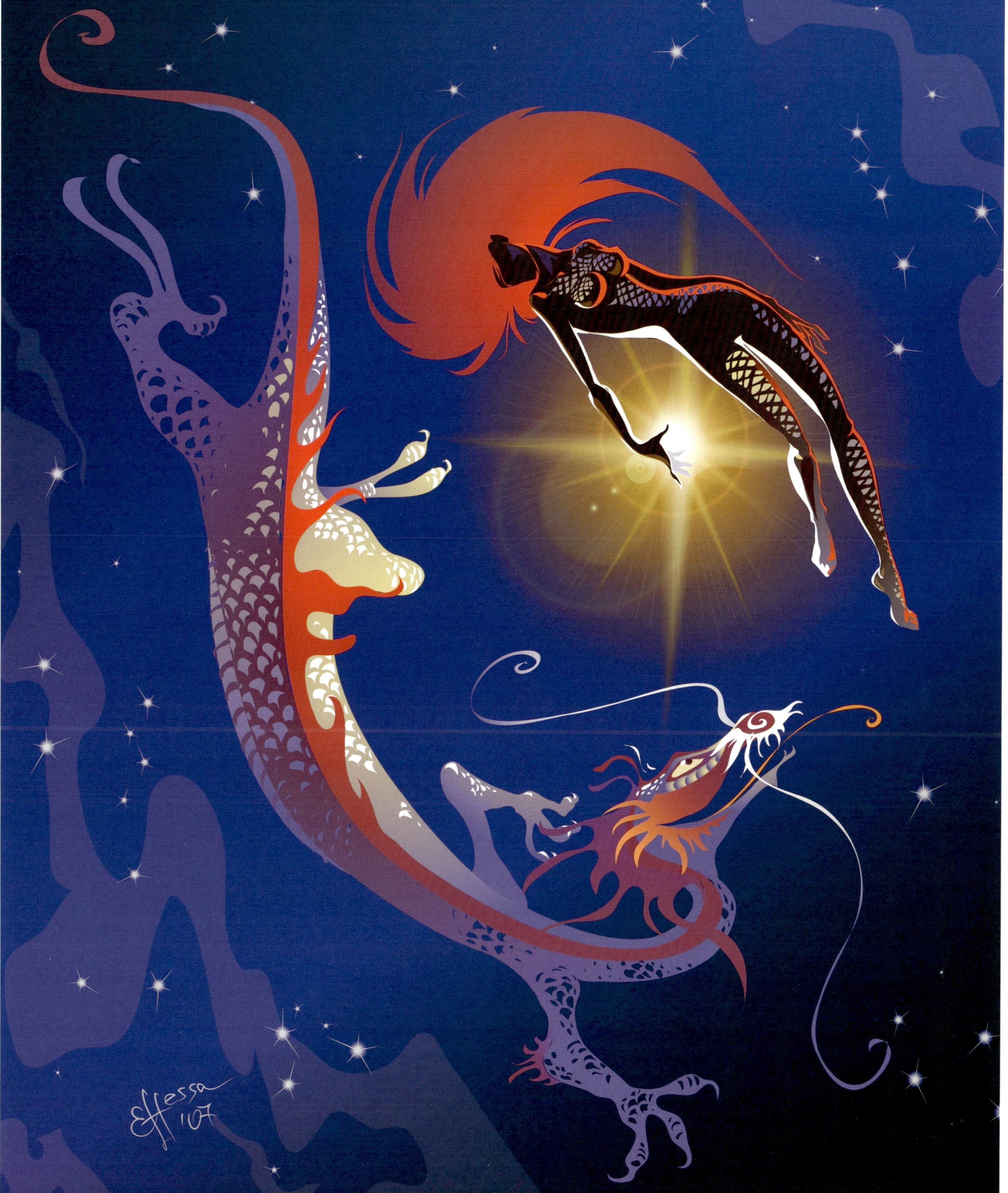
Effessa '07

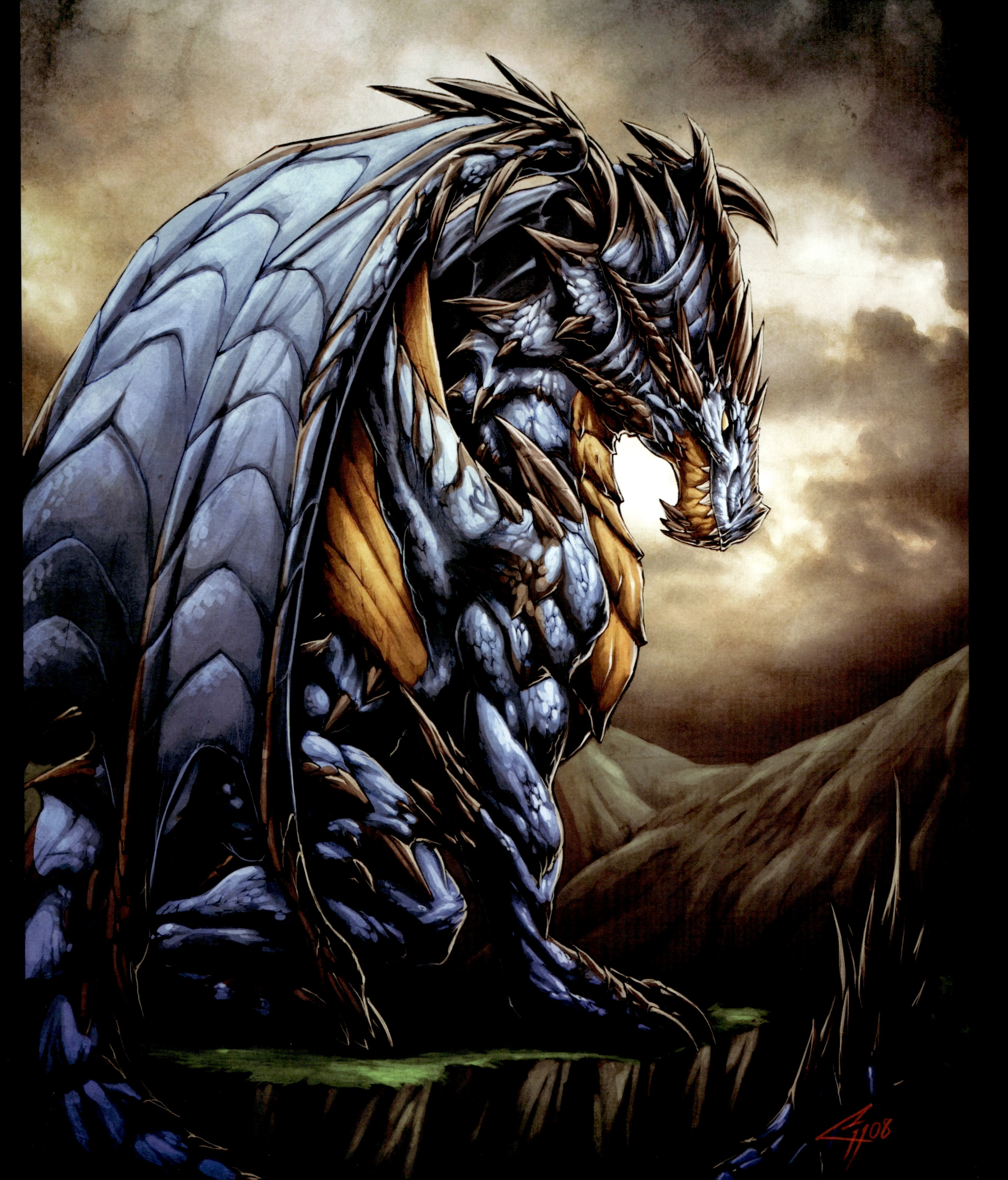

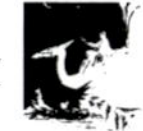

DRAGON CENIZA by Carlos Herrera Portilla
© Carlos Herrera Portilla 2008
Digital media: sketch in pencil, Photoshop
Carlos Herrera Portilla (born in August 1985) is a Chilean illustrator.
He works mostly for Salo's trading card game Myths and Legends, and for some Chilean publishers.
http://hardcolico.deviantart.com

Todd continues, 'If you take the features of a bird, they're very lean and they have huge breast muscles obviously. So dragons with wings that just look like cocktail umbrellas stuck into them annoyed me! What power's in those wings? How do they lift? So I really wanted to look at dragons from the inside out and have them look like real beasts that really lived and not rely on, "oh well, they're magical" as an explanation. [...] That's the science fiction geek in me coming through. If it is a living, breathing animal, then it has to make sense. One of my pet peeves is dragons with human shoulders on their forelimbs. Our shoulders developed from an animal that swung from tree branches. A dragon would never have to do that because it has wings. It makes no sense to me.'

Different Approaches

Bob Eggleton says that he mixes ideas when he goes to draw dragons. He says, 'I do a little bit of everything. I find lizard pictures, I might like the scale patterns and that might inspire something. But ultimately they come out of a shape. I start drawing an interesting shape that might come out of nowhere, and then if I'm going to refine it, I start around the eye. Because the eye really tells you what the beast is going to look like.'

Tracy Trowbridge begins with the surroundings. 'Typically before I begin working on a dragon piece, the first elements I'll think about are its surroundings. So the environment, what kind of pose it will have, whether it will be standing or crouched, or in attack or in flight. A lot of times before I even start working I'll even listen to a song, or it will be after I've watched a film or something. But typically that's how I'll begin. [...] After I get a rough sketch of the environment that it's in and what kind of pose it's in, I'll start sketching out the different details it will have.'

Imagination v. References

Alan Lathwell used to use a lot more reference material than he currently does. 'I used to use models a lot more than I do now. I recommend for beginners to use models, definitely, but I do think, if you paint a figure enough, you can make it up. Hands are tricky, but you just have a mirror by the side of your workspace and if you're having trouble with a hand, you just go to the mirror.'

There is a caveat, however. 'Generally I try not to use photographs or anything, because in fantasy art, you're aiming to distort the figure if anything. You really want to push it to its limit. So if anyone does use models, I'd say just use it as a guide. Don't stick rigidly to it. I think it's much better to use the imagination and push those figures to the limit. That would be my advice.'

It is similar for Jon Hodgson. 'I definitely use references but in quite an indirect way. I look at things like charging tigers, things like birds taking flight and landing, lizard skin; all that stuff is well worth looking at. That informs what you do and makes it much more believable. But I tend to use a lot of imagination if

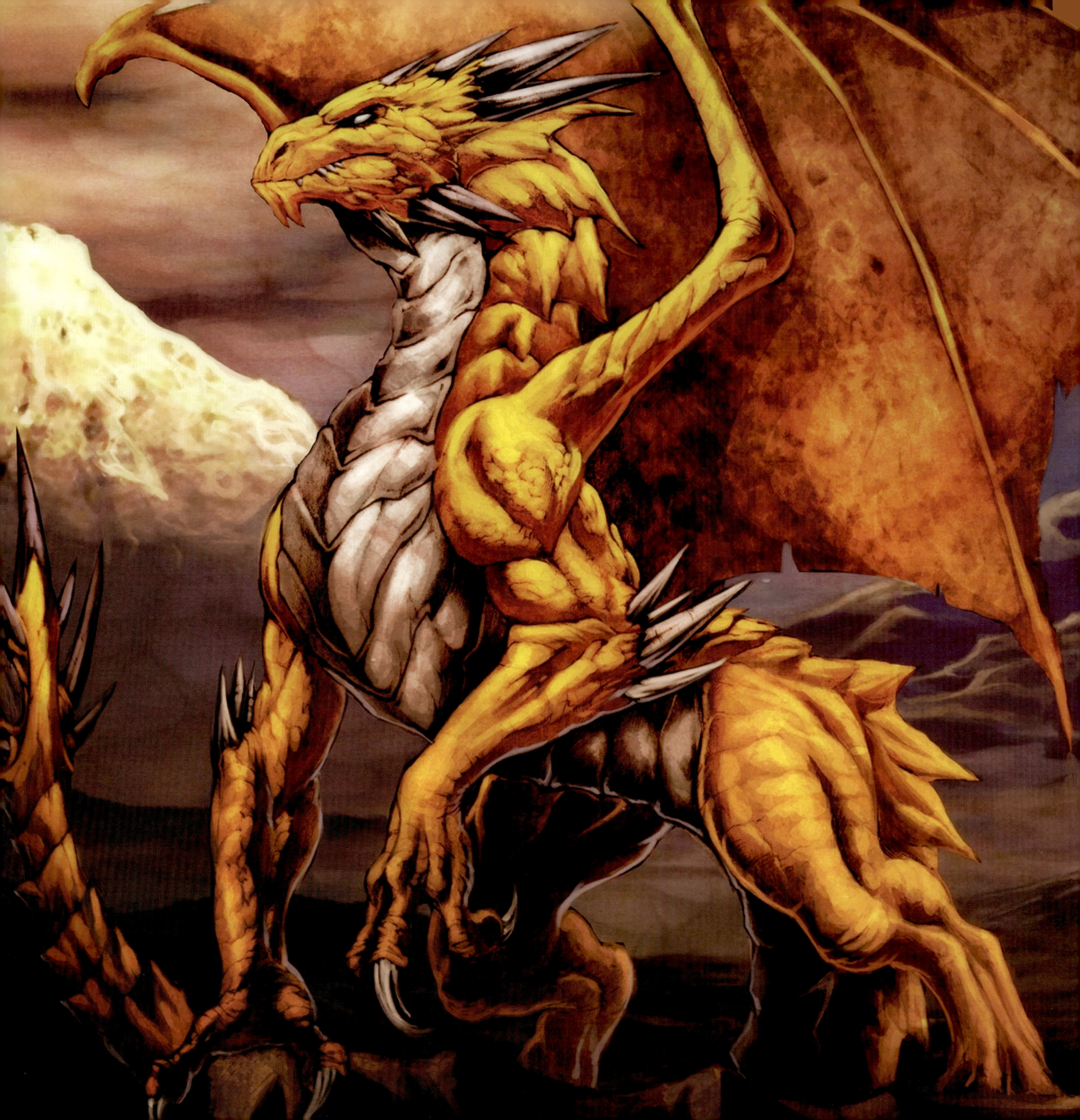

I'm honest. I don't paint with pictures right next to me. I definitely like to get it into my head. I think that informs what I do but I don't stick to it slavishly. Within fantasy if you've got a good idea that looks cool, and it works then I go with that.'

Reference in the Mind

The self-taught Janny Wurts also recalls how she learned her discipline, 'How did I learn to paint? I went to museums and saw how the masters did it, I read books on their techniques, I went to conventions where other illustrators had their originals up and I asked them, I went to publishers' offices and saw the original paintings. The knowledge exists in books and in people's minds. You've just got to put yourself into the environment where it's happening and observe and learn from it. Then you go home and practise, practise, practise.'

But of her actual technique, she says, 'I will go and look at a lot of different things. I live on a country property. I'll go out into the woods, I'll go out into the wilderness. I have a big picture album in my mind and I'll flip through all kinds of images. But then when I sit down to assemble something, I can visualize my own creation. So from a written manuscript, either

Golden Dragon by Carlos Herrera Portilla
© Carlos Herrera Portilla 2007
Digital media: sketch in pencil, Photoshop
Created for a Chilean board game, Arcana, created by Jose Luis Flores.
http://hardcolico.deviantart.com

Black Dragon by Carlos Herrera Portilla
© Carlos Herrera Portilla 2007 · Traditional drawing: pencil
http://hardcolico.deviantart.com

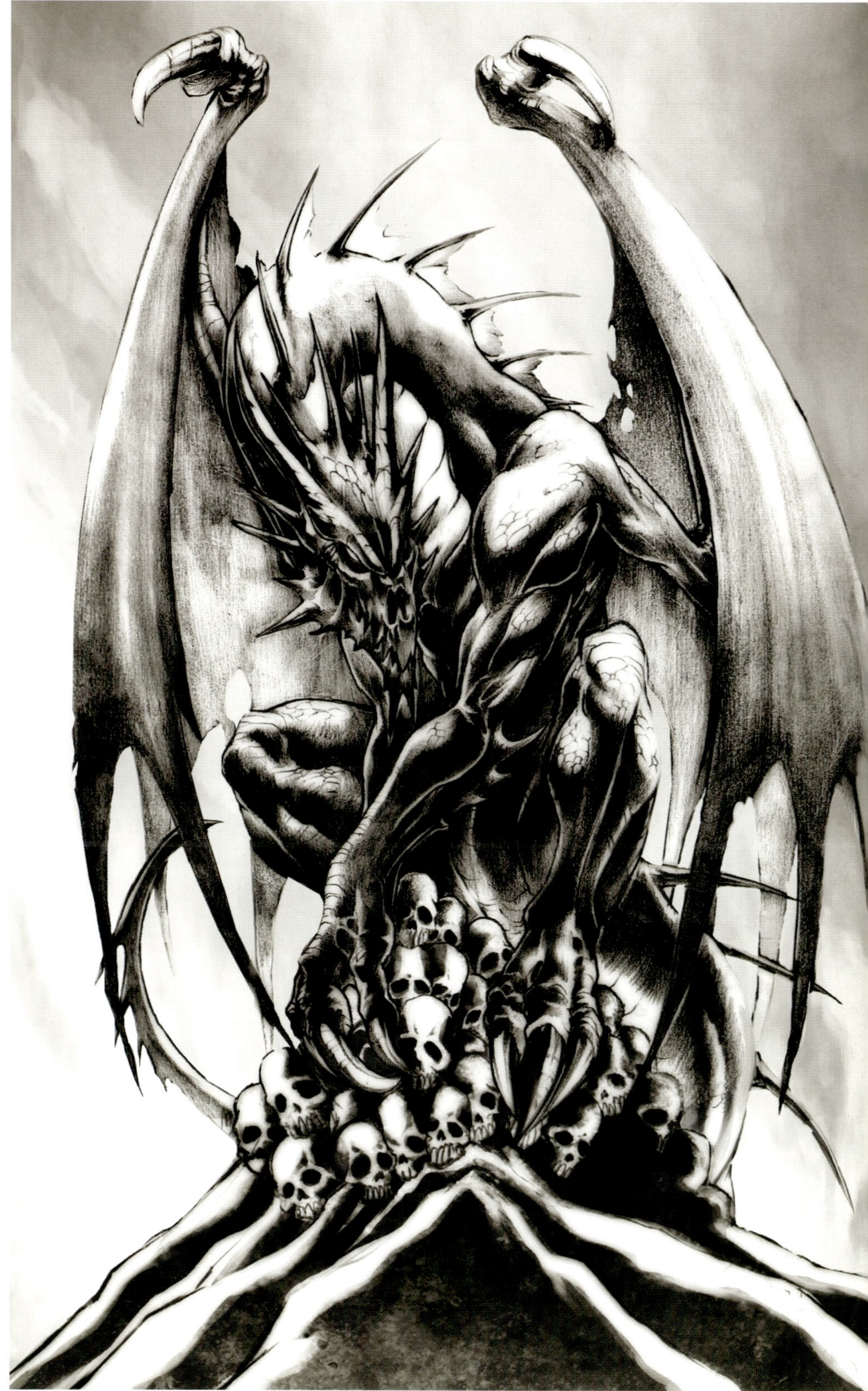

I read it and I saw a visual out of it or I wrote it and I know what it looks like. I do not have models for my characters. I know what they look like.' She continues, 'I sit down with a pencil and keep drawing until it looks like what I pictured, and then I transfer it into paint. So it drives some people crazy because I don't go the whole nine yards and get a model and pull in all this extra research. Very, very occasionally I'll be doing something with a complex bit of drapery and I'll need to put it into a very odd lighting situation or an odd piece of perspective. I will draw the entire picture, draw the entire drapery then I might put a model in that costume just to verify that something wasn't totally out of line, but that's extremely rare. Usually I just draw it.'

Ciruelo considers it more a case of watching a sort of internal motion picture. 'When I work on a commission, for a book cover for instance, I have to restrict myself to someone else's ideas. But when I create for myself I only need to pay attention to the "screen" I have in my mind. Sometimes I project characters or scenes [on to] that mental screen and "move" them until I get the image I want to draw. But many other times, all of a sudden, I watch a projection that I don't know where it comes from, as in a movie, and then try to capture parts of that "film" in my creations. That's when I have more fun and when my art is more creative.'

A Muse with a Life of its Own

Michele-lee Phelan discusses the art in terms of her muse. She says, 'Dragons usually appear on the page, and I simply release them. I don't often "sketch" things as each drawing usually becomes something I use. I have very few sketches, and literally hundreds of finished line works that were all developed fully and refined to a point where I then decided if I would put them aside or paint them. Those I decide to paint are then cleaned up by removing any extraneous lines, and then transferred to a sheet of watercolour paper for painting. I have always preferred heavy watercolour paper as opposed to canvas due to the fact that I do not like texture on my canvas. I prefer not to have to spend hours painting and sanding a canvas in order to make it smooth enough for my needs, and so I don't. I enjoy the finish I achieve by using acrylics on paper.

'The canvas is then taped to a large support sheet of MDF, which I can take to wherever I feel like painting. Most of the time, I sit in my living room with the board supported on my lap and paint while I listen to music or talk to my partner or children. Depending upon the size of the artwork and level of detail involved, a painting can take me between 30 and 300 hours to paint.'

Technology and Art

To return to the notion of journeys and the journey of art itself: art has always been about technology and discovery, whether that is the creation of better writing tools, technology for paper, the knowledge of mixing dyes or paints or even the technology that is the airbrush. But there is something more fundamental

DRAGON BATTLE by Garfield Chan
© Garfield Chan 2008 · Digital media: Photoshop
http://chan1985.cgsociety.org

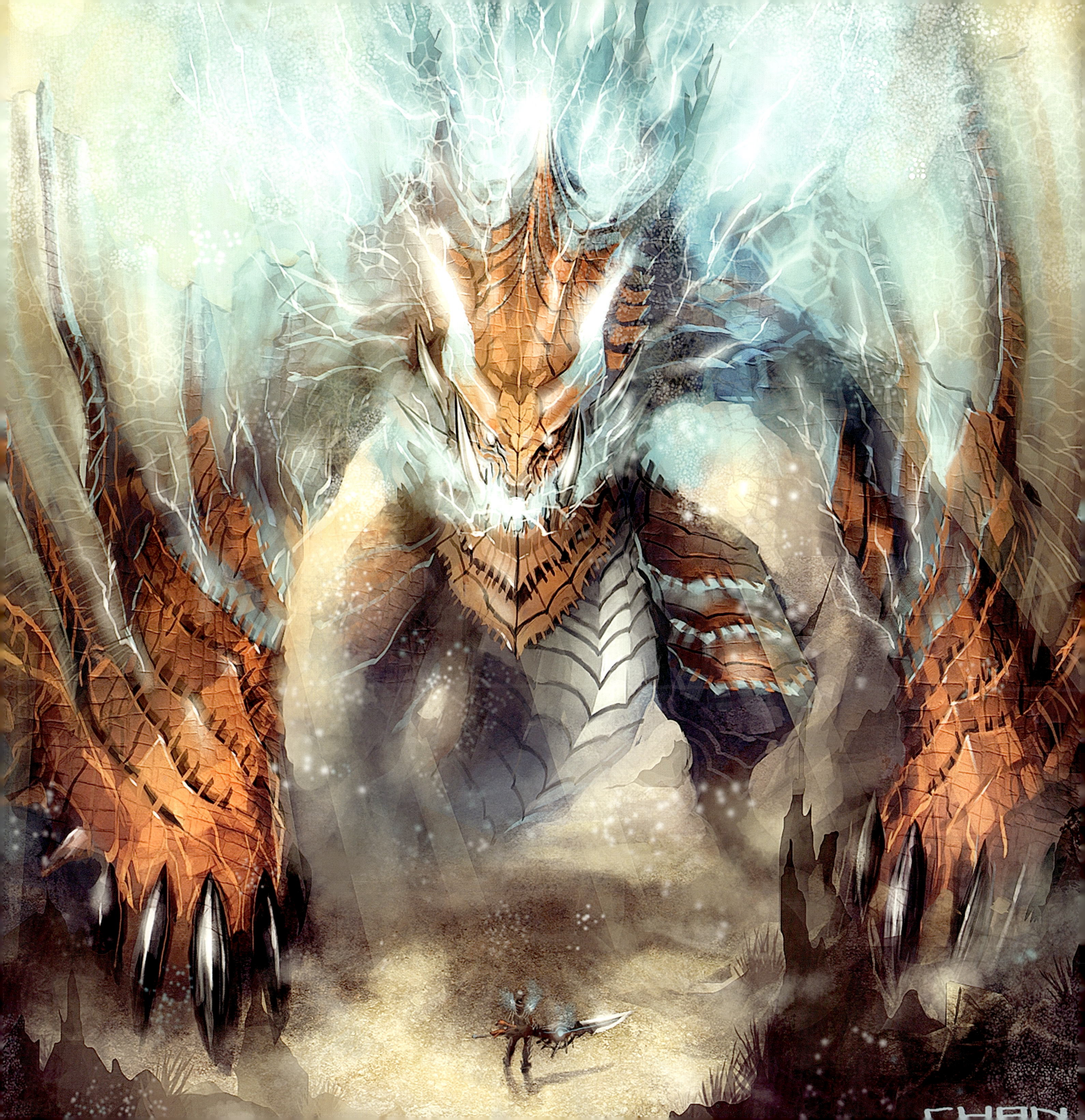

The Dragon Princess by Tony Moy

© Tony Moy 2007; Digital media: Photoshop; Inspired by Chinese mythology and based on a concept created by Tony – the princess is a metaphor for hope and the dragon is a metaphor for living one's dreams; http://tmartist.cgsociety.org

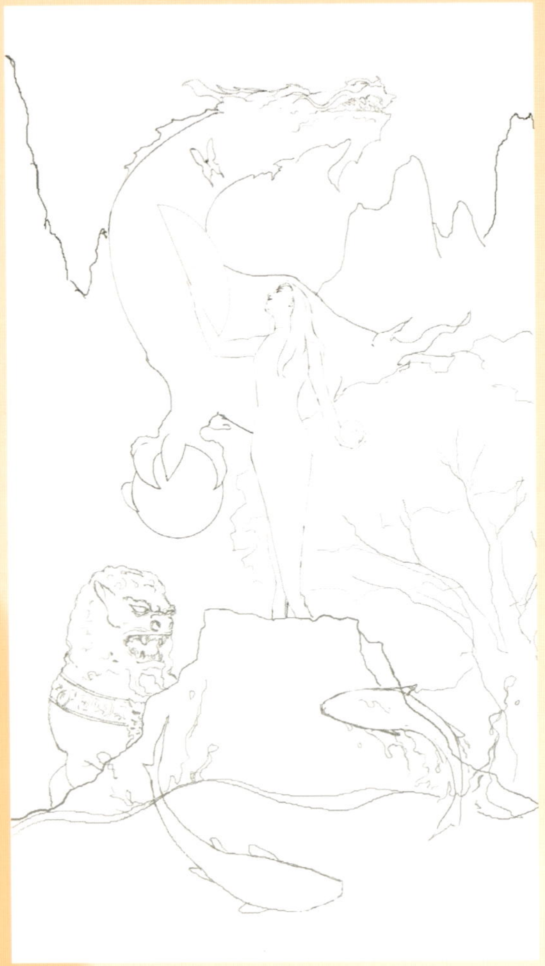

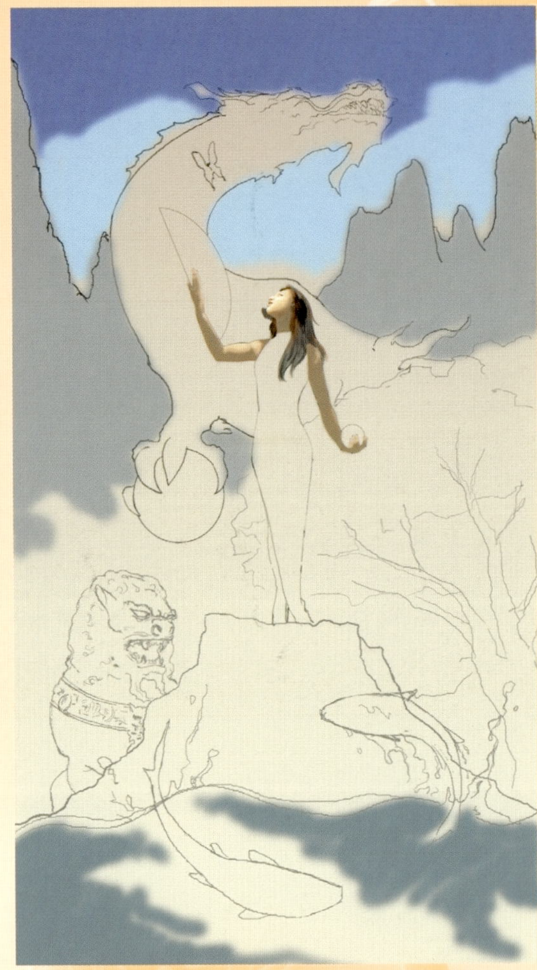

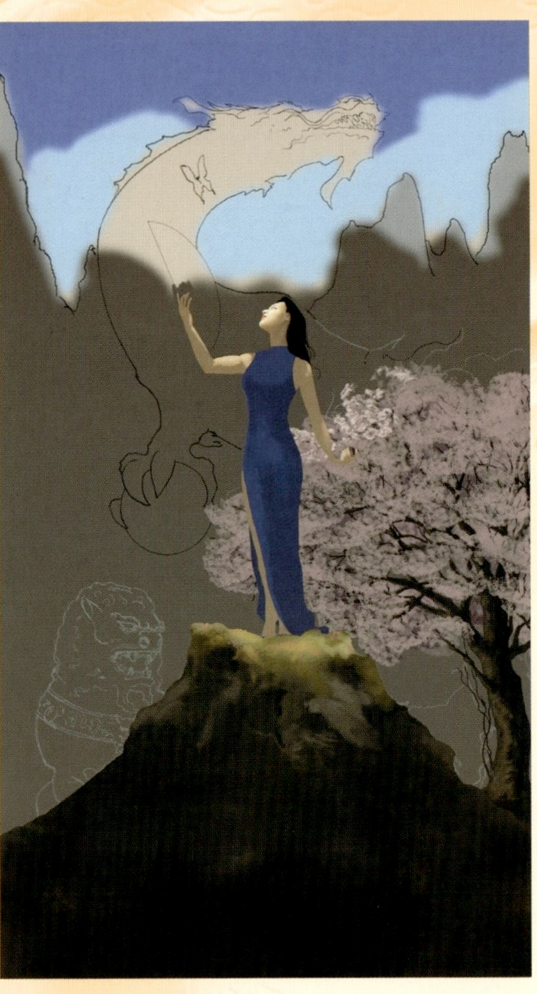

SAMPLE STEP 1. This painting was essentially the beginning of my journey into digital art. It began first with a concept sketch using traditional paper and pencil, which I scanned to use as a basis for creating the digital line art, with a few compositional changes along the way.

SAMPLE STEP 2. Once the line art was established, I created layers over it and began the painting process. I first toned the canvas with a light sepia tone – the idea is to get rid of all the white space, which enables colour development more easily. Then I laid down what I thought would be good foundational colours for the main elements.

SAMPLE STEP 3. I then put in some facsimiles for a cherry blossom and a land mass. I use photo references to help me stay true to realistic lighting and checks on form.

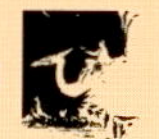

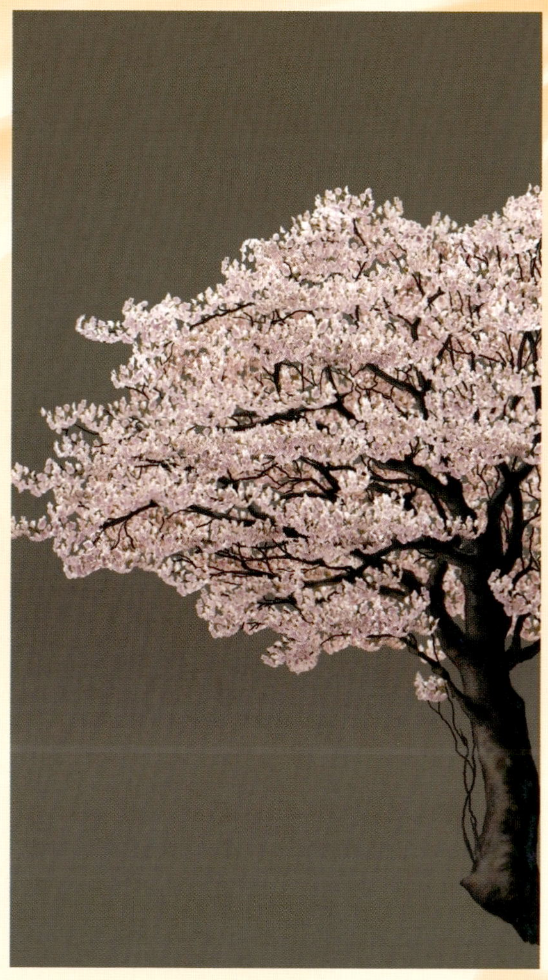

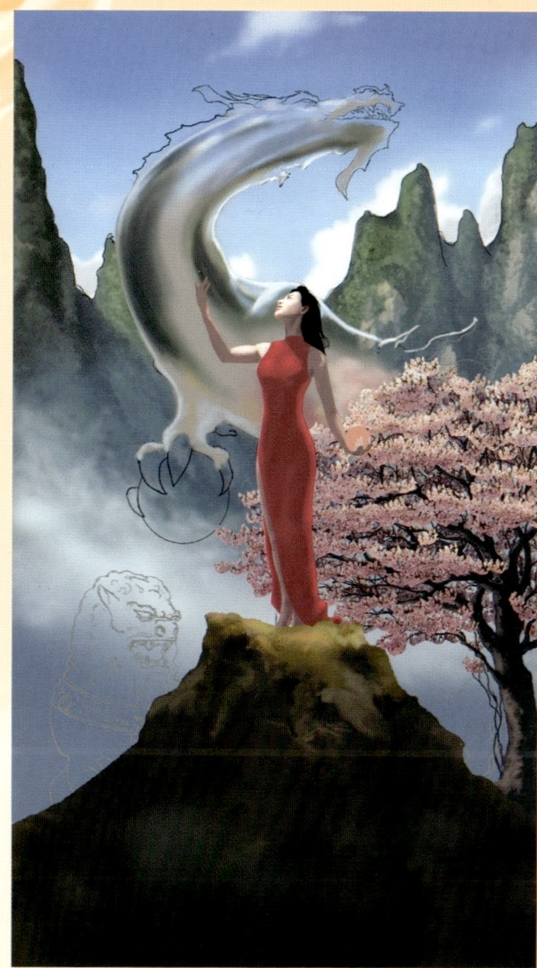

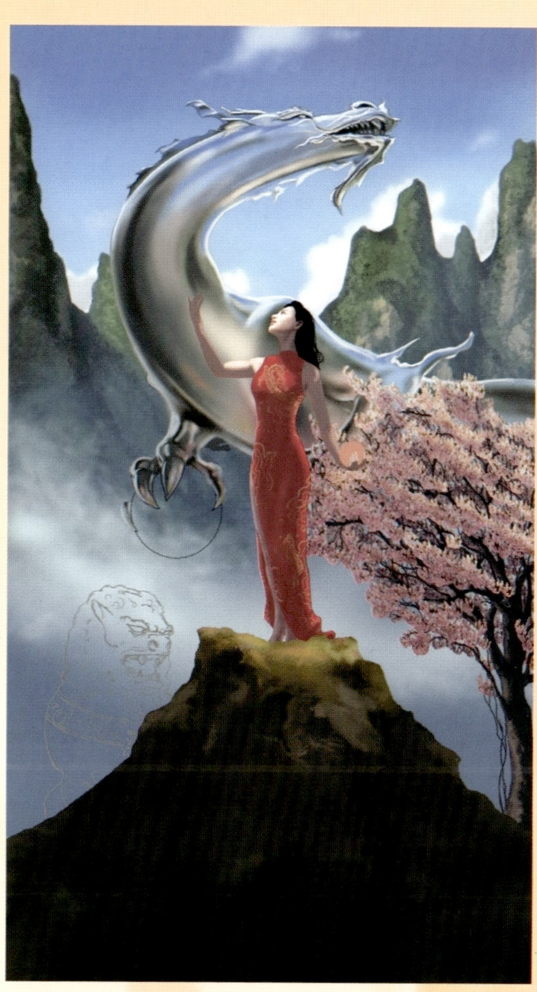

SAMPLE STEP 4. I created the cherry tree, petal by petal, in a separate file as my original image was getting too big. In Photoshop I could duplicate several masses and morph them and adjust their colour so that I could create unique flower masses in a relatively short period of time. I then flattened the image and imported it into the main painting.

SAMPLE STEP 5. I decided then to shift everything to match the brighter tone of the tree; the dress changed from blue to red. For the dragon, I began by loosely pulling colour and forms from the foreground and background to form its metallic skin.

SAMPLE STEP 6. In order to enhance the sense of motion, I warped the cherry tree into a similar pattern as the flow of the dragon's flight. This was done simply using the transform and liquify tools within Photoshop. I then added the Foo Dog and intensified some of the colours and added further elements.

The Dragon Princess by Tony Moy (Continued)

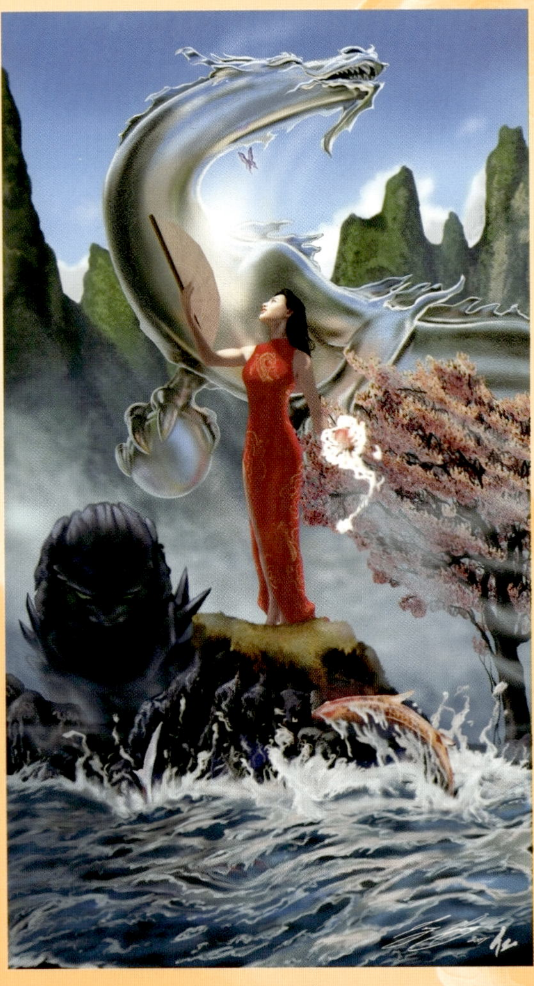

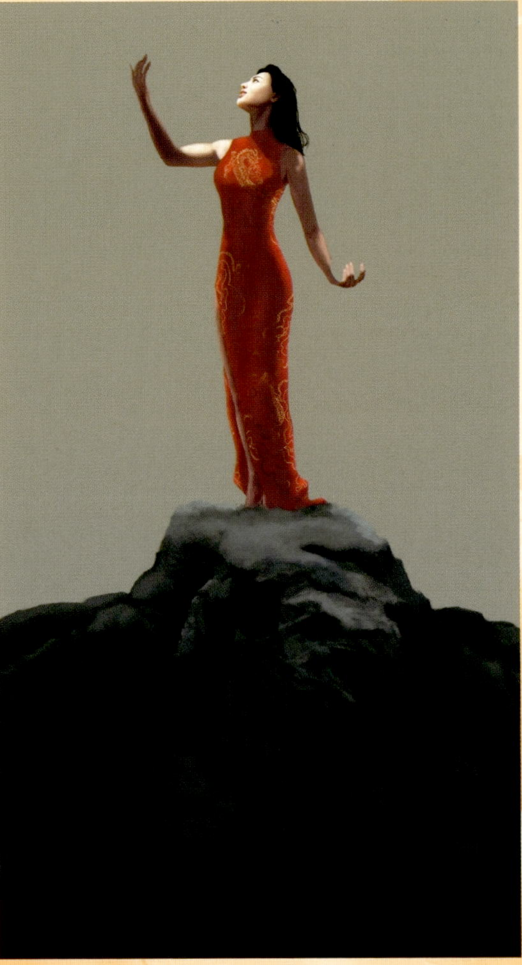

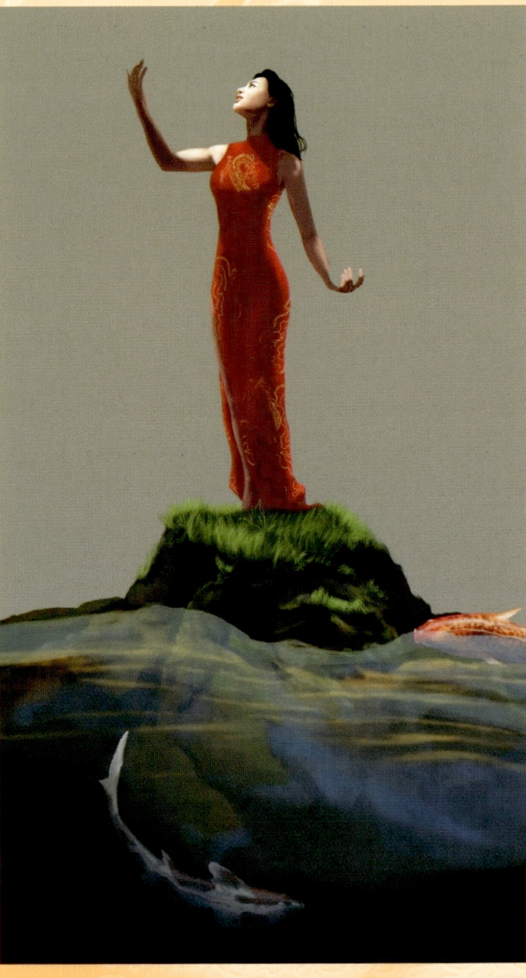

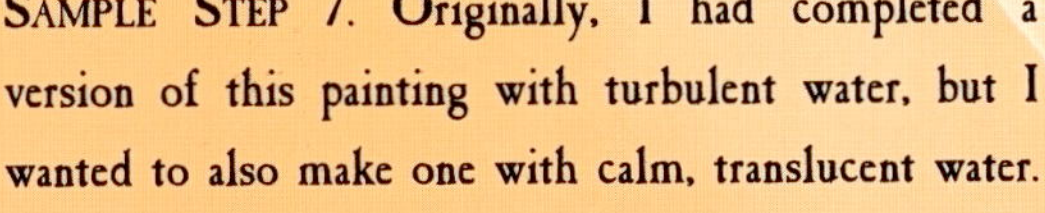

SAMPLE STEP 7. Originally, I had completed a version of this painting with turbulent water, but I wanted to also make one with calm, translucent water.

SAMPLE STEP 8. I exported the Dragon Princess to another canvas in Photoshop and built the landmass from monotone form to full colour.

SAMPLE STEP 9. I then created a variety of layers with different modes (overlay, etc) to form the water.

FINISHING TOUCHES (RIGHT). The final painting was pulled together by importing the Princess with new landmass and water elements back into the original canvas and adjusting colours and tones to harmonize everything.

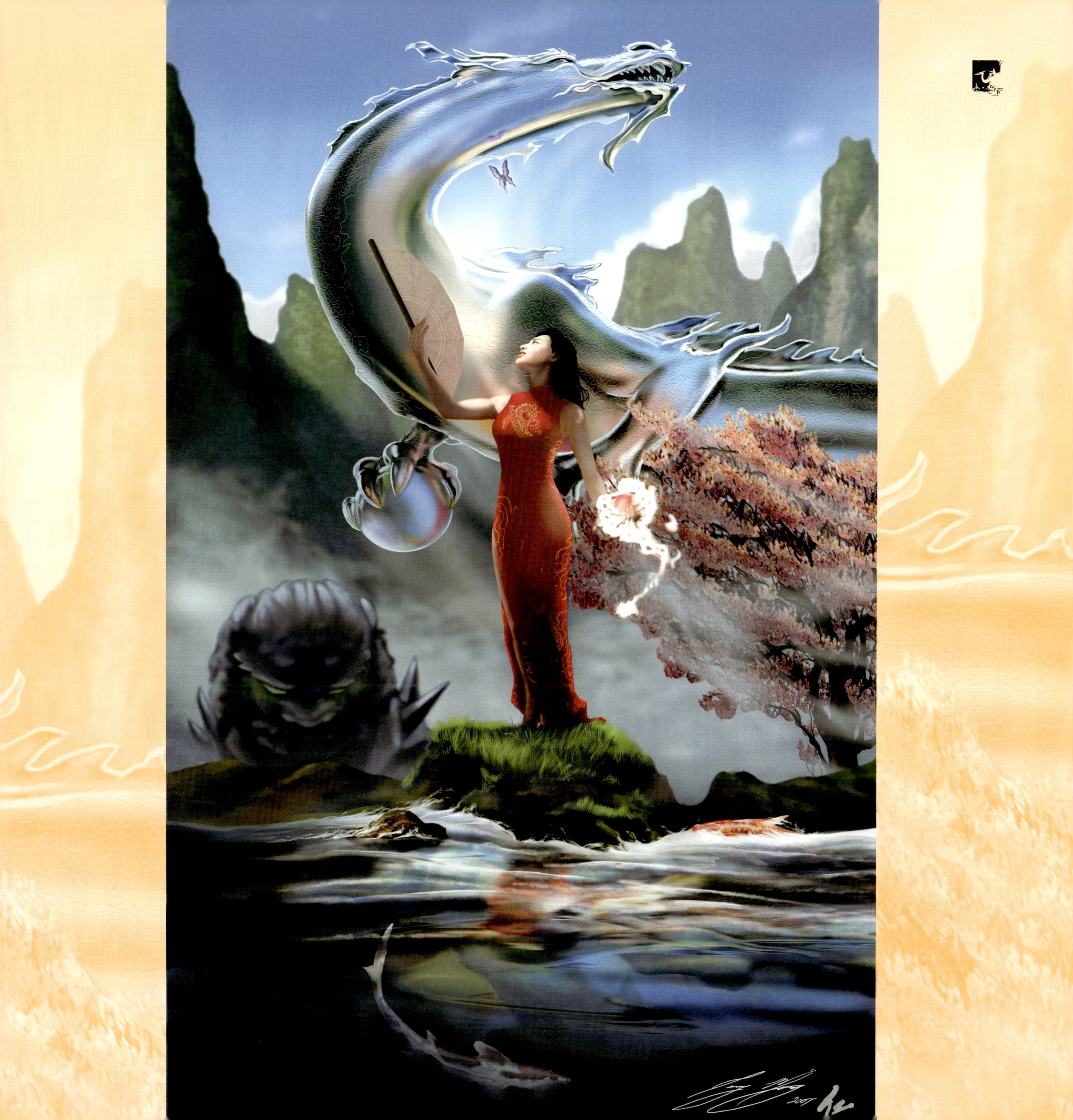

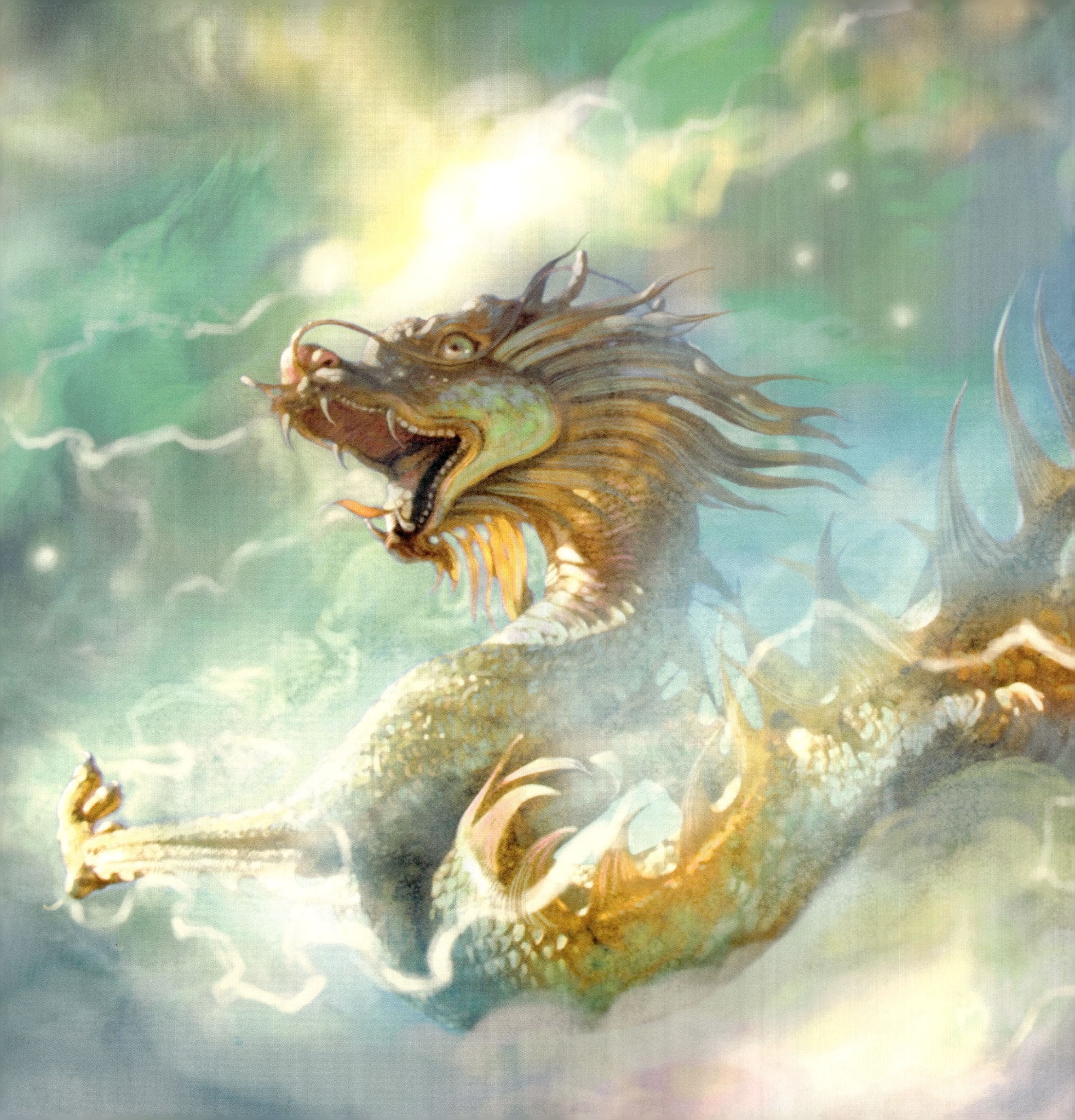

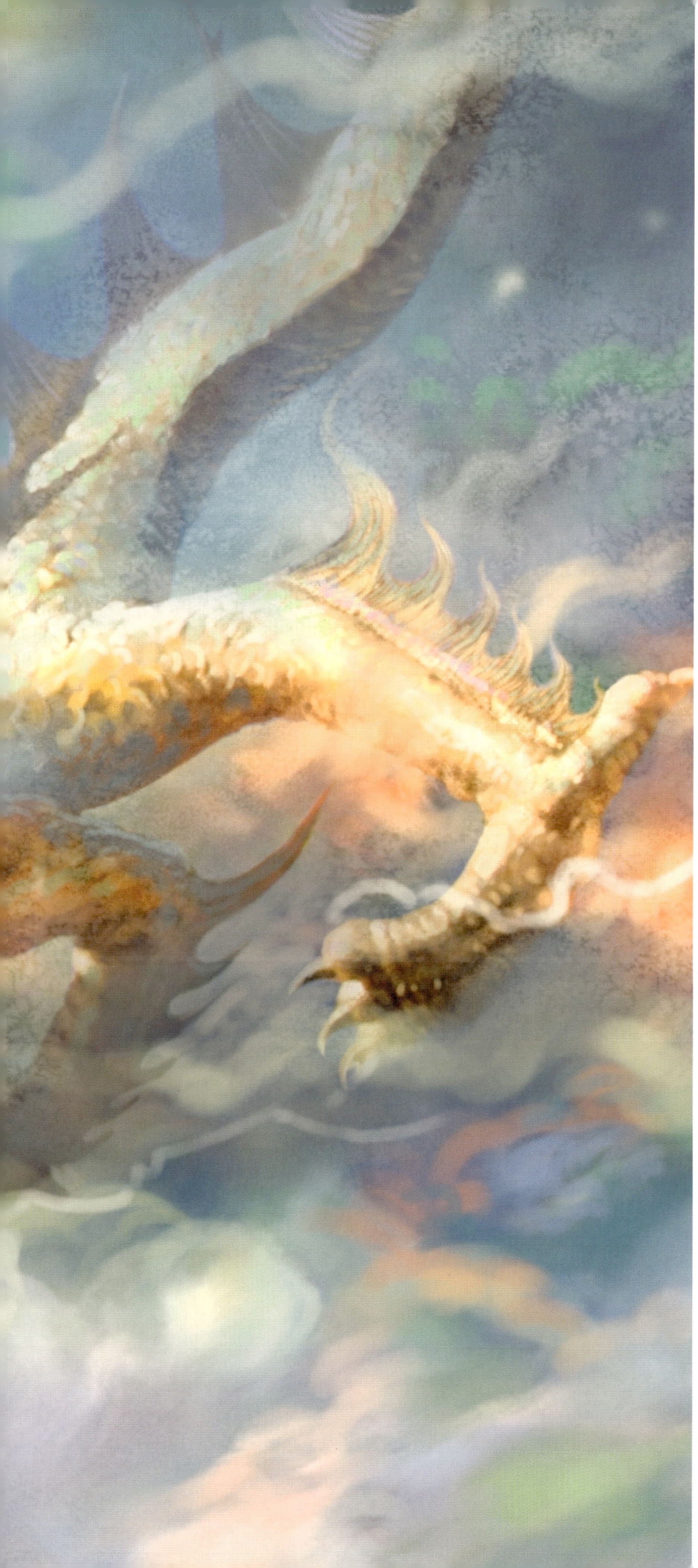

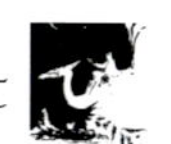

DRAGON OF SANBOUMAO by Thammasak Aueragsakul
(aka 'Mai' or 'Tigermyuou')
 · Digital media: Photoshop
Thammasak is a successful painter and the assistant dean of the Faculty of Art and Design at Rangsit University, Thailand.
http://tigermyuou.deviantart.com

happening to fantasy art at the moment. Computers are gradually changing what Marx might refer to as the 'means of production'. Acrylic may be a plastic-age paint, but the end product is still a physical painting. Similarly, airbrushing leaves a physical artefact that can be hung, stored, admired or even painted over.

The new technology of computer art, using software such as Adobe Photoshop and Corel Painter, does not quite work that way. They leave the artist with a digital file that essentially lives on a computer. There is not a single final version of the art from which others are reproductions. Instead, with a computer, the painting becomes a long list of instructions for a computer: this might mean producing an image on screen, or instructing a printer where to disperse dots on a substrate that might be a sheet of plastic or a paperback book cover. This can have many advantages: there is no paint to dry, no turpentine in the air, no end product to photograph or store. However, the lack of physicality can mean there is something lacking for the artist. Artists have their own opinions of the rise of the computer as a method of producing art.

Computer as Enabler

Todd Lockwood has plenty to say on the subject. 'I'm not a computer person by nature, but when I was in advertising I saw Photoshop change lives. If you could afford a computer and enjoyed

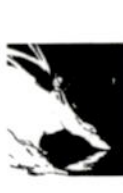

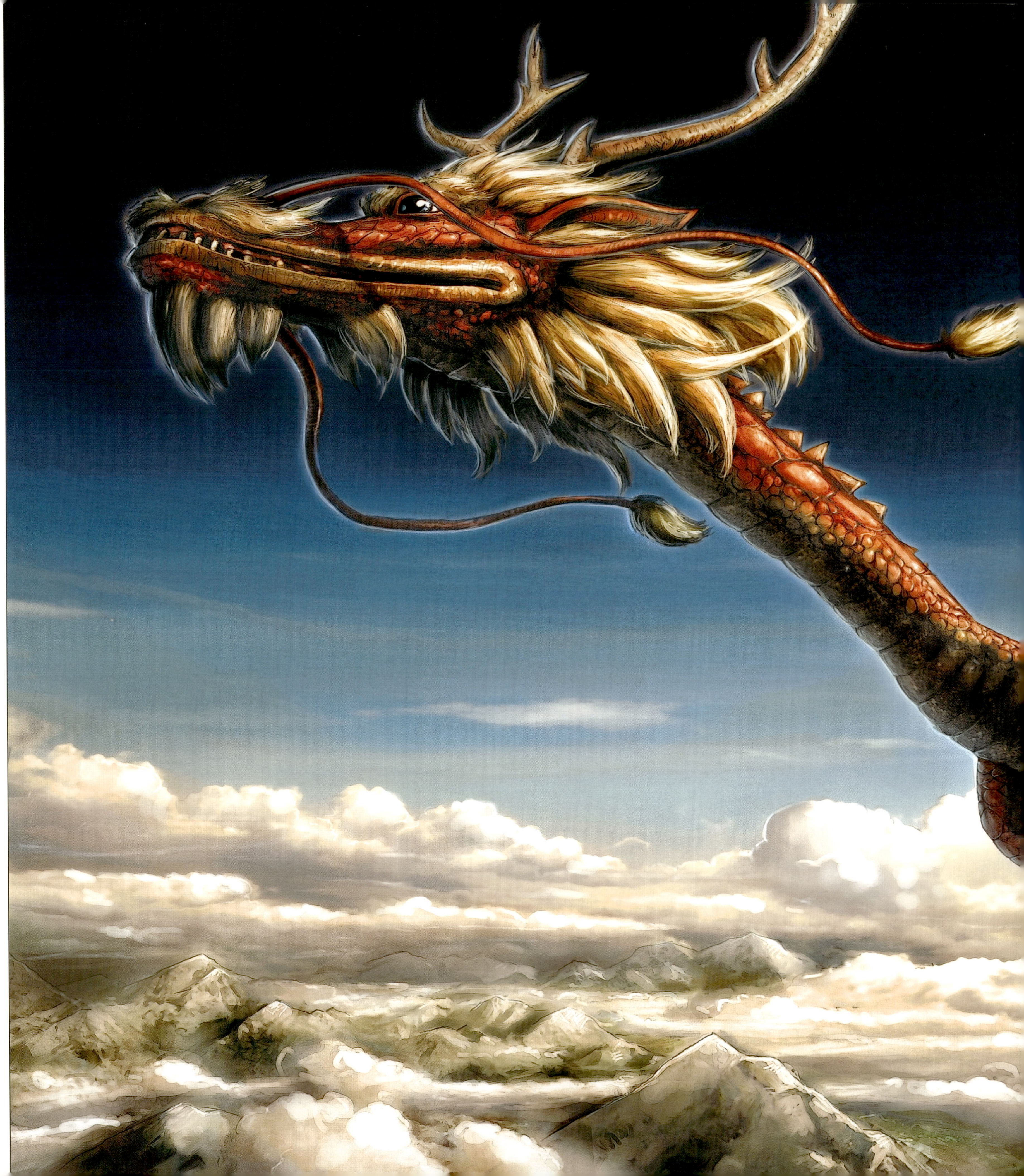

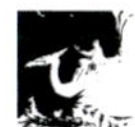

working with that sort of thing, it opened doors. But if you were a traditionalist or had found a niche that computers couldn't fit, you disappeared. I saw tons go out of business. I felt sort of rescued by the fantasy industry because it still used paintings and relied on artwork that looked traditional. When Painter come along and I saw digital work come along that looked like paintings, I knew I'd better get on board because this was going to be another seismic shift in the industry, and it happened. Now everybody wants digital files. Nobody really wants to scan a painting or be bothered with shipping it. It can be a deal breaker in some cases.'

Todd continues, 'So from that point of view, I was carried in kicking and screaming, but Painter does have some features that make it really hard not to work that way. It really is fun. And I'm satisfied because my paintings still look like my paintings. They don't have a digital look and a traditional look. I can still paint the way I paint and see the way I see. So in that regard it's a very happy truce. The only thing I miss is having paintings.'

Open to Alteration

Janny Wurts is somewhat ambivalent. 'When I started out it was all done in paint. Digital art has really come in hard and fast and it's here whether we want it or not. I'm still a traditional painter because I get the best results that way. I've always been very hands-on and I find that there's a value to that original painting that a digital artwork cannot have.

TIAGO 2008 DA SILVA

DRAGON KING AO-KUANG by Tiago da Silva
© Tiago da Silva 2008 · Digital media: Photoshop
http://grafik.deviantart.com/gallery

The Dragonfish by Angela Acquah

© Angela Acquah 2008; Digital media: Photoshop; 'Dragonfish was my take of an 'atypical' dragon; one that resides in the murky depths of the river and masquerades as a giant golden fish'; http://nerversis.blogspot.com

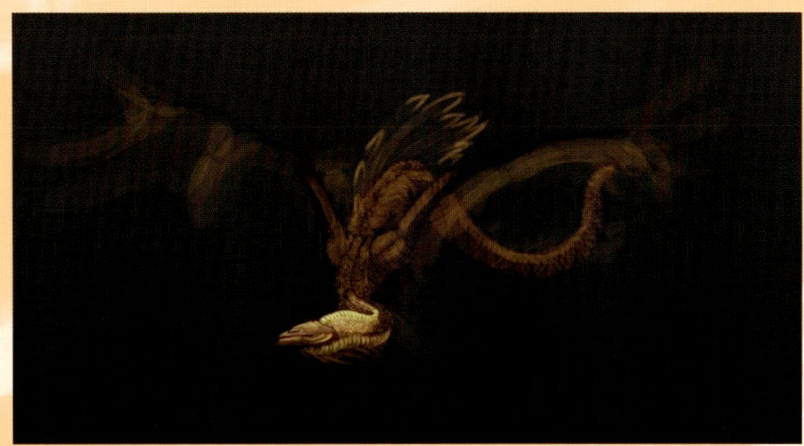

SAMPLE STEP 1. Base colours were put down and the scales were roughly assorted to give me a general idea of what I wanted to achieve.

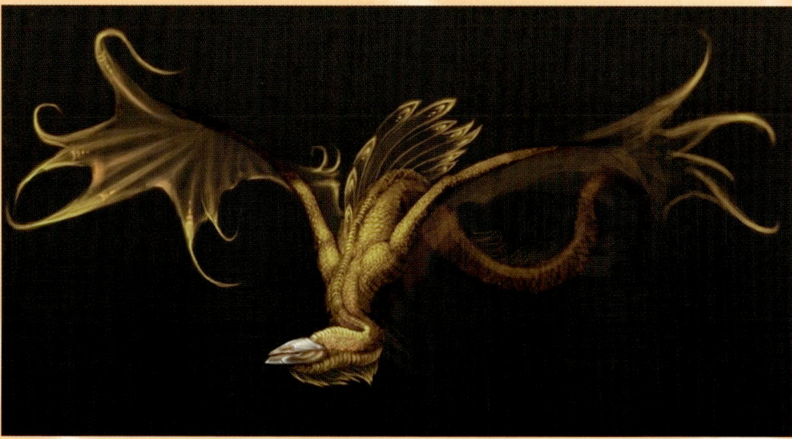

SAMPLE STEP 2. This is the completed base. This was achieved by using the eye-dropper tool in Photoshop to pick the colours I had already put on to the image (opposed to choosing the colours over and over).

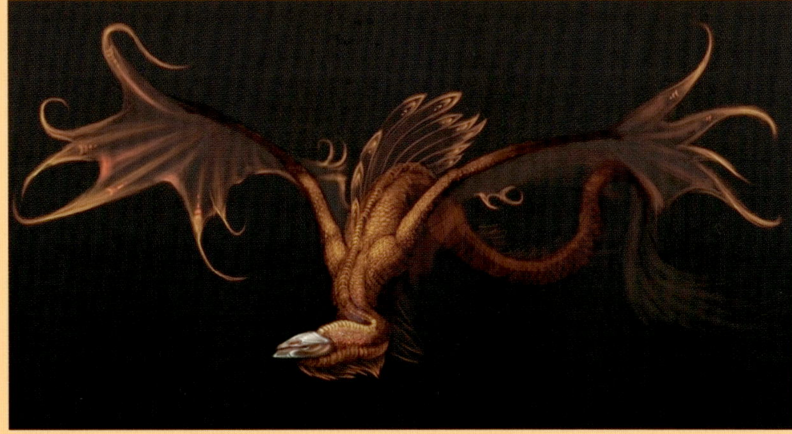

SAMPLE STEP 3. I adjusted the image's colour via the 'edit adjustments hue/saturation' option, making it more 'red' and turning its saturation up.

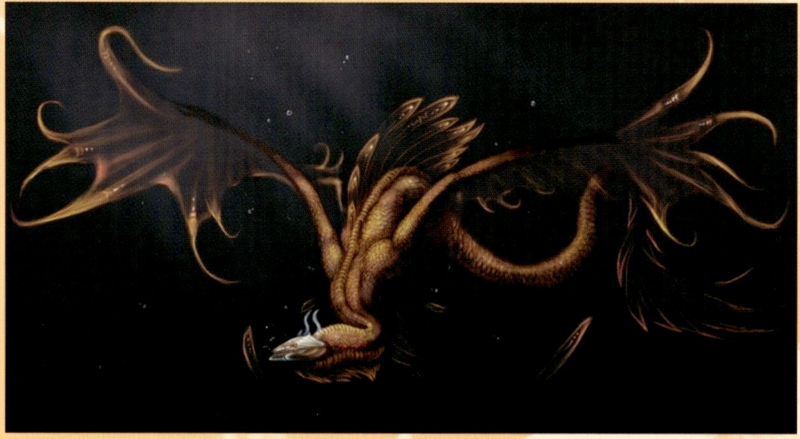

SAMPLE STEP 4. At this stage more refining was done: darker shadows, bubbles and a background colour change were added.

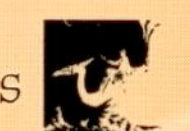

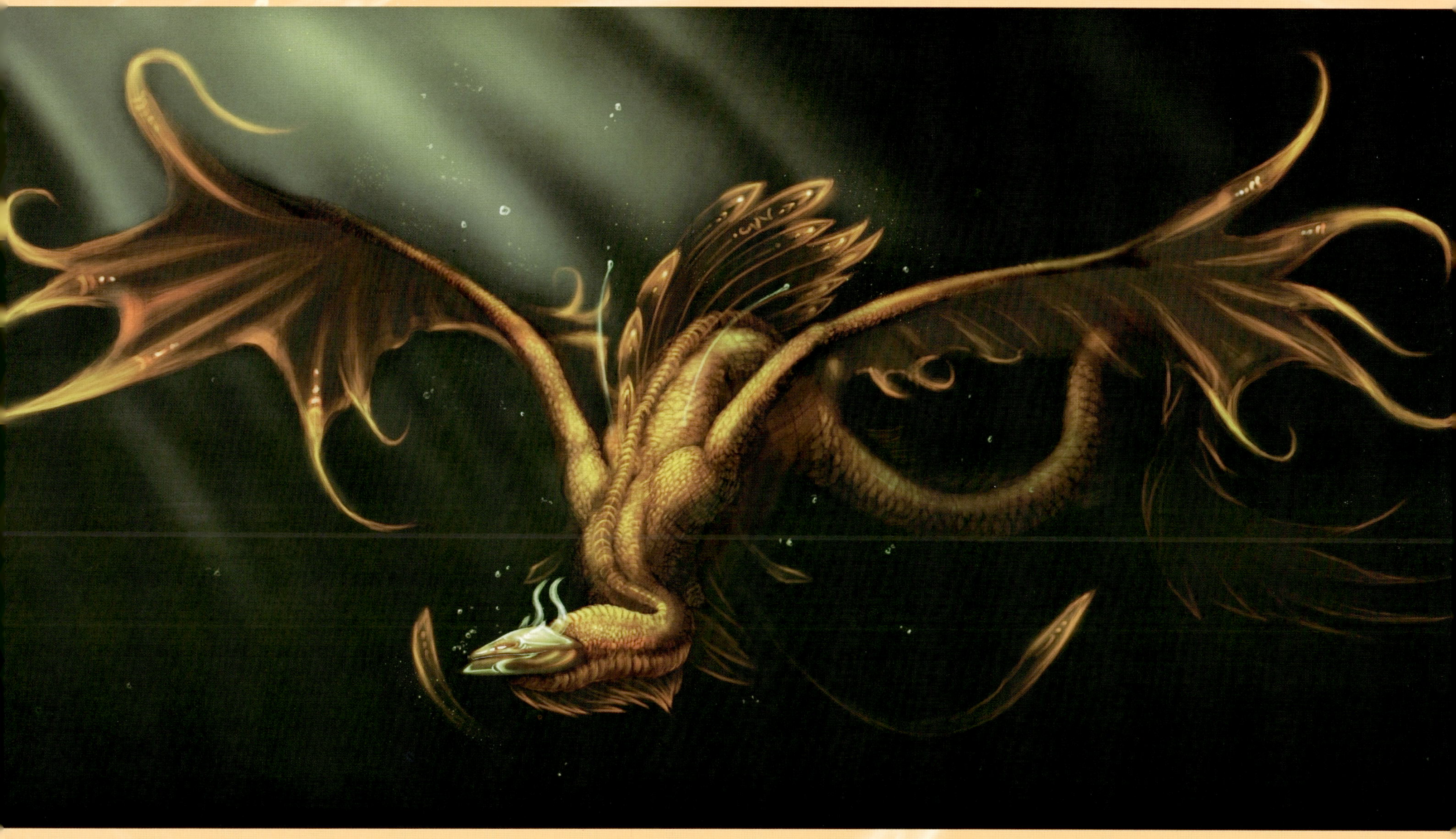

FINISHING TOUCHES. A green gradient was placed on top of everything, and the rays of light were made more pronounced. A large brush, set to dodge, was passed over the areas I wanted to 'stick out' and be affected by the light.

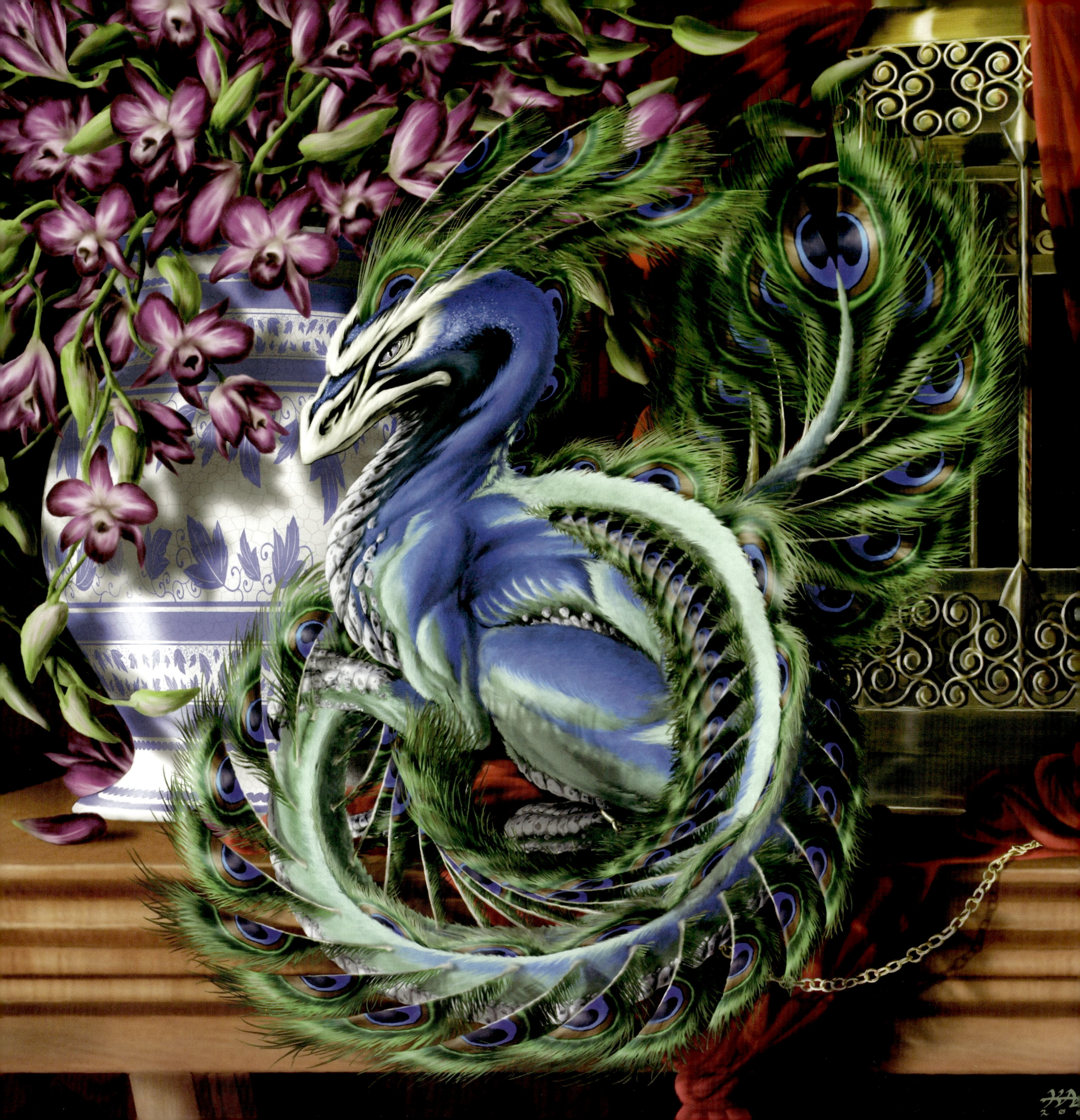

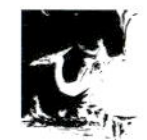

'The digital art, once you create it, it's on a computer, it's in pixels. First of all you can't see it without turning on a switch. Because as the artist created it, it was on a lit screen, when you print it, it goes flat. You can never tell whether the original artist painted it or who the original artist was because when you send a painting in, sometimes someone else will digitally alter it. There's no record. You cannot tell what was the digital alterer or what was the artist. You can't even tell if that was the colour he used because this green and that green don't align. Where painting is valuable is, if I hang a painting on the wall here and the light changes throughout the day, it's a different painting every 10 minutes. The mood of that painting changes according to the ambient light.' She continues, 'You know exactly what I was doing because you can see the brush strokes and you can tell by the materials if somebody else altered it. I think there's a value in that.'

Traditional and Digital in Partnership

For Kerem Beyit, a computer is very much a necessary tool for the job. He says, 'I started with pen and paper. I also worked with acrylics, markers and watercolours, but because I think digital is the most suitable medium for an artist who works for the publishing sector, I only produce digital works now. When you consider its advantages, it's the best medium. However, a good digital artist should always exercise with pencils to remain fit and on form.'

Tracy Trowbridge likes to balance both traditional and digital techniques. With traditional media, there is always that end product, from which you can stand back and see the piece. It does not matter, she says, whether it is a full-blown painting or a ballpoint pen drawing, which is a favourite type of art for her.

GUILDED CAGED by Keith Decesare
© KAD Creations, Inc. 2008 · Digital media: SketchUp, Photoshop
A 'Guilded' is a small dragon with beautifully coloured feathers running along its whole body and ending in a bright display at the tail. They are usually kept by wealthy and/or royal persons for the aforementioned traits.
www.pen-paper.net/artgallery/KeithDeCesare/

But, she describes painting digitally as liberating because it enables the painter to mix and match different ideas in a way that might be difficult in the real world. She says, 'I use a Wacom tablet, and it's fun to be able to experiment with. You have a lot of options with digital art, and there's so many different things you can do. If there's something you want to change it's nice to be able to have layers.'

Ciruelo agrees. He explains, 'I am a traditional painter working mainly with oils on canvas and I will continue to produce most of my art through this means. However, I appreciate and use the advantages of the digital technology since I think it opens new possibilities. One big advantage of painting with the computer is that you don't have to worry about dealing with brushes and mixing paints so your creativity flows faster and with no obstacles. You also have many tools to change colours and add effects with no effort. The traditional media, on the other hand, gives you a different feeling that, for certain artists like me, is very inspiring in itself.'

Disadvantages

But virtual production has its very own real-world drawbacks. Bob Eggleton points out, 'The other problem with [computer technology] is that [it is] endlessly expensive to maintain. In other words, you're constantly having to upgrade all of your storage. You've got to get CDs, and you've got to get good CDs to begin with; if that doesn't happen, the images will degrade on the CD or the technology gets to the point where the CD is no longer readable, so you've got to upgrade. And you've got to keep buying into this technology. That's a very endlessly frustrating thing.'

Bob adds, 'Also, the basic problem is that you're working on a painting – this has happened to me – you're working on a deadline and the power goes out. I could work by either good candlelight or torches in the studio, or by sunlight. I don't need power to do a painting. Unfortunately you need electrical power to do computer artwork.'

DRACO ARBOREA (PARVUS) by Radoslaw Walachnia
© Radoslaw Walachnia 2005 · Digital media: Photoshop
This illustration was created for a 'Dragons' contest organized by a Polish publisher. It won the main prize in the digital category.
www.walachnia.com

but they just don't know how to photograph a painting. So there are frustrations but there are gains. I've had to learn how to do it, but I really don't care for it because you're a whole step removed. You have to choose the technique, and then you have to choose the colour and then you have to choose the touchpad or a keyboard to select all this stuff. Whereas when you grab a brush, you just reach for it and then you slam it in the paint.'

There is also the loss of time spent having to tweak digital images. Janny Wurts says, 'What I'm finding is in the time I save sending the digital image to the other side of the world so that somebody in Russia can print the piece, I lose because in the old days I just had a transparency shot and then went on to the next painting. Now I have to know Photoshop, I have to alter it, size it and get it to what they want, so a tremendous amount of time is being chewed up digitally messing with the pictures to make them look like the picture.'

Janny adds, 'We're losing the people who know how to photograph paintings. They know how to photograph digitally

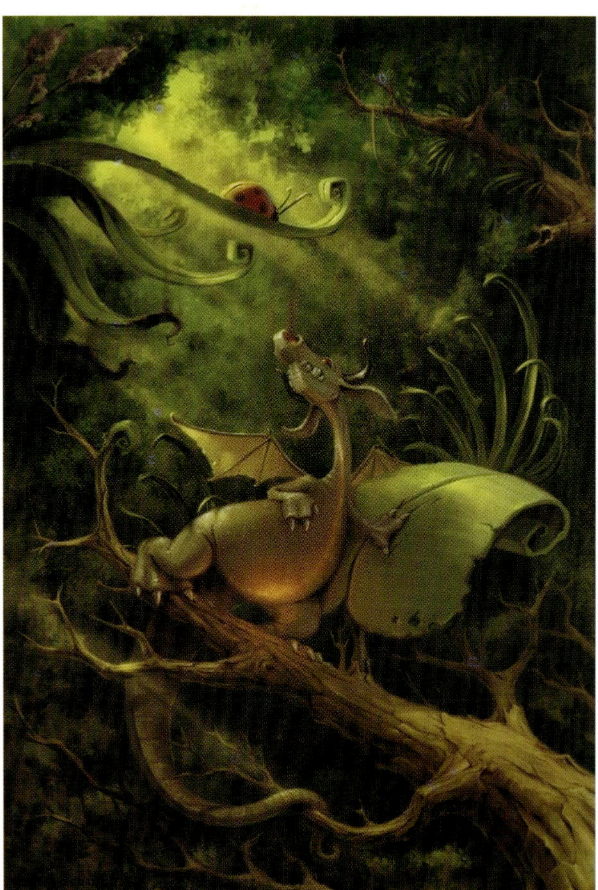

Learning New Skills

Digital art also requires additional skills from the artist, as German artist Nathie points out: 'I still do use traditional media. I paint murals, and I also love sketching just with pencils. A lot of people think that you don't need knowledge or skills to paint digitally. That is definitively not true and makes me furious. It helped me a lot that I painted with traditional media almost 20 years before I started digital. The advantage of digital painting is the zoom factor, you can get far more detail in. The hard thing is to master the painting programme. Photoshop, my main painting programme, is very

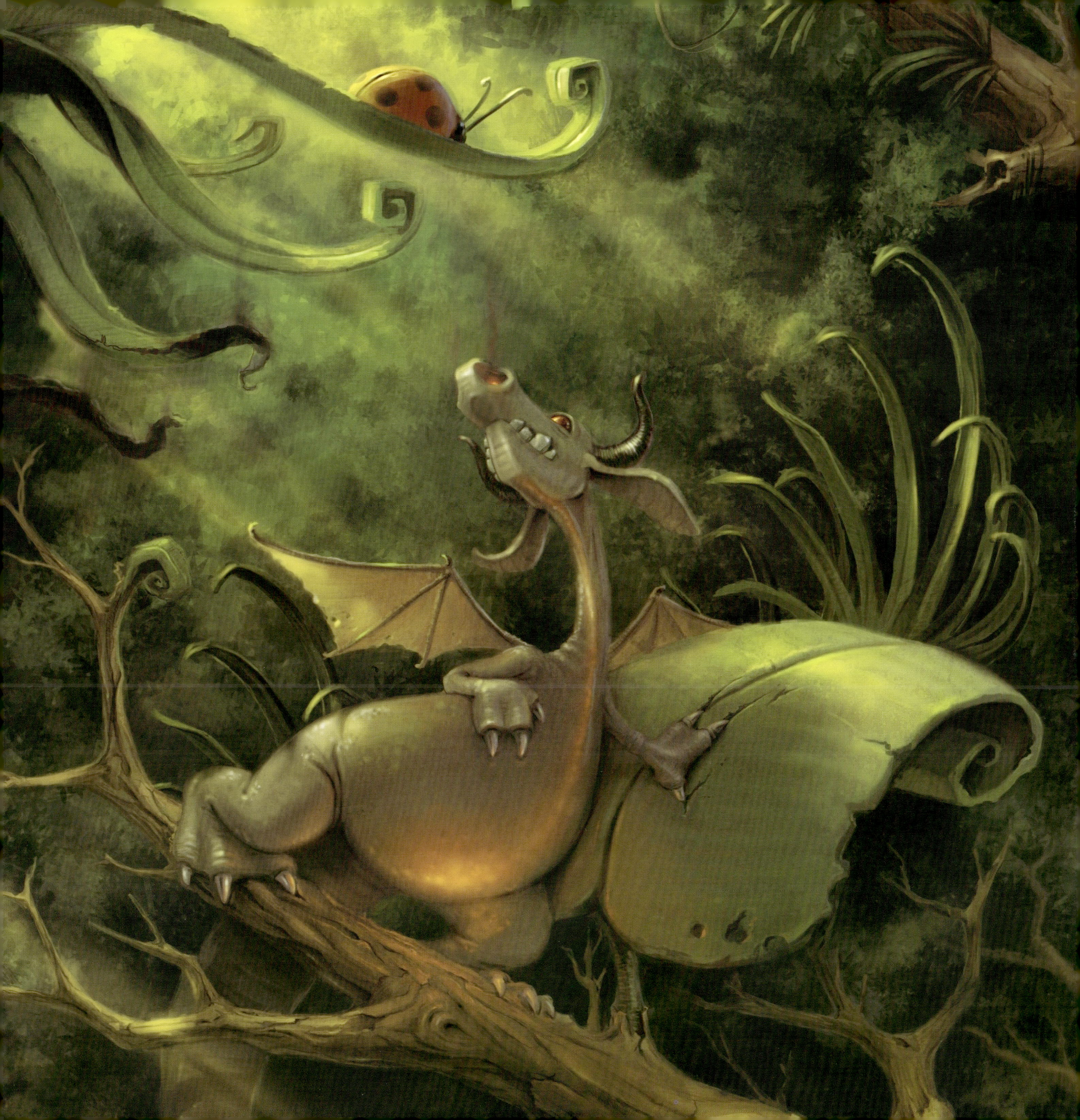

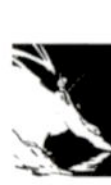

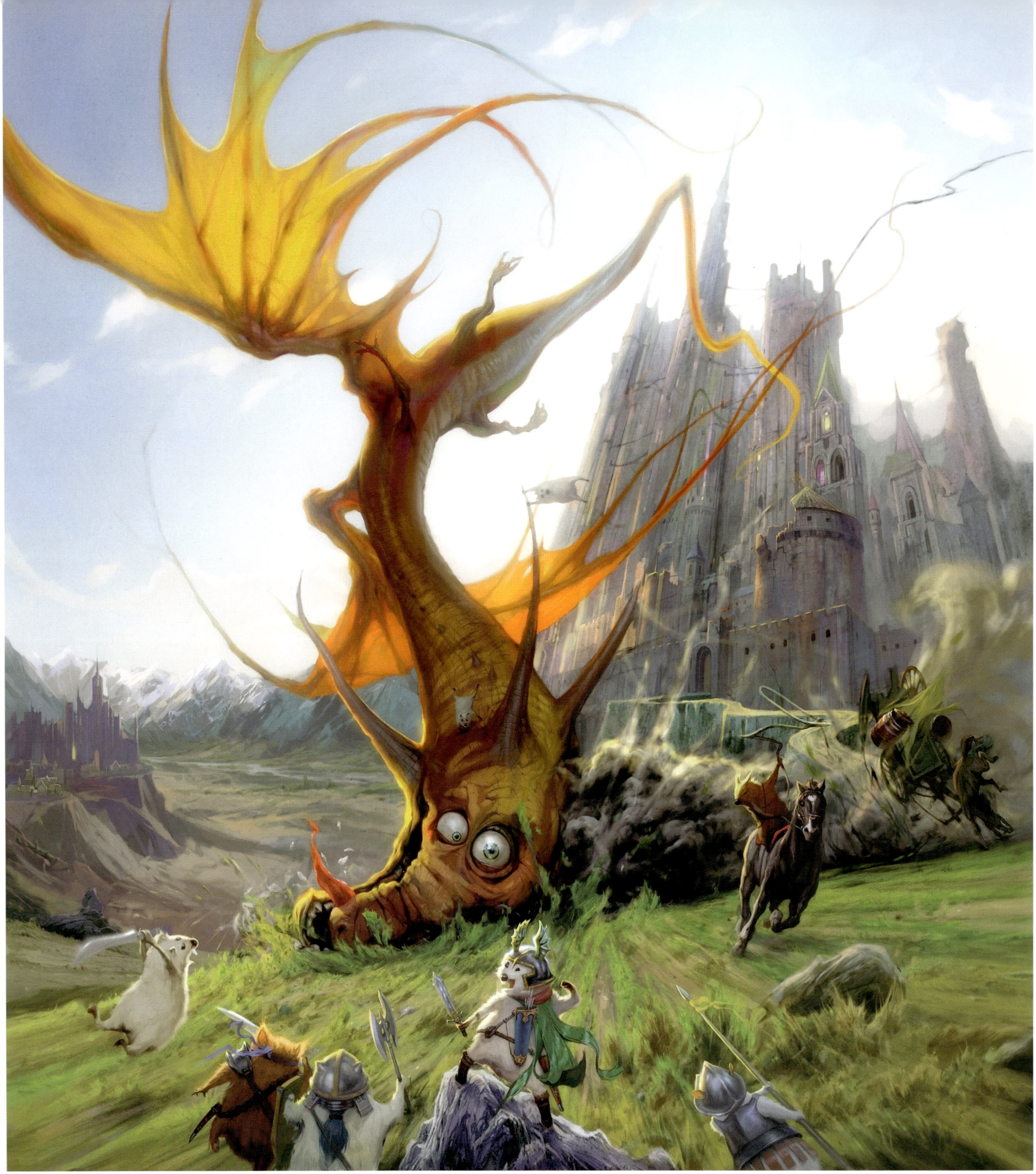

comprehensive, and there is so much more than a simple brush. So if you paint digitally you don't only need to have technical painting knowledge like anatomy, lighting, shading and perspective, you also need to know how to use your tools and tablet.'

In addition, it is not an-all-or-nothing migration, as Alan Lathwell testifies. 'I've only been digital for about four years, and it was a slow progress. I actually started painting in oils and then scanning that in, and modifying it. Then I started doing the pencil, scanning that in and colouring it. Then, I did away with the pencil and now it's just pure digital. The reason why is purely speed. As a commercial illustrator, I have to knock a picture up in two days. I haven't got the time for scanning in things. Painting in oils is obviously time-consuming. You have to wait two days for the background to dry before you can do the figures, most of the time, whereas with digital, it's instant.'

He adds that drawing digitally using a Wacom tablet, for instance, means that he can work much faster. Not only that, it is the flexibility the digital medium gives you. He says, 'If I draw a figure and feel that the head is a little bit too big for that body, as opposed to having to redraw the entire head, I can just cut it out and transform it into a smaller head. You can flip it backwards, forwards; it's incredible really. It's definitely the way of the future. Although I do still love oil painting, working digitally is more practical.'

Art and the Web

Digital art is also advantageous when combined with the Internet. For those who work on book covers or other subsectors of the publishing industry, finding work is a matter of visiting potential clients in person, bringing in portfolios in the search for new work. However, the net means that a well-designed website with a decent gallery can certainly attract new clientele. It is true that one need not create digitally to have a working gallery online, but it certainly does not hurt.

A Double-Edged Sword

But sometimes, it is a case of be careful what you wish for. Amending a digital painting is so easy that it can become a curse. Michele-lee Phelan has been forced, by carpal tunnel syndrome, to return to traditional painting techniques, particularly favouring acrylics and coloured pencils. She says, 'I could do so much more digitally than I could traditionally. Being able to undo mistakes was a real blessing, but it also made me lazy and less inclined to be careful. It also meant that a painting that should have taken me only 50 hours to complete was taking me upwards of 200 hours because I was constantly changing things and experimenting.

'Painting traditionally removes an element that, for me, is a distraction, while giving me something real and tangible and unique which I can offer to my clientele. So, I am the reverse of many artists. While many traditional artists make the transition to digital software, I have gone the other way and moved from digital to traditional.'

DRAGON CRASH by Viktor Titov
© Viktor Titov 2005 · Digital media: Photoshop
http://HamsterFly.cgsociety.org / www.hamsterfly.com

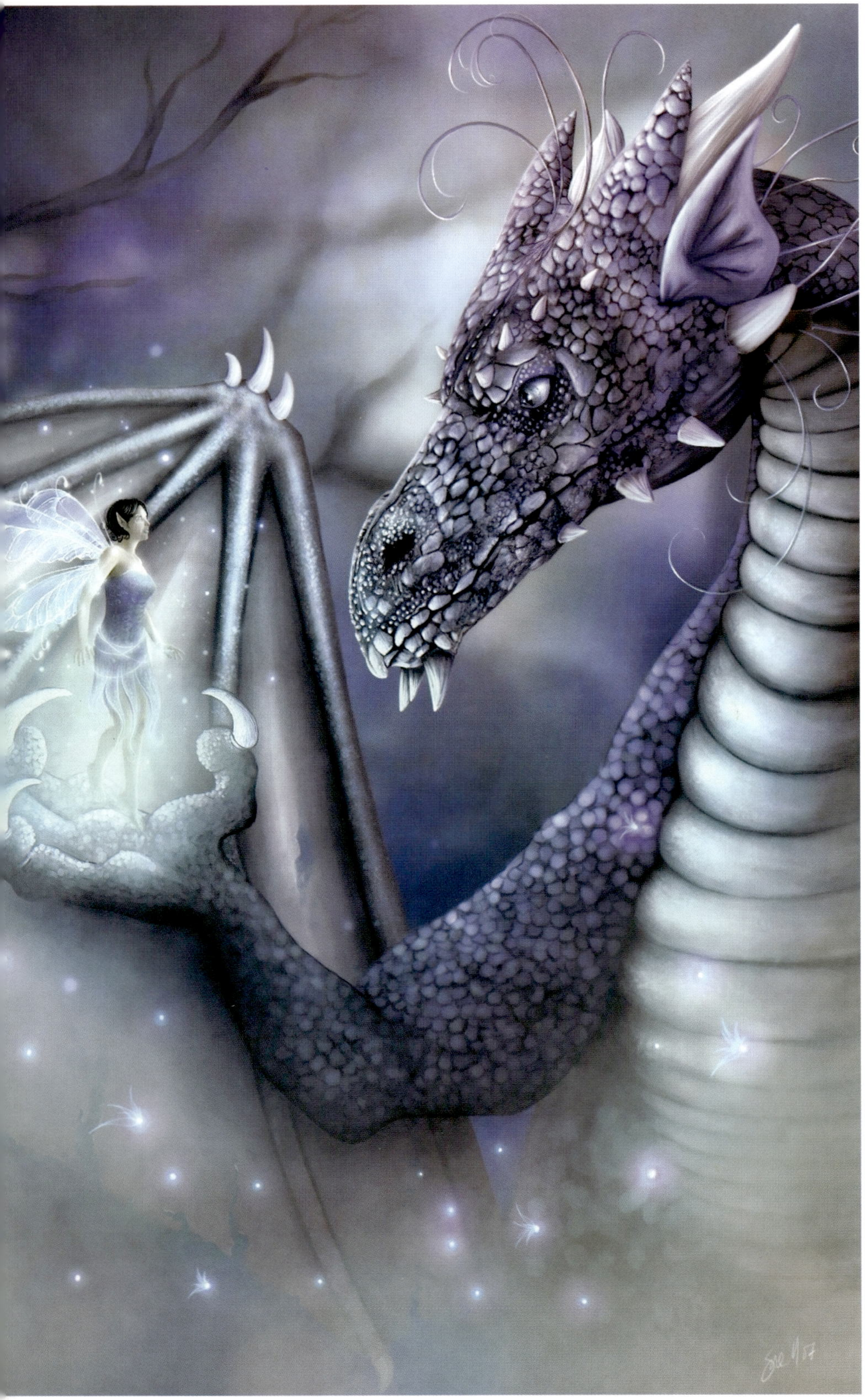

THE STARING CONTEST by Susan McKivergan
© Susan McKivergan 2007 · Digital media: Poser, Photoshop
Susan is a freelance digital artist.
www.thedigitalmuse.net

The Debate Continues

But can the digital medium detract from the sense of fantasy, or even the 'art' of it? After all, part of the joy of looking at a painting is the joy of seeing the brush strokes and textures that brush on paper or oil on canvas makes. Janny Wurts answers, 'I think every artist chooses the medium that suits them, and there's some phenomenal work being done digitally. But I will sit there with just a blank sheet of paper and a pencil and a box of paints and create it straight out of my imagination. That's the way I work.'

Bob Eggleton leaves us with the thought, 'But that all said, there are some absolute masters who do computer artwork, and there are some amazing people who do good work using traditional methods. But there are also some incredibly bad artists who do incredibly bad work, which illustrates the point that it doesn't matter what medium you work in; if [...] you've got the talent, your talent and style will shine through, no matter whether it's an oil painting or a digital painting. It doesn't matter.'

DRAGON'S CAVE by Rafal Hrynkiewicz
© Rafal Hrynkiewicz and Mazer Corporation 2006
Digital media: Painter
www.Angstyboy.com

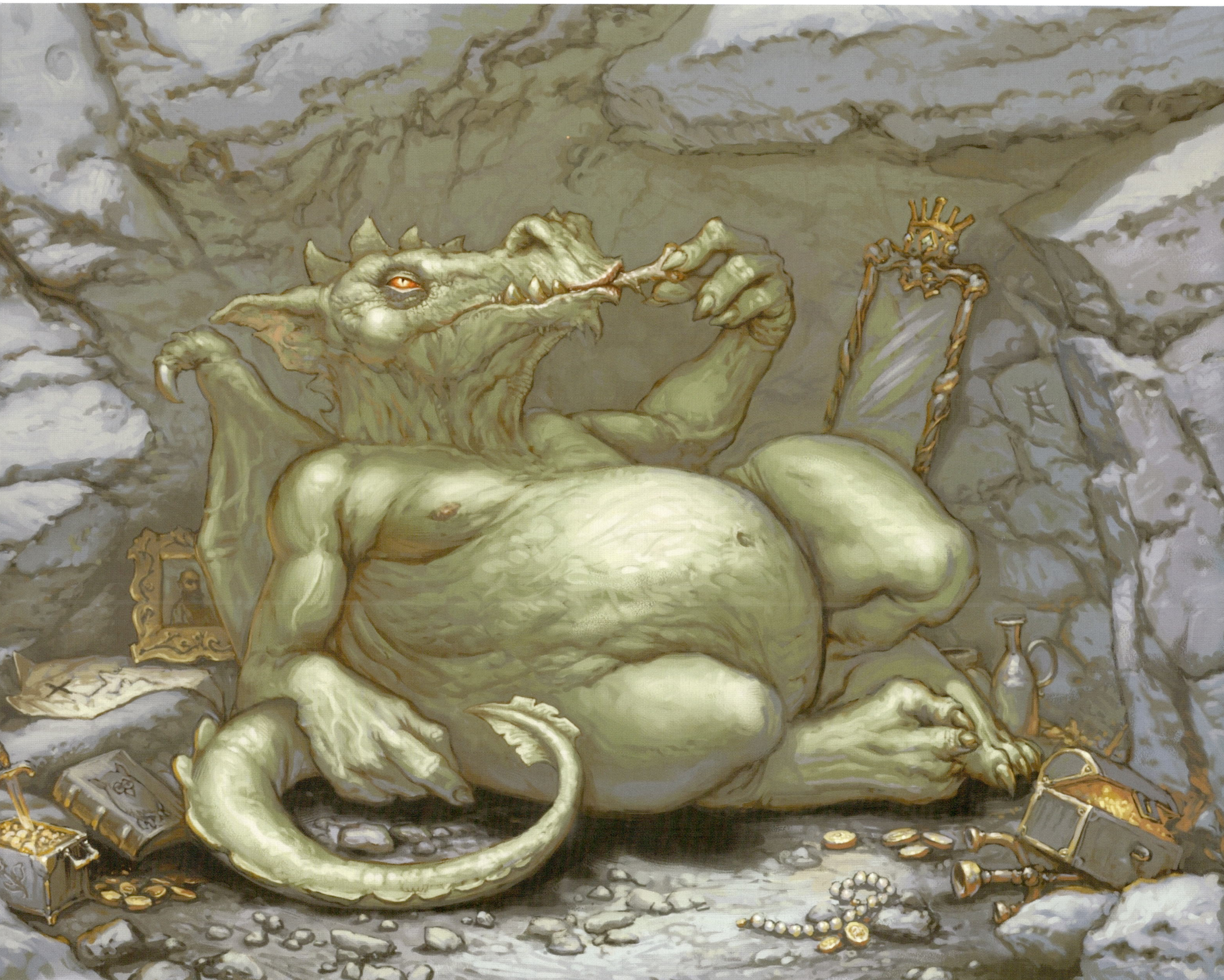

Bibliography

Allardice, Pamela, *Myths, Gods and Fantasy: A Sourcebook*, Prism (Bridport, UK), 1990

Fraes, Kelly and Polly (Eds.), *Wonderworks: Science Fiction and Fantasy Art by Michael Whelan*, Donning (Virginia Beach, VA, USA), 1979

Giebelhause, Michaela, *Painting the Bible: Representation and Belief in Mid-Victorian Britain*, Ashgate Publishing (Farnham, UK), 2006

Hammond, Wayne G. and Scull, Christina, *The JRR Tolkien Guide*, HarperCollins (London, UK), 2006

Herron, Don, *The Dark Barbarian: The Writings of Robert E. Howard*, Greenwood Press (Westport, CT, USA), 1984

Howe, John, *Myth & Magic: The Art of John Howe*, HarperCollins (London, UK), 2001

Joshi, S.T., *A Dreamer and a Visionary: H.P. Lovecraft in His Time*, Liverpool University Press (Liverpool, UK), 2001

Jude, Dick, *Fantasy Art Masters: The Best in Fantasy and SF Art Worldwide*, Collins (London, UK), 2002

Kirchoff, Mary (Ed.), *The Art of the Dragonlance Saga*, TSR Inc. (Lake Geneva, WI, USA), 1987

McKenna, Martin (Ed.), *Fantasy Art Now: The Very Best in Contemporary Fantasy Art and Illustration*, Ilex (Lewes, UK), 2007

Parker, John, *A Formal and Historical Sociology of Western Picture-making with Special Reference to J.M.W. Turner, Power, Space and Light*, The Edwin Mellen Press (Lampeter, Wales, UK), 1998

Reed, Carol, *Giants, Dragons and Monsters*, ABC-CLIO (Santa Barbara, USA), 2000

Tolkien, J.R.R. and Anderson, Douglas A., *The Annotated Hobbit*, Unwin Hyman (London, UK), 1989

Wright, Beth S. (Ed.), *The Cambridge Companion to Delacroix*, Cambridge University Press (Cambridge, UK), 2001

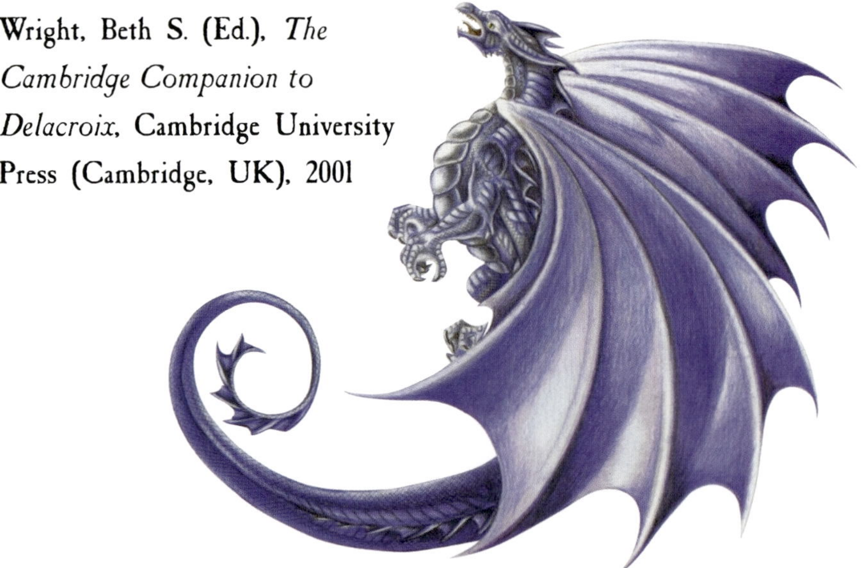

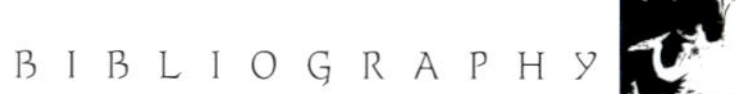

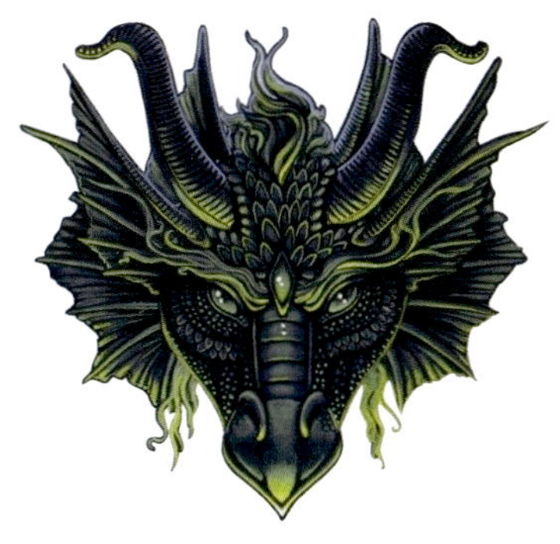

Further Reading

Burns, Michael, *Digital Fantasy Painting: A Step-by-Step Guide to Creating Visionary Art on Your Computer*, Watson-Guptill Publications, 2002

Burns, Michael, *Digital Sci-fi Art: A Step-by-step Guide to Creating Stunning, Futuristic Images*, Ilex (Lewes, UK), 2004

Ciruelo, *The Book of the Dragon*, Union Square Press (New York, NY, USA), 2005

Eggleton, Bob and Grant, John, *Dragonhenge*, Paper Tiger (London, UK), 2002

Fenner, Cathy and Arnie, *Spectrum 15: The Best in Contemporary Fantastic Art*, Underwood Books (Nevada City, CA, USA), 2008

Howe, John, *John Howe Fantasy Art Workshop*, Impact Books (USA), 2008

Howe, John, *John Howe Forging Dragons*, Impact Books (USA), 2009

Lea, Derek, *Creative Photoshop: Digital Illustration and Art Techniques*, Focal Press (St. Louis, MO, USA), 2009

Lippincott, Gary A., *The Fantasy Illustrator's Technique Book*, David & Charles (Newton Abbot, UK), 2007

McKenna, Martin, *Digital Fantasy Painting Workshop*, Ilex (Lewes, UK), 2004

Peffer, Jessica, *DragonArt: How to Draw Fantastic Dragons and Fantasy Creatures*, Impact Books (USA), 2005

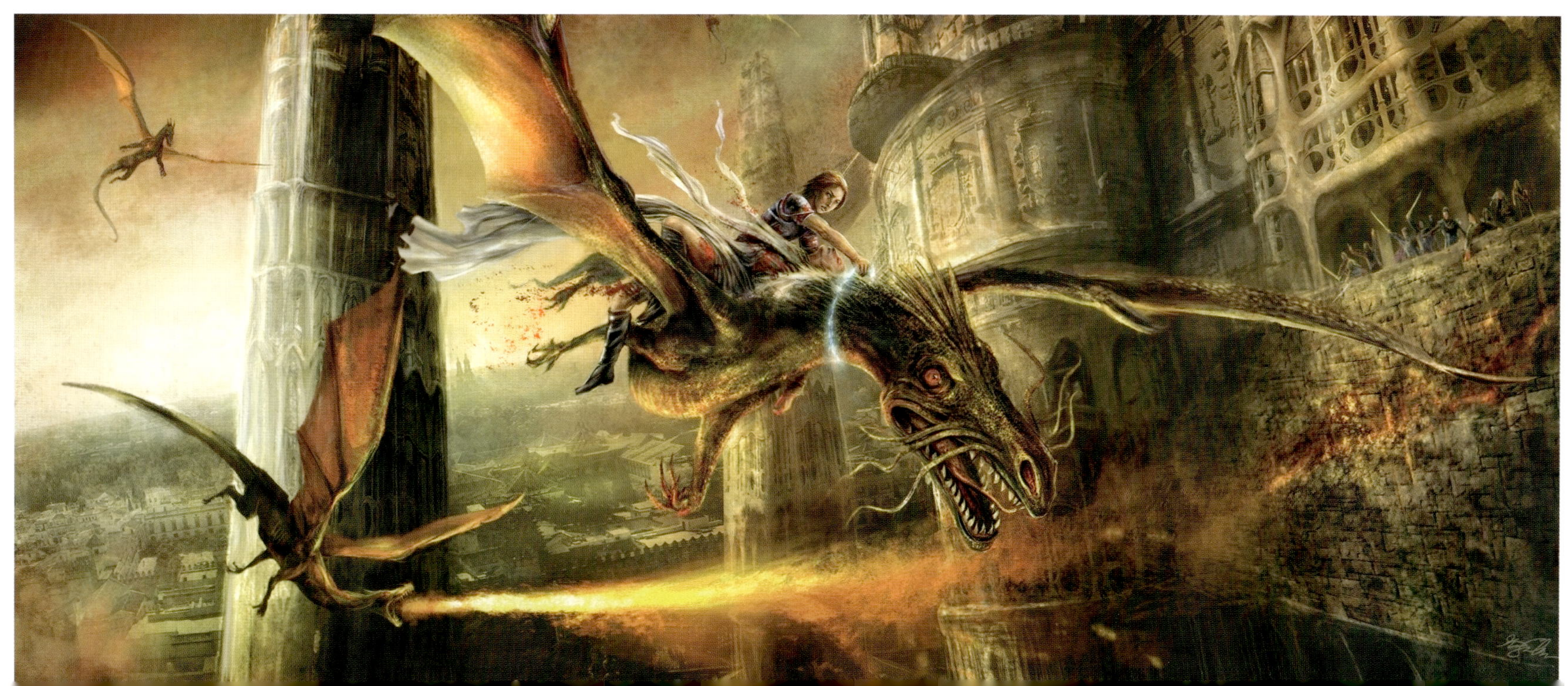

Index

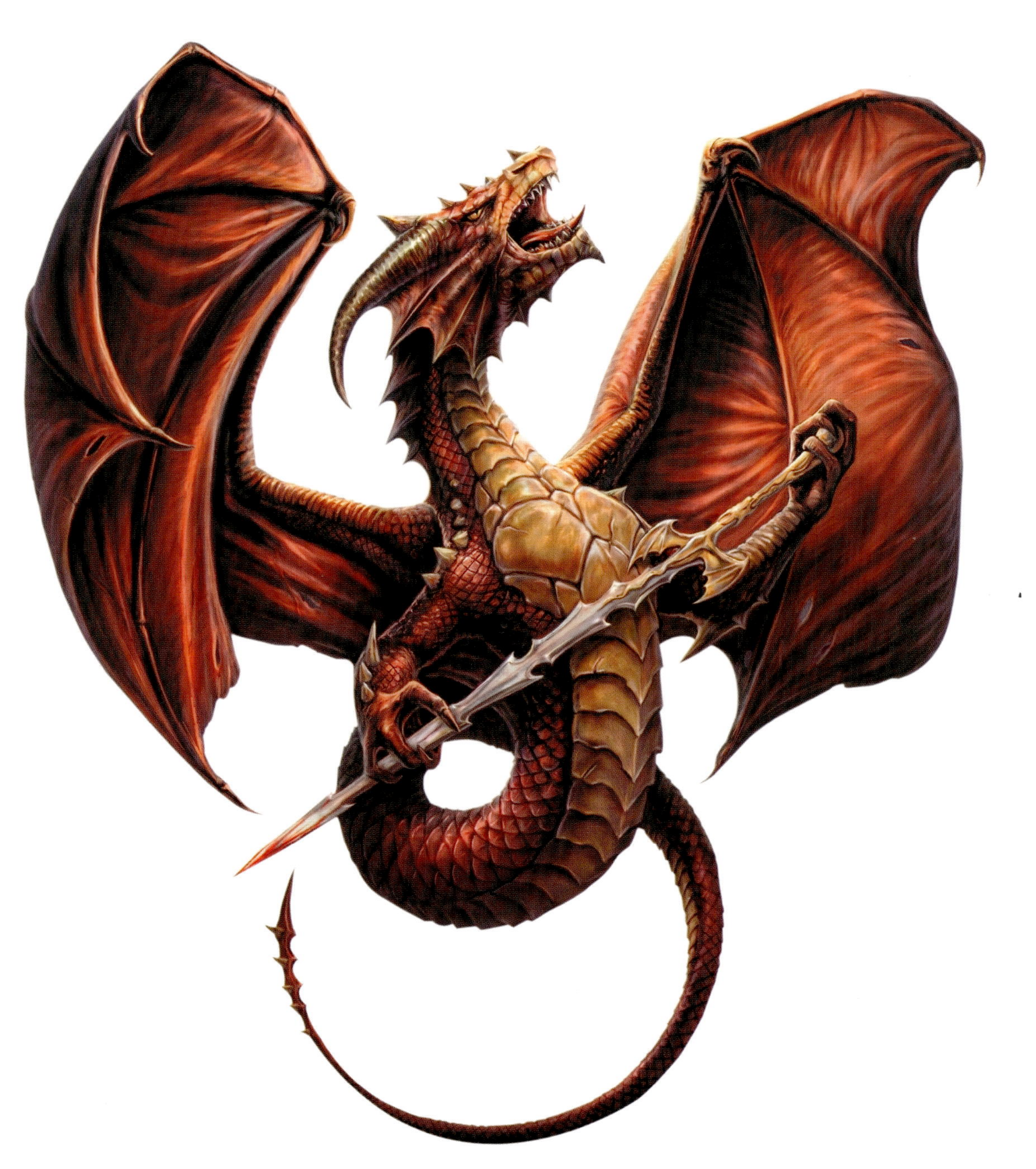